Bed & Breakfast Stops in Britain

2009

- For Holidaymakers and Business Travellers
- Overnight Stops and Short Breaks

Fairwater Head Hotel, Hawkchurch, near Axminster, Devon, (page 23)

Contents

Tourist Board Ratings   316, 342

SOUTH WEST ENGLAND   7
Cornwall and Isles of Scilly, Devon, Dorset, Gloucestershire, Somerset, Wiltshire

LONDON & SOUTH EAST ENGLAND   83
London, Berkshire, Hampshire, Isle of Wight, Kent, Surrey, East Sussex, West Sussex

EAST OF ENGLAND   119
Bedfordshire, Cambridgeshire, Essex, Hertfordshire, Norfolk, Suffolk

MIDLANDS   136
Derbyshire, Herefordshire, Leicestershire & Rutland, Lincolnshire, Northamptonshire, Nottinghamshire, Shropshire, Staffordshire, Warwickshire, West Midlands, Worcestershire

YORKSHIRE   169
East Yorkshire, North Yorkshire, South Yorkshire, West Yorkshire

NORTH EAST ENGLAND   196
Durham, Northumberland, Tyne & Wear

NORTH WEST ENGLAND   121
Cheshire, Cumbria, Lancashire, Merseyside

FHG Guides
publish a large range of well-known accommodation guides.
We will be happy to send you details or you can use the order form
at the back of this book.

Contents

SCOTLAND

Aberdeen, Banff & Moray	253
Angus & Dundee	257
Argyll & Bute	258
Ayrshire & Arran	265
Borders	273
Dumfries & Galloway	278
Edinburgh & Lothians	282
Fife	286
Glasgow & District	288
Highlands	289
Lanarkshire	301
Perth & Kinross	303
Renfrewshire	308
Stirling & The Trossachs	309
Scottish Islands	311

WALES

Anglesey & Gwynedd	319
North Wales	322
Carmarthenshire	324
Ceredigion	325
Pembrokeshire	326
Powys	330
South Wales	332

COUNTRY INNS

335

SPECIAL WELCOME SUPPLEMENTS

Non-Smoking	343
Special Diets	344
Accessible Holidays	345
Website Directory	347
Index of Towns/Counties	363

Please note

All the information in this book is given in good faith in the belief that it is correct. However, the publishers cannot guarantee the facts given in these pages, neither are they responsible for changes in policy, ownership or terms that may take place after the date of going to press. Readers should always satisfy themselves that the facilities they require are available and that the terms, if quoted, still apply.

© FHG Guides Ltd, 2009
ISBN 978-1-85055-414-1

Maps: ©MAPS IN MINUTES™ / Collins Bartholomew 2007

Typeset by FHG Guides Ltd, Paisley.
Printed and bound in China by Imago.

Distribution. Book Trade: ORCA Book Services, Stanley House,
3 Fleets Lane, Poole, Dorset BH15 3AJ
(Tel: 01202 665432; Fax: 01202 666219)
e-mail: mail@orcabookservices.co.uk
Published by FHG Guides Ltd., Abbey Mill Business Centre,
Seedhill, Paisley PA1 ITJ (Tel: 0141-887 0428 Fax: 0141-889 7204).
e-mail: admin@fhguides.co.uk

Bed & Breakfast Stops is published by FHG Guides Ltd,
part of Kuperard Group.

Cover design: FHG Guides
Cover Picture: with thanks to Arches Guesthouse, Whitby, North Yorkshire.

symbols

	Totally non-smoking			Pets Welcome
	Children Welcome		**SB**	Short Breaks
	Suitable for Disabled Guests			Licensed

England

Langley Oast B&B, Langley, Maidstone, Kent, page 104

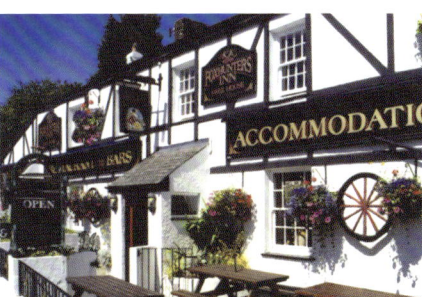
The Foxhunters Inn, West Down, near Ilfracombe, Devon, page 35

Beckfoot Country House, near Penrith, Cumbria, page 228

Ravenscourt Manor, Ludlow, Shropshire, page 157

Cornwall
Boscastle

Cornwall

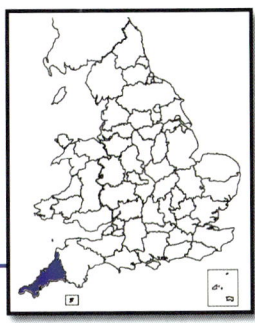

Non-smoking • No pets • No children

Set in own grounds (parking). En suite accommodation. Tea/coffee, TV in rooms. Overlooking Boscastle village, with views of coast and Lundy Island; close to sandy beaches, surfing. 3 miles Tintagel, King Arthur Country. Haven for walkers. Two minutes' walk to local 16th century inn, with real ales and good food. Open Easter to end October. Terms from £28pppn.

Tel: 01840 250606

Mrs P. E. Perfili, Trefoil Farm, Camelford Road, Boscastle PL35 0AD
e-mail: trefoil.farm@tiscali.co.uk • www.thisisnorthcornwall.com

Home Farm, Minster, Boscastle PL35 0BN

Home Farm is a beautifully situated working farm overlooking picturesque Boscastle and its Heritage coastline. The farm is surrounded by National Trust countryside and footpaths through unspoilt wooded valleys to Boscastle village, restaurants and harbour. Traditional farmhouse with beautiful furnishings has three charming en suite rooms with colour TV with satellite link, tea-making facilities; cosy guest lounge with log fire.
Good home cooking; walled garden; plenty of friendly farm animals. Beaches, golf courses, riding stables, coastal paths and many other activities for you to enjoy.

A warm welcome awaits you.

Contact: Mrs Jackie Haddy • Tel & Fax: 01840 250195
e-mail: homefarm.boscastle@tiscali.co.uk • www.homefarm-boscastle.co.uk

The Old Coach House

Relax in a 300 year old former coach house now tastefully equipped to meet the needs of the new millennium with all rooms en suite, colour TVs, refreshment trays and central heating. Good cooking. This picturesque village is a haven for walkers with its dramatic coastal scenery, a photographer's dream, and an ideal base to tour both the north and south coasts. The area is famed for its sandy beaches and surfing whilst King Arthur's Tintagel is only three miles away. Come and enjoy a friendly holiday with people who care. Large garden and patio area.
Bed and Breakfast from £27-£32pp • Non-smoking • Accessible for disabled guests.

Geoff and Jackie Horwell, The Old Coach House, Tintagel Road, Boscastle PL35 0AS
Tel: 01840 250398 • Fax: 01840 250346 • e-mail: stay@old-coach.co.uk • www.old-coach.co.uk

SOUTH WEST ENGLAND

Cornwall — Bude

STRATTON GARDENS HOUSE

Cot Hill, Stratton, Bude, Cornwall EX23 9DN

This charming 16th century Listed house in historic Stratton offers quality accommodation, fine food and friendly, traditional hospitality. Enjoy the comforts of the spacious en suite bedrooms, all of which are individually furnished and have colour television, tea/coffee making facilities and hairdryers.

Relax and feel at home in our comfortable lounge and sample the delights of the licensed restaurant and attractive terraced gardens. Stratton Gardens House is a peaceful hideaway, only one-and-a-half miles from Bude's wonderful beaches and dramatic coastline, an ideal base for bird-watching, walking, exploring the coast or moors, or simply unwinding.

Tel: 01288 352500 • Fax: 01288 359153
e-mail: moira@stratton-gardens.co.uk • www.stratton-gardens.co.uk

---

TRENCREEK farmhouse

St. Genny's, Bude, Cornwall EX23 0AY
01840 230219

Comfortable farmhouse offering homely and relaxed family atmosphere. Situated in quiet and peaceful surroundings yet within easy reach of Crackington Haven. Well placed for easy access to coastal and countryside walks. Family, double and twin-bedded rooms, most en suite, all with tea/coffee making facilities. Two comfortable lounges. Games room. Separate diningroom. Generous portions of freshly prepared, home-cooked farmhouse food.
Children welcome, special rates for unders 12s.
Spring and Autumn breaks available. Non-smoking.

**Margaret and Richard Heard,
Trencreek Farmhouse, St Gennys, Bude EX23 0AY**
e-mail:enquiries@trencreekfarmhouse.com • www.trencreekfarmhouse.com

Cornwall

SOUTH WEST ENGLAND

Bude

West Nethercott Farm, North Cornwall

 SB

Personal attention and a warm welcome await you on this dairy and sheep farm. Watch the cows being milked, scenic farm walks. Short distance from sandy beaches, surfing and the rugged North Cornwall coast. Ideal base for visiting any part of Devon or Cornwall. We are located in Cornwall though our postal address is Devon. The traditional farmhouse has four bedrooms, two en suite; diningroom and separate lounge with TV. Plenty of excellent home cooking. Access to the house at anytime. Bed and Breakfast from £22-£28, Evening Meal available. Children under 12 years reduced rates. Weekly terms available.

Mrs Pearl Hopper, West Nethercott Farm, Whitstone, Holsworthy (Devon) EX22 6LD • 01288 341394
pearl@westnethercott.fsnet.co.uk • www.westnethercott.co.uk

SB

Situated on the Devon/Cornwall border six miles from the surfing beaches at Bude and Widemouth Bay, we are ideally placed for touring both Devon and Cornwall. Guests are welcome to wander on our 205 acre mixed farm. Three large and tastefully furnished family rooms sleeping up to four - two rooms en suite, all rooms are south facing and enjoy views of the surrounding farmland. Children are welcome. Tea making facilities and TV in all rooms. Full English breakfast served daily; ample four course meal available. Numerous sandy beaches nearby and the picturesque villages of Clovelly and Tintagel are within half an hour's drive.

Open from March to November. B&B from £25 per person.

Mrs Sylvia Lucas, Elm Park Farmhouse Bed & Breakfast, Bridgerule, Holsworthy, Devon EX22 7EL • 01288 381231

Highbre Crest, Whitstone, Holsworthy, Near Bude EX22 6UF

SB

Stunning views to coasts and moors make this very spacious house a special destination for your holiday. With the added bonus of peace, tranquillity and delicious breakfasts, how can you resist paying us a visit? We are well situated for the coast and moors in Devon and Cornwall, including The Eden Project. Two double and one twin room - all en suite. Lounge with full size snooker table, dining room and comfortable large conservatory with spectacular coastal views. Garden for guests' use. Car parking space. Non-smoking establishment. Children over 12 welcome. Bed and Breakfast from £30. Open all year.

Mrs Cole • 01288 341002

symbols

 Totally non-smoking

 Children Welcome

 Suitable for Disabled Guests

 Pets Welcome

SB Short Breaks

 Licensed

SOUTH WEST ENGLAND

Cornwall
Callington, Falmouth

Hampton Manor

This six-bedroom country house hotel offers high quality accommodation, food and service in a beautiful setting in the Tamar valley which borders Devon and Cornwall. We are within easy reach of north and south coasts, the Eden Project, many interesting gardens and National Trust properties, and a good variety of challenging walks on Bodmin Moor and Dartmoor.

It's an ideal place to 'get away from it all' – and be spoilt!

B&B from £35pp
3-night break DB&B from £120pp.

Alston, Near Callington PL17 8LX • Tel: 01579 370494
e-mail: hamptonmanor@supanet.com • www.hamptonmanor.co.uk

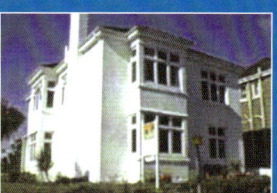

Just a step away from Falmouth seafront and beaches, Palms Guesthouse is a beautiful, family-run home providing a very warm welcome. All our rooms are en suite with either a power shower or bath, tastefully furnished with antique furniture, big beds, hospitality trays, colour TVs and lovely sea views We are non-smoking, all the better to enjoy the lovely sea air.
An ideal spot for discovering this part of Cornwall. Near Castle Beach, Pendennis Castle, many shops and restaurants, and the new award-winning Maritime Museum.

11 Castle Drive, Falmouth, Cornwall TR11 4NF
Tel: 01326 314007 • Mobile: 07812 498 970
e-mail: j_miller99@hotmail.com • www.thepalmsguesthouse.co.uk

The Palms guesthouse

Heritage House
1 Clifton Terrace, Falmouth TR11 3QG

We offer visitors a warm, friendly welcome at our comfortable family-run guesthouse. Centrally located for town and beaches. En suite single, twin, double and family bedrooms, all tastefully decorated, with colour TV, free tea/coffee, vanity basins and central heating. Access available at all times throughout the day. Children are welcome, with cot and highchair available. Bed and full English or vegetarian breakfast from £24 per person nightly. Reduced rates for longer stays. On-street parking available with no restrictions. Open all year (except Christmas).

Proprietor: Lynn Grimes
Tel: 01326 317834
e-mail: heritagehouse@tinyonline.co.uk
www.heritagehousefalmouth.co.uk

Cornwall

SOUTH WEST ENGLAND

Falmouth, Helston, Launceston

Rosemullion Hotel

Gyllyngvase Hill, Falmouth TR11 4DF • 01326 314690 • Fax: 01326 210098

Built as a gentleman's residence in the latter part of the 19th century, Rosemullion Hotel offers you a holiday that is every bit as distinctive as its Tudor appearance. Rosemullion is a house of great character and charm, appealing strongly to the discerning guest. The emphasis is very much on that rarest of commodities in today's world – peace. That is why we do not cater for children and do not have a bar of our own. A family-owned hotel continually being refurbished and updated to first class accommodation. Fully centrally heated with 13 bedrooms, some with glorious views over the bay. Free wifi available. Large parking area.

Non-smoking • B&B £35–£45 single; £33.50–£38pppn in double room.

e-mail: gail@rosemullionhotel.demon.co.uk
www.SmoothHound.co.uk/hotels/rosemullion.html

Hendra Farm, just off the main Helston/Falmouth road, is an ideal centre for touring Cornwall; three miles to Helston, eight to both Redruth and Falmouth. Safe sandy beaches within easy reach – five miles to the sea.

Two double, one single, and one family bedrooms with washbasins and tea-making facilities; bathroom and toilets; sittingroom and two diningrooms.

- Cot, babysitting and reduced rates offered for children.
- No objection to pets • Car necessary, parking space.
- Open all year except Christmas • Evening Dinner optional • Tea and homemade cake before bed.

Bed and Breakfast only from £20 per night.

Mrs P. Roberts, Hendra Farm, Wendron, Helston TR13 0NR (01326 340470)

ROCKLANDS

"Rocklands" is situated overlooking part of Cornwall's superb coastline and enjoys uninterrupted sea views. The Lizard is well known for its lovely picturesque scenery, coastal walks and enchanting coves and beaches, as well as the famous Serpentine Stone which is quarried and sold locally. Open Easter to October. Generations of the Hill family have been catering for visitors on the Lizard since the 1850s. Three bedrooms with sea views, two en suite, tea/coffee making facilities and electric heaters; sittingroom with TV and video; sun lounge; diningroom with separate tables. Children and well trained pets welcome.

Bed and Breakfast £23pppn, en suite £25pppn; reductions for children under 10 years.

Mrs D. J. Hill, "Rocklands", The Lizard, Near Helston TR12 7NX • Tel: 01326 290339

Hurdon Farm
Launceston PL15 9LS
01566 772955

Elegant Listed 18th century farmhouse, idyllically tucked away amidst our 500 acre mixed working farm. Centrally positioned on Devon/Cornwall border, it is ideally located for exploring the many attractions in both counties. Near the Eden Project.

AA ★★★★ FARMHOUSE HIGHLY COMMENDED

Six luxurious and spacious en suite bedrooms, all with colour TV, radio, tea/coffee facilities and central heating. Comfortable guests' lounge. Superb English breakfasts and delicious four-course dinners, freshly prepared and cooked, are served at separate tables in the dining room.

Open May till November • B&B from £25

SOUTH WEST ENGLAND — Cornwall
Liskeard, Looe

Nebula Hotel
ETC ★★★

27 Higher Lux Street, Liskeard PL14 3JU

Relax in your home from home friendly hotel. Old English atmosphere in a Grade II Listed building. Unwind by our large granite fireplace in the lounge area with licensed bar. Eight spacious comfortable en suite rooms, single, double, twin and family, all with TV and tea/coffee facilities. Free WiFi internet. Large car park. Liskeard is ideally placed to tour Cornwall and Plymouth. Near the moors, coast, gardens, golf courses, Eden Project and museums. Enjoy! We also have family cottages available. Terms from £30. *SOUTH WEST TOURISM, CORNWALL TOURIST BOARD*

Tel: 01579 343989 • e-mail: info@nebula-hotel.com • www.nebula-hotel.com

---

Little Larnick Farm
Pelynt, Looe, Cornwall PL13 2NB

Telephone: **01503 262837**

SB

Little Larnick is situated in a sheltered part of the West Looe river valley. Walk to Looe from our working farm and along the coastal path to picturesque Polperro. The character farmhouse and barn offers twin and double en suite rooms. The bedrooms are superbly equipped and decorated to a high standard. Our newly renovated barn offers three self-contained bedrooms with their own lounge areas. Cycling shed, drying room and ample parking. No pets. No smoking. Bed and Breakfast from £30–£33pppn (minimum stay 2 nights). Open all year. Contact: **Mrs Angela Eastley**.

e-mail: littlelarnick@btclick.com
www.littlelarnick.co.uk

Bay View Farm
"Enjoy our little piece of paradise"

AA ★★★★

SB

In a spectacular location, enjoying uninterrupted views of Looe and St George's Island, our coastal farm is a haven for the walker and birdwatcher – you can meet our Shire horses too. This beautifully decorated and furnished bungalow has three spacious en suite bedrooms, two with their own large conservatory with lovely valley views. They offer every comfort, including colour TV, central heating and beverage trays. There is ample parking, and wheelchair access if required. Savour delicious meals whilst gazing across the water, relax in the lounge or on the patio and watch the sun setting over Looe.

- Exceptional location
- Luxury rooms with sea or rural view
- 10 minute walk down to the South West Coastal Path to Millendreath Beach
- Prize-winning Shire Horses
- Ample parking
- Wheelchair-friendly
- No Smoking

Mrs E. Elford
Bay View Farm Guest House
St Martins, Looe, Cornwall PL13 1NZ
Tel/Fax: 01503 265922 • Mobile: 07967 267312
www.looedirectory.co.uk/bay-view-farm.htm

B&B from £30.00 • Evening Meal from £17.50
AA Highly Commended 2007-2008

Cornwall
SOUTH WEST ENGLAND 13
Looe, Mawgan Porth, Mevagissey

• Bake Farm •
Pelynt, Looe, Cornwall PL13 2QQ • 01503 220244

This is an old farmhouse, bearing the Trelawney Coat of Arms (1610), situated midway between Looe and Fowey. Two double and one family bedroom, all en suite and decorated to a high standard, have tea/coffee making facilities and TV. Sorry, no pets, no smoking. Open from March to October. A car is essential for touring the area, ample parking. There is much to see and do here – horse riding, coastal walks, golf, National Trust properties, the Eden Project and Heligan Gardens are within easy reach. The sea is only five miles away and there is shark fishing at Looe.

SB

Bed and Breakfast from £27 to £30 • Brochure available on request.
e-mail: bakefarm@btopenworld.com • www.bakefarm.co.uk

Blue Bay HOTEL, RESTAURANT & LODGES
Trenance, Mawgan Porth, Cornwall TR8 4DA
Tel: 01637 860324
e-mail: hotel@bluebaycornwall.co.uk
www.bluebaycornwall.co.uk

- Beautifully situated in tranquil location between Padstow and Newquay, overlooking Mawgan Porth beach.
- **Hotel** has two garden suites, one family suite, one family room and five double rooms, all en suite. Twin and single rooms available.
- Dogs welcome; Mawgan Porth beach is dog-friendly.
- 4 individually designed Cornish **Lodges**, all fully equipped (sleep 4-8). All have own balcony or patio area. Linen, towels, electricity incl. Laundry room. Dogs welcome.

Hotel prices from £33pppn
Lodge prices from £50 per Lodge per night.

B&B accommodation with magnificent views over the village and harbour, and only a short three/four minute walk to the harbour itself.
All rooms en suite or have private facilities with colour TV/tea and coffee making facilities. Centrally heated and double glazed. Sauna and a south-facing sun deck. Private off-road parking.
Ideal touring base. Special promotion for Heligan Gardens or Eden Project tickets (ring for details).
For further information telephone **Helen Blamey**.

Tregorran, Cliff Street, Mevagissey PL26 6QW • Tel: 01726 842319
e-mail: patricia@parsloep.freeserve.co.uk • www.tregorran.homestead.com/home.html

SOUTH WEST ENGLAND — Cornwall

Mevagissey, Newquay

SB 🐕

Kilbol
Country House Hotel & Cottages
Polmassick, Mevagissey PL26 6HA

A small, cottage-style country hotel set in 5-acre grounds. Dating back to the 16th century, it has been fully refurbished and offers 8 rooms, as well as two self-catering cottages. Two miles from the Lost Gardens of Heligan and Mevagissey, and close to the Eden Project. Outdoor swimming pool, riverside walk, wooded area. No children under 12 years in the hotel. Pets welcome.

Winter & Christmas Breaks available.

Tel: 01726 842481
e-mail: Hotel@kilbol-hotel.co.uk
www.kilbol-hotel.co.uk

'Perfect Peace in Hidden Cornwall'

Lancallan is a large 17th century farmhouse on a working 700-acre dairy and beef farm in a beautiful rural setting, one mile from Mevagissey. We are close to Heligan Gardens, lovely coastal walks and sandy beaches, and are well situated for day trips throughout Cornwall. Also six to eight miles from the Eden Project (20 minutes' drive). Enjoy a traditional farmhouse breakfast in a warm and friendly atmosphere.

Accommodation comprises one twin room and two double en suite rooms (all with colour TV and tea/coffee facilities); bathroom, lounge and diningroom.

Terms and brochure available on request. SAE please.

Mrs Dawn Rundle, Lancallan Farm, Mevagissey, St Austell PL26 6EW
Tel & Fax: 01726 842284
e-mail: dawn@lancallan.fsnet.co.uk • www.lancallanfarm.co.uk

Aquarius Guest House • 29 Henver Road, Newquay, Cornwall TR7 3DG
Tel: 01637 851471 • Mobile : 07967 351572
E-mail : info@aquariusnewquay.co.uk
www.aquariusnewquay.co.uk

Welcoming and tastefully decorated, Aquarius guest house is in a quiet location within walking distance from Newquay town centre and beaches. The Guesthouse is open all year round and is fully centrally heated. We have six family rooms, all en suite with TV, tea / coffee making facilities and use of an iron and hairdryer on request. Most rooms are on the ground floor. There is a double jacuzzi and a comfortable lounge and sun lounge. No smoking in bedrooms, but there is a designated smoking area.
Prices range from £22 - £35pppn and include a full English Breakfast or a vegetarian alternative.

Cornwall

SOUTH WEST ENGLAND

Newquay, Penzance

Take a break in the heart of Cornwall

A warm and friendly welcome awaits you at Pensalda. Situated on the main A3058 road, an ideal location from which to explore the finest coastline in Europe. Close to airport and the Eden Project. Double and family rooms available, all en suite, all with TV, tea/coffee making facilities, including two chalets set in a lovely garden.

- Fire certificate • Large car park
- Licensed • Central heating
- Non-smoking.

Bed and Breakfast from £23
Special offer breaks
November to March
(excluding Christmas and New Year).

Karen and John, Pensalda Guest House, 98 Henver Road, Newquay TR7 3BL • Tel & Fax: 01637 874601
e-mail: karen_pensalda@yahoo.co.uk
www.pensalda-guesthouse.co.uk

Tradewinds Tel/Fax: 01736 330990
21 Regent Terrace, Penzance TR18 4DW

Family-run guest house in seafront location, convenient for Isle of Scilly boat and parking. TV, tea/coffee making facilities. Two generously sized en suite bedrooms - one twin and one very large double/family room. Full English breakfast, vegetarians welcome. Non-smoking. Proprietor: Mrs L. Matthews.
From £26pppn • Reductions for children.

e-mail: lynette.tradewinds@googlemail.com

TORWOOD HOUSE HOTEL 01736 360063
ALEXANDRA ROAD, PENZANCE TR18 4LZ

Torwood is a small, family-run Victorian hotel, situated in a beautiful tree-lined avenue 500 metres from the seafront and town centre. All rooms en suite, with TV/DVD, tea/coffee makers, central heating and radios. Comfortable dining area where a generous full English breakfast is served - other options available on request. Dinner available on request. Well behaved pets by arrangement. B&B from £25 - £29 pppn, evening meal £18.

For further details telephone LYNDA SOWERBY

e-mail: Lyndasowerby@aol.com • ww.torwoodhousehotel.co.uk

SOUTH WEST ENGLAND — Cornwall
Perranporth, Polzeath, Port Isaac

Chy an Kerensa — Licensed Guest House situated by Coastal Path, directly overlooking miles of rolling surf, golden sands, rocks and heathland. Only 200 metres from beach and village centre, which has various restaurants, shops and pubs to suit all tastes and ages. Also tennis, bowls, wetsuit and surfboard hire, with golf and horse riding nearby. Our comfortable bedrooms, most en suite, have colour TV, central heating and tea/coffee making facilities. Many have panoramic sea views, as do our lounge/bar and dining room. Bed and Breakfast from £26 to £32pppn, room only from £22pppn.

Please write or telephone for further details -
Wendy Woodcock, Chy An Kerensa, Cliff Road, Perranporth TR6 0DR • 01872 572470
mobile: 07881 710157

Seaways is a small family guest house, 250 yards from safe, sandy beach. Surfing, riding, sailing, tennis, squash, golf all nearby. All bedrooms with en suite or private bathrooms, comprising one family, two double, two twin and a single room. Sittingroom; dining room. Children welcome (reduced price for under 10s). Cot, high chair available. Comfortable family holiday assured with plenty of good home cooking. Lovely cliff walks nearby. Padstow a short distance by ferry. Other places of interest include Tintagel, Boscastle and Port Isaac.

Non-smoking establishment. Open all year round.
Bed and Breakfast £38pppn.

Mrs P. White, Seaways, Polzeath PL27 6SU
Tel: 01208 862382
e-mail: pauline.white@seaysguesthouse.co.uk • www.seaysguesthouse.com

LONG CROSS HOTEL & VICTORIAN GARDENS
TRELIGHTS, PORT ISAAC PL29 3TF

Lovely Victorian country house hotel with four acres of restored gardens set in beautiful tranquil location overlooking the coast. Close to the area's best beaches, golf courses and other attractions. Spacious, comfortable interior, with newly refurbished en suite bedrooms and suites.

Tel: 01208 880243 • www.longcrosshotel.co.uk

Visit the FHG website
www.holidayguides.com
for details of the wide choice of accommodation featured in the full range of FHG titles

Cornwall
Redruth, St Agnes

Crossroads Travel Inn and Conference Centre
Scorrier, Redruth, Cornwall TR16 5BP
Tel: 01209 820551 Fax: 01209 820392
e-mail: info@crossroadstravelinn.co.uk
www.crossroadstravelinn.co.uk

- In the heart of Cornwall, just 3 miles from Porthtowan Beach
- All bedrooms en suite with excellent modern facilities
- Superb restaurant with table d'hôte and à la carte menus
- Excellent Sunday lunches.
- Conference and function facilities ideal for private and business events

This small, detached, family-run Victorian hotel stands in the heart of the picturesque village of St Agnes, convenient for many outstanding country and coastal walks. Set in mature gardens and having a separate children's play area we can offer peace and relaxation after the beach, which is approximately half-a-mile away. Accommodation is provided in generous sized rooms, mostly en suite and all with colour TV. Public rooms comprise lounge, bar, dining rooms and small games room. Private parking. Evening set menu.

- B&B from £28pppn (sharing).
- Non-smoking
- Regret no pets
- Self-catering annexe available

e-mail: tedellis@cchotel.fsnet.co.uk

Cleaderscroft Hotel
16 British Road, St Agnes TR5 0TZ
Tel: 01872 552349 • Ted & Jeanie Ellis

Penkerris

A creeper-clad B&B/guest house with lawned garden in unspoilt Cornish village. A home from home offering real food, comfortable bedrooms, four en suite and three standard, with facilities (TV, radio, kettle, H&C). Dining room serving breakfast, with dinner available by arrangement. Bright cosy lounge with a log fire in winter - colour TV, video and piano. Licensed. Ample parking. Dramatic cliff walks, sandy beaches, surfing - one km/10 minutes' walk. Easy to find on the B3277 road from big roundabout on the A30 and just by the village sign. Smoking in garden only. Open all year.

ETC ★★ Guest House

B&B from £20 to £40 per night
Dinner available from £17.50

Self-catering in Perranporth also available

SB

Dorothy Gill-Carey, Penkerris, Penwinnick Road, St Agnes TR5 0PA
Tel & Fax: 01872 552262
e-mail: info@penkerris.co.uk • www.penkerris.co.uk

SOUTH WEST ENGLAND — Cornwall
St Austell

The Pier House Hotel & Restaurant

Harbour Front, Charlestown, St Austell PL25 3NJ
Tel: 01726 67955
www.pierhousehotel.com
pierhousehotel@btconnect.com

The Hotel has 26 bedrooms, a bar/bistro and an à la carte restaurant. The patio area has wonderful views across the harbour and St Austell Bay. Our hotel bar is a freehouse and serves a wide selection of locally brewed ales. Our bedrooms are all en suite, with colour TV, direct-dial telephone and tea/coffee making facilities. Many rooms have superb sea and/or harbour views and wireless internet access. We are 3½ miles away from the Eden Project and 6 miles away from the Lost Gardens of Heligan. There are many moors, gardens and places of interest, all within an easy drive.

Elms B&B

The Elms

14 Penwinnick Road, St Austell
Cornwall PL25 5DW

Georgian-style guest house within walking distance of the town centre. The Eden Project and the Lost Gardens of Heligan are approximately five miles away. Ideally situated for visiting the numerous other attractions in Cornwall and close to sandy beaches.

Traditional English breakfast served; three-course evening dinners are available; licensed. Three double en suite bedrooms, all completed to a very high standard for guests' comfort and enjoyment.

Prices from £30 to £35 pppn.
Open all year.

Tel & Fax: 01726 74981
e-mail: pete@edenbb.co.uk
www.edenbb.co.uk

Cornwall
St Austell

Traditional Family Pub and B&B

This former coaching inn lies at the centre of the village of Bugle, between Bodmin and St Austell.

- Comfortable bedrooms, all en suite, with colour TV, telephone and tea/coffee making.
- Good selection of ales, lagers, spirits and fine wines
- Bar snacks, daily specials and a full à la carte pub menu. Authentic Indian cuisine available to eat in or takeaway. Non- smoking dining area.

Ideal for attactions such as the Eden Project (3 miles); the Cornish Riviera, Mevagissey and the Lost Gardens of Heligan are all within a short distance.

The Bugle Inn
**Fore Street, Bugle, St Austell PL26 8PB
Tel: 01726 850307 • e-mail: bugleinn@aol.com**

CORNERWAYS GUEST HOUSE

Centrally situated, and ideal for touring both the North and South Coasts of Cornwall. Ideal for rambling and walking holidays, and for visiting many nearby tourist attractions such as The Eden Project, or the Leisure centre in St Austell, with full size pool, squash courts and fitness centre. There is a choice of double, twin or single bedrooms, some of which are en suite; ironing board, iron and hairdryer available. Full English or Continental Breakfast offered and Bed and Breakfast prices start from £22.

**Penwinnick Road, St Austell, Cornwall PL25 5DS
Tel: Bookings 01726 61579
Visitors: 01726 71874 • Fax: 01726 66871**

Polgreen is a family-run dairy farm nestling in the Pentewan Valley in an Area of Outstanding Natural Beauty. One mile from the coast and four miles from the picturesque fishing village of Mevagissey. A perfect location for a relaxing holiday in the glorious Cornish countryside. Centrally situated, Polgreen is ideally placed for touring all of Cornwall's many attractions; Cornish Way Leisure Trail adjoining farm. Within a few minutes' drive of the spectacular Eden Project and Heligan Gardens. All rooms with private facilities, colour TV, tea/coffee making facilities. Guest lounge. Children welcome.
Terms from £28 per person per night.

**Mrs Liz Berryman, Polgreen Farm, London Apprentice, St Austell PL26 7AP Tel: 01726 75151
e-mail: polgreen.farm@btinternet.com
www.polgreenfarm.co.uk**

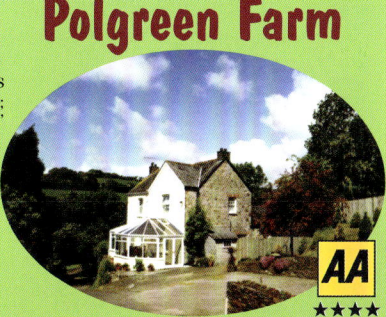

Polgreen Farm

SB

Cornwall

St Ives, Truro

Horizon Guest House •••• St Ives

Do you want a holiday with first-class accommodation, and to feel at home instantly?

With beautiful sea view rooms overlooking Porthmeor Surf beach. We are close to the Coastal Footpath to Zennor, yet only five minutes from the Tate Gallery, Town Centre and beaches, and have some private parking. There is access to your rooms at any time; guests' lounge with colour TV. Option of home-cooked dinner. All rooms en suite. Private parking.

Three-night breaks, early and late season £90.
Brochure and colour postcard available.
Julie Fitzgerald, Horizon Guest House, 5 Carthew Terrace, St Ives TR26 1EB • 01736 798069

Trewey Farm

Zennor, St Ives TR26 3DA

01736 796936

On the main St Ives to Land's End road, this attractive granite-built farmhouse stands among gorse and heather-clad hills, half-a-mile from the sea and five miles from St Ives. The mixed farm covers 300 acres, with Guernsey cattle and fine views of the sea; lovely cliff and hill walks. Guests will be warmly welcomed and find a friendly atmosphere.

Five double, one single and three family bedrooms (all with washbasin); bathroom, toilets; sittingroom, dining room. Cot, high chair and babysitting available.
Pets allowed • Car essential, parking
Open all year • Electric heating.
Bed and Breakfast only
SAE for terms, please.

Mrs N.I. Mann

THE *New Inn*

Veryan, Truro, Cornwall TR2 5QA

Set in a picturesque village on the Roseland Peninsula, the New Inn is a small granite pub, originally consisting of two cottages and was built in the 16th century.

Visitors are welcome to enjoy the atmosphere in our local village bar and we are locally renowned for our good food and cask ales, a wide range of food being served in the bar.

Accommodation consists of spacious and comfortable rooms – one double and one twin en suite. St Austell and Truro are nearby, and we are situated close to the beautiful sandy beaches of Pendower and Carne.

Tel: 01872 501362
e-mail: dennisrohrer@hotmail.com • www.newinnveryan.co.uk

Cornwall
SOUTH WEST ENGLAND

Truro, Wadbridge

TRENONA FARM Ruan High Lanes, Truro, Cornwall TR2 5JS

Enjoy a relaxing stay on this mixed farm, on the unspoilt Roseland Peninsula midway between Truro and St Austell (home of the Eden Project). Victorian farmhouse with four guest bedrooms, all of which are double/family rooms with colour TV, mini-fridge, tea/coffee making facilities, with either en suite or private bathroom. Separate TV lounge and dining room, together with gardens and a patio. Brochure available. Children welcome. Pets welcome by arrangement. .

Open March to November.

SB

Tel: 01872 501339 • e-mail: info@trenonafarmholidays.co.uk • www.trenonafarmholidays.co.uk

A Listed Georgian farmhouse on a working dairy farm, in a quiet location overlooking wooded valleys. Tastefully decorated and centrally heated throughout, offering one double and one twin room, both en suite with TV, radio, hairdryer and beverage trays. Full English breakfast, using mainly local produce, is served in the traditional style diningroom. Special diets by prior arrangement. Comfortable lounge with TV/video. Large garden with outstanding views for relaxing. B&B from £26. Static caravan also available.

SB

Mrs E. Hodge, Pengelly Farm, Burlawn, Wadebridge PL27 7LA • Tel: 01208 814217
e-mail: hodgepete@hotmail.com • www.pengellyfarm.co.uk

An ideal walking, touring and cycling base, only six miles from the coast, with sailing, surfing, golf, riding and coastal walks; Camel Trail, the Saints' Way and Pencarrow House nearby. The Eden Project 35 minutes' drive, Padstow 20 minutes, Wadebridge one and a half miles, with shopping, pubs, restaurants, leisure facilities and The Camel Trail.

Looking for Holiday Accommodation?

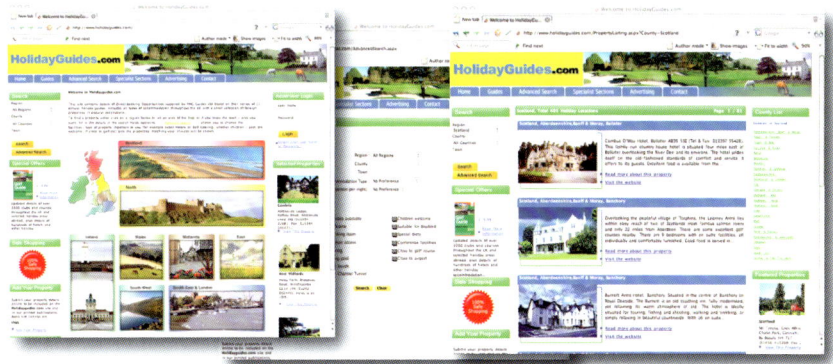

for details of hundreds of properties throughout the UK, visit our website

www.holidayguides.com

Devon

Ashprington

The Durant Arms
Ashprington, Totnes, Devon TQ9 7UP

Nestling amidst the verdant beauty of the Dart Valley, this attractive inn has all the virtues of a traditional English country inn with the comforts of the contemporary holiday-maker in mind. The cuisine is worthy of special mention, with a wide range of main courses catering for all tastes, plus an interesting selection of imaginative desserts. Just three miles past the Elizabethan town of Totnes, this is a fine overnight stop and several beautifully appointed bedrooms suit the purpose admirably.

Tel: 01803 732240 • e-mail: info@thedurantarms.com • www.thedurantarms.com

Please note

All the information in this book is given in good faith in the belief that it is correct. However, the publishers cannot guarantee the facts given in these pages, neither are they responsible for changes in policy, ownership or terms that may take place after the date of going to press. Readers should always satisfy themselves that the facilities they require are available and that the terms, if quoted, still apply.

Fairwater Head Hotel
3 Star Accommodation at Sensible Prices

Located in the tranquil Devon countryside and close to Lyme Regis, this beautiful Edwardian Country House Hotel has all you need for a peaceful and relaxing stopover.

Dogs Most Welcome and Free of Charge
Countryside location with panoramic views • AA Two Rosette Restaurant

The Fairwater Head Hotel
Hawkchurch, Near Axminster, Devon EX13 5TX
Tel: 01297 678349 • Fax: 01297 678459
e-mail: stay@fairwaterheadhotel.co.uk
www.fairwaterheadhotel.co.uk

SOUTH WEST ENGLAND — Devon

Barnstaple

Elizabethan Manor House in secluded gardens, surrounded by rolling countryside. Run by family for 40 years. Friendly and relaxing atmosphere. One mile from local pub serving excellent food.
Easy access to coast and moor and Marwood Hill Gardens.
All bedrooms are large and face South, overlooking the valley.
One four-poster, one double and one twin.
All en suite with colour TV and tea/coffee making facilities in rooms.

Bed and Breakfast from £29pppn, two or more nights from £26pppn.

LEE HOUSE
Marwood, Barnstaple
EX31 4DZ
Tel: 01271 374345

SB

Near Barnstaple • Farmhouse B&B

Mrs J. Ley,
West Barton,
Alverdiscott, Near Barnstaple,
Devon EX31 3PT
Tel: 01271 858230

Our family working farm of 240 acres, with a pedigree herd of suckler cows and sheep, is situated in a small rural village between Barnstaple and Torrington, the Tarka Trail and Rosemoor Gardens. Six miles to the nearest beaches. Double room en suite, twin bedroom also available.
Guest lounge with TV and tea/coffee making facilities.
Good farmhouse cooking.
Ample parking • No pets • Non-smoking

B&B £25pppn. Reduced rates for children under 12; weekly terms on request.

Devon
Barnstaple, Bideford

Lower Yelland Farm Guest House

Situated half way between Barnstaple and Bideford, this delightfully modernised 17thC farmhouse accommodation is part of a working farm. The farm is centrally located for easy access to the many attractions of North Devon, its beautiful beaches, varied walks and sports facilities including golf, surfing, fishing, riding etc. Its proximity to both Exmoor and Dartmoor makes this location perfect for those who wish to explore. Instow with its sandy beach, pubs and restaurants is a just mile away. It lies adjacent to the Tarka Trail, part of the South West Coastal Footpath, and RSPB bird sanctuary.

The bed and breakfast accommodation comprises 3 twin/super king-size and 2 rooms with four-poster beds, 1 double room and 2 single rooms; all rooms en suite, with TV and tea/coffee making facilities. Breakfast includes eggs from our free-range chickens, home-made bread, jams and marmalade. The delightful sitting room has a large selection of books for those who want to relax and browse.

Winner Golden Achievement Award of Excellence for Devon Retreat of the Year

Please visit our website for further details
www.loweryellandfarm.co.uk

**Lower Yelland Farm Guest House, Fremington, Barnstaple EX31 3EN
Tel: 01271 860101 • e-mail: peterday@loweryellandfarm.co.uk**

The Mount, Northdown Road, Bideford EX39 3LP Tel: 01237 473748

A warm welcome awaits you at The Mount in the historic riverside town of Bideford. This small, interesting Georgian building is full of character and charm and is set in its own semi-walled garden, with a beautiful Copper Beech, making it a peaceful haven so close to the town. Within five minutes easy walking, you can be in the centre of the Old Town, with its narrow streets, quay, medieval bridge and park. The Mount is also an ideal centre for exploring the coast, countryside, towns and villages of North Devon. The quiet, restful bedrooms, (single, double, twin and family) are all en suite. Tea and coffee making facilities are available.
All rooms have TV. Non-smoking.
Bed and Breakfast £33 to £38 per person per night.
Golfing breaks – discounted green fees
e-mail: andrew@themountbideford.co.uk
www.themountbideford.co.uk

West Titchberry Farm

Situated on the rugged North Devon coast, West Titchberry is a traditionally run stock farm, half a mile from Hartland Point. The South West Coastal Path skirts around the farm making it an ideal base for walkers.
Pick ups and kit transfers available.

The three guest rooms comprise an en suite family room; one double and one twin room. All rooms have colour TV, radio, hairdryer, tea/coffee making facilities; bathroom/toilet and separate shower room on the same floor. Outside, guests may take advantage of a sheltered walled garden and a games room for the children. Sorry, no pets.

Hartland village is 3 miles away, Clovelly 6 miles, Bideford and Westward Ho! 16 miles and Bude 18 miles.

Tel & Fax: 01237 441287

B&B from £24–£30pppn • Evening meal £14 • Children welcome at reduced rates for under 11s • Open all year except Christmas
Mrs Yvonne Heard, West Titchberry Farm, Hartland Point, Near Bideford EX39 6AU

SOUTH WEST ENGLAND — Devon

Brayton, Brixham

Little Bray House · North Devon

Situated 9 miles east of Barnstaple, Little Bray House is ideally placed for day trips to North and East Devon, the lovely sandy surfing beaches at Saunton Sands and Woolacombe, and many places of interest both coastal and inland. Exmoor also has great charm. Come and share the pace of life and fresh air straight from the open Atlantic and be sustained by a good healthy breakfast. One twin-bedded flatlet with bathroom, or use the Self Catering accommodation in Orchard Cottage and Barn Cottage. Reasonable rates.

Brayford, near Barnstaple EX32 7QG
Tel: 01598 710295
e-mail: holidays@littlebray.co.uk
www.littlebray.co.uk

Brookside Guest House Bed & Breakfast

in Brixham is a contemporary, stylish boutique guest house with elegantly appointed luxury rooms, in the beautiful harbour town of Brixham. Bordering Paignton and Torquay, Brixham is a wonderful base to explore the beautiful scenery of South Devon's English Riviera.

- Great location, close to Brixham town and harbour
- The only Gold Award Guest House in Brixham
- Passionate about personal attention and detail
- Beautiful, stylish interiors and award-winning garden
- Free car parking
- Sun trap large decked patio area
- Fresh, organic, locally sourced breakfast
- 5 quality rooms with complimentary toiletries
- Free Wi-Fi Internet access in all rooms
- Pleasant smoke-free environment • No under 16s

Brookside Guest House
160 New Road, Brixham, Devon TQ5 8DA
01803 858858 • holidays@brooksidebrixham.co.uk
www.brooksidebrixham.co.uk

symbols

	Totally non-smoking			Pets Welcome
	Children Welcome		**SB**	Short Breaks
	Suitable for Disabled Guests			Licensed

Devon

SOUTH WEST ENGLAND 27

Brixham, Chudleigh, Colebrook

Devon • The English Riviera
WOODLANDS GUEST HOUSE
Parkham Road, Brixham, South Devon TQ5 9BU

Overlooking the beautiful Brixham Harbour

Victorian House with large car park at rear and unrestricted on-road parking to the front. All bedrooms en suite, with colour TV, tea/coffee making facilities, mini fridges etc. Four-Poster bedroom with panoramic views over Brixham Harbour and Torbay. Just a short walk away from the picturesque harbour, ancient fishing port with its quaint streets full of varied shops, pubs and restaurants. Ideal holiday base from which to explore the glorious South-West, romantic Dartmoor, boat trips, Paignton and Dartmouth Steam Railway.

Walkers can explore the marvellous Devon countryside. Fishing trips available from the harbour. Bed and Breakfast from £25pppn.
We hope to see you soon and make your stay a memorable one.

Phone 01803 852040, Paul and Rita Pope
for free colour brochure and details
www.woodlandsdevon.co.uk • e-mail: woodlandsbrixham@btinternet.com

SB

★★★★ GUEST HOUSE

GLEN COTTAGE

17th century thatched cottage idyllically set in secluded garden, with stream surrounded by woods. Adjoining a beauty spot with rocks, caves and waterfall. A haven for wildlife and birds; kingfishers and buzzards are a common sight. Outdoor swimming pool. Central for touring the moors or sea. Bed and Breakfast from £25. Tea/coffee all rooms.

Jill Shears, Glen Cottage, Rock Road, Chudleigh TQ13 0JJ (01626 852209)

The Oyster is a modern bungalow in the pretty, peaceful village of Colebrooke in the heart of Mid Devon. There is a spacious garden for children to play around or sit on the patio. Comfortable accommodation with tea/coffee making facilities, with TV in bedroom and lounge. Bedrooms en suite or with private bathroom - two double and one twin. Walking distance to the New Inn, Coleford, a lovely 13th century free house. Dartmoor and Exmoor are only a short drive away. Central heating. Open all year. Ample parking. Terms from £24 per person for Bed and Breakfast. Children and pets welcome. Smoking accepted.

To find us take the Barnstaple road (A377) out of Crediton, turn left after one-and-a-half miles at sign for Colebrooke and Coleford. In Coleford village turn left at the crossroads, then in Colebrooke village take the left hand turning before the church, the Oyster is the second on the right.

Pearl Hockridge, The Oyster, Colebrooke, Crediton EX17 5JQ

The Oyster
01363 84576

Devon

Crediton, Croyde, Dartmoor

Hayne Farm, Cheriton Fitzpaine, Crediton EX17 4HR

Guests are welcome to our 17th century working beef and sheep farm, situated between Cadeleigh and Cheriton Fitzpaine. Exeter nine miles, Tiverton eight miles. South and North coast, Exmoor and Dartmoor within easy reach. Full cooked breakfast. Local pubs nearby. Extensive gardens: summer house overlooking duck pond. No smoking or pets. Bed and Breakfast from £25, reduction for children.

Mrs M Reed - Tel: 01363 866392

Crowborough Farmhouse

Open all year • Rest and Relax in North Devon

A beautifully quiet, peaceful old farmhouse, Crowborough is only 2 miles from the seaside village of Croyde, 4 miles from Saunton Championship Golf Course, and just 8 minutes' walk from Georgeham village. Enjoy exploring the nearby beaches, coastal walks and North Devon countryside, return to the peace and quiet that Crowborough offers, freshen up, then take a leisurely walk to one of the two excellent inns (good food, wine and ale) in the village.

Three bedrooms • Two bathrooms • Breakfast/sitting room with TV • wood burner in winter • No children or pets • Tariff from £30 pppn.

Georgeham, Braunton, North Devon EX33 1JZ

Tel: Audrey Isaac 01271 891005 • www.crowboroughfarm.co.uk

The Edgemoor
Country House Hotel
Haytor Road, Lowerdown Cross,
Bovey Tracey, Devon TQ13 9LE
Tel: 01626 832466

**Charming Country House Hotel in peaceful wooded setting adjacent Dartmoor National Park.
Many lovely walks close by.
All rooms en suite. Excellent food.
Dogs (with well-behaved owners) welcome.**

For more information, photographs, current menus and general information about the area see our website.

www.edgemoor.co.uk or e-mail: reservations@edgemoor.co.uk

Devon
Dartmouth, Dawlish

Welcome to our cosy farmhouse with a friendly service. Easy level parking. Working farm. Farm walks with sea views. Relax in our large beautiful garden, and listen to the birdsong while watching our sheep, cattle and wildlife nearby.
A real oasis yet just four miles to Dartmouth and beaches and one mile to Dartmouth Golf Club and Woodlands Leisure Park.
Three comfortable en suite double or twin rooms with all facilities.
Bed and full English breakfast (Aga cooked) from £30 per person per night. Reductions for longer stays.
Self catering cottage for four also available..

Mrs Stella Buckpitt, Middle Wastray Farm, Blackawton, Totnes, Devon TQ9 7DD
Tel: **01803 712346**
stella.buckpitt1@btopenworld.com
www.middle-wadstray-farm.com

SB

Ocean's Guest House • Dawlish

Sea front location. All rooms en suite with tea/coffee facilities and colour TV. Ground floor rooms available with wheelchair access for people with walking disabilities.

No smoking. Open April to October.

£45-£55 double room. Children £16 each (up to 14 years of age). 10% discount for Senior Citizens in October.

Mrs Henley, Ocean's Guest House, 9 Marine Parade, Dawlish EX7 9DJ • 01626 888139

The South Devon Hotel with a Different Outlook...

- Family Friendly
- 66 En suite Bedrooms
- Indoor & Outdoor pools
- Magnificent Sea Views
- Relaxation Therapies
- Fitness Room
- Hairdresser • Tennis • Snooker
- Table Tennis
- Licensed Bars
- Extensive Lounges
- 19 Acres of Grounds

Langstone Cliff Hotel

AA ★★★ Hotel

Dawlish • South • Devon • EX7 0NA
Telephone **01626 868000**
www.langstone-hotel.co.uk

SOUTH WEST ENGLAND

Devon
Dunsford, Exeter

THE ROYAL OAK INN
Dunsford, Near Exeter EX6 7DA
Tel: 01647 252256

Enjoy a friendly welcome in our traditional Country Pub in the picturesque thatched village of Dunsford. Quiet en suite bedrooms are available in the tastefully converted cob barn. Ideal base for touring Dartmoor, Exeter and the coast, and the beautiful Teign Valley. Real Ale and home-made meals are served.

Well-behaved children and dogs are welcome

Regular dog Kizzy • Resident dog Connie   *Please ring Mark or Judy Harrison for further details.*

Culm Vale Guest House, Stoke Canon, Exeter EX5 4EG

A fine old country house of great charm and character, giving the best of both worlds as we are only three miles to the north of the Cathedral city of Exeter, with its antique shops, yet situated in the heart of Devon's beautiful countryside on the edge of the pretty village of Stoke Canon. An ideal touring centre. Our spacious comfortable Bed and Breakfast accommodation includes full English breakfast, colour TV, tea/coffee facilities, washbasin and razor point in both rooms. Full central heating. Ample free parking. Bed and Breakfast £20 to £27.50 pppn according to room and season. Credit cards accepted.

Telephone & Fax: 01392 841615
e-mail: culmvale@hotmail.com
www.SmoothHound.co.uk/hotels/culm-vale.html

WOODBINE GUESTHOUSE
1 Woodbine Terrace, Exeter, Devon EX4 4LJ
Tel: 01392 203302   Fax: 01392 254678

A small, friendly **non-smoking** guesthouse situated in quiet city centre location, within walking distance of shopping precincts, train/bus stations, University, museum and the historic Cathedral. Modern en suite rooms with hospitality tray, colour TV and shaver points. **Wireless internet access**, hairdryer, ironing facilities and some off-street parking available. Highly recommended. Please check website for up to date terms.

www.woodbineguesthouse.co.uk
e-mail: bookings@woodbineguesthouse.co.uk

Enjoy a peaceful break in beautiful countryside. Close to the Exe Estuary and Powderham Castle, and only two miles to the nearest sandy beach. Take a stroll to the village (only half a mile) to discover many eating places, or a little further to some specially recommended ones. Birdwatching, golf, fishing, racing, etc. all nearby, and centrally situated for exploring all the lovely countryside and coastline in the area. Good shopping in Exeter. Comfortable rooms, guests' lounge, English breakfast. Nice garden. Plenty of parking. NON- SMOKING.
Bed and Breakfast from £24pppn; weekly rates available.

Stile Farm
Starcross, Exeter EX6 8PD
Tel & Fax: 01626 890268
www.stile-farm.co.uk

White Hart
Hotel • Exeter

One of Exeter's most historic inns, the White Hart Hotel retains much of its heritage and charm and yet offers the business or leisure visitor all the facilities and amenities of modern living.

The White Hart boasts 55 en suite rooms. Located in a central position within the old city walls, it's ideally situated to enjoy all the city has to offer, from its famous Gothic Cathedral to the newly opened shopping centre.

The White Hart offers meeting and function rooms with a choice of eating areas, a walled secret garden, an extensive selection of freshly cooked meals, fine cask ales and a comprehensive wine list – all tastes are catered for.

White Hart Hotel
66 South Street, Exeter EX1 1EE
Tel: 01392 279897 • Fax: 01392 250159
E-mail: whitehart.exeter@marstons.co.uk

Staghunters Inn/Hotel
Brendon, Exmoor EX35 6PS

- A friendly family-run Exmoor village inn with frontage to the East Lyn River.
- Beautiful landscaped garden to the rear.
- 12 en suite bedrooms.
- Varied menu of home-made foood using fresh local produce.
- Log fires, fine wines and local cask ales.
- A walkers' paradise in the Doone Vallley, close to Watersmeet, Lynton and Lynmouth.
- Ample off-road parking.
- B&B from £30

Owners: The Wyburn Family.
e-mail: stay@staghunters.com
www.staghunters.com
Tel: 01598 741222
Fax: 01598 741352

Standing in four acres of mature subtropical gardens, overlooking two miles of sandy beach, yet within easy reach of Dartmoor and Exeter, Devoncourt provides an ideal base for a family holiday.

BEDROOMS: The accommodation is in 52 single, double or family rooms, all with private bathroom, colour TV, tea and coffee making facilities and telephone.

LEISURE: Swimming pool, sauna, steam room, whirlpool spa, solarium and fitness centre, snooker room, hair and beauty salon. For those who prefer to be out of doors there is a tennis court, croquet lawn, attractive outdoor heated pool, 18 hole putting green and golf practice area, all within the grounds.

DINING: Attractive lounge bar and restaurant overlooking the fabulous gardens, with fantastic sea views from the large picture windows. Children's menus and vegetarian options available.

DEVONCOURT HOTEL
Douglas Avenue, Exmouth, Devon EX8 2EX
Tel: 01395 272477 • Fax: 01395 269315
e-mail: enquiries@devoncourt.com • www.devoncourt.com

Devon
Honiton
SOUTH WEST ENGLAND 33

As far away from stress as it is possible to be!

Odle Farm

We have two Bed and Breakfast rooms in our family home. Our double room has its own private bathroom and views across the valley; the twin-bedded room has an en suite shower room and views over the courtyard and gardens. Tea and coffee making facilities are in both rooms and a TV in the double room. You are welcome to use the lounge downstairs during your stay which has a TV with DVD and Freeview. Your full English breakfast using local produce and our own free range eggs is served in our conservatory, which has amazing views of the Otter Valley.

No pets • Non-smoking

There is a cosy pub in the village of Upottery and several other excellent hostelries in the vicinity. Odle Farm provides a convenient stop if you are passing through Devon or an ideal base for a short break. B&B £32.50-£40.00pp.

Odle Farm, New Road, Upottery, Near Honiton EX14 9QE
Tel: 01404 861105 • www.odlefarm.co.uk

SB

A most attractively situated working farm. The house is a very old traditional Devon farmhouse located just three miles east of Honiton and enjoying a superb outlook across the Otter Valley. Enjoy a stroll down by the River Otter which runs through the farmland. Try a spot of trout fishing. Children will love to make friends with our two horses. Lovely seaside resorts 12 miles, swimming pool, adventure parks and garden nearby. Traditional English breakfast, colour TV, washbasin, heating, tea/coffee facilities in all rooms.

Bed and Breakfast £20-£25 • Reductions for children.

Mrs June Tucker,
Upottery, Honiton EX14 9QP
Tel: 01404 861680

Devon
Ilfracombe

WENTWORTH HOUSE

Wentworth House, a friendly, family-run private hotel built as a gentleman's residence in 1857, standing in lovely gardens only a stone's throw from the town and minutes from the sea, harbour and Torrs Walks. En suite rooms with colour TV and tea/coffee making facilities. Family rooms sleeping up to four persons. Home-cooked food with packed lunches on request. Spacious bar/lounge. Secure storage for bicycles etc. Private parking in grounds. Open all year. No smoking.

Bed & Breakfast from £22.00
Bed, Breakfast & Evening Meal £32.00.
Discounted rates for weekly bookings.

Stay a few days or a week,
Geoff & Sharon will make your visit a pleasant one.

2 Belmont Road, Ilfracombe EX34 8DR
Tel & Fax: 01271 863048 • e-mail: wentworthhouse@tiscali.co.uk
www.hotelilfracombe.co.uk

Varley House,
Chambercombe Park,
Ilfracombe EX34 9QW

Tel: 01271 863927 • Fax: 01271 879299
e-mail: info@varleyhouse.co.uk
www.varleyhouse.co.uk

ETC/AA ★★★★

Built at the turn of the 20th century for returning officers from the Boer War, Varley generates a feeling of warmth and relaxation, combined with an enviable position overlooking Hillsborough Nature Reserve. Winding paths lead to the Harbour and several secluded coves. Our attractive, spacious, fully en suite bedrooms all have colour TV, central heating, generous beverage tray, hairdryer and clock radio alarm. Superb food, beautiful surroundings and that special friendly atmosphere so essential to a relaxing holiday. Cosy separate bar. Car park. Children over 5 years of age. Dogs by arrangement. NON-SMOKING.
Bed and Breakfast from £30pp. Weekly from £189pp.
Low season 3 day breaks from £78pp.

Devon
Ilfracombe

SOUTH WEST ENGLAND

The Foxhunters Inn
West Down, Near Ilfracombe EX34 8NU

- 300 year-old coaching Inn conveniently situated for beaches and country walks.
- Serving good local food.
- En suite accommodation.
- Pets allowed in bar areas and beer garden, may stay in accommodation by prior arrangement. Water bowls provided.

Tel: 01271 863757 • Fax: 01271 879313
www.foxhuntersinn.co.uk

ILFRACOMBE. St Brannocks House, St Brannocks Road, Ilfracombe EX34 8EQ (Tel & Fax: 01271 863873).
A lovely relaxing home which is open all year. A level walk to the nearby town, shops and harbour. Great food, cosy bar and comfy lounge. Large car park.
• Children and Pets welcome.
VisitBritain ★★★★ *GUEST ACCOMMODATION*.
e-mail: barbara@stbrannockshouse.co.uk
www.stbrannockshouse.co.uk

SB

Please note

All the information in this book is given in good faith in the belief that it is correct. However, the publishers cannot guarantee the facts given in these pages, neither are they responsible for changes in policy, ownership or terms that may take place after the date of going to press. Readers should always satisfy themselves that the facilities they require are available and that the terms, if quoted, still apply.

BLACKWELL PARK
LODDISWELL • KINGSBRIDGE

Bed, Breakfast and Evening Meal is offered in Blackwell Park, a 17th century farmhouse situated 5 miles from Kingsbridge. Six bedrooms, some en suite, and all with washbasins and tea-making facilities. Large garden, also adjoining 54 acres of woodland/Nature Reserve. Ample food with choice of menu. Pets welcome FREE of charge. Dogsitting available.

Dartmoor, Plymouth, Torbay, Dartmouth and many beaches lie within easy reach.
Same family ownership since 1971.

Bed and Breakfast • Evening Meal optional
Proprietress: Mrs B. Kelly • Tel: 01548 821230
Blackwell Park, Loddiswell, Devon TQ7 4EA

SB

The fully licensed Garden Room Restaurant provides tasty traditional home cooking with fresh quality produce. Large and small functions can be catered for in a friendly, relaxed atmosphere.

You and your family can be assured of a warm welcome from Anne Rossiter.

For **B&B** the farmhouse offers a choice of tastefully decorated family, double, twin or single rooms, all en suite, centrally heated and equipped with tea/coffee making facilities and TV. This is a non-smoking zone.

For **Self-Catering** there are two and three bedroomed cottages, with fully equipped kitchens, colour TV/video, night storage heaters and beautiful stone-built fireplaces. They have large gardens, perfect for children and parents alike.

BURTON FARMHOUSE Galmpton, Kingsbridge TQ7 3EY
Tel: 01548 561210 • Fax: 01548 562257
e-mail: anne@burtonfarm.com • www.burtonfarmhouse.co.uk

CENTRY FARM

SB

Centry is located in a peaceful, secluded valley just a mile from Kingsbridge, the centre of the South Hams. Beautiful views across the gardens to fields beyond. The area is well known for its lovely scenery, beaches, and cliff and moorland walks, and is ideal for touring with Salcombe, Dartmouth and Totnes within 11 miles, and Plymouth and Torquay 20 miles.

Centry offers comfort and cleanliness in double en suite rooms, with king size beds, TV, tea/coffee trays, hairdryer, radio/alarm. There is a lounge with TV, and

books and maps of the area, plus a separate diningroom where you can enjoy a delicious farmhouse breakfast. Fridge for guests' use. Gardens, patio, and ample car and boat parking. Regret no pets.
B&B from £27.50pppn.

Centry Farm, Kingsbridge TQ7 2HF
Tel: 01548 852037 • Mobile: 07790 569864
e-mail: pam@centry.plus.com
www.centry.plus.com

Devon
Lifton, Lynmouth

SOUTH WEST ENGLAND 37

The Lifton Hall Hotel and Village Inn
Lifton, Devon PL16 0DR

A family-run hotel where old-fashioned values of service, style and comfort can still be enjoyed. On the Devon/Cornwall border, ½ mile off the A30, it offers the perfect opportunity to explore the West Country.

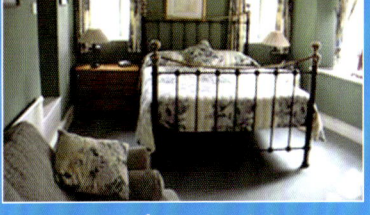

The tastefully furnished bedrooms have en suite bath or shower and a full range of amenities; there is also a light and airy residents' lounge, a stylish dining room and a cosy bar with open fire.

Meals are an essential part of the Lifton Hall experience, with something to suit every taste and appetite, using only the best quality local produce. A carefully chosen and reasonably priced wine list provides the perfect accompaniment.

Tel: 01566 784863 Fax: 01566 784770
relax@liftonhall.co.uk   www.liftonhall.co.uk

SMALL HOTEL

Share the magic of living at the water's edge in an 18th century hotel which stands alone at the harbour entrance. Offering peace and tranquillity, it is the perfect place to relax. All rooms have fantastic views, are centrally heated with en suite facilities. A locally sourced bar and à la carte menu are available with a diverse wine list. A fully licensed bar services the restaurant and gardens.

Ideal for walkers, coastal, woodland and riverside routes with Exmoor a stone's throw away.

Explore the Heritage Coast by boat, great birdwatching and photography.

Visit the Valley of Rocks or the famous Doone Valley.

These are some of the many activities in the area.

AA ★★★★ Guest Accommodation

ROCK HOUSE HOTEL
Lynmouth, North Devon EX35 6EN • Tel: 01598 753508
e-mail: enquiries@rock-house.co.uk • www.rock-house.co.uk

SOUTH WEST ENGLAND — Devon

Lynmouth / Lynton

COUNTISBURY LODGE

Countisbury Hill,
Lynmouth, Devon EX35 6NB
www.countisburylodge.co.uk

A former Victorian vicarage with magnificent views over the Lyn Valley and sea. Extremely quiet and peaceful yet within 5 minutes' walk of the picturesque village of Lynmouth. Licensed bar. All our bedrooms are centrally heated and en suite. Private parking. Pets welcome free of charge.

❖ ALSO SELF CATERING COTTAGE AND APARTMENT AVAILABLE ❖

Brochure/Tariff with pleasure from Pat & Paul Young

Tel: 01598 752388

AA ★★★ Guest Accommodation

Hillside House

SB

Situated on the East Lyn River at Lynmouth, in a perfect position to explore an abundance of coastal, riverside and woodland scenery. Hillside House is ideally suited to the needs of walkers or those of a less strenuous disposition. Double, twin or single rooms are available, each has a TV, hair-dryer, tea/coffee making facilities and either en suite or private bath/shower room. We offer a four-course breakfast in our dining-room where a large selection of books and magazines are available. Well behaved dogs are welcome. Packed lunches on request. Kit transfer can be arranged. Non-smoking.

22 Watersmeet Road, Lynmouth, Devon EX35 6EP
Tel: 01598 753836
E-mail: info@hillside-lynmouth.co.uk
www.hillside-lynmouth.co.uk

Devon

SOUTH WEST ENGLAND 39

Lynmouth / Lynton

The Heatherville

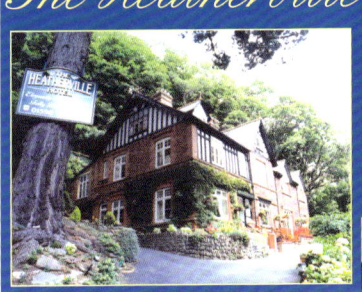

The Heatherville is in a unique location, quiet, secluded and peaceful with breathtaking views, yet only 4 minutes' walk from the pretty harbourside village of Lynmouth.
Mother and daughter team, Jean and Lorraine, run this Victorian house to impeccable standards, reflected in the award of the top grading of five stars for guest accommodation from the AA and VisitBritain.
Our AA award-winning breakfast served in the spacious, stylish dining room is exceptionally good, with all dairy produce being organic.
Beautiful individually styled bedrooms with luxury en suite facilities are a delight to relax in. Private parking. Pet-friendly. Double room from £70.

Tors Park, Lynmouth, Devon EX35 6NB
Tel: 01598 752327
www.heatherville.co.uk
Luxury Accommodation

AA ★★★★

Glenville House, 2 Tors Road, Lynmouth EX35 6ET

Idyllic riverside setting for our delightful Victorian B&B built in local stone, full of character and lovingly refurbished, at the entrance to the Watersmeet Valley. Award-winning garden. Picturesque village, enchanting harbour and unique water-powered cliff railway nestled amidst wooded valleys. Beautiful area where Exmoor meets the sea. Breathtaking scenery, riverside, woodland and magnificent coastal walks with spectacular views to the heather-clad moorland. Peaceful, tranquil, romantic - a very special place.

Tastefully decorated bedrooms, with pretty en suites or private facilities.
Elegant lounge overlooking river.
Enjoy a four-course breakfast in our attractive dining room.
Non-smoking. Licensed. B&B from £29 per person per night.
Tricia and Alan Francis • 01798 752202
e-mail: tricia@glenvillelynmouth.co.uk

www.glenvillelynmouth.co.uk

Woody Bay, Parracombe
Devon EX31 4RA
01598 763224

Moorlands, formerly the Woody Bay Station Hotel, is a family-run Guesthouse in a most beautiful part of North Devon, surrounded by Exmoor countryside and within two miles of the spectacular coastline.

Very comfortable and quiet single, double or family suite accommodation, all en suite with bath or shower, colour TV and beverage making facilities.
Moorlands has a licensed dining room and residents' lounge with open fire, a private outdoor swimming pool, all set in six acres of gardens. A perfect retreat for the country lover to relax in.

Bed and Breakfast £32 - £38pppn.
Evening meals by arrangement £19.50.
Some ground floor rooms and
self-catering apartments available.
Please see our website for special offers.
www.moorlandshotel.co.uk

Blue Ball Inn
formerly The Exmoor Sandpiper Inn

is a romantic Coaching Inn dating in part back to the 13th century, with low ceilings, blackened beams, stone fireplaces and a timeless atmosphere of unspoilt old world charm. Offering visitors great food and drink, a warm welcome and a high standard of accommodation.

The inn is set in an imposing position on a hilltop on Exmoor in North Devon, a few hundred yards from the sea, and high above the twin villages of Lynmouth and Lynton, in an area of oustanding beauty.
The spectacular scenery and endless views attract visitors and hikers from all over the world.

We have 16 en suite bedrooms, comfortable sofas in the bar and lounge areas, and five fireplaces, including a 13th century inglenook. Our extensive menus include local produce wherever possible, such as locally reared meat, amd locally caught game and fish, like Lynmouth Bay lobster; specials are featured daily. We also have a great choice of good wines, available by the bottle or the glass, and a selection of locally brewed beers, some produced specially for us.

Stay with us to relax, or to follow one of the seven circular walks through stunning countryside that start from the Inn. Horse riding for experienced riders or complete novices can be arranged. Plenty of parking. Dogs (no charge), children and walkers are very welcome!

Blue Ball Inn *formerly The Exmoor Sandpiper Inn*
Countisbury, Lynmouth, Devon EX35 6NE
01598 741263
www.BlueBallinn.com • www.exmoorsandpiper.com

Devon
Lynton, Mortehoe, Moretonhampstead

Longmead House — Longmead, Lynton EX35 6DQ

One of Lynton's best kept secrets, with a Silver Award for standards of comfort, hospitality and food. Longmead is a small, friendly, family-run hotel providing old-fashioned hospitality and attention to detail in a relaxed and informal atmosphere, with well equipped, en suite rooms. This delightful house is quietly situated in beautiful surroundings towards the Valley of Rocks, yet close to the village centre, with ample car parking. Imaginative evening menu, in low season • Licensed.

B&B from £25 to £33 pppn. Caroline & Alan Reeves.

e-mail: info@longmeadhouse.co.uk
www.longmeadhouse.co.uk • Tel: 01598 752523

SB

Situated in the pretty village of Mortehoe, The Smugglers offers luxury accommodation from twin rooms to family suites.
Treat yourselves and your pets to beautiful coastal walks and golden beaches, before you sample our delicious home-cooked meals, real ales and warm, year round hospitality.

**The Smugglers Rest Inn,
North Morte Road, Mortehoe,
North Devon EX34 7DR
Tel/Fax: 01271 870891**

info@smugglersmortehoe.co.uk
www.smugglersmortehoe.co.uk

SB

Great Sloncombe Farm
**Moretonhampstead Devon TQ13 8QF
Tel: 01647 440595**

Share the magic of Dartmoor all year round while staying in our lovely 13th century farmhouse full of interesting historical features. A working mixed farm set amongst peaceful meadows and woodland abundant in wild flowers and animals, including badgers, foxes, deer and buzzards. A welcoming and informal place to relax and explore the moors and Devon countryside. Comfortable double and twin rooms with en suite facilities, TV, central heating and coffee/tea making facilities. Delicious Devonshire breakfasts with new baked bread.

Open all year~No smoking~Farm Stay UK
e-mail: hmerchant@sloncombe.freeserve.co.uk • www.greatsloncombefarm.co.uk

SOUTH WEST ENGLAND — Devon

Okehampton, Ottery St Mary

Teachmore Cottage

A friendly and warm welcome awaits at this Bed & Breakfast, peacefully located and surrounded by farmland with views to Dartmoor. An ideal peaceful haven away from the hustle and bustle, suitable for cycling, riding, touring and walking (including the nearby Tarka Trail). Situated between Inwardleigh and Jacobstowe, within 5 minutes' drive of Okehampton, 10 minutes from the A30 and Dartmoor, 30 minutes from Bude, 35 minutes from Exeter.

The popular local pub provides good quality home-cooked food.

Accommodation consists of a self-contained annexe with private shower room/wc, own kitchen area with cooking facilities, central heating and colour TV. Guests are able to relax in our private garden with patio. B&B £25pppn. Discounts available for mini breaks or self-catering guests. Open all year. No smoking and no pets. Reductions for children. e-mail: 12penny@tiscali.co.uk

Penny Roberts, Teachmore Cottage, Inwardleigh, Okehampton, Devon EX20 3AJ (01837 851435)

THE CASTLE INN HOTEL & RESTAURANT

Lydford, Okehampton, Devon EX20 4BH
Tel: 01822 820241 • Fax: 01822 820454
info@castleinnlydford.com • www.castleinnlydford.co.uk

One of the finest traditional wayside inns in the West Country, this romantic Elizabethan, family-run hotel simply oozes character. Featured in Conan Doyle's 'The Hound of the Baskervilles', it nestles on the western slopes of Dartmoor, offering first-class food in a bar and restaurant with slate floors, bowed ceilings, low, lamp-lit beams and fascinating antiques; dining by candlelight from imaginative à la carte menus is a memorable experience. Close by is Lydford Castle, built in 1195, and picturesque Lydford Gorge. Guest rooms, decorated in individual style, are beautifully furnished and equipped. This is a wonderful place to shake off the cobwebs of urban existence and appreciate the really worthwhile things of life.

Peace and Tranquillity are easily found at Fluxton Farm

A delightful 16th century Devon longhouse in the beautiful Otter Valley

Occupying a sheltered position just south of Ottery St Mary, and only 4 miles from the sea at Sidmouth. We are no longer a working farm, but keep ducks, chickens and geese, and have lots of cats.

We have 10 bedrooms, all en suite, and two charming sitting rooms. Our beamed dining room has a large open fire and separate tables, where a full English breakfast is served.

The house stands in peaceful, lawned gardens with a small trout stream flowing through.

As well as peace and quiet, we offer a warm welcome and an easy-going atmosphere, plus a high level of care and attention, comfort and delicious food.

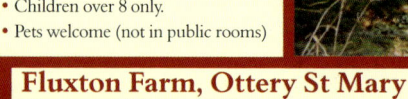

• Children over 8 only.
• Pets welcome (not in public rooms)

Fluxton Farm, Ottery St Mary Devon EX11 1RJ
Tel: 01404 812818 • Fax: 01404 814843   AA ★★
Proprietor Ann Forth • www.fluxtonfarm.co.uk

Devon
Paignton, Plymouth

SOUTH WEST ENGLAND 43

The No Smoking Clifton Hotel Paignton
9-10 Kernou Road, Paignton TQ4 6BA
Tel & Fax: 01803 556545

A licensed, "green" home from home in the heart of the English Riviera. Ideal level location just off the sea front and close to shops and stations. On the SW Coastal Path. All rooms en suite with TV and beverages. Superb evening meals available using mostly organic produce - special diets catered for. Good public transport system for exploring locally and further afield - Exeter, Plymouth, Dartmoor, etc. Open Easter to late September. From £30 per person Bed and Breakfast. *Steve and Freda Bamford Dwane.*

e-mail: bandb@cliftonhotelpaignton.co.uk • www.cliftonhotelpaignton.co.uk

SB

The Cranbourne
278/282 Citadel Road,
The Hoe, Plymouth PL1 2PZ
Tel: 01752 263858/661400/224646
Fax: 01752 263858

- Equidistant City Centre and Hoe Promenade • All bedrooms beautifully decorated, heated, with colour TV, tea/coffee facilities • ¼ mile Ferry Terminal • Keys for access at all times
- Licensed Bar • Pets by prior arrangement (No charge) • Large secure car park

Under the personal supervision of The Williams Family

AA Guest Accommodation ★★★★

e-mail: cran.hotel@virgin.net • www.cranbournehotel.co.uk

Other specialised holiday guides from FHG

PUBS & INNS OF BRITAIN
COUNTRY HOTELS OF BRITAIN
WEEKEND & SHORT BREAKS IN BRITAIN & IRELAND
THE GOLF GUIDE WHERE TO PLAY, WHERE TO STAY
PETS WELCOME!
SELF-CATERING HOLIDAYS IN BRITAIN
500 GREAT PLACES TO STAY IN BRITAIN
CARAVAN & CAMPING HOLIDAYS IN BRITAIN
FAMILY BREAKS IN BRITAIN

Published annually: available in all good bookshops or direct from the publisher:
FHG Guides, Abbey Mill Business Centre, Seedhill, Paisley PA1 1TJ
Tel: 0141 887 0428 • Fax: 0141 889 7204
e-mail: admin@fhguides.co.uk • www.holidayguides.com

PORT LIGHT
Hotel, Restaurant & Inn

As featured in Times, Guardian, Mail, Telegraph, Express, and many pet-friendly internet sites

- Luxury en suite rooms, easy access onto the gardens
- Close to secluded sandy cove, 20 minutes' walk
- No charge for pets which are most welcome throughout the hotel
- Outstanding reputation for service and superb home-cooked fayre
- Set alongside the famous National Trust Salcombe to Hope Cove coastal walk
- Fully licensed bar - log burner - real ale
- Large free car park ◆ Open Christmas & New Year ◆ Self-catering cottages

A totally unique location, set amidst acres of National Trust coastal countryside with panoramic views towards Cornwall, Dartmoor and France.

Doggies' Heaven, Walkers' Paradise, Romantics' Dream

Bolberry Down, Malborough, Near Salcombe, South Devon TQ7 3DY
e-mail: info@portlight.co.uk • www.portlight.co.uk
Tel: (01548) 561384 or (07970) 859992 • Sean & Hazel Hassall

Devon · Seaton, Sidmouth · **SOUTH WEST ENGLAND** 45

Beaumont, Castle Hill, Seaton EX12 2QW

Spacious and gracious Victorian, seafront guesthouse in a quiet East Devon town on England's only World Heritage coastline. Shopping, restaurants and leisure facilities nearby. Unrivalled views over Lyme Bay and Beer Cliffs. Half-mile promenade just yards away.
All five rooms en suite with TV, wifi access, tea and coffee making facilities, radio and hairdryer.
Parking available. Bed and Breakfast from £30 per person per night.
Special weekly rate. A warm welcome is assured.

Tony and Jane Hill • 01297 20832
e-mail: tony@lymebay.demon.co.uk
www.smoothhound.co.uk/hotels/beaumon1.html

SB

Pinn Barton, Peak Hill, Sidmouth EX10 0NN

Peace, comfort and a warm welcome where we offer the little extras that attract guests back time and time again. Two miles from Sidmouth seafront. Lovely coastal walks and views from the farm. Warm and comfortable en suite bedrooms with TV, fridge, beverage trays and access at all times.

Open all year • No smoking • Children welcome

One twin, one double and one family room available.
Terms from £28 to £32 per person.

Mrs Betty S. Sage • Tel & Fax: 01395 514004
e-mail: betty@pinnbartonfarm.co.uk
www.pinnbartonfarm.co.uk

LOWER PINN FARM Peak Hill, Sidmouth EX10 0NN
Tel: 01395 513733
e-mail: liz@lowerpinnfarm.co.uk • www.lowerpinnfarm.co.uk

19th century built farmhouse on the World Heritage Jurassic Coast, two miles west of the unspoilt coastal resort of Sidmouth and one mile to the east of the pretty village of Otterton. Ideally situated for visiting many places, and for walking, with access to coastal path.

Comfortable, centrally heated en suite rooms with colour television and hot drink making facilities. Guests have their own keys and may return at all times throughout the day. Good hearty breakfast served in the dining room. Ample off-road parking. Children and pets welcome. Lower Pinn is a no smoking establishment. Open all year.

Bed and Breakfast from £28 to £35

SB

BRAMLEY LODGE GUEST HOUSE
Vicarage Road, Sidmouth EX10 8UQ

A family-owned and run guest house, in a town house only half-a-mile level walk via the High Street to the sea front. Relax in the residents' garden, backing on to the River Sid and The Byes Parkland. Enjoy breakfast in our dining room before exploring Sidmouth and East Devon's attractions. Six comfortable bedrooms; single, double and family rooms, each with hot drinks facilities and TV; most with en suite facilities. Optional home-cooked evening meals. Private parking at rear. Bed and Breakfast from £28.50 to £32.00 per person. Child reductions. Pets by arrangement. For further information or to book ring Linda and David on 01395 515710.
e-mail: haslam@bramleylodge.fsnet.co.uk

The Longhouse • Salcombe Hill, Sidmouth

Formerly a part of the Norman Lockyer Observatory, The Longhouse has been lovingly restored and recently updated to provide the benefits of modern living. Surrounded by woodland, it is just under a mile from the town centre and sea front in easy reach of the town's facilities.

- Ample private off-road parking available.
- All rooms have en suite showers.
- Tea/coffee making facilities, TV and DVD.
- Aga-cooked full English breakfast, using fresh local produce.
- Towels and linen supplied.

A warm welcome is guaranteed, please phone and speak to Lynne or Pete Vincent for further booking information, tariff and availability.
Tel: 01395 577973 • www.holidaysinsidmouth.co.uk

The Groveside

The Groveside is a privately owned and run Guest House, entirely non-smoking, currently offering Bed and Breakfast throughout the year. We are a few minutes' level walk from the town centre and seafront.

Spacious, centrally heated en suite bedrooms have colour television, clock radio and tea and coffee making facilities. The guest lounge is comfortably furnished, with many personal touches. It is the perfect place to relax, read a book, watch the television, or plan your day out in Sidmouth or the surrounding area.

In the dining room enjoy a leisurely breakfast, with a wide choice from the buffet table followed by a full English breakfast.

We offer ample private car parking, but with Sidmouth shops, beaches and gardens all within easy walking distance from our Bed and Breakfast, who needs their car? The Groveside is our home and as our guests we hope you will enjoy your stay with us.

Vicarage Road, Sidmouth EX10 8UQ • Tel: 01395 513406
www.eastdevon.net/groveside

Partridge Arms Farm
Yeo Mill, West Anstey, South Molton, North Devon EX36 3NU

Now a working farm of over 200 acres, four miles west of Dulverton, "Partridge Arms Farm" was once a coaching inn and has been in the same family since 1906. Genuine hospitality and traditional farmhouse fare await you. Comfortable accommodation in double, twin and single rooms, some of which have en suite facilities. There is also an original four-poster bedroom.
Children welcome • Animals by arrangement • Residential licence • Open all year
Fishing and riding available nearby • FARM HOLIDAY GUIDE DIPLOMA WINNER.

Bed and Breakfast from £25; Evening Meal from £14.   Hazel Milton • 01398 341217
Fax: 01398 341569 • e-mail: bangermilton@hotmail.com
TOURIST ASSOCIATION

Devon

SOUTH WEST ENGLAND 47

Tiverton, Torquay

The Mill

A warm welcome awaits you at our converted mill, beautifully situated on the banks of the picturesque River Exe. Close to the National Trust's Knightshayes Court and on the route of the Exe Valley Way. Easy access to both the north and south coasts, Exmoor and Dartmoor. Only two miles from Tiverton. Relaxing and friendly atmosphere with delicious farmhouse fare. En suite bedrooms with TV and tea/coffee making facilities.

Bed and Breakfast from £26.

Mrs L. Arnold, The Mill, Lower Washfield, Tiverton EX16 9PD • 01884 255297
e-mail: themillwashfield@hotmail.co.uk • www.themill-tiverton.co.uk

SB

The Glenorleigh
26 Cleveland Road
Torquay
Devon TQ2 5BE
Tel: 01803 292135
Fax: 01803 213717
As featured on BBC Holiday programme
David & Pam Skelly
AA ★★★★

Situated in a quiet residential area, Glenorleigh is 10 minutes' walk from both the sea front and the town centre.
• Delightful en suite rooms, with your comfort in mind.
• Good home cooking, both English and Continental, plenty of choice, with vegetarian options available daily.
• Bar leading onto terrace overlooking Mediterranean-style garden with feature palms and heated swimming pool. • Discounts for children and Senior Citizens. • Brochures and menus available on request. • B&B £30–£40; Dinner £14.

e-mail: glenorleighhotel@btinternet.com • www.glenorleigh.co.uk

Heathcliff House 16 Newton Road, Torquay, Devon TQ2 5BZ
Telephone: 01803 211580 • Owners: Adrian & Terri Bailey

This former vicarage is now a superbly appointed family-run B&B equipped for today yet retaining its Victorian charm. All the bedrooms have full en suite facilities, colour TV and drink making facilities. The elegant licensed bar boasts an extensive menu and unlike many establishments', the car park has sufficient space to accommodate all vehicles to eliminate roadside parking. Torquay's main beach, high street shops, entertainment and restaurants are all nearby and with full English breakfast included, it is easy to see why guests return time after time.

Tariff for B&B ranges between £23 and £37pppn.

e-mail: heathcliffhouse@btconnect.com
www.heathcliffhousehotel.co.uk

SB

Aveland House

Just a short walk to Babbacombe seafront and St Marychurch Village
Close to shops, theatres, restaurants and attractions
An ideal location for holidays and short breaks

- AA 4 Star Guest Accommodation
- Licensed
- All rooms en-suite
- Special diets catered for
- Evening meal optional
- Children welcome
- Car park and gardens
- Non Smoking Silver Award
- Free wi-fi internet access
- All major credit cards accepted

Aveland Road, Babbacombe, Torquay, Devon, TQ1 3PT
Tel: 01803 326622   Fax: 01803 328940
email: avelandhouse@aol.com   Website www.avelandhouse.co.uk

SB

48 SOUTH WEST ENGLAND

Devon
Torquay

SEA POINT HOTEL

Lovely Grade II Listed family-run hotel ideally situated in a quiet location just 10 minutes' walk to the harbour and the town's many other attractions. En suite rooms with colour TV and beverage-making facilities.

B&B from £17-£25pppn • Children under 13 half price, under 2s free. 5% discount on weekly bookings • 4 nights for 3 Special Breaks

• Licensed bar • Off-road parking • Open all year

Please ring Dave or Kim for bookings or brochure.

Old Torwood Road, Torquay TQ1 1PR • Tel: 01803 211808
e-mail: seapointhotel@hotmail.com • www.seapointhotel.co.uk

Silverlands Guest House

27 Newton Road, Torquay TQ2 5DB
Telephone: 01803 292013

Silverlands is a family-run guest house with a warm welcome and comfortable bedrooms. We cater for couples and families. All rooms have colour television, hairdryer and complimentary drinks-making facilities. We serve a full English breakfast or, if you prefer a lighter breakfast, we can accommodate your wishes; we also cater for vegetarians and coeliac diets. We are a 25 minute walk from Torquay and the Marina, where you will find a number of places to visit.

Please check our website for more information.

enquiries@silverlandsguesthouse.co.uk
www.silverlandsguesthouse.co.uk

Looking for Holiday Accommodation?

FHG KUPERARD

for details of hundreds of properties throughout the UK, visit our website

www.holidayguides.com

Devon SOUTH WEST ENGLAND 49

Totnes, Umberleigh, Yelverton

ORCHARD HOUSE
Horner, Halwell, Totnes, Devon TQ9 7LB
Telephone: 01548 821448
e-mail: Helen@orchard-house-halwell.co.uk
www.orchard-house-halwell.co.uk

Tucked away in a rural valley of the South Hams, only a short drive from sandy beaches and Dartmoor. With mature gardens and private parking surrounding the house, it is a peaceful location from which to enjoy your stay.
Luxury accommodation in three spacious and beautifully furnished rooms, all en suite with colour TV, clock radio, hair dryer and tea/coffee tray. Full central heating, sitting area has a log burner. Ample and varied breakfast using local produce. No smoking or pets.

From £27.50 to £30 pppn

BOUCHLAND FARM
. John and Eileen Chapple welcome you to spend a holiday on their family-run working farm, one mile off the A377 overlooking the lovely Taw Valley.

Delicious home-cooking using fresh farm produce - full English breakfasts and varied four-course evening meal (optional). Family, double and twin rooms with washbasins, tea-making facilities and colour TV. En suite available. Lounge with TV, separate dining room, games room with snooker, darts and table tennis.

Ideal for exploring North Devon's sandy beaches, moors and many local places of interest.
Bed and Breakfast from £27.50 per person per night, reductions for children.

Bouchland Farm, Burrington, Umberleigh EX37 9NF • 01769 560394

Callisham Farm B&B
Meavy, Near Yelverton PL20 6PS
Tel/Fax: 01822 853901

Rustic charm in rural Devon countryside
Esme Wills and her family extend a warm welcome to their guests all year round. Feel at home in one of the three comfortable en suite bedrooms, with tea/coffee tray, clock radio and TV. Relax in the warm and cosy guests' lounge. A superb English breakfast is the perfect beginning to the day; vegetarian and special diets catered for on request. With easy access to rolling moorland, Callisham is a perfect base for riding, fishing, golf, and touring the beautiful coasts of Devon and Cornwall. In the nearby village of Meavy, the Royal Oak offers a selection of real ales and fine food; other pubs within a mile and a half; Plymouth 12 miles.
www.callisham.co.uk • esme@callisham.co.uk

symbols

🚭	Totally non-smoking	🐕	Pets Welcome
🎠	Children Welcome	**SB**	Short Breaks
♿	Suitable for Disabled Guests	🍷	Licensed

50 SOUTH WEST ENGLAND

Dorset

Beaminster, Bournemouth

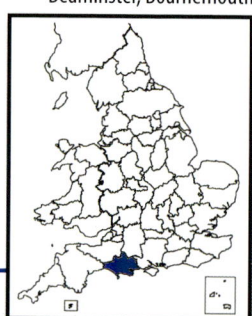

Dorset

Watermeadow House Tel: 01308 862619
Bridge Farm, Hooke, Beaminster, Dorset DT8 3PD

You are assured of a warm welcome at Watermeadow House, on the edge of the small village of Hooke, near Beaminster. We offer high quality accommodation in a friendly atmosphere. Two well furnished bedrooms with many facilities, and breakfast served in the attractive sunroom. A large lawned garden surrounds the house, where guests are welcome to enjoy the peace and tranquillity of the countryside. No smoking. Prices from £30 per person including full English breakfast. Children from £15.

e-mail: enquiries@watermeadowhouse.co.uk
www.watermeadowhouse.co.uk

Silver Award

SB

Lynne and John welcome you to their family-run guest house. Comfortable lounge with colour television. Good home cooking. Tea and coffee making facilities in all rooms. Rooms with showers available, full English Breakfast. Children welcome. Senior Citizens' reductions. Access 24 hours. Close to beach, shops and bus routes. Strictly no smoking. No stag or hen parties.
Terms £18 to £26 pppn.

**Lynne and John Scott, Balmer Lodge,
23 Irving Road, Southbourne BH6 5BQ
Tel: 01202 428545**
e-mail: john.wscott@hotmail.co.uk
or lynne.vscott@hotmail.co.uk

DENEWOOD HOTEL
**40 Sea Road,
Bournemouth BH5 1BQ
Tel: 01202 309913
Fax: 01202 391155
www.denewood.co.uk**

Warm, friendly hotel in excellent central location, just 500 yards from the beach and close to the shops. Good parking. Single, twin, double and family rooms available, all en suite. Residential and restaurant licence. TV, tea/coffee and biscuits in rooms. Health salon and spa on site. Open all year. Children and pets welcome. Please check out our website.

**Bed and Breakfast from £22.50-£30.
Special weekly rates available
and Short Break discounts.**

Dorset
Bournemouth

Gervis Court Hotel
38 Gervis Road, Bournemouth BH1 3DH

Gervis Court is a detached Victorian villa set in its own grounds, yet it is only a few minutes' walk to the town centre. The clean sandy beach, B.I.C., shops, attractions and clubs being so close allows you to leave your car in our car park. All rooms are en suite with TV and kettles. Prices start from £25-£33 per person depending on availability and season. For more information please look us up on our website.

Tel: 01202 556871 • Fax: 01202 467066
enquiries@gerviscourthotel.co.uk
www.gerviscourthotel.co.uk

The Golden Sovereign Hotel
97 Alumhurst Road, Alum Chine, Bournemouth BH4 8HR

Charming Victorian hotel close to award-winning beaches and wooded Chine walks. Experience our unique atmosphere. Cosy bar. En suite rooms all with tea/coffee making facilities, television, clock/radio alarm and internet access. Sorry, no pets.

Our priority? – Your comfort and happiness

- Prices from £25pppn.
- Brochure on request.
- Families welcome
- Private parking

Tel: 01202 762088
Fax: 01202 762417
e-mail: scott.p@talk21.com
www.goldensovereignhotel.com

★★★★ GUEST HOUSE

THE VINE HOTEL
22 Southern Road, Southbourne
Bournemouth BH6 3SR
Telephone: 01202 428309

A small, family, award-winning non-smoking Hotel only three hundred yards from dog-friendly beach and shops.

All rooms en suite; tea/coffee making facilities and colour TV. Residential licence with attractive bar. Full central heating. Forecourt parking. Open all year.

Pets Welcome – Free of Charge
FHG Diploma

52 SOUTH WEST ENGLAND

Dorset
Bournemouth

Bed & Breakfast at Tiffany's

Set in its own spacious grounds with ample parking, Tiffany's is centrally situated within minutes' walk of the town centre with unrivalled shopping, fine restaurants and lively nightlife. A leisurely stroll will take you to the promenade and miles of clean, safe beaches.

Relax in the hotel's elegant Breakfast Room and enjoy an English breakfast. The 15 beautifully appointed en suite bedrooms have colour TV, hairdryer and tea/coffee making facilities. Family rooms and non-smoking rooms available.

An excellent base for exploring the New Forest and the South Coast.

Tiffany's Bed & Breakfast, Chine Crescent, West Cliff, Bournemouth BH2 5LB
Tel: 01202 551424 • Fax: 01202 318559
e-mail: tiffanyshotel@aol.com • www.tiffanysbb.co.uk

A small, friendly, family-run, licensed, **NON-SMOKING** guest house, situated in one of the most pleasant parts of Southbourne, in a quiet tree-lined road. We are within two minutes of European award 'Blue Flag' beach, offering seven miles of sandy beaches and safe bathing. The promenade can be reached by either a zig-zag path or the popular cliff lift. The Woodside is in a wonderful position for cliff top walks, with panoramic views over the Isle of Wight and the Purbeck Hills. All rooms are en suite, with tea/coffee making facilities, colour TV and shaver points.

**Hazel & Keith Ingram,
The Woodside,
29 Southern Road, Southbourne,
Bournemouth BH6 3SR
Tel: 01202 427213**

AA ★★★★ Guest House

e-mail: enquiries@woodsidehotel.co.uk
www.the-woodside.co.uk

Mayfield, 46 Frances Road, Knyveton Gardens, Bournemouth BH1 3SA

SB

Sandra and Mike Barling make your comfort, food and relaxation their concern, offering a high standard of catering and comfort. Ideally situated overlooking Knyveton Gardens with bowls, petanque, tennis and sensory garden. Handy for sea, shops, shows, rail and coach stations.
All rooms are en suite, with colour TV, teamaking, central heating, hairdryer, trouser press, fridge and radio alarm. Own keys. Parking.
Bed and Breakfast from £26 to £30 daily.
Bed, Breakfast and Evening Dinner from £170 to £200 weekly per person.
Bargain Breaks October/April.

Tel: 01202 551839 • www.hotelmayfield.co.uk

Registered with Bournemouth Quality Standards

SOUTHERNHAY HOTEL
**42 Alum Chine Rd,
Westbourne,
Bournemouth
BH4 8DX**

Tel & Fax:
01202 761251

enquiries@southernhayhotel.co.uk
www.southernhayhotel.co.uk

ETC ★★★

The Southernhay Hotel provides warm, friendly, high standard accommodation with a large car park. All rooms have colour TV, tea/coffee making facilities, hairdryer and radio alarm clock. The hotel is ideally situated at the head of Alum Chine (a wooded ravine) leading down to the sea and miles of safe sandy beaches.
The Bournemouth International Centre, cinemas, theatres, restaurants, clubs and pubs are all within easy reach; minutes by car or the frequent bus service. Seven bedrooms, five en suite. Open all year. Details from Tom and Lynn Derby.

2 for 1 Golf deals available

Bed and Breakfast from £20 to £30 per adult per night.

Dorset
Bridport

SOUTH WEST ENGLAND 53

New House Farm
Bed & Breakfast

SB

Situated in beautiful countryside, set in the rural Dorset hills, comfortable farmhouse with large garden where you are welcome to sit or stroll around. Two large rooms available, both en suite, with lovely views. Each room has television, fridge and tea/coffee making facilities. Discover the charm of Bridport, the Chesil Beach and the World Heritage Coastline. Seaside, golf courses, fossil hunting, gardens, wonderful walking, lots to see and do – including our own Coarse Fishing Lake, well stocked with carp, roach and tench. Tickets available from New House Farm.

Bed and Breakfast from £26

Jane Greening, New House Farm, Mangerton Lane, Bradpole, Bridport DT6 3SF
Tel & Fax: 01308 422884 • e-mail: mangertonlake@btconnect.com
www.mangertonlake.co.uk

Situated ten minutes' walk from the market town of Bridport, two miles from the Jurassic Coast, ten miles from Lyme Regis and ten miles from the sub-tropical gardens at Abbotsbury, near Weymouth.
Bedrooms with TV, tea making facilities and washbasin. Parking space available.

Mrs K.E. Parsons
179 St Andrews Road, Bridport • 01308 422038

We invite you to relax and enjoy a carefree holiday in our 16th/17th century farmhouse on a working farm with cows, sheep and some chickens. The heated bedrooms are all en suite, with radio clock alarm, TV and tea/coffee making. There is a lounge with colour TV. This is an ideal base for touring the South West, and the historic market town of Bridport is 4 miles away. The surrounding area offers activities such as horse riding , golf and fishing.

SB

Dunster Farm

Broadoak, Bridport DT6 5NR • Tel: 01308 424626 • Fax: 01308 423544
E-mail: dunsterfarm@surfree.co.uk • www.dunsterfarm.co.uk

Dorset
Bridport

Britmead House Hotel

West Bay Road,
Bridport DT6 4EG
Tel: 01308 422941
Fax: 01308 422516
e-mail: britmead@talk21.com
www.britmeadhouse.co.uk

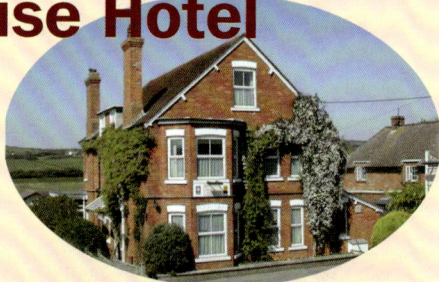

An elegant Edwardian house, family-run and ideally situated between Bridport and West Bay Harbour, with its beaches, golf course, Chesil Beach and Dorset Coastal Path. We offer full en suite rooms (two ground floor), all with TV, tea/coffee making facilities, and hairdryer. South facing lounge and dining room overlooking the garden.
Private parking • Non-smoking.

Wisteria Cottage
Morcombelake, West Dorset

Stunning panoramic views from our comfortable, well equipped en suite guest rooms.
A friendly welcome and good food. Vegetarian and special diets also catered for.
An ideal base for exploring the Jurassic World Heritage Coast and historic towns of Lyme Regis and Bridport.
A walkers' paradise or just an idyllic spot for people seeking tranquillity and fresh country air. Fossil hunting equipment available for our guests' use.
Off road parking. Visit Britain Four Star award.
Open all year except Christmas and New Year.
Rooms from £50 - £70 per night for two persons sharing, £40 – 50 single occupancy. Low season midweek breaks also available. Call now for a brochure, or visit our website.

Contact Details:
Taylors Lane, Morcombelake, Dorset DT6 6ED
Tel: 01297 489019
www.dorsetcottage.org.uk
E-mail: dave@dorsetcottage.org.uk

Dorset

SOUTH WEST ENGLAND 55

Bridport, Charmouth, Chideock, Dorchester

17th Century Frogmore Farm

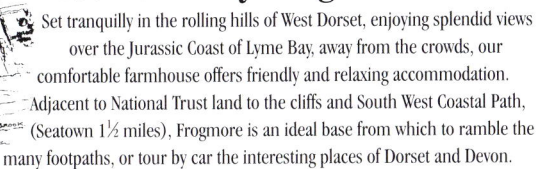

Set tranquilly in the rolling hills of West Dorset, enjoying splendid views over the Jurassic Coast of Lyme Bay, away from the crowds, our comfortable farmhouse offers friendly and relaxing accommodation. Adjacent to National Trust land to the cliffs and South West Coastal Path, (Seatown 1½ miles), Frogmore is an ideal base from which to ramble the many footpaths, or tour by car the interesting places of Dorset and Devon. En suite bedrooms, TV and tea-making facilities; guests' dining room and cosy lounge with woodburner. Well behaved dogs very welcome. *Open all year.* Car essential. Bed & Breakfast from £27. Brochure and terms free on request.

Contact Mrs Sue Norman, Frogmore Farm, Chideock, Bridport DT6 6HT
Tel: 01308 456259 • E-mail: bookings@frogmorefarm.com • www.frogmorefarm.com

SB

Kingfishers

Come to Kingfishers and relax on your large sunny balcony overlooking the river and gardens. Set in beautiful surroundings on the banks of the River Char, Kingfishers offers a secluded setting yet is only a short stroll to the beach and village amenities.
• 2 miles Lyme Regis • Adjoining National Trust land
• South Coast Path • Free access • Ample parking
• Home-cooked food including clotted cream teas available throughout the day. *Open all year.*

**Mrs C.Reeves,
Kingfishers, Newlands Bridge,
Charmouth, Dorset DT6 6QZ
Tel: 01297 560232**

Bay Tree House, Duke Street, Chideock DT6 6JW

Situated in the coastal village of Chideock, with its 13thC Parish Church and dramatic views of Eype Down and Thorncombe Beacon. An ideal location for walking holiays; close to the South West Coastal Path, with footpaths crossing the village. Bay Tree House has two Bed and Breakfast rooms, both appointed and maintained to the highest standard. The double room has an en suite bathroom and the twin room has an en suite shower room. Each bedroom has tea and coffee making facilities, TV, and comfortable armchairs to relax in. To set you up for a good start to the day we serve a hearty English breakfast, which can be enjoyed on the veranda on sunny days. 
Bay Tree House is a non smoking establishment.

Tel: 01297 489336 • Mobile 07817 115080 • www.baytreechideock.co.uk

DORCHESTER. Mrs V.A. Bradbeer, Nethercroft, Winterbourne Abbas, Dorchester DT2 9LU (01305 889337).
This country house with its friendly and homely atmosphere welcomes you to the heart of Hardy's Wessex. Central for touring the many places of interest that Dorset has to offer, including Corfe Castle, Lyme Regis, Dorchester, Weymouth, Lulworth Cove, etc. Lovely country walks and many local attractions. Two double rooms, one single, en suite or separate bathroom. TV lounge, dining room. Large garden. Open all year. Central heating. Car essential, ample parking. Take the A35 from Dorchester, we are the last house at the Western edge of the village.
Rates: Bed and Breakfast from £25 per person.
www.nethercroft.com

SB

e-mail: v.bradbeer@ukonline.co.uk

SOUTH WEST ENGLAND

Dorset
Dorchester

Brambles
Bed & Breakfast accommodation in Dorset

Set in beautiful, tranquil countryside, Brambles is a pretty, thatched cottage offering every comfort, superb views and a friendly welcome. There is a choice of en suite, twin, double or single rooms, all very comfortable and with colour TV and tea/coffee making facilities. Pretty garden available for relaxing in. Full English or Continental breakfast served. Occasional evening meals available by arrangement. Parking available. There are many interesting places to visit and wonderful walks for enthusiasts. B&B from £25 single pppn, £35 double/twin pppn.

Woolcombe, Melbury Bubb, Dorchester DT2 0NJ
Tel: 01935 83672 • www.bramblesdorset.co.uk
e-mail: bramblesbandb@hotmail.co.uk

ETC ★★★★ Guest House

CHURCHVIEW GUEST HOUSE
Winterbourne Abbas, Dorchester, Dorset DT2 9LS   Tel/Fax: 01305 889296

Our 17th century Guest House, noted for warm hospitality, delicious breakfasts and evening meals, makes an ideal base for touring beautiful West Dorset. Our character bedrooms are comfortable and well-appointed. Meals, served in our beautiful dining room, feature local produce, with relaxation provided by two attractive lounges and licensed bar. Hosts, Jane and Michael Deller, are pleased to give every assistance, with local information to ensure a memorable stay. Short breaks available. Non-smoking.

Terms: Bed and Breakfast: £35–£40; Dinner, Bed and Breakfast: £53–£60.
e-mail: stay@churchview.co.uk • www.churchview.co.uk

Westwood House
29 High West Street, Dorchester DT1 1UP
01305 268018 • www.westwoodhouse.co.uk
reservations@westwoodhouse.co.uk

Personally run by owners, Tom and Demelza Stevens, Westwood House offers comfortable, informal, non-smoking accommodation.
Each bedroom has digital TV, complimentary wi-fi, and tea/coffee making. Breakfast is served in the light and airy conservatory.
A variety of pubs, restaurants and cafes are just a short stroll away. The lovely market town of Dorchester has many places of historical interest, and is an ideal base for exploring the Dorset coast and countryside.

Dorset   SOUTH WEST ENGLAND 57
Dorchester, Lulworth, Lulworth Cove

Bay Tree House

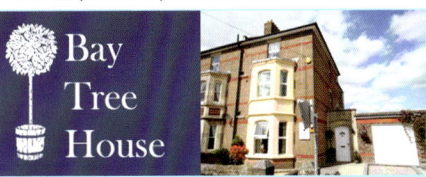

Nicola & Gary Cutler welcome you to their family-run B&B in a quiet residential area within a few minutes' walk of the town centre.
Spacious and light twin-bedded and double rooms are available, all en suite or with private bathroom. A farmhouse-style breakfast is served in the open-plan kitchen/dining area. Non-smoking. Off-road parking. Short Breaks available.

Athelstan Road, Dorchester DT1 1NR • Tel: 01305 263696
e-mail: info@baytreedorchester.co.uk • www.bandbdorchester.co.uk

AA ★★★★ Bed & Breakfast

SB

Bramlies Bed & Breakfast
107 Bridport Road, Dorchester DT1 2NH
www.bramlies.co.uk • 01305 265778

A warm welcome awaits you at Bramlies, which is conveniently situated in Dorchester, the historic county town of Dorset, and home of Thomas Hardy. We are within easy reach of both the stunning Jurassic Coast and the beautiful countryside. We offer three en suite rooms, two of which are detached and set in our pretty garden. All our rooms are furnished to a high quality. A delicious breakfast prepared from high quality produce will get your day off to the perfect start.

AA Highly Commended ★★★ Bed & Breakfast 2008-2009

SB

Luckford Wood Farmhouse
**Church Street, East Stoke
Wareham, Dorset BH20 6AW**

In the heart of Dorset countryside, warm welcome, very peaceful. Extensive classical farmhouse breakfast served in the dining room, conservatory (or garden). Ideal for cyclists, walkers, beach lovers and golfers. Tank Museum, Monkey World, Lulworth nearby. B&B from £30pppn, open all year. Caravan and camping available and storage.

Tel: 01929 463098 • Mobile: 07888 719002
e-mail: luckfordleisure@hotmail.co.uk • www.luckfordleisure.co.uk

SB

Lulworth Cove, Dorset
Cromwell House Hotel

Catriona and Alistair Miller welcome guests to their comfortable family-run hotel, set in secluded gardens with spectacular sea views. Situated 200 yards from Lulworth Cove, with direct access to the Jurassic Coast. A heated swimming pool is available for guests' use from May to October. Accommodation is in 20 en suite bedrooms, with TV, direct-dial telephone, and tea/coffee making facilities; most have spectacular sea views. There is disabled access and a room suitable for disabled guests. Self-catering flat and cottage available. Restaurant, bar wine list.

*B&B from £40. Two nights DB&B (fully en suite) from £120 pp.
Off-peak mid week breaks all year except Christmas.*

**Cromwell House Hotel, Lulworth Cove, Dorset BH20 5RJ
Tel: 01929 400253/400332 • Fax: 01929 400566
ETC/AA ★★**

www.lulworthcove.co.uk

SB

SOUTH WEST ENGLAND — Dorset

Lyme Regis, Portland, Sherborne, Shillingstone

Providence House

SB

Friendly and comfortable accommodation on the edge of historic Lyme Regis in 200 year old character house with open beamed fireplace, raised gallery area and roof garden. 25 minutes' walk from the sea. Ideal for artists, fossil hunting, walking etc. Easy access by road. Axminster five miles with main line connection to Waterloo.

Accommodation comprises one single, one double, one double en suite; all with TV and tea/coffee making facilities. Full English Breakfast and vegetarian option. Secure courtyard area available for bikes/motor bikes, etc.
Rooms available from £25pppn.

Mrs L. Brown, Providence House,
Lyme Road, Uplyme, Lyme Regis
DT7 3TH • Tel: 01297 445704

Alessandria Hotel

71 Wakeham, Easton, Portland DT5 1HW
Highly recommended by our guests
Good old fashioned service and value

15 BEDROOMS • MOST EN SUITE. 2 on ground floor.
All with tea/coffee, colour television, some rooms with sea views
4 spacious en suite family rooms.
Comfortable accommodation • Friendly atmosphere
Quiet location • Reasonable prices • Free Parking
Vegetarians catered for. • Under same management for 18 years

AA/VisitBritain ★★

Tel: Giovanni 01305 822270 • Fax: 01305 820561 • www.s-hystems.co.uk/hotels/alessand.html

Stoneleigh Barn

SB

This handsome 18th century stone barn is situated in some of the most picturesque of Dorset's countryside. Set in its own secluded, landscaped gardens, the barn has been extensively modernised to provide high quality accommodation at affordable prices. There are two large en suite guest suites on the second floor and a third suite on the ground floor with disabled access. The rooms are all newly refurbished to a high standard, each with television, hairdryer, footspa and hospitality tray. Wifi access. Heated outdoor swimming pool in grounds. *Mrs Penny Smith.*

RED & BREAKFAST ★★★★ — Silver SILVER AWARD

North Wootton, Sherborne, Dorset DT9 5JW
Tel: 01935 815964 • www.stoneleighbarn.com
e-mail: stoneleighbarn@aol.com

Pennhills Farm

Pennhills Farmhouse, set in 100 acres of unspoiled countryside, is situated one mile from the village of Shillingstone in the heart of the Blackmore Vale, an ideal peaceful retreat, short break or holiday. It offers spacious comfortable accommodation for all ages; children welcome, pets by arrangement. One downstairs bedroom. All bedrooms en suite with TV and tea/coffee making facilities, complemented by traditional English breakfast with home produced bacon and sausages. Vegetarians catered for. Good meals available locally. Brochure sent on request. A warm and friendly welcome is assured from your host Rosie Watts. From £27 per person.

AA ★★★ Farmhouse

Mrs Rosie Watts, Pennhills Farm, Sandy Lane,
Off Lanchards Lane, Shillingstone, Blandford DT11 0TF
Tel: 01258 860491

Dorset

SOUTH WEST ENGLAND

Sturminster Newton, Swanage, Wareham

Come and have a relaxing holiday at on our 400 acre working farm, staying in our lovely Listed farmhouse (pictured here) mentioned in Nikolaus Pevsner and Dorset books for its architectural interest.

We offer excellent full breakfasts, tea/coffee making in the bedrooms which are en suite or private bathroom. We have a guest lounge for you to relax in. There are lots of very good eating places around and we have a range of menus to tempt you or we can offer a light supper tray.

We are within easy reach of the coast and all Dorset National Trust properties and beauty spots, also the Jurassic Coast. Children welcome, dogs by arrangement (never in the bedrooms). You can walk along the country lanes and across the field. Riding or fishing can be arranged nearby. Weekly and childrens terms by arrangement.

LOWER FIFEHEAD FARM
Fifehead, St Quinton,
Sturminster Newton
Dorset DT10 2AP

B&B from £25-£35 pppn

Contact Mrs Jill Miller, Lower Fifehead Farmhouse
Tel/Fax: 01258 817335

You can be sure of a warm welcome with good home-cooking whenever you stay at Sandhaven. We wish to make sure your stay is as relaxing and enjoyable as possible. All bedrooms are en suite and equipped with tea and coffee making facilities; all have colour TV. There is a residents' lounge, diningroom and conservatory for your comfort. The Purbeck Hills are visible from the guest house, as is the beach, which is only 100 metres away.

- Bed and Breakfast is available from £30 to £35.
- Non-smoking bedrooms.
- Open all year except Christmas.

Janet Foran, Sandhaven Guest House.
5 Ulwell Road, Swanage BH19 1LE • 01929 422322
e-mail: mail@sandhaven-guest-house.co.uk

Sandhaven Guest House

SB

Breachfield Bed & Breakfast

Breachfield is a friendly and traditional B&B set in the heart of Wool, in the beautiful county of Dorset. It is ideally located as an excellent base to get to all the sights and attractions this area has to offer. The world famous Monkey World Ape Rescue Centre is just 2 minutes away. Our warm, cosy, country-syle rooms offer a superb base where you can unwind at the end of an action-packed day. We have a variety of rooms to suit all accommodation needs, ranging from single occupancy to family rooms, and we offer both en suite and private bathroom facilities.

Breachfield B&B, 9 Breachfield, Wool, Wareham BH20 6DQ
www.breachfieldbedandbreakfast.co.uk • e-mail: matt@matthart9.wanadoo.co.uk • tel: 012929 405308

SB

Dorset

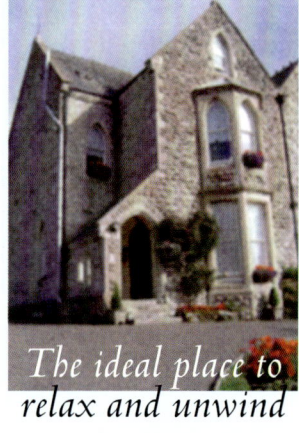

West Lulworth, Weymouth

GRAYBANK
BED & BREAKFAST

Built in 1871, Graybank is set in the picturesque village of West Lulworth, a beautiful, quiet location just a short walk from the spectacular Lulworth Cove and the World Heritage coastline. One double en suite; one family, two double, one twin and one single bedroom, all with private facilities. All rooms have colour TV and tea/coffee making facilities. Full breakfast menu with vegetarian options. Good choice of pubs, cafes and restaurants within walking distance. Free parking for all guests. Non-smoking throughout. Open from February to November. Children aged 4 and over welcome. We do not accept pets. Bed and Breakfast from £30 per person per night.

The ideal place to relax and unwind

Val and Barry Burrill, Graybank Bed and Breakfast,
Main Road, West Lulworth BH20 5RL Tel: 01929 400256

Corfe Gate House

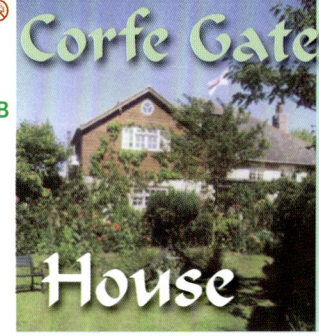

Set in the picturesque hamlet of Coryates, Corfe Gate House offers a warm welcome to all guests. Accommodation consists of a galleried diningroom, sittingroom and three bedrooms, all tastefully decorated and furnished to a high standard. Colour TV and hospitality tray in each bedroom. Secluded gardens and off-road parking. Full English or Continental Breakfast is provided and there is a choice of pubs and restaurants in the area to suit all tastes. Within easy driving distance of interesting towns and villages including Dorchester and Weymouth.
Prices from £55 per room, based on two people sharing.

Maureen & Mark Adams, Corfe Gate House
Coryates, Weymouth, Dorset DT3 4HW
Tel: 01305 871583 • Mob: 07798904602
E-mail: Corfegatehouse@aol.com
www.corfegatehouse.co.uk

Publisher's note

While every effort is made to ensure accuracy, we regret that FHG Guides cannot accept responsibility for errors, misrepresentations or omissions in our entries or any consequences thereof. Prices in particular should be checked.
We will follow up complaints but cannot act as arbiters or agents for either party.

Gloucestershire

Bristol, Cheltenham

Gloucestershire

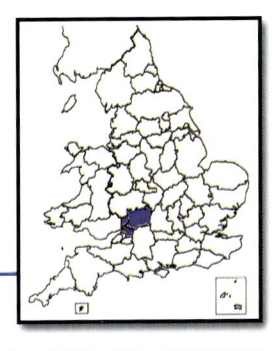

BRISTOL. Pool Farm, Bath Road, Wick, Bristol BS30 5RL (0117 937 2284).
Welcome to our 350 year old Grade II Listed farmhouse on a working farm. On A420 between Bath and Bristol and a few miles from Exit 18 of M4, we are on the edge of the village, overlooking fields, but within easy reach of pub, shops and golf club. We offer traditional Bed and Breakfast in one family and one twin room with tea/coffee facilities and TV. Central heating. Ample parking.
Rates: Bed and Breakfast from £22 per person per night.
• Open all year except Christmas.

Roylands Farm Cottage Bed & Breakfast

Fernhill, Almondsbury, Bristol, Gloucs BS32 4LU • Tel: 07791 221102 • 07768 286924

ROYLANDS FARM COTTAGE is a comfortable home-from-home situated within a working farm, with classic styling to blend in with its rural surroundings. Rooms are spacious, bright and welcoming with all usual en suite and private facilities, lounge and kitchen. One single, one twin and a double bedroom, all with full English breakfast, towels, TV and tea and coffee making facilities. Uniquely guests can take advantage of their own lounge, or relax and take in the beautiful views of the Severn estuary and the surrounding countryside from the adjoining conservatory or large country garden. Ample secure and secluded off-road parking. From £35 single per night. ETC ★★★★

e-mail: jane@roylandfarmcottage.co.uk • www.roylandfarmcottage.co.uk

Parkview is a fine Regency guesthouse which stands in Cheltenham's nicest area, only 10 minutes' walk from the centre. The bedrooms are large and airy and have TV, tea, coffee and provide views onto Pittville Park. Cheltenham is famous for horse racing and festivals of music and literature, and two theatres provide a regular programme of entertainment.
Nearby Prestbury is the most haunted village in England, the Cotswold villages stand in the surrounding hills, and Stratford is one hour's drive.

Parkview Guesthouse

4 Pittville Crescent, Cheltenham GL52 2QZ • Tel: 01242 575567
e-mail: stay@parkviewguesthouse.me.uk • www.parkviewguesthouse.me.uk

The FHG Directory of Website Addresses

on pages 347-362 is a useful quick reference guide for holiday accommodation with e-mail and/or website details

62 SOUTH WEST ENGLAND

Gloucestershire
Chipping Campden, Fairford

'Brymbo'

ETC ★★★★

Honeybourne Lane, Mickleton,
Chipping Campden,
Gloucestershire GL55 6PU
Tel: 01386 438890
Fax: 01386 438113
enquiries@brymbo.com
www.brymbo.com

A warm and welcoming farm building conversion with large garden in beautiful Cotswold countryside, ideal for walking and touring.

All rooms are on the ground floor, with full central heating. The comfortable bedrooms all have colour TV and tea/coffee making facilities. Sitting room with open log fire. Breakfast room. Children and dogs welcome. Parking. Two double, two twin, one family. Bathrooms: three en suite, two private or shared.
Bed and Breakfast: single £27 to £42; double £45 to £60. Brochure available.
Credit Cards accepted.

Close to Stratford-upon-Avon, Broadway, Chipping Campden and with easy access to Oxford and Cheltenham.

CHIPPING CAMPDEN. Mr J. Hutsby, Holly House, Ebrington, Chipping Campden GL55 6NL (01386 593213). Holly House is set in the centre of the picturesque thatched Cotswold village of Ebrington. Ideally situated for touring the Cotswolds and Shakespeare's country. Two miles Chipping Campden and Hidcote Gardens, five miles Broadway, 11 miles Stratford-upon-Avon, 19 miles Warwick. Double, twin and family rooms available, all beautifully appointed with en suite facilities. TV and tea and coffee. Laundry facility available. Private parking. Lovely garden room at guests' disposal. Village pub serves meals. Bike hire available locally. From Chipping Campden take the B4035 towards Shipston on Stour, after half-a-mile turn left to Ebrington, we are in the centre of the village.

Rates: Bed and Breakfast from £60-£70 double, £45-£60 single, £70-£90 family, child reductions.
AA ★★★★
e-mail: hutsbybandb@aol.com
www.hollyhousebandb.co.uk

SB

17th century private manor house set in peaceful gardens.
Fine reception rooms, lovely garden, home-grown vegetables, excellent home cooking.
Ideal setting for weddings, receptions, long or short stays.
Two double bedrooms, one en suite,
one with private facilities.
Three miles from Fairford, Cirencester nine miles.
Easy access to M4 and M5.
Terms from £40 single, £60-£70 double,
children up to 14 years £15. Open all year.

Kempsford Manor, Near Fairford GL7 4EQ
Tel & Fax: 01285 810131 • Mrs Z.I. Williamson
e-mail: ipek@kempsfordmanor.co.uk • www.kempsfordmanor.co.uk

Gloucestershire

SOUTH WEST ENGLAND 63

Forest of Dean, Gloucester, Lechlade on Thames, Parkend

DRYSLADE FARM
Bed & Breakfast

ENGLISH BICKNOR, COLEFORD GL16 7PA • Tel/Fax: 01594 860259

AA ★★★★ • HIGHLY COMMENDED

Daphne and Phil warmly welcome you to this 18th century farmhouse on their family-run working farm. Situated in Royal Forest of Dean and close to Symonds Yat, ideal for walking, cycling and canoeing.
Excellent traditional farmhouse breakfast using local produce served in conservatory overlooking gardens.
Cosy guest lounge • Well behaved dogs welcome • All rooms in house non-smoking.
Terms from £30 - £36 • Reductions for children.

www.drysladefarm.co.uk

Tel & Fax: 01452 840224

Quality all ground floor accommodation. "Kilmorie" is Grade II Listed (c1848) within conservation area in a lovely part of Gloucestershire. Double, twin, family or single bedrooms, all having tea tray, colour digital TV, radio, mostly en suite. Very comfortable guests' lounge, traditional home cooking is served in the separate diningroom overlooking large garden. Perhaps walk waymarked farmland footpaths which start here. Children may "help" with our pony, and "free range" hens. Rural yet perfectly situated to visit Cotswolds, Royal Forest of Dean, Wye Valley and Malvern Hills. Children over five years welcome. No smoking, please. Ample parking.

Bed and full English Breakfast from £24 per person

**S.J. Barnfield, "Kilmorie Smallholding", Gloucester Road, Corse, Staunton, Gloucester GL19 3RQ
mobile: 07840 702218 • e-mail: sheila-barnfield@supanet.com**

Situated in an attractive village on the River Thames, this family-run guest house is only eight miles from Burford and 12 miles from Swindon. Ideal base for touring the Cotswolds, with Kemscott Manor and Buscot House and Gardens nearby. We are close to the river and guests can make use of our lovely garden. One family, two double (en suite), two twin (en suite) and two single rooms available. One room with king-size bed and corner bath; two ground floor bedrooms. Breakfast is served in our airy conservatory overlooking the garden.
Non-smoking • Pets by arrangement • Open all year.
B&B: single en suite £45-£55; double/twin en suite £55-£75.
A warm and friendly welcome is assured at Cambrai Lodge.

**Mr and Mrs J. Titchener, Cambrai Lodge, Oak Street,
Lechlade on Thames GL7 3AY • 01367 253173 • Mobile: 07860 150467
e-mail: cambrailodge@btconnect.com • www.cambrailodgeguesthouse.co.uk**

THE FOUNTAIN
INN & LODGE

Parkend, Royal Forest of Dean, Gloucestershire GL15 4JD.

Traditional village inn, well known locally for its excellent meals and real ales. A Forest Fayre menu offers such delicious main courses as Lamb Shank with Redcurrant and Rosemary Sauce and Gloucester Sausage in Onion Gravy, together with a large selection of curries, vegetarian dishes, and other daily specials.
Centrally situated in one of England's foremost wooded areas, the inn makes an ideal base for sightseeing, or for exploring some of the many peaceful forest walks nearby.
All bedrooms (including one specially adapted for the less able) are en suite, decorated and furnished to an excellent standard, and have television and tea/coffee making facilities. Various half-board breaks are available throughout the year.

Tel: 01594 562189 • Fax: 01594 564378 • e-mail: thefountaininn@aol.com • www.thefountaininnandlodge.com

Gloucestershire
Stow-on-the-Wold

South Hill Farmhouse

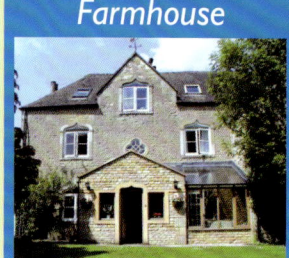

Siân and Mark Cassie welcome you to South Hill Farmhouse. The house is a Listed Cotswold stone farmhouse (no longer a working farm) situated on the ancient Roman Fosse Way on the outskirts of Stow-on-the-Wold. There is ample parking for guests, and it is only 10 minutes' walk to the pubs, restaurants and shops of Stow-on-the-Wold.

Single £50, double/twin £70, family (three) £90, (four) £110 per room per night, including generous breakfast. Non-smoking house.

South Hill Farmhouse, Fosseway, Stow-on-the-Wold GL54 1JU
Tel: 01451 831888 • Fax: 01451 832755
e-mail: info@southhill.co.uk • www.southhill.co.uk

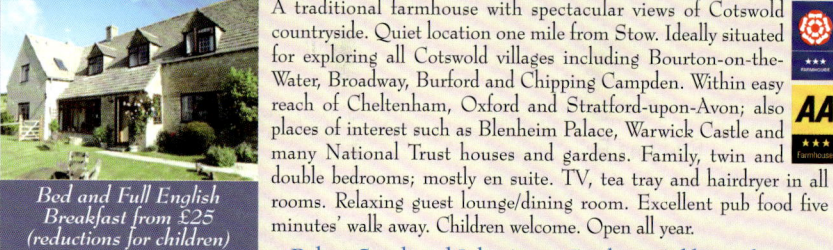

Bed and Full English Breakfast from £25 (reductions for children)

A traditional farmhouse with spectacular views of Cotswold countryside. Quiet location one mile from Stow. Ideally situated for exploring all Cotswold villages including Bourton-on-the-Water, Broadway, Burford and Chipping Campden. Within easy reach of Cheltenham, Oxford and Stratford-upon-Avon; also places of interest such as Blenheim Palace, Warwick Castle and many National Trust houses and gardens. Family, twin and double bedrooms; mostly en suite. TV, tea tray and hairdryer in all rooms. Relaxing guest lounge/dining room. Excellent pub food five minutes' walk away. Children welcome. Open all year.

Robert Smith and Julie-Anne, Corsham Field Farmhouse, Bledington Road, Stow-on-the-Wold GL54 1JH • 01451 831750 • Fax: 01451 832247
e-mail: farmhouse@corshamfield.co.uk • www.corshamfield.co.uk

---

THE Old Stocks Hotel
The Square, Stow-on-the-Wold GL54 1AF

Ideal base for touring this beautiful area. Tasteful guest rooms in keeping with the hotel's old world character, yet with modern amenities. 3-terraced patio garden with smoking area.

Mouth-watering menus offering a wide range of choices.
Special bargain breaks also available.

Tel: 01451 830666 • Fax: 01451 870014
e-mail: fhg@oldstockshotel.co.uk
www.oldstockshotel.co.uk

Gloucestershire Stow-on-the-Wold

THE LIMES

AA ★★★

Large Country House with attractive garden, overlooking fields. Four minutes to town centre. One four-poster bedroom; double, twin or family rooms, all en suite. Tea/coffee making facilities, colour TV in all rooms. TV lounge. Central heating. Children and pets welcome. Car park.

Bed and Full English Breakfast from £25 to £30pppn.
Open all year except Christmas. *Established over 30 years.*

Evesham Road, Stow-on-the-Wold, GL54 1EN Tel: 01451 830034/831056
e-mail: thelimes@zoom.co.uk
www.cotswold.info/webpage/thelimes-stow.htm

Aston House, Broadwell, Moreton-In-Marsh GL56 0TJ

ASTON HOUSE is in the peaceful village of Broadwell, one-and-a-half miles from Stow-on-the-Wold, four miles from Moreton-in-Marsh. It is centrally situated for all the Cotswold villages, while Blenheim Palace, Warwick Castle, Oxford, Stratford-upon-Avon, Cheltenham and Gloucester are within easy reach. Accommodation comprises a twin-bedded and a double room, both en suite on the first floor, and a double room with private bathroom on the ground floor. All rooms have tea/coffee making facilities, radio, colour TV, hairdryer, electric blankets for the colder nights and fans for hot weather. Bedtime drinks and biscuits are provided. Open from March to October. No smoking. Car essential, parking. Pub within walking distance. PC and internet access available. Bed and good English breakfast from £31 to £34 per person per night; weekly from £210 to £221 per person.

Tel: 01451 830475
e-mail: fja@astonhouse.net • www.astonhouse.net
VisitBritain ★★★★ Silver Award • AA ★★★★

SOUTH WEST ENGLAND

Gloucestershire

Stroud, Tewkesbury, Winchcombe

The Withyholt Guest House
Paul Mead, Edge, near Stroud, Gloucestershire GL6 6PG

Modern guesthouse in Gloucestershire close to Gloucester Cathedral, Tetbury, Stroud. Many lovely country walks. Pets welcome. En suite bedrooms, large lounge. Large garden.

Telephone: 01452 813618
Fax: 01452 812375

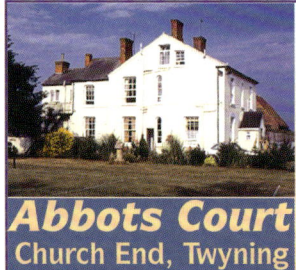

Abbots Court
Church End, Twyning
Tewkesbury
GL20 6DA

A large, quiet farmhouse on a working farm set in 350 acres, built on the site of monastery between the Malverns and Cotswolds, half a mile M5-M50 junction.

Six en suite bedrooms with colour TV and tea making facilities. Centrally heated. Open all year except Christmas. Large lounge with open fire and colour TV. Lawn. Cot and high chair available. Laundry facilities.

Coarse fishing available on the farm
Ideally situated for touring with numerous places to visit
Swimming, tennis, sauna, golf within three miles
Bed and Breakfast from £23 to £26.
Reduced rates for children and Senior Citizens.

Mrs Bernadette Williams • Tel & Fax: 01684 292515
e-mail: abbotscourt@aol.com

Ireley Farm

Ireley is an 18th century farmhouse located in the heart of gentle countryside, one-and-a-half miles from Winchcombe and within easy reach of Cheltenham, Gloucester, Stratford-upon-Avon and Worcester.

The cosy yet spacious guest rooms (one double and two twin) offer either en suite or private bathroom. Relax in the evening beside a traditional open fire and in the morning enjoy a delicious English breakfast. Families are welcome, to enjoy the unique atmosphere of this working farm.

**Mrs Margaret Warmington, Ireley Farm,
Broadway Road, Winchcombe GL54 5PA
Tel: 01242 602445 • e-mail: warmingtonmaggot@aol.com**

B&B from £28.50 per person.

symbols

Symbol	Meaning	Symbol	Meaning
🚭	Totally non-smoking	🐕	Pets Welcome
🐎	Children Welcome	SB	Short Breaks
♿	Suitable for Disabled Guests	🍷	Licensed

Somerset
Bath

Somerset

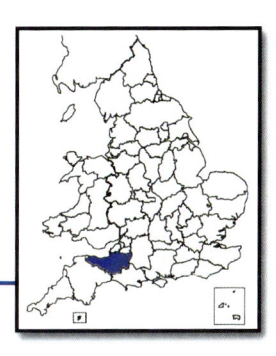

SOUTH WEST ENGLAND 67

Toghill House Farm
Freezing Hill, Wick, Near Bath BS30 5RT

Situated just four miles north of Bath and within a few miles of Lacock, Castle Combe, Tetbury and the Cotswolds.

Stay at Toghill in one of our tastefully decorated rooms offering a high level of comfort. Combine this with a traditional English breakfast and you will soon understand why many guests return time after time. All rooms have en suite bathroom, television and tea/coffee making facilities. Ample car parking.

Self Catering also available in luxury converted 17th century cottages.

Tel: 01225 891261 • Fax: 01225 892128 • www.toghillhousefarm.co.uk

SB

The Kennard is an original Georgian townhouse, carefully maintained and restored and offering all the modern features which are now expected: en suite rooms with showers, telephones with data port, wireless internet connection, satellite television (some rooms now with plasma screens) and beverage trays. The original Georgian kitchen, now a delightful breakfast room, is the setting for a full choice of English or Continental breakfasts. For those arriving by car, free residents' parking permits will be provided. No Smoking. Children over 8 years of age are most welcome. Terms on request.

The Kennard
11 Henrietta Street, Bath BA2 6LL
• Tel: 01225 310472 •

Email: bookings@kennard.co.uk
www.kennard.co.uk

SOUTH WEST ENGLAND

Somerset
Bath

Marlborough House
1 Marlborough Lane, Bath BA1 2NQ
Tel: +44 (0)1225 318175 • Fax: +44 (0)1225 466127

Marlborough House is an enchanting, Victorian Guest House located at the edge of Royal Victoria Park, close to the heart of Georgian Bath and all the major attractions.

Each bedroom is handsomely furnished with antiques and contains either an antique wood four-poster, or a Victorian brass and iron bed. All are comfortable and scrupulously clean, with complimentary sherry and a hostess tray. Each has direct-dial telephone, wifi, alarm/radio, hairdryer, and colour TV.

Served in either the elegant parlour or lovely dining room, breakfasts are cooked to order, using only the highest quality organic ingredients.

www.marlborough-house.net

Eden Vale Farm

nestles down in a valley by the River Frome. Enjoying a picturesque location, this old watermill offers a selection of rooms including en suite facilities, complemented by an excellent choice of full English or Continental breakfasts. Beckington is an ideal centre for visiting Bath, Longleat, Salisbury, Cheddar, Stourhead and many National Trust Houses including Lacock Village. Only a ten minute walk to the village pub, three-quarters of a mile of river fishing. Local golf courses and lovely walks. Very friendly animals. Dogs welcome. Open all year.

Mrs Barbara Keevil, Eden Vale Farm, Mill Lane, Beckington, Near Frome BA11 6SN
Tel: 01373 830571
e-mail: bandb@edenvalefarm.co.uk • www.edenvalefarm.co.uk

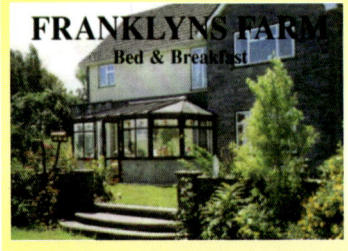

Franklyns Farm,
Chewton Mendip, Near Bath BA3 4NB
Betty Clothier - 01761 241372

Come and relax in peaceful setting, comfortable and cosy farmhouse, set in one acre of garden with hard tennis court. Delicious breakfasts with free range eggs. Ideal for visiting Bath, Glastonbury, Wells, Cheddar, Longleat and the coast is within easy reach. We are just off the A39 on the Emborough B3114 road. Half-a-mile along the road on the right is Franklyns Farm.

Bed and Breakfast from £25 per person.

Somerset
Bath

The White Guest House

Steve and Anna Wynne welcome you to their guest house. Very conveniently located five minutes' walk to the city and all of Bath's famous attractions. Close to the Kennet and Avon canal (Bath in Bloom winners.) All rooms en suite, with central heating, TV, tea/coffee facilities. Traditional cooked breakfast or Continental breakfasts. Ground floor rooms.

B&B single from £35, double/twin from £27pp. Min. 2 nights stay. Free bottle of wine when you mention 'FHG'

23 Pulteney Gardens, Bath BA2 4HG • 01225 426075
e-mail: enquiries@whiteguesthouse.co.uk
www.whiteguesthouse.co.uk

The Old Red House

Welcome to our romantic Victorian "Gingerbread" house which is colourful, comfortable and warm; full of unexpected touches and intriguing little curiosities. The leaded and stained glass windows are now double glazed to ensure a peaceful night's stay. Each bedroom is individually furnished, some with antiques and a king-size bed. All have colour TV, complimentary beverages, radio alarm clock, hairdryer and either en suite shower or private bathroom. Easy access to city centre, via road or river paths. The English breakfast and buffet will keep you going all day. We have private parking. Non-smoking.

Theresa Elly, The Old Red House, 37 Newbridge Road, Bath BA1 3HE • 01225 330464
e-mail: orh@amserve.com • www.oldredhouse.co.uk

Walton Villa • Bath

◆ Our immaculate Victorian family-run B&B offers a relaxed and friendly atmosphere.

◆ Just a short bus journey or 25 minute stroll to town centre, via the beautiful gardens of the Royal Victoria Park.

◆ Our three en suite bedrooms are delightfully decorated and furnished for your comfort, with colour TV, hairdryer and hospitality tray.

◆ Enjoy a delicious Full English or Continental breakfast served in our gracious dining room.

• Off-street parking
• Non-smoking accommodation
• Sorry, no pets • Bed and Breakfast from £35.

**Michael & Carole Bryson, Walton Villa, 3 Newbridge Hill, Bath BA1 3PW
Tel: 01225 482792 • Fax: 01225 313093**
e-mail: walton.villa@virgin.net • www.waltonvilla.co.uk

SOUTH WEST ENGLAND

Somerset
Bath, Bristol

Wellsway Guest House

A comfortable Edwardian house with all bedrooms centrally heated; washbasin and colour television in the rooms. On bus route with buses to and from the city centre every few minutes or an eight minute walk down the hill. Alexandra Park, with magnificent views of the city, is five minutes' walk. Bath is ideal for a short or long holiday with many attractions in and around the city; Longleat, Wells and Bristol are all nearby. Parking available.

Bed and Breakfast from £30 single, £50 double, with a pot of tea to welcome you on arrival

Mrs D. Strong,
Wellsway Guest House,
51 Wellsway,
Bath BA2 4RS
01225 423434

Downs View Guest House

A well established, family-run Victorian guest house situated on the edge of Durdham Downs. All rooms have panoramic views over the city or the Downs. One-and-a-half miles north of the city centre. Plenty of restaurants, shops and buses nearby. Within walking distance of Bristol Zoo and Clifton Suspension Bridge. Nine en suite rooms with tea/coffee making facilities, washbasin, colour TV and central heating. Full English breakfast.

38 Upper Belgrave Road, Clifton, Bristol BS8 2XN • Tel: 0117 9737046 • Fax: 0117 9738169
e-mail: bookings@downsviewguesthouse.co.uk • www.downsviewguesthouse.co.uk

The Model Farm

Model Farm is situated two miles off the A37 in a hamlet nestling under the Dundry Hills. A working arable and beef farm in easy reach of Bristol, Bath, Cheddar and many other interesting places. The spacious accommodation is in two en suite rooms, one family and one double, with tea/coffee facilities. Separate dining room and lounge with colour TV for visitors. Private parking. Open all year (except Christmas and New Year). Bed and Breakfast from £25.

Mrs M. Hasell, The Model Farm, Norton Hawkfield, Pensford, Bristol BS39 4HA • 01275 832144
e-mail: margarethasell@hotmail.com • www.themodelfarm.co.uk

Somerset
SOUTH WEST ENGLAND 71

Churchill, Congresbury, Dulverton

Winston Manor

This newly refurbished, well-appointed Victorian manor house sits in its own secluded walled garden overlooking the Mendip Hills. The hotel is privately owned and offers personal service in traditional style. The 14 bedrooms, all with private bathroom, are equipped with modern comforts. There is a small friendly bar with warming log fires in winter. Close to the M5 (Junctions 21 or 22), Churchill is centrally located for Bath, Bristol, Glastonbury or Wells, and is only four miles from Cheddar Gorge. Bristol Airport is just five miles away, making Winston Manor the ideal country retreat for small business meetings. Children welcome. Residential licence. No smoking accommodation.

Winston Manor Hotel, Bristol Road, Churchill, Winscombe BS25 5NL
Tel: 01934 852348 • Fax: 01934 852033
e-mail: info@winstonmanorhotel.co.uk • www.winstonmanorhotel.co.uk

SB

Brinsea Green Farm

Brinsea Green is a Period farmhouse surrounded by open countryside. Set in 500 acres of farmland, it has easy access from the M5, (J21), A38 and Bristol Airport. Close to the Mendip Hills, the historic towns of Bath, Bristol and Wells, plus the wonders of Cheddar Gorge and Wookey Hole. Beautifully furnished en suite/shower bedrooms offer lovely views, comfortable beds, complimentary hot drinks and biscuits, radio, alarm, toiletries, sewing kit and hairdryer for your convenience. Both guest lounge (with TV) and dining room have inglenook fireplaces providing a warm, home from home atmosphere. Choose from our wide range of books and enjoy real peace and tranquillity.

SINGLE FROM £30   **DOUBLE FROM £50**

**Mrs Delia Edwards, Brinsea Green Farm
Brinsea Lane, Congresbury, Near Bristol BS49 5JN
Tel: Churchill (01934) 852278 • Fax: (01934) 852861**
e-mail: delia@brinseagreenfarm.co.uk
www.brinseagreenfarm.co.uk

Marsh Bridge Cottage.

This superb accommodation has been made possible by the refurbishment of this Victorian former gamekeeper's cottage on the banks of the River Barle. The friendly welcome, lovely rooms, delicious (optional) evening meals using local produce, and clotted cream sweets are hard to resist! Open all year, and in autumn the trees that line the river either side of Marsh Bridge turn to a beautiful golden backdrop. Just off the B3223 Dulverton to Exford road, it is easy to find and, once discovered, rarely forgotten. From outside the front door footpaths lead in both directions alongside the river. Fishing available. Terms from £28pp B&B or £46pp DB&B.

SB

**Mrs Carole Nurcombe, Marsh Bridge Cottage, Dulverton TA22 9QG
01398 323197 • www.marshbridgedulverton.co.uk**

Somerset
Dulverton, Dunster

Winsbere House

Attractive private house set in pretty gardens on the edge of Dulverton, 10 minute walk from the centre and a short drive to Tarr Steps and the moors. Comfortable, tastefully decorated rooms with lovely country views and a friendly informal atmosphere. One double, one twin, both en suite, plus one double/single with private bathroom. Superb full English breakfast.

Cyclists welcome. Route Three West Country Way on doorstep. Ample private parking and lock-up cycle shed.

No dogs • Non-smoking • Children welcome aged 8 or over. • Excellent location for touring Exmoor, West Somerset and North Devon.

Open all year (except Christmas and New Year). Terms: £25 to £30pppn (single from £25).

Mrs M. Rawle, Winsbere House, Dulverton, Exmoor TA22 9HU (01398 323278).
e-mail: info@winsbere.co.uk
www.winsbere.co.uk

In the centre of quaint English village, an ideal location for walking and exploring Exmoor, the surrounding coastline and the many local attractions, The Yarn Market Hotel is a comfortable, family-run hotel which provides a friendly, relaxed atmosphere. All rooms are en suite, with tea and coffee making facilities, and colour TV. Some have four-poster beds, and some have views over the spectacular surrounding countryside. Family rooms are also available. The restaurant offers a mouth-watering selection of dishes featuring local produce whenever possible. Packed lunches available. Drying facilities. Non-smoking. Well-behaved pets are welcome. Party bookings and midweek breaks a speciality. B&B from £35.

THE YARN MARKET HOTEL
High Street, Dunster TA24 6SF
Tel: 01643 821425   Fax: 01643 821475
e-mail: hotel@yarnmarkethotel.co.uk
www.yarnmarkethotel.co.uk

symbols

- Totally non-smoking
- Children Welcome
- Suitable for Disabled Guests
- Pets Welcome
- **SB** Short Breaks
- Licensed

Somerset
Exmoor, Glastonbury, Minehead

SOUTH WEST ENGLAND

North Down Farm

In tranquil, secluded surroundings on the Somerset/Devon Border. Traditional working farm set in 150 acres of natural beauty with panoramic views of over 40 miles. M5 7 miles, Taunton 10 miles. All rooms tastefully furnished to high standard include en suite, TV, and tea/coffee facilities. Double, twin or single rooms available. Dining room and lounge with log fires for our guests' comfort; centrally heated and double glazed. Drying facilities. Delicious home produced food a speciality. Fishing, golf, horse riding and country sports nearby. Dogs welcome.

*Bed and Breakfast from £36 pppn,
B&B and Evening Meal £300 weekly.
North Down Break: three nights B&B and Evening Meal £145 per person.*

*Jenny Cope, North Down Farm, Pyncombe Lane, Wiveliscombe,
Taunton TA4 2BL • Tel & Fax: 01984 623730
e-mail: jennycope@btinternet.com
www.north-down-farm.co.uk*

SB

Meare Manor

200 year old Manor House set in own grounds with beautiful gardens and views over Mendip Hills. Peaceful setting in the heart of King Arthur country. Ideal base for tourist attractions including Glastonbury Abbey, Chalice Well, Wells Cathedral, Cheddar Gorge and Clarks Shopping Village. Warm welcome assured with friendly help and advice. Family rooms available. Hospitality trays, colour TV. Ample car parking.
Open all year. From M5, Junction 23 follow A39 Glastonbury - Street, take B3151 Glastonbury to Wedmore, approximately three miles from Glastonbury. Bed and Breakfast from £70 double occupancy per night.

**Sue Chapman, Meare Manor, 60 St Mary's Road, Meare,
Glastonbury BA6 9SR • Tel 01458 860449 • Fax: 01458 860855
e-mail: reception@mearemanor.com • www.mearemanor.com**

SB

West Porlock House
01643 862880

Imposing country house in Exmoor National Park on the wooded slopes of West Porlock commanding exceptional sea views of Porlock Bay and countryside. Set in five acres of beautiful woodland gardens unique for its variety and size of unusual trees and shrubs and offering a haven of rural tranquillity. The house has large spacious rooms with fine and beautiful furnishings throughout. Two double, two twin and one family bedrooms, all with en suite or private bathrooms, TV, tea/coffee making facilities, radio-alarm clock and shaver point. Non-smoking. Private car park. Sorry, no pets.
Bed and Breakfast from £32 to £34.50 per person. Credit cards accepted.

**Margery and Henry Dyer, West Porlock House,
West Porlock, Near Minehead TA24 8NX
e-mail: westporlockhouse@amserve.com**

Somerset

Minehead, Porlock

Delightful family-run private guest house only a few minutes' level walking distance from sea front

- Delicious home cooking • Full central heating
- 8 en suite bedrooms, all with courtesy tray, remote-control TV, hairdryer
- Children and well behaved pets welcome
- Totally non-smoking

SUNFIELD, 83 Summerland Avenue, Minehead TA24 5BW
Tel: 01643 703565 • www.sunfieldminehead.co.uk

Steps Farmhouse

Bilbrook, Minehead, Somerset TA24 6HE
Tel: 01984 640974
e-mail: stay@stepsfarmhouse.co.uk
www.stepsfarmhouse.co.uk

A traditional 16th century former farmhouse offering wonderful Exmoor bed and breakfast accommodation with off-road parking. Ideally situated for walking, fishing, golfing, cycling or exploring the backwaters of the West Somerset coastline. All the comfortable, en suite, centrally heated bedrooms are in barn conversions with views of Exmoor and the Brendon Hills. Full English breakfast served.
For a week's holiday, a quiet weekend or just an overnight stop you can be assured of a warm welcome at Steps Farmhouse.

Ash Farm

Ash Farm is situated two miles off the main Porlock to Lynmouth road (A39) and overlooks the sea. It is 2½ miles from Porlock Weir, and 11 from Minehead and Lynmouth. Only 10 minutes to the tiny church of "Culbone", and Coleridge is reputed to have used the farmhouse which is 200 to 300 years old. Oare Church, Valley of Rocks, County Gate, Horner Valley and Dunkery Beacon are all within easy reach.
The house has double, single and family bedrooms, all with washbasins; toilet and separate bathroom; large sittingroom and diningroom.
Open from Easter to October.
Bed and Breakfast from £22pppn which includes bedtime drink.

SAE please to: Mrs A.J. Richards, Ash Farm, Porlock, Near Minehead TA24 8JN
Tel: 01643 862414

Somerset
Taunton

SOUTH WEST ENGLAND 75

The Falcon Hotel
Henlade, Taunton
TA3 5DH

You can always expect a warm welcome at this historic villa, with just the right blend of comfortable, spacious accommodation, friendly efficient staff and the personal attention of its family owners. Located one mile from the M5 motorway, it makes an ideal base for business stays, or as a touring centre for this attractive corner of the West Country. Facilities include ten en suite bedrooms with colour TV, tea/coffee making facilities, direct dial telephone, etc. Honeymoon suite, conference facilities, restaurant and ample parking. Superbly accessible to Quantock, Blackdown Hills, Exmoor, North and South Devon coasts.
Our tariff is inclusive of a Full English Breakfast.

Tel: 01823 442502
Fax: 01823 442670

www.hotelfalcon.co.uk • mail@hotelfalcon.co.uk

76 SOUTH WEST ENGLAND

Somerset
Taunton, Theale

Spacious Victorian residence set in large gardens with a swimming pool and large car park. Situated just five minutes' walking distance from Taunton town centre, railway, bus station and Records Office. 25 comfortable bedrooms with washbasin, central heating, colour TV and tea making facilities. Five of the bedrooms have traditional four-poster beds, ideal for weekends away and honeymoon couples. Family and twin rooms are available. The majority of rooms have en suite facilities. Large dining room traditionally furnished; full English breakfast/Continental breakfast included in the price.

Please send for our colour brochure.

**Mr and Mrs P.J. Painter
Blorenge House,
57 Staplegrove Road, Taunton TA1 IDG
Tel & Fax: 01823 283005
e-mail: enquiries@blorengehouse.co.uk**

www.blorengehouse.co.uk

The Old Mill
**Bishop's Hull, Taunton TA1 5AB
Tel: 01823 289732
www.theoldmillbandb.co.uk
www.bandbtaunton.co.uk**

Grade II Listed former Corn Mill, situated on the edge of a conservation village just two miles from Taunton. We have two lovely double bedrooms, The Mill Room with en suite facilities overlooking the weir pool, and The Cottage Suite with its own private bathroom, again with views over the river. Both rooms are centrally heated, with TV, generous beverage tray and thoughtful extras. Guests have their own lounge and dining area overlooking the river, where breakfast may be taken from our extensive breakfast menu amidst machinery of a bygone era. We are a non-smoking establishment.

**Double from £27.50 – £30pppn
Single occupancy from £40**

THATCHED COUNTRY COTTAGE & GARDEN B&B

An old thatched country cottage halfway between Taunton and Honiton, set in the idyllic Blackdown Hills, a designated Area of Outstanding Natural Beauty. Picturesque countryside with plenty of flowers and wildlife. Central for north/south coasts of Somerset, Dorset and Devon. Double/single and family suite with own facilities, TV, tea/coffee. Conservatory/Garden Room. Evening Meals also available. Open all year. B&B from £22pppn.

**Mrs Pam Parry, Pear Tree Cottage,
Stapley, Churchstanton, Taunton TA3 7QA
Tel & Fax: 01823 601224
e-mail: colvin.parry@virgin.net
www.SmoothHound.co.uk/hotels/thatch.html** OR **www.best-hotel.com/peartreecottage**

This 17th century farmhouse is equidistant between Wells and Cheddar both approximately eight minutes away by car. The seaside towns of Weston, Burnham and Brean are close by and the cities of Bath and Bristol, both served with park and ride facilities, are approx. 35 minutes' drive. There is a very warm welcome awaiting you at this farm, which has been in the Clark family for over 120 years. Lovely accommodation with en suite facilities, colour TV (one room with video) and full coffee and tea making facilities. Two and three-course home-cooked evening meals available. Children welcome; pets at discretion of the owners.
Please telephone for brochure. From £28 per person per night.

**e-mail: enquiries@yewtreefarmbandb.co.uk
www.yewtreefarmbandb.co.uk**

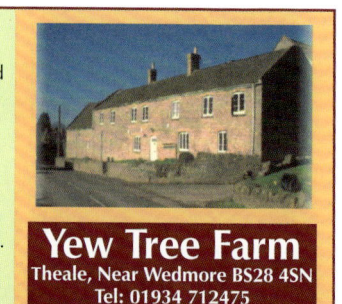

Yew Tree Farm
**Theale, Near Wedmore BS28 4SN
Tel: 01934 712475**
Gilly & Vern Clark

Somerset
Washford, Wells

SOUTH WEST ENGLAND 77

Hungerford Farm

is an attractive 13th century farmhouse on a family-run 350 acre farm with cattle, horses, free range chickens and ducks. We are situated in beautiful countryside on the edge of the Exmoor National Park. Ideal country for walking, riding or cycling. The medieval village of Dunster with its spectacular castle, mentioned in the Domesday Book, and the numerous attractions of Exmoor are all a short distance away. There is a good choice of local pubs within easy reach. Double and twin bedrooms with TV.

- Stabling available for visitors' horses.
- Dogs by arrangement.
- Cyclists welcome.
- From £26 per person.
- Open February to December.

Hungerford Farm, Washford, Somerset TA23 0JZ
Tel: 01984 640285 • e-mail: sarah.richmond@virgin.net

Cadgwith House

Hawkers Lane, Wells BA5 3JH
Tel: 01749 677799
cadgwith.house@yahoo.co.uk
www.cadgwithhouse.co.uk

Cadgwith House is an exceptionally spacious detached house in a quiet location a short walk from the centre of Wells. We back onto a field with a play area accessible from the garden. There are 3 large bedrooms offering double, twin or family accommodation, all with spacious en suite facilities. Each has hospitality tray, television, radio alarm, hairdryer and luggage rack.

We have a dining room/lounge offering digital television and in the winter, a cosy log fire. Start your day with a choice of breakfasts using locally sourced ingredients. There is always fresh fruit salad and home-made bread and preserves. Diets catered for, just let us know your requirements.

We are ideally situated for touring the Mendip Hills, the Somerset Levels, Glastonbury, Cheddar Gorge and Wookey Hole, yet only a few minutes' walk from the centre of Wells with its beautiful cathedral, historic buildings, and the picturesque market place with its twice-weekly market.

WiFi • Private Parking • Well behaved dogs welcome • No Smoking

Somerset
Wells

SB

Modern farmhouse accommodation on a family-run working farm. Comfortable family home in beautiful gardens with views of Somerset Levels and Mendips. Quiet location, off the beaten track in lovely countryside. Breakfast room for sole use of guests. Full English breakfast. Meals available at local pub five minutes' walk away. En suite rooms with fridge, hairdryer, tea/coffee making facilities, shaver point, colour TV and central heating. Non-smoking.

Terms £28pppn, reduced rates for 3 nights or more.

Mrs Sheila Stott:
'LANA'
Hollow Farm,
Westbury-sub-Mendip,
Near Wells,
Somerset BA5 1HH
Tel: 01749 870635
sheila@stott2366.freeserve.co.uk

SB

Danbury

Danbury is situated in walking distance to the city of Wells, near Cheddar and Wookey Hole, and also near Glastonbury. Friendly, welcoming accommodation. Two attractive en suite bedrooms with tea/coffee making facilities and colour TV. Delicious full English breakfast served in the dining room. Bed and Breakfast from £25. Children welcome.

Mrs M. White, Danbury, Haybridge, Near Wells, Somerset BA5 1AJ • Tel: 01749 673295

SB

WELLS. Mrs Sue Crane, Birdwood House, Bath Road, Wells BA5 3EW (01749 679250).
Imposing Victorian house situated on the edge of the Mendip Hills but only one and a half miles from Wells town centre. Accommodation consists of two double en suite rooms, one twin and one single room, all with TV and tea/coffee making facilities. Off-road secure parking. Located close to a walking trail and cycling route; facilities available for cycle storage. Groups and parties welcome.
Rates: Bed and Breakfast from £30 per person.
• Children welcome. • Pets by arrangement. • No smoking.
• Open all year. • Short Breaks available.
AA ★★★
www.birdwood-bandb.co.uk

Somerset
Wells, Weston-Super-Mare

Honeysuckle Cottage, Worth, Near Wells
Bed & Breakfast

Situated on a working farm in rural Somerset, this recent barn conversion maintains an 'olde worlde' charm, and is an ideal base for visiting Wells Cathedral, mystical Glastonbury, and West Country attractions. The cottage has oil-fired central heating, three bedrooms, each with TV. One is en suite, and a double room and adjoining single have a private bathroom. Impressive features include the spacious dining/living room, and old oak beams. This room opens onto a large patio and raised garden which looks out onto the Mendip Hills and surrounding countryside. *Honeysuckle Cottage is strictly non-smoking.*

Tel: 01749 678971

Mrs L. Law, Honeycroft Farm, Worth, Wells BA5 1LW • www.honeycroftfarm.co.uk
e-mail: honeycroft2@aol.com or luana@honeycroftfarm.co.uk

SB

MOORLANDS
Hutton, Near Weston-super-Mare, Somerset BS24 9QH
Tel and Fax: 01934 812283

Enjoy a good breakfast and warm hospitality at this impressive late Georgian house set in landscaped gardens below the slopes of the Western Mendips. A wonderful touring centre, perfectly placed for visits to beaches, sites of special interest and historic buildings. Families with children particularly welcome; reduced terms. Full central heating, open fire in comfortable lounge. Open all year.

Resident host: Mrs Margaret Holt
Rates: single room from £25-£35, double room from £50-£60 per night..

e-mail: margaret-holt@hotmail.co.uk
www.guestaccom.co.uk/35.htm
www.moorlandscountryguesthouse.co.uk

SB

Publisher's note

While every effort is made to ensure accuracy, we regret that FHG Guides cannot accept responsibility for errors, misrepresentations or omissions in our entries or any consequences thereof. Prices in particular should be checked.

We will follow up complaints but cannot act as arbiters or agents for either party.

Wiltshire

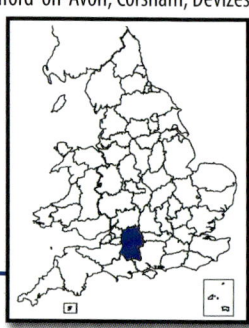

Bradford-on-Avon, Corsham, Devizes

Stillmeadow
18 Bradford Road, Winsley,
Bradford-on-Avon BA15 2HW

A warm welcome is offered in this secluded setting with views among extensive gardens and wildflower meadows. Situated in a picturesque village convenient for Bradford-on-Avon and Bath, it is ideal for relaxing, walking cycling and golf. Excellent local pubs and restaurants.

At Stillmeadow we have three spacious, modern guest bedrooms with en suite facilities and all amenities. There is a choice of Full English or Continental Breakfast and special dietary requirements can be catered for by arrangement. Bed and Breakfast from £50 single.

Tel: 01225 722119 • Fax: 01225 722833
e-mail: sue.gilby@btinternet.com
www.stillmeadow.co.uk

SB

Park Farm Barn, Westrop, Corsham SN13 9QF

Converted 18th century tithe barn with newly constructed Cotswold-style B&B accommodation close by. Park Farm Barn has three en suite bedrooms which are light and spacious with apex ceilings and beams. Ideal base for the many interesting and historic places in and around Corsham, situated in the delightful hamlet of Westrop, one mile from Corsham and seven miles from Junction 17 on the M4. The National Trust village of Lacock is only a short drive away with a number of excellent pubs for evening meals. Castle Combe and Bradford-upon-Avon only 20 minutes, Bath ten miles.

Children over 10 years of age welcome. No smoking. Parking.
Terms from £40-£50 single, £32.50-£35pppn double/twin.
ETC ★★★★, FARM STAY UK MEMBER.

Kate Waldron • Tel: 01249 715911 • Mobile: 07976 827083 • Fax: 01249 701107
e-mail: parkfarmbarn@btinternet.com • www.parkfarmbarn.co.uk

Littleton Lodge
Littleton Panell (A360),
West Lavington, Devizes SN10 4ES
Tel: 01380 813131

Superb Victorian family house set in one acre of private grounds, overlooking vineyard within pretty conservation village. Five minutes' drive from historic Devizes. All rooms en suite with beverage tray, TV and radio/alarms. Choice of scrumptious breakfast. Excellent meals are available at two pubs within five/ten minutes' walk. Stonehenge is only 15 minutes' drive and Littleton Lodge is an ideal base to explore the Wiltshire White Horses, prehistoric Avebury, Georgian Bath (40 mins), Salisbury (20 mins), the National Trust village of Lacock, as well as numerous country houses and gardens, including Longleat. Private parking.

Mastercard, Visa and Switch accepted.
Single occupancy from £45, Double from £65.
e-mail: stay@littletonlodge.co.uk
www.littletonlodge.co.uk

Wiltshire
SOUTH WEST ENGLAND 81
Malmesbury, Marlborough, Mere

Lovett Farm • www.lovettfarm.co.uk
Enjoy traditional hospitality at our delightful farmhouse on a working farm just three miles from the historic town of Malmesbury with its wonderful Norman abbey and gardens and central for Cotswolds, Bath, Stratford, Avebury and Stonehenge.

Two attractive en suite bedrooms with delightful views, each with tea/coffee making facilities, colour TV and radio. Delicious full English breakfast served in our cosy dining room/lounge. Central heating throughout. Bed and Breakfast from £27.50. Credit cards accepted. Non-smoking accommodation. Open all year.

Mrs Susan Barnes

Lovett Farm, Little Somerford, Near Malmesbury SN15 5BP
Tel & Fax: 01666 823268 • Mobile: 07808 858612 • e-mail: sue@lovettfarm.co.uk

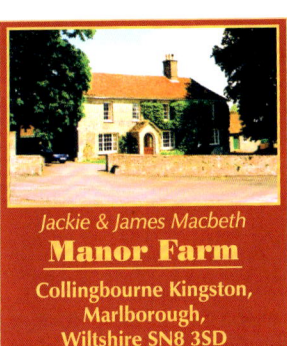

Tel: 01264 850859
e-mail: stay@manorfm.com
www.manorfm.com

Manor Farm B&B

Jackie & James Macbeth
Manor Farm
Collingbourne Kingston, Marlborough, Wiltshire SN8 3SD

- Attractive Grade II Listed farmhouse on working family farm, very easy to find, 12 minutes south of Marlborough on the A338 Salisbury Road.
- Our comfortable, spacious and well equipped rooms are all en suite or private, and include double, twin and family (for four).
- Sumptuous traditional, vegetarian, and other special diet breakfasts.
- Beautiful countryside with superb walking and cycling from the farm.
- Pleasure flights by helicopter from our private airstrip.
- Horses and pets welcome • Ample private parking
- Non-smoking • Credit cards welcome

B&B from £27 pppn

THE GEORGE INN

WCT/AA ★★★
The Square, Mere, Wiltshire BA12 6DR
Tel: 01747 860427 • Fax: 01747 861978

A detour from the busy A303 to sample the relaxing properties of this 16th century inn is heartily recommended. A popular feature of a picturesque little town now enabled to revert to its previous tranquil way of life, the inn, known until recently as the Talbot Hotel, has a stirring history and a just as stirring rebirth, having been carefully refurbished with original features such as exposed beams, stone walls and flagstone floors maintaining its age-old character. In 1651 King Charles II, fleeing from the forces of Oliver Cromwell, dined here en route to safety and exile that lasted eight years. Today, relaxation and the provision of quality chef-inspired fare is the order of the day and handsome overnight en suite accommodation is available at reasonable rates.

una.white@btconnect.com
www.thegeorgeinnmere.co.uk

82 SOUTH WEST ENGLAND   Wiltshire

Salisbury, Westbury

Scotland Lodge Farm, Winterbourne Stoke

Warm welcome at family-run competition yard set in 46 acres of grassland. Lovely views and walks. Stonehenge and Salisbury nearby. Three attractive, comfortable rooms - double with private bathroom; twin and double on ground floor. Conservatory and garden for guests' use. Dogs by arrangement. French, Italian and German spoken. Easy access off A303 with entry through automatic gate. Excellent local pubs.

Scotland Lodge Farm, Winterbourne Stoke
Salisbury SP3 4TF • 01980 621199 • Fax: 01980 621188
e-mail: catherine.lockwood@bigwig.net
www.smoothhound.co.uk/hotels/scotlandl.html

Hayburn Wyke GUEST HOUSE ★★★

Hayburn Wyke is a Victorian house, situated adjacent to Victoria Park, and a ten minute riverside walk from the city centre. Salisbury and surrounding area have many places of interest to visit, including Salisbury Cathedral, Old Sarum, Wilton House and Stonehenge. Most bedrooms have en suite facilities, all have television, and tea/coffee making equipment. Children are welcome at reduced rates. Sorry, no pets (guide dogs an exception). Private car parking for guests. Wi-Fi. Open all year. Credit cards and Switch accepted.

72 Castle Road, Salisbury SP1 3RL • Tel & Fax: 01722 412627
e-mail: hayburn.wyke@tinyonline.co.uk • www.hayburnwykeguesthouse.co.uk

Bed and full English Breakfast from £27

Spinney Farmhouse ~ Thoulstone, Chapmanslade, Westbury BA13 4AQ

Off A36, three miles west of Warminster; 16 miles from historic city of Bath. Close to Longleat, Cheddar and Stourhead. Reasonable driving distance to Bristol, Stonehenge, Glastonbury and the cathedral cities of Wells and Salisbury. Pony trekking and fishing available locally.

- Washbasins, tea/coffee-making facilities and shaver points in all rooms.
- Family room available. • Guests' lounge with colour TV.
- Central heating. • Children and pets welcome.
- Ample parking. • Open all year. • No smoking

*Enjoy farm fresh food in a warm, friendly family atmosphere.
Bed and Breakfast from £25 per night. Reduction after 2 nights.
Evening Meal £12.*
Telephone: 01373 832412 • e-mail: isabelandbob@btinternet.com

symbols

🚭	Totally non-smoking		🐕	Pets Welcome
🐎	Children Welcome		**SB**	Short Breaks
♿	Suitable for Disabled Guests		🍷	Licensed

London (Central & Greater)

Ealing, London

London
(Central & Greater)

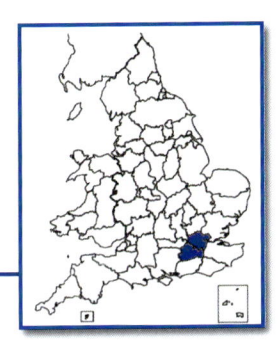

CONVENIENT FOR HEATHROW AIRPORT.
The finest view in Ealing. An oasis of tranquillity in an informal and relaxed family home. Spacious, light rooms with stunning hilltop view over Public Golf Course, 5 minutes walk away. Optional meals in summer on the terrace. Wireless access. Off-road parking. Babysitting. Possible collection from nearest station. Close to Ealing Hospital. Full English or Continental breakfast, or to order. From £40 per night.

Ealing Hanwell Bed & Breakfast
Alured & Tass Darlington

110a Grove Avenue, Hanwell, London W7 3ES
Tel: (44) 020 8567 5015
www.ealing-hanwell-bed-and-breakfast.co.uk
e-mail: TassAnimation@aol.com

SB

BED AND BREAKFAST IN LONDON
IDEAL LONDON LOCATION

Comfortable, centrally located quiet Edwardian home. Great base for sightseeing, close to the river, traditional pubs, lots of local restaurants and antique shops. Excellent transport facilities – easy access to West End, Theatreland, shopping, Harrods, museums, Albert Hall, Earls Court and Olympia Exhibition centres.

Direct lines to Eurostar, Airports: Heathrow, Gatwick (Victoria), Stansted (Liverpool Street).

Bed and Continental Breakfast Prices:
Double/Twin/Triple £25 pppn;
Single £36.00; Children's reductions.
Smoking only in garden.

**Sohel and Anne Armanios
67 Rannoch Road,
Hammersmith, London W6 9SS
Tel: 020 7385 4904
Fax: 020 7610 3235
www.thewaytostay.co.uk**

SB

Gower Hotel

129 SUSSEX GARDENS, HYDE PARK, LONDON W2 2RX
Tel: 0207 262 2262; Fax: 0207 262 2006
E-Mail: gower@stavrouhotels.co.uk   www.stavrouhotels.co.uk

The Gower Hotel is a small family-run Hotel, centrally located, within two minutes' walk from Paddington Station, which benefits from the Heathrow Express train "15 minutes to and from Heathrow Airport".

Excellently located for sightseeing London's famous sights and shops, Hyde Park, Madame Tussaud's, Oxford Street, Harrods, Marble Arch, Buckingham Palace and many more close by.

All rooms have private shower and WC, radio, TV (includes satellite and video channels), direct dial telephone and tea and coffee facilities. All recently refurbished and fully centrally heated. 24 hour reception.

All prices are inclusive of a large traditional English Breakfast & VAT

Discount available on 3 nights or more if you mention this advert

Stavrou Hotels is a family-run group of hotels.
We offer quality and convenience at affordable rates.
A VERY WARM WELCOME AWAITS YOU.

Single Rooms from £30-£79
Double/Twin Rooms from £60-£89
Triple & Family Rooms from £80

Our hotels accept all major Credit cards, but some charges may apply.

Queens Hotel

Stavrou Hotels

33 Anson Road, Tufnell Park, LONDON N7 0RB
Tel: 0207 607 4725; Fax: 0207 697 9725
E-Mail: queens@stavrouhotels.co.uk   www.stavrouhotels.co.uk

The Queens Hotel is a large double-fronted Victorian building standing in its own grounds five minutes' walk from Tufnell Park Station. Quietly situated with ample car parking spaces; 15 minutes to West End and close to London Zoo, Hampstead and Highgate. Two miles from King's Cross and St Pancras Stations. Many rooms en suite.

**All prices include full English Breakfast plus VAT.
Children at reduced prices. Discounts on longer stays**

Stavrou Hotels is a family-run group of hotels.
We offer quality and convenience at affordable rates.
A VERY WARM WELCOME AWAITS YOU.

Single Rooms from £30-£55
Double/Twin Rooms from £40-£69
Triple & Family Rooms from £20 per person

Our hotels accept all major Credit cards, but some charges may apply.

Charlie's Budget Hotel

This elegant Victorian house, built towards the end of the 19th century, is located on the corner of one of London's fine tree-lined residential streets, offering parking.
It is located in the district of Tufnell Park, within walking distance of Tufnell Park Underground station (Northern Line), with Central London just 15 minutes away. Local attractions include Hampstead Heath and Camden Market.

Free WiFi internet connection available
Tourist information and assistance available.
There are pubs, bars and restaurants in the locality offering a variety of cuisine.

Singles • Doubles • Triples • Family Rooms
Discounts available for stays over one week.

Charlie's Budget Hotel is a family-run, friendly bed and breakfast hotel. Our well maintained and comfortable bedrooms are fully centrally heated throughout. Rooms have en suite shower and toilet facilities, and colour television. All prices include a cooked English Breakfast.

63 Anson Road, London N7 0AR
Tel: 0207 607 8375
Mobile: 07772 969316
Fax: 0207 697 8019
e-mail: info@charlieshotel.com
www.charlieshotel.com

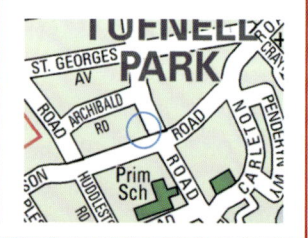

Elizabeth Hotel

Quiet, convenient townhouse overlooking the magnificent gardens of Eccleston Square. Only a short walk from Buckingham Palace and other tourist attractions. Easy access to Knightsbridge, Oxford Street and Regent Street.

Extremely reasonable rates in a fantastic location.

Visa, Mastercard, Switch, Delta and JCB are all accepted.

37 Eccleston Square, Victoria, London SW1V 1PB
info@elizabethhotel.com
www.elizabethhotel.com

Tel: 020 7828 6812
Fax: 020 7828 6814

Barry House
12 Sussex Place, Hyde Park, London W2 2TP

- Comfortable, family-friendly B&B
- En suite, double, triple and family rooms
- Rates include English Breakfast
- Near Hyde Park and Oxford Street
- Paddington Station 4 minutes' walk

www.barryhouse.co.uk
hotel@barryhouse.co.uk
fax: 020 7723 9775

Call us now on: 0207 723 7340

We believe in family-like care

Ask for your B&B Stops discount

The FHG Directory of Website Addresses
on pages 347-362 is a useful quick reference guide for holiday accommodation with e-mail and/or website details

---

Looking for Holiday Accommodation?

FHG · KUPERARD

for details of hundreds of properties throughout the UK, visit our website

www.holidayguides.com

Berkshire
Reading, Windsor

Berkshire

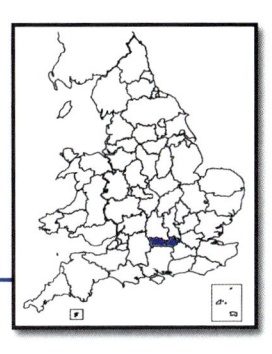

Orchard House

Church Lane, Three Mile Cross, Reading RG7 1HD
Telephone: 01189 884457

Accommodation all year round in this modern, large, homely house close to the Chilterns and Berkshire Downs. An ideal halt for that long journey to Cornwall or Wales, with a wealth of holiday interest to suit all tastes in the area.

Babysitting can be arranged • English or Continental Breakfast Evening Drink/Meal/Light Supper available • Packed Lunches on request.

Pets permitted at extra charge. We accept guests returning/arriving very late. Terms from £20.50 for Bed and Breakfast (we accept euros). Taxi service at moderate rates. SAE, please.

Close to M4 Motorway (Heathrow 30 minutes away, Gatwick 45 minutes; Oxford 30 miles and London 35 miles). Ideal for WOMAD festival or on route to Dover, Portsmouth and Newhaven. Also close to M3, Reading Rock Festival, and Reading football/rugby stadium and the Thames, Kennet and Avon Canal/River for coarse fishing.

WINDSOR. Clarence Hotel, 9 Clarence Road, Wondsor SL4 5AE (01753 864436; Fax: 01753 857060).
High quality accommodation at guest house prices, in town centre location. Licensed bar and steam room. All rooms have en suite bathrooms, TV, tea/coffee making facilities, radio alarms, hairdryers, free wi-fi and internet. Heathrow Airport 25 minutes by car. Convenient for Legoland and trains to London.
ETC/AA ★★★
www.clarence-hotel.co.uk

A useful index of towns/counties appears at the back of this book

Berkshire / Buckinghamshire

Winkfield

BLUEBELL HOUSE
LOVEL LANE, WINKFIELD, WINDSOR SL4 2DG
Tel & Fax: 01344 886828

Charming ex-coaching inn on the outskirts of Windsor and Ascot, and close to Bracknell and Maidenhead. Traditional rooms offering classic accommodation with an added touch of class. All rooms tastefully furnished and have TV, hairdryer, trouserpress, iron, mini-fridge and toaster/food warmer, one room has a four-poster bed.
A very full Continental breakfast is taken in your room.
Private off-road parking.

e-mail: registrations@bluebellhousehotel.co.uk • www.bluebellhousehotel.co.uk

Buckinghamshire

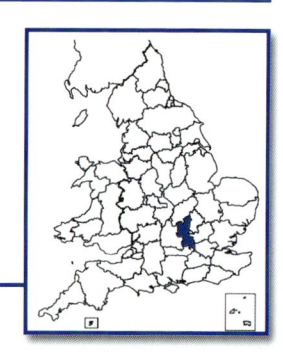

Aylesbury

Poletrees Farm

This working family farm provides spacious, comfortable 4 Star Bed & Breakfast accommodation for couples and individuals, whether on an overnight visit or longer.
• Non-smoking
• En suite bedrooms in 4 cottages with colour TV and tea/coffee tray
The Burnwode Jubilee Way cuts through the farm, and there are many places of historic interest in the area.

**Ludgershall Road, Brill, Near Aylesbury,
Bucks HP18 9TZ • Tel & Fax: 01844 238276**
Bookings will only be taken by phone or fax
www.country-accom.co.uk/poletrees-farm

AA ★★★★ Guest Accommodation

Hampshire

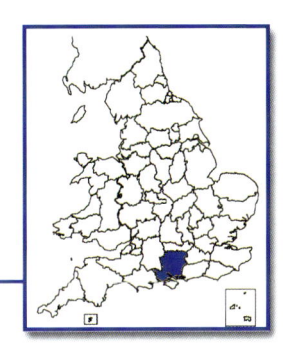

Barton-on-Sea, Brockenhurst

Hampshire

LONDON & SOUTH EAST ENGLAND 91

Ideally situated for the delights of the New Forest, scenic cliff top walks, local beaches, pleasure cruises to the Isle of Wight, the Needles and historic Hurst Castle, horse riding, cycling, golf and a whole host of indoor and outdoor pursuits. Laurel Lodge is a comfortable, centrally heated, converted bungalow, offering twin, double & family rooms. All rooms are fully en suite with tea and coffee making facilities, comfortable chairs, colour TV and alarm clock radio. Ground floor rooms available. Breakfast is served in our conservatory/diningroom with views over the garden.
Bed and Breakfast from £27.50 per person • Special deals for longer breaks • Children welcome, cot and high chair supplied by prior arrangement • Off-road parking for all rooms • Strictly no smoking • Open all year • Please phone for further details.

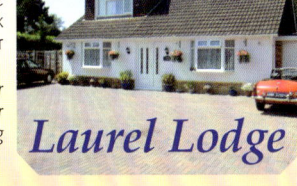

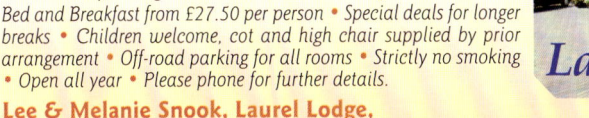

Laurel Lodge

**Lee & Melanie Snook, Laurel Lodge,
48 Western Avenue, Barton-on-Sea, New Milton BH25 7PZ • 01425 618309**

Hilden Bed & Breakfast

**Southampton Road, Boldre,
Brockenhurst SO41 8PT
Tel: 01590 623682
Fax: 01590 624444**

Hilden is a friendly Edwardian home in two-and-a-half acres of gardens and paddock, 50 yards from the open New Forest, offering wonderful cycling, riding and walking. Both the pretty Georgian sailing town of Lymington and the New Forest village of Brockenhurst (80 minutes to Waterloo by train) are about two miles away. There are numerous very good pubs and restaurants nearby, including The Hobler Inn, which serves excellent food, under 200 yards away. Stabling can be arranged, as can cycle hire, and riding from various local stables within five minutes' drive.
Children and dogs welcome.

e-mail: Crystal@buchannan.co.uk • www.newforestbandbhilden.co.uk

LONDON & SOUTH EAST ENGLAND
Hampshire
Eastleigh, Hayling Island

PINEHURST

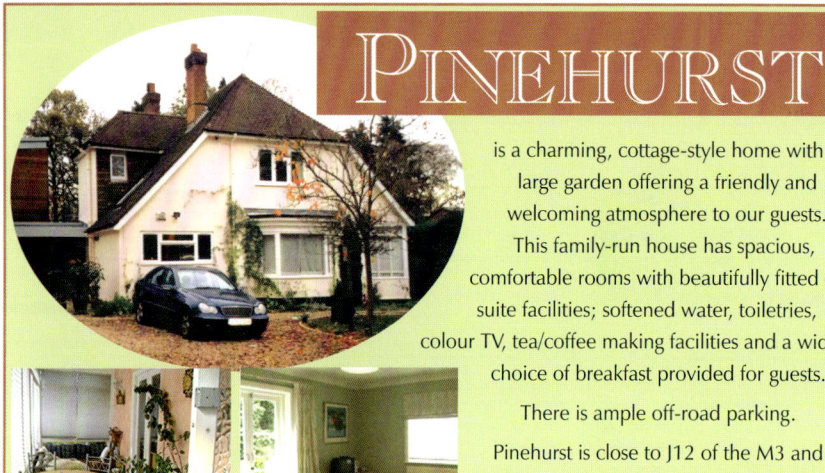

is a charming, cottage-style home with a large garden offering a friendly and welcoming atmosphere to our guests. This family-run house has spacious, comfortable rooms with beautifully fitted en suite facilities; softened water, toiletries, colour TV, tea/coffee making facilities and a wide choice of breakfast provided for guests.

There is ample off-road parking.

Pinehurst is close to J12 of the M3 and convenient for Southampton, Winchester, Romsey, Eastleigh Station and Airport, also M27 and New Forest.

We operate a no smoking policy

Mrs A. Barr, Pinehurst, 287 Hursley Road, Chandler's Ford SO53 5PJ
Tel: 02380 270303 • e-mail: info@pinehurstbandb.co.uk
www.pinehurstbandb.co.uk

Ravensdale

- double room from £66
- single room from £40
- triple room from £90

Jane and Phil welcome you to their home, which is comfortably fitted and in a quiet location within a short walk of the beach and golf course. Two double rooms with en suite facilities, triple room with three single beds, one small double bedroom with use of main bathroom. Central heating, television, tea/coffee making facilities. A full English Breakfast is included and Evening Meal is optional. Car parking. No smoking, and no pets please.

**Jane & Phil Taylor, Ravensdale,
19 St Catherines Road, Hayling Island PO11 0HF**
Tel & Fax: 023 9246 3203 • Mobile: 07802 188259
www.ravensdale-hayling.co.uk

Hampshire
Hook, Lymington

LONDON & SOUTH EAST ENGLAND 93

OAKLEA GUEST HOUSE

London Road,
Hook RG27 9LA
Tel: 01256 762673
Fax: 01256 762150
Please quote FHG

Friendly, family-run Guest House. All bedrooms en suite with TV and hospitality tray. Guest lounge with SKY TV, licensed bar. Easy access from J5 M3, London 55 minutes by train. Free wireless internet access available via own equipment.

GOLF: Many excellent courses within 10-mile radius.
HORSE RACING at Sandown, Ascot and Goodwood.
SHOPPING at The Oracle, Reading and Festival Place, Basingstoke.
DAYS OUT: Thorpe Park, Chessington, Legoland, Windsor Castle, Hampton Court, RHS Wisley, Milestones.

AA ★★★★ Guest House

e-mail: reception@oakleaguesthouse.co.uk • www.oakleaguesthouse.co.uk

Harts Lodge

AA ★★★★ Guest Accommodation

Bungalow (non-smoking), set in three acres. Large garden with small lake. Quiet location. Three miles west of Lymington. Friendly welcome. Double, twin and family en suite rooms, each with tea/coffee making facilities and colour TV. Delicious four-course English breakfast. The sea and forest are five minutes away by car. Horse riding, golf and fishing are nearby. The village pub, ½ mile serves excellent meals. Sorry, no pets. Bed and Breakfast from £27.50 per person.

242 Everton Road, Everton, Lymington, Hampshire SO41 0HE

Tel: 01590 645902

SB

symbols

- 🚭 Totally non-smoking
- 🐴 Children Welcome
- ♿ Suitable for Disabled Guests
- 🐕 Pets Welcome
- **SB** Short Breaks
- 🍷 Licensed

94 LONDON & SOUTH EAST ENGLAND

Hampshire

Lymington, Milford-on-Sea, New Forest

Efford Cottage
Everton, Lymington, Hampshire SO41 0JD
Tel: 01590 642315 • Fax: 01590 641030
e-mail: effordcottage@aol.com • www.effordcottage.co.uk

Guests receive a warm and friendly welcome to our home, which is a spacious Georgian cottage. All rooms are en suite with many extra luxury facilities. We offer a four-course multi-choice breakfast with homemade bread and preserves. Patricia is a qualified chef and uses our home-grown produce. An excellent centre for exploring both the New Forest and the South Coast with sports facilities, fishing, bird watching and horse riding in the near vicinity. Private parking.

Dogs welcome. Sorry no children. **Bed and Breakfast from £25–£35 pppn.** *Mrs Patricia J. Ellis.*

Winner of "England For Excellence 2000"
FHG Diploma 1997/1999/2000/2003 / Michelin / Welcome Host
Awards Achieved: Gold Award / RAC Sparkling Diamond & Warm Welcome
Nominated Landlady of Year & Best Breakfast Award.

Set in its own grounds in a quiet location, this delightful 1912 period house offers a friendly and relaxed atmosphere, a high standard of accommodation and ample parking.

A delicious choice of breakfasts is served in the spacious residents' dining room.

Only five minutes' walk from the High Street and Quay area, ideal for mariners and for travellers catching Isle of Wight ferries.

Delightful forest and coastal walks.
Open all year.

The Rowans, 76 Southampton Road, Lymington SO41 3GZ
Tel: 01590 672276 • Fax: 01590 688610 • e-mail: therowans@totalise.co.uk

---

Ha'penny House

A delightful character house with a warm, friendly atmosphere. Set in a quiet area of the unspoilt village of Milford-on-Sea and just a few minutes' walk to both sea and village, it is ideally situated for visiting the New Forest, Bournemouth, Salisbury and the Isle of Wight. The comfortable bedrooms are all en suite, with TV, DVD, hospitality tray and many extra touches. Award-winning breakfast menu with many choices. Large sunny diningroom and cosy guest lounge. Attractive gardens and summer house. Ample private parking. Non-smoking. Self-catering apartment also available. Open all year.

£68-£80 per room per night, double or twin, including breakfast.

Carolyn and Roy Plummer, Ha'penny House, 16 Whitby Road, Milford-on-Sea, Lymington SO41 0ND • 01590 641210
e-mail: info@hapennyhouse.co.uk • www.hapennyhouse.co.uk

VB ★★★★★ SILVER AWARD • AA ★★★★★ BREAKFAST AWARD

NEW FOREST. Mrs J. Pearce, "St Ursula", 30 Hobart Road, New Milton BH25 6EG (01425 613515).
Large detached family home offering every comfort in a friendly relaxed atmosphere. Off Old Milton Road, New Milton. Ideal base for visiting New Forest with its ponies and beautiful walks; Salisbury, Bournemouth easily accessible. Sea one mile. Leisure centre with swimming pool etc, town centre and mainline railway to London minutes away. Twin (en suite), double, family, single rooms, all with handbasin, TV and tea-making facilities. High standards maintained throughout; excellent beds. Two bathrooms/showers, four toilets. Cot etc, available. Pretty garden with barbecue which guests are welcome to use. Lounge with large colour TV. Two diningrooms. Smoke detectors installed. Full central heating.
Rates: Bed and Breakfast from £27.50.
• Downstairs twin bedroom suitable for disabled persons. • Children and pets welcome. • Open all year.
ETC ★★★, *NATIONAL ACCESSIBLE SCHEME LEVEL 1.*

Hampshire

LONDON & SOUTH EAST ENGLAND 95

Portsmouth, Ringwood

Hamilton House
Bed & Breakfast • Portsmouth

Delightful Victorian townhouse B&B, centrally located five minutes by car from Continental and Isle of Wight Ferry Terminals, M27/ A27, Stations, City Centres, University, Seafront, Historic Ships/ Museums and all the tourist attractions that Portsmouth, and its resort of Southsea, has to offer.

Bright, modern, centrally heated rooms with remote-control colour TV, hairdryer, clock, cooler fan and generous tea/coffee making facilities. All rooms have en suite or private facilities. Ideal touring base for Southern England.

Full English, Vegetarian and Continental breakfasts are served in lovely Spanish-style dining room. Also Continental breakfasts served from 6am (for early morning travellers). Nightly/weekly stays welcome all year. Totally non-smoking.

B&B £30 to £32pp nightly in standard rooms • £32 to £35pp in en suite rooms.

Graham & Sandra Tubb, "Hamilton House", 95 Victoria Road North, Portsmouth PO5 1PS • Tel & Fax: 023 928 23502

ETC / AA ★★★★

e-mail: sandra@hamiltonhouse.co.uk • www.hamiltonhouse.co.uk

Fraser House

Tel: 01425 473958

Fraser House is situated one mile from the market town of Ringwood, overlooking the Avon Valley. This comfortable family house is on the edge of the New Forest, famous for its ponies, deer and pleasant walks. It is ten miles from Bournemouth and the South Coast, and is convenient for visiting Southampton, Stonehenge and the cathedral city of Salisbury. All rooms have en suite bath or shower facilities, central heating, comfortable beds, colour TV, hairdryer, tea/coffee making facilities. Guest lounge with colour TV. Fishing and water sports available nearby.

Ample parking space • Open all year • Most major credit cards accepted
Bed and Breakfast from £33 per person per night • Non-smokers preferred

e-mail: mail@fraserhouse.net • www.fraserhouse.net
Mr Michael Burt, Fraser House, Salisbury Road, Blashford, Ringwood BH24 3PB

Joan and Brian warmly welcome you to Old Stacks, their delightful spacious bungalow where home from home hospitality awaits. The twin en suite room with its own garden entrance and patio and the double room with its large private bathroom adjoining have colour TV and tea and coffee facilities and are both attractively decorated and comfortable. Relaxation awaits in their lovely garden.

A country inn is conveniently close by and Ringwood with its weekly Wednesday market and many excellent restaurants and pubs is a mile away. Explore the beautiful New Forest and walk along Bournemouth's sandy beaches, 15 minutes' drive by car.

An ideal centre for your holiday. For non-smokers only. Bed and Breakfast from £30 per person.

Joan and Brian Peck, Old Stacks, 154 Hightown Road, Ringwood BH24 1NP
Tel: 01425 473840 • e-mail: oldstacksbandb@aol.com
www.SmoothHound.co.uk/hotels/oldstacks.html

AA ★★★★ Guest Accommodation

---

symbols

Symbol	Meaning
🚭	Totally non-smoking
🐴	Children Welcome
♿	Suitable for Disabled Guests
🐕	Pets Welcome
SB	Short Breaks
🍷	Licensed

Hampshire

Romsey, Southampton

Southernwood is a family-run Bed and Breakfast in the beautiful countryside of the New Forest, Hampshire. It is in a secluded location surrounded by farmland, with ample parking, on the A36 between Southampton and Salisbury and 4 miles from Romsey town.

We have comfortable accommodation including a family area, double en suite and single rooms. Included in the price is a full English breakfast. Horse riding, golf, fishing and swimming are available locally and it is 5 minutes' walk from New Forest countryside.

There are several fine inns, all offering good food, close by.

For enquiries please telephone (quoting FHG)

01794 323255

Southernwood@lycos.co.uk

Salisbury Road, Plaitford, Near Romsey, Hampshire SO51 6EE

Southernwood

Twin Oaks Guest House

A family-run guest house with a reputation for providing an excellent service in a friendly and efficient manner.

- Bed & Breakfast • Tea/coffee making facilities
- Car parking • No smoking • Central heating

Near Junction 7 of M27 (Hedge End) • Close to all amenities and superstores

43 Upper Northam Road, Hedge End, Southampton SO30 4EA
Tel: 01489 690054 • Mobile: 07840 816052
e-mail: penny@twinoaksguesthouse.co.uk • www.twinoaksguesthouse.co.uk

Visit the FHG website
www.holidayguides.com
for details of the wide choice of accommodation featured in the full range of FHG titles

Hampshire

LONDON & SOUTH EAST ENGLAND

Winchester

Acacia

First class Tourist Board inspected accommodation in a peaceful location on the edge of the countryside, yet only a five minute drive from Winchester city centre. Excellent and easy access to road and rail communications to many tourist areas, all within one hour including London (by rail), Portsmouth, the New Forest, Salisbury, Stonehenge, etc. The accommodation consists of two doubles and one twin bedroom, all of which have en suite or private bathroom and tea/coffee making facilities. Charming sitting room with satellite TV. Excellent choice of breakfast. Non-smokers only. Off-street parking.

Leave Winchester by the Romsey road, Kilham Lane is right at the second set of traffic lights. "Acacia" is 200 metres on the right.

Bed and Breakfast from £60 to £65 double; single £46 to £48.

Mrs S. Buchanan, "Acacia", 44 Kilham Lane, Winchester SO22 5PT
Tel: 01962 852259 • Mobile: 07801 537703
e-mail: ericbuchanan@btinternet.com
www.btinternet.com/~eric.buchanan

VisitBritain ★★★★
Silver Award

Lang House
www.langhouse.co.uk

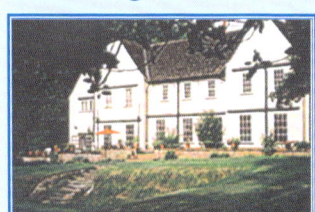

Winchester is one of the most beautiful cities in Britain and somewhere that demands exploration. Good accommodation is a must, and that is to be found at Lang House. Built at the beginning of the 20th century it has all the graciousness of buildings of that time. You will be warm in winter and enjoy the cool airy rooms in summer. Ample parking in the grounds and the house overlooks the Royal Winchester Golf Course. All bedrooms have en suite facilities and are comfortable and well furnished with colour TV and tea/coffee making facilities. You can be assured of a warm and friendly welcome and Winchester has a plethora of good eateries.

Single from £50, double from £70.
Lang House, 27 Chilbolton Avenue, Winchester SO22 5HE
Tel & Fax: 01962 860620

Visit the FHG website
www.holidayguides.com

for details of the wide choice of accommodation featured in the full range of FHG titles

Isle of Wight

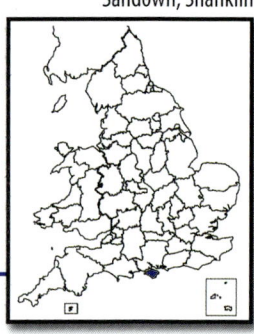

Sandown, Shanklin

The Sandhill
Sandown, Isle of Wight

The Sandhill offers spacious accommodation in a quiet residential area of Sandown. The beautiful beach, town centre and mainline linked railway station are all within a few minutes walk. We offer all the comfort and facilities to allow our guests of all ages to enjoy their ideal holiday in a friendly and relaxing family atmosphere. All rooms are ensuite and offer colour television, hospitality tray and direct dial telephones with Free WiFi internet access. Enjoy a drink in our well stocked licensed bar and relax in our comfortable lounge or sun lounge. Evening meals are always available from our varied menus. Family rooms cater for up to 2 adults and 4 children with space for a cot.

Full details and Special Offers on web site

B&B £25-£35pp
Kathy, Stacey & Steve
6 Hill Street, Sandown. PO36 9DB
email: sandhillsandown@aol.com
Web: www.sandhill-hotel.co.uk

01983 403635 fax :01983 403695

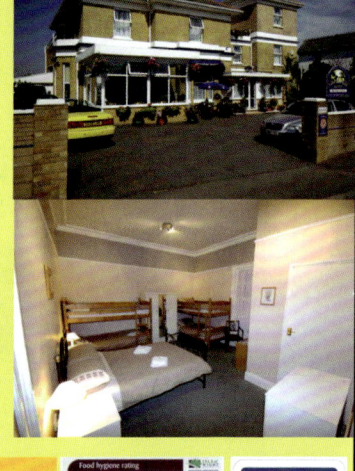

---

4 Chine Avenue,
Shanklin Old Village,
Isle of Wight PO37 6AQ

BEDFORD LODGE

Nestled in the heart of the Old Village, we are close to quaint shops and thatched pubs. We have 12 standard en suite rooms and two Premier rooms. We warmly welcome dog owners, and our ground floor rooms have access directly into our private gardens. The park is opposite and the beach is at the end of the road. We have a guest car park and a licensed bar.

Tel: 01983 862416 • e-mail: mail@bedfordlodge.co.uk
www.bedfordlodge.co.uk

Isle of Wight
Shanklin, Totland

LONDON & SOUTH EAST ENGLAND 99

❖ HAYES BARTON ❖
7 Highfield Road, Shanklin, Isle of Wight PO37 6PP

Hayes Barton has the relaxed atmosphere of a family home, with well equipped en suite bedrooms and comfortable public areas. Dinner is available from a selection of home-cooked dishes and there is a comfortable guests' lounge. The old village, beach and promenade are all within walking distance. Pets welcome in bedrooms and public areas but not dining room. Parking.

Tel: 01983 867747
e-mail: williams.2000@virgin.net • www.hayesbarton.co.uk

AA ★★★★ Guest Accommodation

Frenchman's Cove
Alum Bay Old Road, Totland, Isle of Wight PO39 0HZ

Our delightful family-run guesthouse is set amongst National Trust downland, not far from the Needles and safe sandy beaches. Ideal for ramblers, birdwatchers, cyclists and those who enjoy the countryside

We have almost an acre of grounds. Cots and high chairs are available. All rooms are en suite, with colour TV and tea/coffee making facilities. Four ground floor bedrooms suitable for most disabled guests. Guests can relax in the attractive lounges.

GREEN ISLAND AWARDS Gold

Also available is the Coach House, a well appointed self-catering apartment for two adults and two children. No smoking. No pets.

Please contact Sue or Chris Boatfield for details.
Tel: 01983 752227
www.frenchmanscove.co.uk

symbols

Symbol	Meaning	Symbol	Meaning
🚭	Totally non-smoking	🐕	Pets Welcome
🐎	Children Welcome	SB	Short Breaks
♿	Suitable for Disabled Guests	🍷	Licensed

Little Span Farm

Rew Lane, Wroxall, Ventnor, Isle of Wight PO38 3AU

Sheep farm in an Area of Outstanding Natural Beauty, close to footpaths, golf course and holiday attractions. Ideal for family holidays. Bed and Breakfasters can stay in the stone 17th century, centrally heated farmhouse or the Harvesters Cottage. Three en suite double bedrooms and one twin en suite. Each double room has a colour television and tea and coffee making facilities. Traditional English farmhouse breakfast or Vegetarian option by arrangement.

Tel/Fax: 01983 852419 • Freephone 0800 2985819
E-mail: info@spanfarm.co.uk • www.spanfarm.co.uk

Farmhouse B&B

Other specialised holiday guides from FHG

PUBS & INNS OF BRITAIN

COUNTRY HOTELS OF BRITAIN

WEEKEND & SHORT BREAKS IN BRITAIN & IRELAND

THE GOLF GUIDE WHERE TO PLAY, WHERE TO STAY

PETS WELCOME!

SELF-CATERING HOLIDAYS IN BRITAIN

500 GREAT PLACES TO STAY IN BRITAIN

CARAVAN & CAMPING HOLIDAYS IN BRITAIN

FAMILY BREAKS IN BRITAIN

Published annually: available in all good bookshops or direct from the publisher:
FHG Guides, Abbey Mill Business Centre, Seedhill, Paisley PA1 1TJ
Tel: 0141 887 0428 • Fax: 0141 889 7204
e-mail: admin@fhguides.co.uk • www.holidayguides.com

Kent

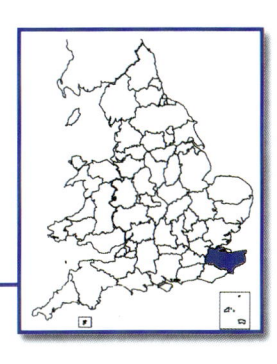

Ashford, Broadstairs

LONDON & SOUTH EAST ENGLAND 101

Heron Cottage

Peacefully situated in own grounds of six acres amidst acres of arable farmland, boasting many wild animals and birds, a stream and pond for coarse fishing. Within easy reach of Leeds Castle and many National Trust Properties including Sissinghurst Castle. You can choose between six tastefully furnished rooms with en suite and TV, or one room with separate bathroom. All rooms are centrally heated and have tea/coffee making facilities. There is a residents' lounge with log fire. Evening meals by arrangement.

Bed and Breakfast from £30-£35 per person per night.

Mrs Susan Twort, Heron Cottage, Biddenden, Ashford TN27 8HH
Tel: 01580 291358

Bolden's Wood Fiddling Lane, Stowting, Near Ashford, Kent TN25 6AP

Between Ashford/Folkestone. Friendly atmosphere – modern accommodation (one double, one single) on our Smallholding, set in unspoilt countryside. No smoking throughout. Full English breakfast. Country pubs (meals) nearby. Children love the old-fashioned farmyard, free range chickens, friendly sheep and... Llamas, Alpacas and Rheas. Treat yourself to a Llama-led Picnic Trek to our private secluded woodland and downland and enjoy watching the bird life, rabbits, foxes, badgers and occasionally deer. Easy access to Channel Tunnel and Ferry Ports.

Bed and Breakfast £25.00 per person.
Contact: Jim and Alison Taylor
e-mail: StayoverNight@aol.com

Tel & Fax: 01303 812011

SB

Keston Court Hotel

14 Ramsgate Road, Broadstairs CT10 1PS
Tel: 01843 862401

Welcome to our family-run hotel, renowned for the quality of its accommodation and service, which incorporates an alternative therapeutic health care salon. Most rooms have colour TV, and all have hospitality trays. There is a large, quiet lounge for relaxation, and breakfast is served in the dining room, where there is also a cosy bar. Ideal for exploring this scenic area; Canterbury 30 mins drive.

SB

e-mail: kestoncourt@tinyonline.co.uk
www.SmoothHound.co.uk/hotels/keston.html

102 LONDON & SOUTH EAST ENGLAND — Kent

Canterbury, Dover, Faversham

Upper Ansdore

Beautiful secluded Listed Tudor farmhouse with various livestock, situated in an elevated position with far-reaching views of the wooded countryside of the North Downs. The property overlooks a Kent Trust Nature Reserve, is five miles south of the cathedral city of Canterbury and only 30 minutes' drive to the ports of Dover and Folkestone. The accommodation comprises one family, three double and one twin-bedded rooms. All have shower and WC en suite and tea making facilities. Dining/sitting room, heavily beamed with large inglenook. Pets welcome. Car essential.

Tel: 01227 700672

Bed and Breakfast from £29 per person. Credit cards accepted.

Mr and Mrs R. Linch, Upper Ansdore, Duckpit Lane, Petham, Canterbury CT4 5QB
e-mail: rogerd@talktalk.net • www.bedandbreakfastupperansdore.co.uk

Great Field Farm

Stelling Minnis, Canterbury, Kent CT4 6DE
Tel: 01227 709223

Situated in beautiful countryside, 10 minutes' drive from Canterbury, Channel Tunnel and Folkestone, our spacious farmhouse provides friendly, comfortable accommodation. Full central heating and double glazing. Hearty breakfasts with home-grown produce. All rooms en suite with colour TV, courtesy tray and free internet access. Cottage suite with its own entrance. Both annexe suite (sleeps 2) and new detached ground floor geo-thermally heated Sunset Lodge (sleeps 4/5) are ideal for B&B or self-catering.
Ample off-road parking • Good pub food nearby
Non-smoking establishment • **B&B from £30 per person.**

Bed & Breakfast • Self-Catering • www.great-field-farm.co.uk

Bleriot's ★★★ Dover

Our AA Highly Commended three gold star non-smoking Victorian residence is set in a tree-lined avenue, in the lee of Dover Castle, within easy reach of trains, bus station, town centre, ferries and cruise terminal. Channel Tunnel approximately 10 minutes' drive. Off-road parking. We specialise in one night 'stop-overs' and mini-breaks. Single, double, twin and family rooms with full en suite. All rooms have colour TV, tea and coffee making facilities, and are fully centrally heated. Full English breakfast served from 7am. Reduced rates for room only. Open all year. MasterCard and Visa accepted. AA Centenary Awards B&B Friendliest Landlady Finalist.

Bed and Breakfast £26 to £30 per person per night.
Mini-Breaks January to March and October to December £24 per person per night.

Bleriot's, 47 Park Avenue, Dover CT16 1HE • Tel: 01304 211394
e-mail: info@bleriots.net • www.bleriots.net

Tenterden House
B&B from £25pp

Stay in one of the en suite bedrooms (one double, one twin) in this delightful gardener's cottage and stroll through the shrubbery to the 16th century diningroom, in the main house, for a traditional English breakfast, beneath the Dragon Beam. Close to Canterbury, Whitstable and the Channel Ports. It makes an ideal base for exploring Kent, then walk to one of the historic inns in the village for your evening meal. Tea/coffee making facilities. Off-road parking. Open all year.

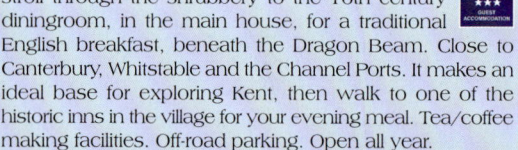

Mrs Prudence Latham, Tenterden House, The Street, Boughton, Faversham ME13 9BL (01227 751593).
e-mail: platham@tesco.net
www.faversham.org/tenterdenhouse

Kent
Folkestone, Headon

LONDON & SOUTH EAST ENGLAND

Linda Dowsett welcomes you to her comfortable, family-run Guest House.

Home-made English breakfast and Continental
- Coffee/tea making facilities and colour TV in each room
- En suite rooms • Private car park
- Five minutes town centre, two minutes Folkestone Central railway station, 10 minutes Channel Tunnel, 20 minutes to Dover for France and Belgium
- Children welcome • Early starters catered for
- Own keys • B&B from £25

Sunny Lodge Guest House

85 Cheriton Road, Folkestone CT20 2QL
Tel/Fax: 01303 251498
e-mail: linda.dowsett@btclick.com
www.sunnylodge.co.uk

Waterkant

Waterkant is a small guest house in a tranquil 16th century Kent Wealdon Village of olde worlde charm. A warm and friendly welcome and the relaxed and informal atmosphere is complemented by excellent service and comfortable surroundings. Bedrooms have private or en suite bathrooms, four-poster beds, tea/coffee making facilities, TV and are centrally heated and double glazed. Sitting room with TV. The beautifully landscaped Mediterranean-style gardens bounded by a stream provides a large pond, summerhouse for visitors' use and ample parking. Fast trains to London and a wealth of historic places to visit nearby. Open all year. *Visitors return year after year. Bed and Breakfast from £20 per person, with reduced rates for children, Senior Citizens, midweek and winter season bookings, and referrals from FHG. Participants in ETC's Quality Assurance schemes.*

**Mrs Dorothy Burbridge, Waterkant Guest House,
Moat Road, Headcorn, Ashford TN27 9NT
Tel: 01622 890154 • Mobile: 07785 534530
e-mail: colin@waterkant.freeserve.co.uk • www.headcornbb.co.uk**

Kent

Maidstone, Pluckley

Luxuriously converted Kentish oasthouse set in a quiet, picturesque hamlet of about 12 houses, off A274 south of Maidstone and close to Leeds Castle. Ideal touring base for all of Kent's attractions, and for London. Also makes a good stopover to or from Europe.

Stay in one of our two large Roundel rooms, one with Jacuzzi bath, or in a twin or double room with half-tester canopy.

B&B from £27.50 to £47.50 per person,

Langley Oast B&B

Langley Park, Langley, Maidstone, Kent ME17 3NQ
Tel & Fax: 01622 863523
e-mail: margaret@langleyoast.freeserve.co.uk

Bramley Knowle Farm

A warm welcome awaits you at our modern farmhouse built in the style of a Kentish Barn, set in 45 acres of land surrounded by peaceful countryside. Only 10 minutes' drive from M20, J8, it is an ideal central location, close to Leeds Castle, Sissinghurst, Canterbury. London one and a quarter hours by train, Dover one hour by car. One double room en suite, one family suite (single/twin and double with shared bathroom), all with tea/coffee making facilities, TV, central heating, wireless broadband. Ample off-road parking.

B&B from £27.50 per person. Self-catering also available.

Mr & Mrs Leat, Bramley Knowle Farm, Eastwood Road, Ulcombe, Maidstone, Kent ME17 1ET
Tel: 01622 858878 • E-mail: diane@bramleyknowlefarm.co.uk • www.bramleyknowlefarm.co.uk

Elvey Farm

Elvey Lane, Pluckley, Kent TN27 0SU
Tel: 01233 840 442
bookings@elveyfarm.co.uk • www.elveyfarm.co.uk

Elvey Farm is a medieval farmstead in the village of Pluckley. The Hall House was built in 1430 and little has changed since then. Once used as a 75-acre farm for cereals and sheep, Elvey is now run as a small country hotel. Guests stay in the converted stable block and barn, and enjoy brand new contemporary bathrooms and excellent personal service, with glorious views over the Kent countryside. Whether you're sipping champagne on the veranda outside your suite, or you're riding your own horse through our excellent bridleways, you'll be surrounded by the quietest, the prettiest and the most idyllic countryside in Kent.

At breakfast you have fresh eggs, crispy bacon, sausages and tomatoes from local farms. In the evenings, you can sample wine or cider from Kent's vineyards, and admire crafts from local artists.

Elvey has been run by local people for centuries.
That's why we say Elvey is Kentish to the core.

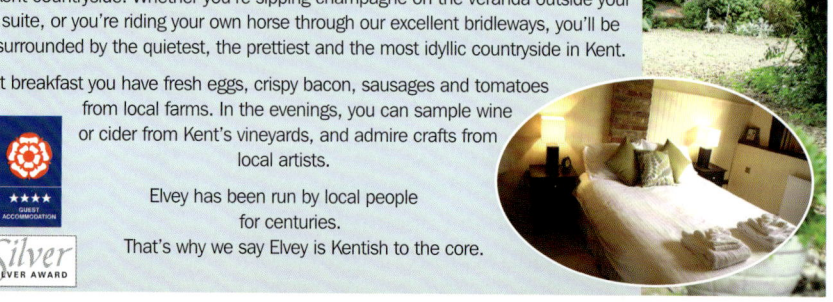

Oxfordshire

Banbury, Henley-on-Thames

Oxfordshire

NEW FARMHOUSE situated on edge of village off A423 Southam Road, three miles north of Banbury overlooking the beautiful Cherwell Valley. Ideally situated for touring Cotswolds, Stratford, Warwick, Oxford, Blenheim Palace. Local pubs serving evening meals Tuesdays to Saturdays.

Very comfortable accommodation comprising one twin room, one family room (one double and one single bed). Tea/coffee making facilities, hair dryers; central heating; shower room with electric shower; guests' sittingroom with colour TV. All rooms fully carpeted. Non-smoking. Parking.

Sorry, no pets.

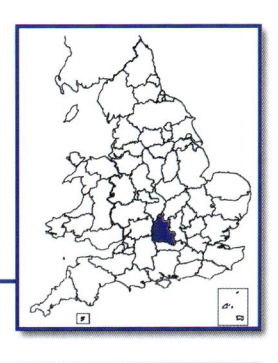

Bed and Breakfast from £25
Child under 10 sharing family room £12
A warm welcome awaits you

Mrs Rosemary Cannon
High Acres Farm
Great Bourton
Banbury OX17 1RL
Tel & Fax: 01295 750217

Abbottsleigh

A large comfortable house in a quiet location near town and River Thames. Very good for short breaks and visits to Oxford, Windsor and London, and river trips along the famous Henley Regatta course. Plenty of places to eat. Good area for walking. Easy to get to Heathrow. All rooms have colour TV, tea/coffee making facilities, washbasin, most en suite. Full central heating. Full English breakfast. Regret no dogs. Good parking, some off-road. Open all year.

Single room from £38, double/twin £65 to £75 per night.
Single occupancy in double room £38 to £55 per night.

**Mrs K. Bridekirk, Abbottsleigh,
107 St Marks Road, Henley-on-Thames RG9 1LP**

e-mail: abbottsleigh@hotmail.com
Tel & Fax: 01491 572982 • Mobile: 07958 424337

LONDON & SOUTH EAST ENGLAND — 106 — **Oxfordshire**

Henley-on-Thames, Long Hanborough, Minster Lovell, Oxford

THE OLD BAKERY
Skirmett, Near Henley-on-Thames RG9 6TD

This welcoming family house is situated on the site of an old bakery, seven miles from Henley-on-Thames and Marlow; half-an-hour from Heathrow and Oxford; one hour from London. It is in the beautiful Hambleden Valley in the Chilterns, with many excellent pubs. Village pub in Skirmett, within easy walking distance, serves superb food in the restaurant. One double en suite, one twin-bedded room and one double with use of own bathroom, all with TV and tea making facilities. Open all year. Parking for six cars (car essential). Children and pets welcome. Outstandingly beautiful garden/vegetable garden overlooking woodlands and farmland. B&B from £35 single; £60 double, £80 en suite.

e-mail: lizzroach@aol.com
Tel: 01491 638309 • Office: 01491 410716
Fax: 01491 638086

The Close Guest House
Witney Road
Long Hanborough
Oxfordshire
OX29 8HF

We offer comfortable accommodation in house set in own grounds of one-and-a-half acres. Three family rooms, four double rooms; all en suite; one double and one single.

All have colour TV and tea/coffee making facilities. Full central heating. Use of garden and car parking for eight cars. Please mention FHG when booking.

Close to Woodstock, Oxford and the Cotswolds.
Open all year except Christmas. Bed and Breakfast from £25.
Mrs I.J. Warwick (01993 882485).

Hill Grove Farm
Crawley Road, Minster Lovell, Witney
Oxon OX29 0NA • 01993 703120

HILL GROVE is a mixed 300-acre working farm situated in an attractive setting with rural views overlooking the River Windrush Valley. Good walking area and easy access to Oxford, Woodstock (Blenheim Palace), Witney, and Burford (Gateway to the Cotswolds and renowned for its Wildlife Park). Our animals include 2 gorgeous donkeys fostered from the Devon Donkey Sanctuary.
Hearty breakfasts and a warm welcome.
Open all year except Christmas. Non-smoking.
B&B: one double room with private shower £31-£32pp
• one double en suite £32-£33pp • one double/twin en suite £32-£34pp.
Mrs Katharine Brown
e-mail: katharinemcbrown@btinternet.com
www.countryaccom.co.uk/hill-grove-farm

The Bungalow
Cherwell Farm, Mill Lane,
Old Marston,
Oxford OX3 0QF
Tel: 01865 557171
Bed and Breakfast from £25 to £30 per person.

Modern bungalow on five acres set in countryside but only three miles from the city centre. Offering comfortable accommodation and serving traditional breakfast. Colour TV, tea/coffee facilities in all rooms. Non-smoking. Private parking. Not on bus route.
ros.bungalowbb@btinternet.com • www.cherwellfarm-oxford-accom.co.uk

Oxfordshire
Oxford, Souldern

Arden Lodge

Modern detached house in select part of Oxford, within easy reach of Oxford Centre.

Excellent position for Blenheim Palace and for touring Cotswolds, Stratford, Warwick etc.

Close to river, parks, country inns and golf course. Easy access to London.

All rooms have tea/coffee making and private facilities. Parking.

Bed and Breakfast from £27 per person per night.

Mr and Mrs L. Price, Arden Lodge, 34 Sunderland Avenue (off Banbury Road), Oxford OX2 8DX
Tel: 01865 552076 • Fax: 01865 512265 • mobile: 07702 068697

Nanford Guest House

Period guest house located five minutes on foot from Oxford University. Wide range and number of rooms at budget prices. All rooms have private shower and toilet, colour TV and tea making equipment. Private off-street parking. Check in time 2pm or later.

Prices per night: single £30, double £40, twin single £40, family room £60, quadruple £80.

MR B. CRONIN, NANFORD GUEST HOUSE, 137 IFFLEY ROAD, OXFORD OX4 1EJ
Tel: 01865 244743 • Fax: 01865 249596
e-mail: b.cronin@btinternet.com • www.nanfordguesthouse.com

SB

Tower Fields
Tusmore Road, Near Souldern, Bicester OX27 7HY

Ground floor en suite rooms, all with own entrance and ample parking. Rooms have power showers, tea/coffee making facilities, fridges, Freeview TV, etc. Breakfast using local produce.

Easy reach of Banbury, Oxford, Stratford-upon-Avon, many National Trust houses. Motor racing at Silverstone, horse racing at Towcester or a leisurely cruise down the Oxford Canal. Shopaholics catered for at nearby Bicester Village retail shopping outlet.

A friendly welcome awaits you - dogs and horses welcome by arrangement. Children over 10 years only.

Contact: Toddy and Clive Hamilton-Gould - 01869 346554
e-mail: toddyclive@towerfields.com • www.towerfields.com

SB

Oxfordshire
Woodstock

Hamilton House

Highly recommended Bed and Breakfast establishment with parking, overlooking Blenheim Park, Blenheim Palace and the town centre with good selection of restaurants, pubs and shops within walking distance.

Comfortable and relaxed atmosphere with informative and very hospitable hostess. Ideal base for Blenheim Palace, Bladon, the Cotswolds, Stratford-upon-Avon, Oxford and major airports. Access off A44 northern end of Woodstock, one-third-of-a-mile up the hill from the Black Prince Pub.

• TV & WiFi in all rooms • Telephone available • En suite facilities in all rooms • Tea and coffee making facilities • Ironing facilities • Children welcome • Hairdryer available • Special diets catered for • Non-smoking. • Parking available. • Credit cards accepted. • Dogs welcome by arrangement

Double bed single occupancy with breakfast £40 to £60
Double/Twin Bed with Breakfast from £50.00 to £65.00 per room
Triple Bed / Family Room with Breakfast from £60.00 to 75.00 per room • Long term rates negotiable
For immediate response please call landline first, then mobile if ansaphone comes on.

Mrs Kay Bradford, Hamilton House, 43 Hill Rise, Old Woodstock, Oxfordshire OX20 1AB
Tel: 01993 812206 • Mobile: 07778 705568
e-mail: kay@hamiltonhousewoodstock.co.uk • www.hamiltonhousewoodstock.co.uk

---

Beautifully restored 16th century home. High priority to cleanliness and quality. Large en suite rooms. Banquet breakfast using fresh local produce, homemade jams and bread. Many super walks including Roman Villa. Close to Blenheim Palace, all Cotswold towns and villages and Oxford City. Open all year. Two double en suite bedrooms.

B&B from £48-£70 single, £70-£72 double.

Elbie House
East End, North Leigh,
Near Witney OX29 6PX • 01993 880166
e-mail: mandy@cotswoldbreak.co.uk
www.cotswoldbreak.co.uk

Please note
All the information in this book is given in good faith in the belief that it is correct. However, the publishers cannot guarantee the facts given in these pages, neither are they responsible for changes in policy, ownership or terms that may take place after the date of going to press. Readers should always satisfy themselves that the facilities they require are available and that the terms, if quoted, still apply.

Surrey

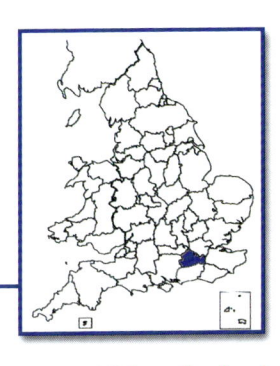

Godalming, Gomshall

GODALMING. Mrs Langdale, Heath Hall Farm, Bowlhead Green, Godalming GU8 6NW (01428 682808).
Converted stable courtyard surrounded by its own farmland on edge of village of Bowlhead Green. Countryside charming with outstanding walking. Ideal base for many famous historic attractions - Losely House, Petworth House, Wisley RHS Garden, Arundel Castle, Midhurst (Cowdray Castle), historic Portsmouth. Plenty in locality to visit with children. Central for golf courses; polo at Midhurst. Close to South and North Downs. Relaxed atmosphere in house, domestic pets, cattle, sheep, ducks and chooks. All rooms have en suite bathrooms, TV, tea/coffee making facilities. Wire-free computer access, security encrypted. Three rooms on ground floor. Ample car parking. Warm welcome with friendly help and advice.

Rates: £32 per person per night (£37 if one night only), £10 per child (up to 12 years), £15 per child (13 years and over). Cot provided on application (£10 per night).
- Dogs welcome if kept under control and with prior arrangement (£5 per dog per night) • Children welcome
- Open all year • Cards accepted

e-mail: heathhallfarm@btinternet.com   www.heathhallfarm.co.uk

The COMPASSES Inn
Purveyors of fine food, ale and .....music!

SB

This attractive inn was once known as the 'God Encompasses' but through time and mispronunciation is now simply known as the 'Compasses'.

Known for its appetising selection of home-cooked dishes and supporting local Surrey Hills Brewery, this friendly hostelry has a warm ambience accentuated by its exposed oak beams and horse brasses.

There is good traditional home-cooked food in the bar and the restaurant. Live music from 9pm every Friday. Situated beneath the North Downs, there is a popular beer garden through which runs the Tillingbourne Stream.

Station Road, Gomshall, Surrey GU5 9LA
Tel: 01483 202 506
www.thecompassesinn.co.uk

Surrey

Horley, Kingston-on-Thames, Lingfield

The Lawn Guest House
"Everything for the Gatwick Airport Traveller"

30 Massetts Road, Horley, Surrey RH6 7DF
Tel: 01293 775751 • Fax: 01293 821803
E-mail: info@lawnguesthouse.co.uk
www.lawnguesthouse.co.uk

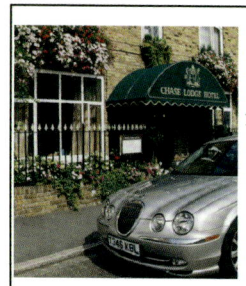

Imposing Victorian house set in pretty gardens. Five minutes by car from Gatwick airport and only 2 minutes walk to the centre of Horley. Main line rail station is 300 yards; London (Victoria) 40 minutes. Comfortable en suite bedrooms, some with both bath and shower; TV, hairdryers, tea/coffee/chocolate trays, d/d phones, computer modem sockets and fully adjustable central heating. Full English or Continental breakfast available. Residents' on-line computer. Overnight parking. Long term parking and airport transfers by arrangement.

Twin/Double £60 per room, Triple £70 per room, Family room for 4, £80 per room, Family room for 5, £85. All inclusive of English breakfast and tax.

Chase Lodge Hotel
An Award Winning Hotel
with style & elegance, set in tranquil surroundings at affordable prices

10 Park Road Hampton Wick Kingston-Upon-Thames KT1 4AS
Tel: 020 8943 1862 . Fax: 020 8943 9363
E-mail: info@chaselodgehotel.com Website: www.chaselodgehotel.com
and
www.surreyhotels.com

Quality en suite bedrooms
Full Buffet Continental Breakfast

Licensed bar
Wedding Receptions
Honeymoon suite
available with jacuzzi & steam area
20 minutes from Heathrow Airport
Close to Kingston town centre & all major transport links.

★★★

All major credit cards accepted

Stantons Hall Farm
is an 18th century farmhouse, set in 18 acres of farmland and adjacent to Blindley Heath Common. Family, double and single rooms, most with WC, shower and wash-hand basins en suite. Separate bathroom. All rooms have colour TV, tea/coffee facilities and are centrally heated. Enjoy a traditional English breakfast in our large farmhouse kitchen.

Conveniently situated within easy reach of M25 (London Orbital), Gatwick Airport (car parking for travellers) and Lingfield Park racecourse.

- Bed and Breakfast from £30 per person, reductions for children sharing • Cot and high chair available
- Well behaved dogs welcome by prior arrangement • There are plenty of parking spaces.

Mrs V. Manwill, Stantons Hall Farm, Eastbourne Road, Blindley Heath, Lingfield RH7 6LG • 01342 832401

Oaklands
is a spacious country house of considerable charm dating from the 17th century. It is set in its own grounds of one acre and is about one mile from the small town of Lingfield and three miles from East Grinstead, both with rail connections to London. It is convenient to Gatwick Airport and is ideal as a "stop-over" or as a base to visit many places of interest in south-east England. Dover and the Channel Ports are two hours' drive away whilst the major towns of London and Brighton are about one hour distant. One family room en suite, one double and one single bedrooms with washbasins; three bathrooms, two toilets; sittingroom; diningroom. Cot, high chair, babysitting and reduced rates for children. Gas CH. Open all year. Parking. *B&B from £23.*

*Mrs Vivienne Bundy, Oaklands, Felcourt Road, Lingfield RH7 6NF
Tel: 01342 834705 • e-mail: oaklands@ukonline.co.uk*

Surrey
LONDON & SOUTH EAST ENGLAND

Merstham, Surbiton

Little Orchard Bed and Breakfast

A warm welcome is offered to business and holiday guests at this comfortable, friendly home from home B&B situated close to M25 and M23, and Redhill, Reigate and Croydon. Colour TV and tea/coffee facilities. Evening Meal available if required.
24 hour transfer to Gatwick or Heathrow, plus holiday parking. The perfect way to start and finish a business trip or holiday.
Heated swimming pool in summer months.
Bed and Breakfast from £40pppn, DB&B from £50pppn.
Self-catering also available.

SB

152 London Road North, Merstham RH1 3AA • Tel: 01737 558707 • Fax: 0208 657 7263
e-mail: jackie@littleorchardbandb.co.uk • www.littleorchardbandb.co.uk

---

Villiers Lodge

Mrs Menzies, 1 Cranes Park, Surbiton, Surrey KT5 8AB
Telephone: 020 8399 6000

Excellent accommodation in small Guest House. Tea/coffee making facilities in all rooms. Close to trains and buses for London, Hampton Court, Kew, Windsor and coast. Ham House is a favourite visiting place and Merton Abbey Mills is a wonderful place for a day shopping and exploring. Excellent accommodation in small Guest House. Close to trains and buses for London, Hampton Court, Kew, Windsor and coast. Ham House is a favourite visiting place and Merton Abbey Mills is a wonderful place for a day shopping and exploring.

- Children welcome • Colour television in all bedrooms
- Ground floor bedrooms available
- Tea & coffee making facilities in all bedrooms
- Central heating throughout • Car parking • Off site parking

B&B from £25pppn Euros accepted

---

symbols

🚭	Totally non-smoking	🐕	Pets Welcome
🐎	Children Welcome	**SB**	Short Breaks
♿	Suitable for Disabled Guests	🍷	Licensed

East Sussex
Brighton

East Sussex

Paskins town house

PASKINS is a small, green hotel that has found its own way. It's a sort of eclectic, environmentally friendly hotel with nice and sometimes amusing rooms, and brilliant breakfasts. You arrive at the Art Nouveau reception to be shown to one of the 19 slightly out of the ordinary rooms, each individual in design, perhaps a little quirky, but not at the expense of being comfortable. For example, one room has a genuine Victorian brass bed with several mattresses, just as Queen Victoria's did, which enabled her to sleep higher than all her subjects. Having been welcomed royally, you will sleep like a monarch, and come down to a regal spread at breakfast, prepared with mainly organic, fair trade or locally sourced produce. The Art Deco breakfast room continues the charming theme of the hotel, and has a menu of celebrated choice, including a variety of imaginative vegetarian and vegan dishes, some intriguing signature dishes, and a blackboard full of specials.   AA ★★★★ • Green Tourism Gold Award

PASKINS TOWN HOUSE • • 18/19 Charlotte Street, Brighton BN2 1AG
Tel: 01273 601203 • Fax: 01273 621973 • www.paskins.co.uk • welcome@paskins.co.uk

MAON HOTEL

26 Upper Rock Gardens,
Brighton BN2 1QE
Tel: 01273 694400
e-mail: maonhotel@aol.com
www.maonhotel.co.uk

This is a completely non-smoking Grade II Listed building run by proprietors who are waiting with a warm and friendly welcome. Established over 25 years. Our standard of food has been highly recommended by many guests who return year after year. Two minutes from the sea and within easy reach of conference and main town centres.

- All nine bedrooms are furnished to a high standard with matching Dorma linen, and have colour TV, fan, mini-fridge, radio alarm clock, hospitality tray and hairdryer and most are en suite.
- A lounge with colour TV is available for guests' convenience; diningroom.
- Full central heating. Access to rooms at all times.
- No children.   TOTALLY NON-SMOKING.

Maon Hotel

East Sussex
LONDON & SOUTH EAST ENGLAND 113
Burwash, Eastbourne

Woodlands Farm
Burwash, Etchingham TN19 7LF

Woodlands Farm stands one third of a mile off the road, surrounded by fields and woods.

This peaceful and beautifully modernised 16th century farmhouse offers comfortable and friendly accommodation.

Sitting/dining room; two bathrooms, one en suite, double or twin-bedded rooms (one has four-poster bed) together with excellent farm fresh food.

This is a farm of 108 acres with a variety of animals and is situated within easy reach of 20 or more places of interest to visit and half an hour from the coast.

Open all year • Central heating • Literature provided to help guests. Children welcome • Dogs allowed if sleeping in owner's car. Parking • Evening Meal optional • Non-smoking.

Bed and Breakfast from £40 single and from £60-£70 double. Telephone or SAE, please • Mrs E. Sirrell • Tel & Fax: 01435 882794

e-mail: liz_sir@lineone.net
www.SmoothHound.co.uk/hotels/woodlands.html

Far End GUEST HOUSE

From the moment you arrive you are assured of a warm welcome and real "home from home" atmosphere. Our centrally heated bedrooms with colour TV and tea/coffee making facilities are tastefully decorated, most have en suite facilities and sea views. Residents have their own lounge and private car park. Enjoy freshly prepared traditional home cooking. Special diets can be catered for. Credit cards accepted.

We are adjacent to the popular Princes Park with boating lake, lawns, bowling greens and pitch'n'putt, close by you can enjoy sailing, fishing, bowling, tennis and swimming. We are in easy reach of Beachy Head, the South Downs and Newhaven. We will be delighted to provide information on the many local attractions and services, and shall do our best to make your stay as memorable and pleasant as possible. Open all winter, including Christmas.

SB

Bed and Breakfast from £28
Evening Meal available Mon-Fri
Low season short breaks.
Please call or write for colour brochure.

AA
★★★★
Guest Accommodation

Far End Guest House
139 Royal Parade, Eastbourne
East Sussex BN22 7LH
Tel: 01323 725666
www.farendhotel.co.uk
farendguesthouse@hotmail.com

114 LONDON & SOUTH EAST ENGLAND — East Sussex

Eastbourne, Hailsham, Hartfield

EBOR LODGE HOTEL — 71 Royal Parade, Eastbourne BN22 7AQ

Ebor Lodge has a warm, friendly atmosphere, offering accommodation at realistic prices.

Recently refurbished, all rooms are en suite and furnished to a high standard, fully centrally heated with hospitality trays, colour TVs, clock radios, bedside lights and hairdryers. A ground floor room is adjacent to the dining room and guest lounge. Front rooms boast sea views with one having a private balcony. Open all year. We offer off-peak reductions for Senior Citizens. Opposite the Redoubt and bowling greens, it is a short walk to Prince's Park, tennis courts, putting greens and children's amusements.

Tel: 01323 640792

The Boship Farm

Lower Dicker, Near Hailsham, East Sussex BN27 4AT
Tel: 01323 844826
Fax: 01323 843945

A lovely old farmhouse dating from 1652 forms the hub of the Boship Farm Hotel, set in the Sussex Weald, an Area of Outstanding Natural Beauty. There are several golf courses within 20 minutes of the hotel.
All bedrooms are en suite, with colour TV, telephone, trouser press, hairdryer and courtesy tray. Most enjoy lovely views across fields and countryside. Relax in the Health Suite, which has a sauna, jacuzzi, solarium, rowing machine and exercise cycle. The hotel restaurant 'Cromwells' is renowned locally for its high standard of traditional English Fayre.

www.boshipfarmhotel.co.uk • info@boshipfarmhotel.co.uk

Situated in quiet private country lane one mile north of the market town of Hailsham with its excellent amenities including modern sports centre and leisure pool, surrounded by footpaths across open farmland. Ideal for country lovers. The coast at Eastbourne, South Downs, Ashdown Forest and 1066 country are all within easy access.

The non-smoking accommodation comprises one twin room, double room en suite; family room en suite and tea/coffee making facilities.

Bed and Breakfast from £25pp.

Tel & Fax: 01323 841227
www.longleysfarmcottage.co.uk

David and Jill Hook, Longleys Farm Cottage
Harebeating Lane, Hailsham BN27 1ER

Bolebroke Castle

Henry VIII's hunting lodge, Bolebroke Castle is set on a beautiful 30 acre estate with lakes, woodlands and views to Ashdown Forest, where you will find 'Pooh Bridge'. Antiques and beamed ceilings add to the atmosphere. Four-poster suite available. B&B or Self-Catering options. Please call for our brochure.

In the heart of "Winnie the Pooh" country.

www.bolebrokecastle.co.uk

Bolebroke Castle, Hartfield,
East Sussex TN7 4JJ
Tel: 01892 770061

East Sussex

Hastings, Lewes

Westwood Farm

Farm with pigs, sheep, chickens, etc. Quiet rural location off country lane half-a-mile from B2093 approximately two miles from seafront and town centre. Golf course nearby. Central position for visiting places of interest to suit all ages. Elevated situation with outstanding views over Brede Valley.

Double, twin, family rooms with en suite and private facilities. Colour TV, tea/coffee in all rooms, two bedrooms on ground floor. Full English breakfast. Off-road parking.

Bed and Breakfast from £28pp for two persons sharing. Reduced rates for weekly booking. Also available six-berth self-catering caravan – details on request.

Mr & Mrs S. York
Westwood Farm
Stonestile Lane
Hastings
TN35 4PG

- Tel & Fax: 01424 751038 • mobile: 07837 271797
- e-mail: westwoodfarm@talktalk.net
- www.SmoothHound.co.uk/hotels/westwoodf.html

★★★ FARMHOUSE

Grand Hotel

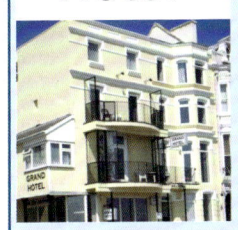

Seafront family-run hotel, half-a-mile west of Hastings Pier. Spacious lounge, licensed bar, central heating throughout. Radio/room-call/baby-listening. En suite rooms with Freeview/DVD player/TV also available. Free access at all times. Unrestricted/ disabled parking in front of hotel. In the heart of 1066 country close to Battle, Bodiam and Hever Castles, Kipling's Batemans and Rye, plus Hastings Castle, Caves, Aquarium, local golf courses and leisure centres.

Hastings & St.Leonards Hotels & Tourism Association

★ HOTEL

Wi-fi broadband throughout • Non-smoking throughout
Children welcome, half price when sharing room • Open all year

GRAND HOTEL, GRAND PARADE, ST LEONARDS, HASTINGS TN38 0DD
Tel & Fax: 01424 428510
e-mail: info@grandhotelhastings.co.uk
www.grandhotelhastings.co.uk

**B&B from £25
Evening Meal
from £15**

Behind the Georgian facade of the White Hart lies an historic Tudor building which has been substantially extended to create a lively county town hotel.

♦ *53 bedrooms, all en suite with colour TV, telephone, tea-making. Some rooms have views of the Downs; some with disabled access.*

♦ *Wide range of meals and snacks available daily - à la carte, carvery, bar meals, light snacks, teas and coffees.*

♦ *Leisure Centre and Health Spa with heated indoor pool, fully equipped gym, sauna, aerobics studio, beauty clinic etc.*

White Hart Hotel, High Street, Lewes BN7 1XE • Tel: 01273 476694
Fax: 01273 476695 • info@whitehartlewes.co.uk • www.whitehartlewes.co.uk

---

Visit the FHG website
www.holidayguides.com
for details of the wide choice of accommodation featured in the full range of FHG titles

LONDON & SOUTH EAST ENGLAND

East Sussex
Polgate, Rye, Seaford

Homely private house. Quiet location; large enclosed garden. Parking space. Ideally situated for walking on South Downs and Forestry Commission land. All rooms, washbasins and tea/coffee making facilities.

Bed and Breakfast. Pets very welcome.

**MRS P. FIELD,
20 ST JOHN'S ROAD,
POLEGATE BN26 5BP • 01323 482691**

SB

Situated in a quiet road, just ten minutes' walk from the centre of medieval Rye, Little Saltcote is an Edwardian family home which offers off-road parking and four comfortable rooms (one at ground floor), all with TV/DVD, radio and beverage tray. We welcome families and are pleased to offer tourist advice or arrange bike hire. Ideally located for touring Sussex and Kent's varied attractions, including everything from sandy beaches to castles, historic houses and gardens. Rates include acclaimed full English or vegetarian breakfast. B&B from £31.50 per person. Pets welcome by arrangement. No smoking.

Barbara and Denys Martin,
Little Saltcote,
22 Military Road, Rye TN31 7NY
01797 223210 • Fax: 01797 224474
e-mail: info@littlesaltcote.co.uk • www.littlesaltcote.co.uk

AA ★★★★ Guest Accommodation

AA Pet-Friendly Establishment of the Year 2005

THE SILVERDALE
**21 Sutton Park Road, Seaford BN25 1RH
Tel: 01323 491849**

e-mail info@silverdaleseaford.co.uk • www.silverdaleseaford.co.uk

The Silverdale is perfectly situated in the heart of Seaford. Renowned for first class home cooking, all breakfasts are freshly cooked from a substantial breakfast menu. This award-winning guest house was voted AA Pet Friendly Hotel of the Year in 2005, and has been a continuous holder of the Clean Catering Award since it opened. At the time of writing, it is the only AA and Quality in Tourism 4 Star graded guest house in Seaford offering guests remote colour TV and video, direct-dial telephone, clock radio, tea and filter coffee tray, welcome cosmetic basket, mini-bar, canopied or four-poster bed, and en suite facilities in every room. A warm and friendly welcome awaits you at The Silverdale.

*SEEDA award winner 2003, Clean Catering Award winner for 15 years   ETC/AA ★★★★
Green Tourism Business Scheme Gold Award*

West Sussex
Arundel, Bognor Regis

West Sussex

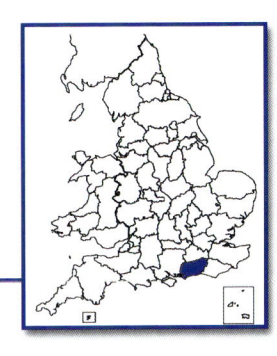

LONDON & SOUTH EAST ENGLAND 117

• Woodacre •

offers Bed and Breakfast in a traditional family home with accommodation for up to 10-12 guests. The house is set in a beautiful garden surrounded by woodland. We are well positioned for Chichester, Arundel, Goodwood and the seaside and easily accessible from the A27. Our rooms are clean and spacious and two are on the ground floor. We serve a full English breakfast in our conservatory or diningroom overlooking the garden. Plenty of parking space. Everyone is very welcome.
Credit cards accepted.

Mrs Vicki Richards,
Woodacre, Arundel Road,
Fontwell, Arundel BN18 0QP
Tel: 01243 814301
e-mail: wacrebb@aol.com
www.woodacre.co.uk

SB

Bed and Breakfast from £27.50 per person.
3 nights for the price of 2 November to March.

A charming 17th century Priory restored to its former glory with a blend of historic charm. Situated in a picturesque rural village close to Bognor Regis, Chichester, Arundel, Goodwood, Fontwell and within easy access of Portsmouth, Brighton, Continental ferry port and all major commuting routes. Facilities include superb en suite rooms equipped to 4 star standard, four-poster water bed with jacuzzi bath, secluded outdoor swimming pool. Homemade bread and jams.
Open all year.

Single £40, doubles from £30.00 to £50 per person per night inclusive of full English Breakfast

Deborah S. Collinson, The Old Priory, 80 North Bersted Street, Bognor Regis PO22 9AQ
01243 863580 • Fax: 01243 826597 • e-mail: old.priory@btinternet.com

West Sussex

Chichester, Henfield, Worthing

SUFFOLK HOUSE HOTEL

3 East Row, Chichester PO19 1PD

This Georgian hotel, once the town residence of the Dukes of Richmond, has been tastefully modernised and retains many beautiful features. It is situated a few minutes' walk from the town centre, making it the perfect venue for social and business occasions.

The restaurant is open to non-residents and offers a choice of freshly cooked food.

There is also a comfortable bar lounge with a wide selection of wines, spirits and liqueurs. All the comfortable bedrooms are en suite and have tea/coffee making facilities, telephone, clock radio, trouser press and hairdryer.

METRO HOTEL

Tel: 01243 778899 • Fax: 01243 787282
e-mail: shouse@suffolkhousehotel.co.uk
www.suffolkhousehotel.co.uk

THE SQUIRRELS — Albourne Road, Woodmancote, Henfield BN5 9BH

The Squirrels is a country house with lovely large garden set in a secluded area convenient for south coast and downland touring. Brighton and Gatwick 20 minutes. Good food at pub five minutes' walk. One family, one double, one twin and one single rooms, all with colour TV, washbasin, central heating and tea/coffee making facilities. Ample parking space. A warm welcome awaits you. Open all year. Directions: from London take M25, M23, A23 towards Brighton, then B2118 to Albourne. Turn right onto B2116 Albourne/Henfield Road – Squirrels is approx. one-and-a-half miles on left.

Tel: 01273 492761
pound@squirrels500.fsnet.co.uk

Tudor Lodge

25 Oxford Road, Worthing BN11 1XQ
Tel: 01903 234401
tudorlodgeguesthouse@btinternet.com

Large Victorian house in central position near all amenities offering spacious accommodation.
Colour TV, tea/coffee facilities, central heating.
Access at all times.
Some off-street parking. No smoking.
Bed and Breakfast from £32pppn.

SB

Bedfordshire

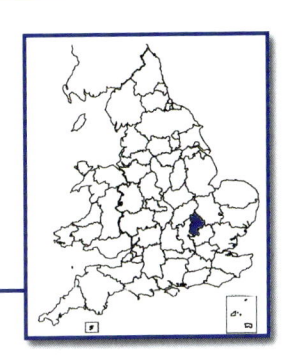

Aspley Guise

Bedfordshire

EAST OF ENGLAND

Moore Place Hotel

is located less than a mile from M1 Junction 13. Set in the picturesque village of Aspley Guise in the heart of the Bedfordshire countryside, Moore Place Hotel offers guests an informal and relaxing break.

We are pleased to announce our Golf Break packages in partnership with the nearby Aspley Guise Golf Club.

2 Day Golf Breaks from £115 pp including one night's accommodation sharing double/twin bedroom, three-course evening meal, full English breakfast, and two rounds of golf at nearby Aspley Guise Golf Course located less than half a mile from the hotel.

**Moore Place Hotel, The Square, Aspley Guise,
Milton Keynes, Bedfordshire MK17 8DW
Tel: 01908 282000 • Fax: 01908 281888
e-mail: events@mooreplace.com • www.mooreplace.com**

symbols

Totally non-smoking	Pets Welcome
Children Welcome	**SB** Short Breaks
Suitable for Disabled Guests	Licensed

120　EAST OF ENGLAND　　　　　　　　　　　　　　　　　　　　Bedfordshire
Luton

Wicks Bed & Breakfast

Bed and Breakfast accommodation situated just 10 minutes from Luton Airport, just off the M1 Junction 10 and close to the A505. Near town centre and railway stations (Town Centre and Parkway); 25 minutes' train journey to Central London. Large bungalow with double rooms; tea/coffee making equipment and colour TV. Overnight parking available. Close to local pubs, restaurants and shops. Children welcome. A warm welcome awaits.

Bedfordshire • Mr & Mrs Wicks
19 Wigmore Lane, Luton LU2 8AA • Tel: 01582 423419
e-mail: wicks-bandb@hotmail.co.uk
Mobile: 079 722 14929

Looking for Holiday Accommodation?

FHG
KUPERARD

for details of hundreds of properties throughout the UK, visit our website

www.holidayguides.com

Cambridgeshire

Burwell, Cambridge

Cambridgeshire

EAST OF ENGLAND

THE MEADOW HOUSE
2a High Street, Burwell, Cambridge CB5 0HB
Tel: 01638 741926 • Fax: 01638 741861

e-mail: hilary@themeadowhouse.co.uk

The Meadow House is a magnificent modern house set in two acres of wooded grounds offering superior Bed and Breakfast accommodation in spacious rooms, some with king-size beds. The variety of en suite accommodation endeavours to cater for all requirements; a suite of rooms sleeping six complete with south-facing balcony; a triple room on the ground floor with three single beds and the Coach House, a spacious annexe with one double and one single bed; also one double and two twins sharing a well equipped bathroom. All rooms have TV, central heating and tea/coffee facilities. Car parking. No smoking
Family rate available on request.

www.themeadowhouse.co.uk

Victoria Guest House

57 Arbury Road, Cambridge CB4 2JB

- Wiithin walking distance of city centre.
- Single, double/twin and family bedrooms, all en suite.
- All rooms with colour TV, hairdryer, tea/coffee making facilities, iron etc.
- Varied breakfast menu served in dining room overlooking picturesque garden.
- On-site parking; easy access to A14, M11, A10.

Tel: 01223 350086
www.victoria-guesthouse.co.uk
e-mail: victoriahouse@ntlworld.com

DORSET HOUSE

35 Newton Road, Little Shelford, Cambridge CB2 5HL • Tel: 01223 844440
e-mail: dorsethouse@msn.com
www.SmoothHound.co.uk

Just four miles from the historic city of Cambridge, **DORSET HOUSE** is situated in its own extensive grounds. The house has open fireplaces and wooden beams, and each luxury bedroom is individually decorated. Some rooms are en suite and all have colour TV and tea/coffee facilities. Breakfast is served in our lovely dining room.

If you are looking for the best:
Bed & Breakfast £48-£60 Single, £68-£75 Double & Twin, £75-£90 Family.

Manor Farm
Landbeach
Cambridge CB25 9FD
Tel: 01223 860165

Manor Farm is a lovely Georgian house with large spacious bedrooms, all with en suite or private bathroom, and a light airy sitting room that guests may use. Wifi available. Guests are welcome to relax in the large walled garden or take a walk on the farm.

Landbeach is a small, pretty village about six miles north of Cambridge and ten miles south of Ely. There are many local pubs and restaurants, although none are within walking distance - why not bring a bicycle and cycle along the tow path into Cambridge?

Local bus service from the village, Park-and-Ride 2 miles, railway station 2 miles (Waterbeach to London 1 hour) Ample off road parking.

Terms from £40 per room single, £55 double and £70 triple.

e-mail: vhatley@btinternet.com
www.manorfarmcambridge.co.uk

Cambridgeshire

Horseheath, Wisbech

Chequer Cottage

Streetly End, Horseheath CB21 4RP • 01223 891522

Luxurious 15thC country cottage set in gentle rolling countryside just 15 miles south east of Cambridge. Our spacious, annexed double en suite room provides total comfort and privacy. It overlooks our pretty cottage garden where you can relax and take afternoon tea, play croquet or explore the local countryside; take a stroll down the Roman Road or hop on a bicycle and search out nearby villages with pub stops en route! Enjoy our home-cooked breakfast serving locally sourced or home-grown produce, with eggs from our neighbour's happy hens. A gracious and warm welcome awaits your stay with us in our treasured home

e-mail: stay@chequercottage.com • www.chequercottage.com

Four Winds is a charming house situated four miles from the historic market town of Wisbech. It offers one en suite double room, one en suite twin room, and two single rooms with the use of a bathroom with Airspa bath. Small double room also available in high season. Comfortable guests' lounge.
Ample off-road parking.
Spacious gardens with summer house.
Bikes and helmets available for hire.
B&B from £27 pppn. Evening Meals (£10) by arrangement.

Four Winds
Mill Lane, Newton,
Near Wisbech, Cambs
PE13 5HZ
Tel: 01945 870479
Mrs Jayne Manger
jayne.best@talktalk.net

Please note

All the information in this book is given in good faith in the belief that it is correct. However, the publishers cannot guarantee the facts given in these pages, neither are they responsible for changes in policy, ownership or terms that may take place after the date of going to press. Readers should always satisfy themselves that the facilities they require are available and that the terms, if quoted, still apply.

Essex

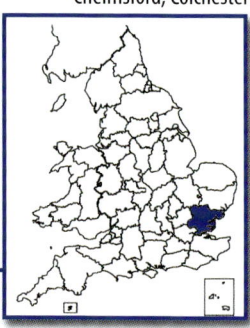

Chelmsford, Colchester

The Windmill Inn & Restaurant
01245 361188

- Bed & Breakfast accommodation on the Essex Way
- Lovely double and twin rooms - all en suite
- Free Wi-Fi
- Traditional home cooked food
- A la carte evening menu, all freshly prepared to order
- Friendly and relaxed cosy atmosphere
- Sunday Lunch - Booking advisable

Chatham Green, Near Little Waltham, Chelmsford, Essex CM3 3LE
www.windmillmotorinn.co.uk

Seven Arches Farm

Georgian farmhouse set in large garden close to the ancient town of Colchester. The farm extends to 100 acres and supports both arable crops and cattle. Private fishing rights on the River Colne, which runs past the farmhouse. This is a good location for visits to North Essex, Dedham and the Stour Valley which have been immortalised in the works of John Constable, the landscape painter.

- Children welcome.
- Open all year.
- ◆ Bed and Breakfast from £30
- ◆ Evening Meal from £5
- ◆ Twin room £50

**Mrs Jill Tod, Seven Arches Farm, Chitts Hill, Lexden, Colchester CO3 9SX
01206 574896**

The Old Manse
15 Roman Road, Colchester CO1 1UR • 01206 545154
e-mail: wendyanderson15@hotmail.com • www.theoldmanse.uk.com

Award-winning spacious Victorian family home situated in a quiet square beside the Castle Park. Only three minutes' walk from bus/coach station or through the Park to town centre.
We promise a warm welcome and a friendly, informal atmosphere. All rooms have central heating, TV and tea/coffee making facilities. One twin and one double room, both en suite, and one twin with private facilities. Full, varied English Breakfast.
B&B from £40 single, £34pppn double.
Only 30 minutes' drive from Harwich and Felixstowe. Within easy reach of Constable country and one hour's train journey from London.
Sorry, no smoking • Mrs Wendy Anderson

Essex / Hertfordshire

EAST OF ENGLAND 125

Kelvedon

KELVEDON. Mrs D. Bunting, Highfields Farm, Highfields Lane, Kelvedon CO5 9BJ (Tel & Fax: 01376 570334).
Set in a quiet area on a 700 acre working farm. This makes a peaceful overnight stop on the way to Harwich or a base to visit historic Colchester and Constable country. Convenient for Harwich, Felixstowe and Stanstead Airport. Easy access to A12 and main train lines to London. The accommodation comprises two twin and one double bedrooms, all en suite, all with TV and tea/coffee making facilities. Residents' lounge. Good English breakfast is served in the oak beamed dining room. Ample parking.
Rates: Bed and Breakfast from £38 single and from £58 twin or double.
VisitBritain ★★★★ *GUEST ACCOMMODATION.*
e-mail: highfieldsfarm@tiscali.co.uk   www.highfieldsfarm.co.uk

Hertfordshire

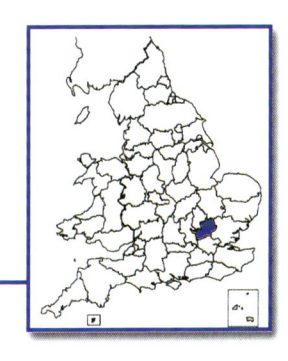

Bishop's Stortford, Much Hadham

Friars is a working farm that has been home to the Hockley family for over a century. The ivy-clad 19th century farmhouse is situated on a quiet country lane just outside the village of Hatfield Heath. The accommodation consists of two double rooms with en suite facilities and a twin room with private shower room. There is also a private sitting room for all visitors to use. Guests are welcome to sit in or wander around the garden, or make use of the many footpaths over the surrounding farmland. No smoking in the house.

Friars Farm

Hatfield Heath, Bishop's Stortford CM22 7AP
Tel & Fax: 01279 730244
www.friarsfarmbedandbreakfast.co.uk

Silver SILVER AWARD

Full English or Continental breakfast is included in the overnight prices as follows:
Double room £80, single occupancy £40;
Twin room £70, single occupancy £37.50.

High Hedges is a family-run B & B in the village of Green Tye, 20 minutes from Stansted Airport, M11, Junction 8 and 5 minutes from the village of Much Hadham. Accommodation consists of comfortably furnished double/single rooms (cot available on request), all with en-suite or private bathrooms, coffee/tea making facilities, hair dryer and TV. Local produce is used wherever possible for breakfast, and long stay parking is available by arrangement.
We now offer holistic therapies from a qualified therapist. So you can enhance your stay by relaxing and enjoying a luxury therapy to take your mind off the stresses of daily life.

Green Tye, Much Hadham, Herts SG10 6JP
Tel: 01279 842505
e-mail: info@high-hedges.co.uk • www.high-hedges.co.uk

AA Bed & Breakfast ★★★★

Norfolk

Attleborough, Aylsham

Manor Farm is situated in a rural location only five minutes from the A11 (20 minutes from Norwich). We are within easy reach of the many and varied places of interest East Anglia has to offer. Set in a large garden backing on to a young woodland, the farmhouse offers a peaceful, relaxing environment. The house has great character with inglenook fireplace and exposed beams. Every effort is made to ensure guests' comfort and the rooms are spacious and well appointed. Further details and terms on request.

Mrs Liz Rivett, Manor Farm, Hingham Road,
Great Ellingham, Attleborough NR17 1JE
Tel & Fax: 01953 453388
e-mail: e.rivett@manorfarmnorfolk.co.uk

THE OLD PUMP HOUSE, Holman Road, Aylsham, Norwich NR11 6BY
01263 733789 • theoldpumphouse@btconnect.com • www.theoldpumphouse.com

This comfortable 1750s house, owned by Marc James and Charles Kirkman, faces the old thatched pump and is a minute from Aylsham's church and historic marketplace. It offers five bedrooms (including one four-poster and two family rooms) in a relaxed and elegant setting, with colour TV, tea/ coffee making facilities, wireless internet access, hair dryers and CD radio alarm clocks in all rooms. English breakfast with free-range eggs and local produce (or vegetarian breakfast) is served in the pine-shuttered sitting room overlooking the peaceful garden. Aylsham is central for Norwich, the coast, the Broads, National Trust houses, steam railways and unspoilt countryside. Well behaved children and dogs welcome.
B&B from £60.00 single and £75.00 twin/double. Dinner by prior arrangement from October to May. Non-smoking. Off road parking for six cars.

symbols

- Totally non-smoking
- Children Welcome
- Suitable for Disabled Guests
- Pets Welcome
- **SB** Short Breaks
- Licensed

Norfolk
Dereham, Diss

EAST OF ENGLAND 127

Scarning Dale

Dale Road, Scarning, East Dereham NR19 2QN
Tel: 01362 687269

A wonderful heavily timbered house with inglenook fireplaces that dates back to the 17th century. Ideal for a delightfully different holiday experience, an overnight stay in peaceful countryside, or an unusual venue for that special party. Guests at Scarning Dale may use the heated indoor swimming pool (free use for 1 hour per day), play snooker (full-size table) or table tennis. The 25 acres of pretty countryside surrounding Scarning Dale is a birdwatcher's paradise and an inspiration to painters.

We have accommodation for six people in the house. Guests can relax in the Music Room, enjoy a book in the Library or perhaps have a quiet game of snooker or table tennis, or simply spend the evening in front of a blazing log fire in the winter, or sit in the garden on a summer evening.

All meals are home-cooked and we always use fresh vegetables grown in our own kitchen garden, depending on the season.

There are also available in the grounds of Scarning Dale six self catering cottages. Each cottage has its own garden, equipped with garden furniture.

Pets are allowed with the owner's permission provided guests clear up after their animals at all times.

www.scarningdale.co.uk

The Rookery

B&B from £28.00

Listed Georgian Farmhouse on a family-run dairy and arable farm situated on the Suffolk/Norfolk border. The twin room and one of the double rooms are situated in the recently renovated east wing of the house. The third room is a fully draped four-poster. All rooms have been beautifully decorated and furnished to a high standard and are en suite. Breakfast is a choice of full English or continental and is served in the spacious dining room. A large, comfortable lounge with TV and open fire is available for guests. Ideally placed for the many delights of East Anglia. The stunning coastline is a short distance away, as are numerous National Trust properties and tourist attractions.

Maureen Ling, The Rookery, Wortham, Diss, Norfolk IP22 1RB
Tel & Fax: 01379 783236 • mobile: 07788 455688
E-mail: russell.ling@ukgateway.net
www.polymerclaypit.co.uk/Rookery/home.html

Norfolk

Happisburgh, King's Lynn

THE Hill House
Happisburgh NR12 0PW
Tel & Fax: 01692 650004

This attractive free house on the lonely Norfolk coast at Happisburgh (pronounced 'Hazeborough') was once the favourite haunt of the remarkable Sir Arthur Conan Doyle, creator of Sherlock Holmes. Clues may be found in that the coastline here is renowned for its ghosts and has been a graveyard for ships over the years which have foundered on the formidable Haisborough Sands, some seven miles off-shore. However, conviviality and good fare is provided by a visit to the inn's beamed bar and restaurant.

Excellent accommodation is available in spacious rooms and there is a large garden in which a double en suite room has been created in a converted signal box overlooking the sea. Different!

ETC ★★★

HOLMDENE FARM
BEESTON, KING'S LYNN PE32 2NJ

17th century farmhouse situated in central Norfolk within easy reach of the coast and Broads. Sporting activities available locally, village pub nearby. One double room, one twin and two singles. Pets welcome. Bed and Breakfast from £22.50 per person; Evening Meal from £15. Weekly terms available and child reductions. Two self-catering cottages. Sleeping 4/8. Terms on request.

MRS G. DAVIDSON • Tel: 01328 701284
e-mail: holmdenefarm@farmersweekly.net
www.holmdenefarm.co.uk

The Beeches Guest House

The Beeches is an established, family-run guest house located in historic King's Lynn. All bedrooms are en suite or have a private bathroom, and are equipped with colour TV, hairdryer, and tea/coffee making facilities. We offer a superb breakfast menu, and evening meals by arrangement.

Mrs Hilary Sellers, The Beeches Guest House, 2 Guanock Terrace, King's Lynn PE30 5QT • 01553 766577 • www.beechesguesthouse.co.uk

Norfolk

EAST OF ENGLAND 129

Long Stratton, Mundesley, North Walsham

Woodgreen, Long Stratton
Norwich NR15 2RR

Period 17th century farmhouse on 30 acre common with ponds and natural wildlife, 10 miles south of Norwich (A140). The beamed sittingroom with inglenook fireplace invites you to relax. A large sunny dining room encourages you to enjoy a leisurely traditional breakfast. All en suite bedrooms (two double/twin) are tastefully furnished to complement the oak beams and period furniture, with tea/coffee facilities and TV. Full size snooker table and all-weather tennis court for guests' use. Jo is trained in therapeutic massage, aromatherapy and reflexology and is able to offer this to guests who feel it would be of benefit. Come and enjoy the peace and tranquillity of our home.

Greenacres Farmhouse

Bed and Breakfast from £30. Reductions for two nights or more. Non-smoking.

Tel: 01508 530261 • www.abreakwithtradition.co.uk

A warm welcome to all pets and their owners at "Whincliff" by the sea. Family/en suite, twin or single room available. Tea/coffee facilities, TV in all rooms, private parking, sea views, unspoilt beach and coastal walks to enjoy. **Anne & Alan Cutler.**

WHINCLIFF
Bed & Breakfast
CROMER ROAD,
MUNDESLEY NR11 8DU
Tel: 01263 721554

e-mail: cutler.a@sky.com

Friendly welcome from the proprietor, Gloria Faulkner, in this bungalow accommodation. Bed and Breakfast in a village setting just two-and-a-half miles from beaches. Many rural walks locally; within easy reach of all Norfolk's attractions including the Norfolk Broads. Golfing, horse riding and swimming nearby. All rooms en suite, with tea/coffee making facilities, TV, hairdryer. Enquiries by telephone only please.

DOLPHIN LODGE

Mrs G. Faulkner, Dolphin Lodge,
3 Knapton Road, Trunch, North Walsham
NR28 0QE • 01263 720961 • 07901 691084
e-mail: dolphin.lodge@btopenworld.com • www.dolphinlodge.net

OAKBROOK HOUSE • South Norfolk's Guest House
The ideal base to explore East Anglia & The Norfolk Broads

Simon and Heather welcome you to this former village school, fully refurbished in 2005, with views over the quiet Tas Valley, south of Norwich. Oakbrook House is the ideal touring base for East Anglia for work or leisure, centrally situated in the region. Nine warm comfortable rooms of various sizes and prices to match individual budget and comfort, each with en suite wc and basin, colour TV, clock radio and hospitality tray, en suite or private shower. All diets catered for, central heating, smoke-free, pets by arrangement. Evening meals and daytime use of the facilities available.

Contact us for brochure. Long stay discounts. B&B from £19 pppn.

Oakbrook Guest House, Frith Way, Great Moulton, Norwich NR15 2HE
Tel: 01379 677359 • mobile: 07885 351212
e-mail: oakbrookhouse@btinternet.com • www.oakbrookhouse.co.uk

Edmar Lodge

64 Earlham Road, Norwich NR2 3DF
Tel: 01603 615599 • Fax: 01603 495599

A family-run guest house where you will receive a warm welcome from Ray and Sue. We are situated only 10 minutes' walk from the city centre. All rooms have en suite facilities and digital TV. We are well known for our excellent breakfasts that set you up for the day.

e-mail: edmarlodge.co.uk
www.edmarlodge.co.uk

THE OLD HALL INN
Freehouse & Restaurant

The Old Hall Inn is an old world character freehouse/restaurant situated on the coast road between Cromer and Great Yarmouth. It is in the middle of the village and just five minutes' walk from one of the best beaches along the Norfolk coast. There are six letting rooms, three of which are en suite, all have tea/coffee making facilities and TV. There is a non-smoking à la carte restaurant and bar meals are also available. Wireless internet available. Well behaved children and pets are welcome.

Prices start at £35 for a single room, inclusive of full English breakfast, and £50 for a double room (two persons) per night.

The Old Hall Inn, Sea Palling NR12 0TZ
Tel: 01692 598323 • Fax: 01692 598822

Norfolk
Wroxham, Wymondham

EAST OF ENGLAND 131

Friendly Bed and Breakfast in an elegant Victorian house, in Wroxham 'Capital of Norfolk Broads'. Ideal for touring, day boats and boat trips on the beautiful Broads, fishing, steam railways, National Trust Houses, Wroxham Barns. Near north Norfolk coast, Great Yarmouth and Norwich. Good local restaurants and pubs. Guests arriving by train can be met. All rooms en suite, tea/coffee, colour TV. Hearty breakfasts. Large garden, car park, central heating and public telephone. Ring for brochure

Bed and Breakfast from £28 per person.
• Non-smoking • Open all year

Tel: 01603 782991
www.wroxhamparklodge.com

Wroxham Park Lodge
142 Norwich Road,
Wroxham NR12 8SA

Home Farm

Comfortable accommodation set in four acres, quiet location, secluded garden. Conveniently situated off A11 between Attleborough and Wymondham, an excellent location for Snetterton and only 20 minutes from Norwich and 45 minutes from the Norfolk Broads. Accommodation comprises two double rooms and one twin-bedded room, all with TV, tea/coffee facilities and central heating. Children over five years old welcome, but sorry no animals and no smoking. Fishing lakes only ½ mile away.

Bed and Breakfast from £26 to £28 pppn.

Mrs Joy Morter, Home Farm,
Morley, Wymondham NR18 9SU
Tel: 01953 602581

SB

Looking for Holiday Accommodation?

FHG
KUPERARD

for details of hundreds of properties throughout the UK, visit our website

www.holidayguides.com

Suffolk

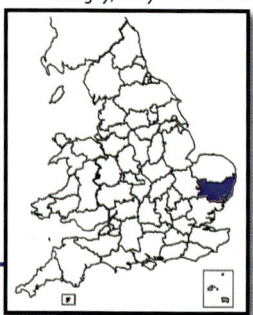

Bungay, Bury St Edmunds

George's House

A charming 17th century cottage in six-acres and working forge/blacksmith's showroom, situated in the centre of the village, just off the main Norwich to Bungay road.

Wonderful holiday area, ideal for touring Norfolk and Suffolk

Within 10 miles is historic Norwich, with its castle, cathedral, theatre and excellent shops. Coast 18 miles. Excellent pub meals available 100 yards.

Guest accommodation comprises three bedrooms – two double and one twin, all en suite. Dining room, lounge/TV, sun room. Ample parking.
B&B from £28pppn.
Mrs J. Read, George's House, The Nurseries, Woodton,
Near Bungay NR35 2LZ • Tel: 01508 482214
e-mail: julietpeter@googlemail.com
www.rossmag.com/georges

BURY ST EDMUNDS. Ann & Roy Dakin, **Dunston Guest House/Hotel, 8 Springfield Road, Bury St Edmunds IP33 3AN (01284 767981; Fax: 01284 764574).**
Dunston Guest House is a delightful Victorian house, five minutes from the town centre, situated in a quiet, tree-lined road. Seventeen individually decorated rooms, many en suite, all with colour TV, tea/coffee tray. Ground floor rooms available in the Coach House. Well furnished guests' lounge with colour TV. Car Parking. Garden.
AA/ETC ★★★
website: www.dunstonguesthouse.co.uk

**Manorhouse, The Green, Beyton,
Near Bury St Edmunds IP30 9AF • 01359 270960**

You will find a welcoming and relaxed atmosphere at this lovely timbered 15th century farmhouse, set in large gardens overlooking the village green.

Pretty, spacious, en suite bedrooms – two twin and two king-size, with sofas; all with colour TV, tea-making, radio and hairdryer. Choice of breakfasts; individual tables.

Parking. Good local inns.
Terms from £34 pppn. Beyton signposted off A14.

ETC ★★★★★ GOLD AWARD
WINNER BEST B&B IN SUFFOLK

e-mail: manorhouse@beyton.com
www.beyton.com

The FHG Directory of Website Addresses
on pages 347-362 is a useful quick reference guide for holiday accommodation with e-mail and/or website details

Suffolk

EAST OF ENGLAND 133

Clare, Felixstowe, Framlingham

Clare is an historic market town and the area abounds in history and ancient buildings, with many antique shops and places of interest to visit. The house is within easy walking distance of the ancient castle and country park, and the town centre with pubs and restaurants which provide excellent food.

Within the pretty walled garden is the charming beamed twin-bedded en suite cottage with private access. The cottage has central heating, fridge, colour TV and tea/coffee making facilities.

Bed and Breakfast from £35pppn.

Easy parking. We are strictly non-smoking.

SB

Alastair and Woolfy Tuffill, Cobbles, 26 Nethergate Street, Clare, Near Sudbury CO10 8NP
01787 277539 • e-mail: cobbles@tuffillverner.com

The Grafton Guest House

Situated by the sea front, the Grafton offers quality Bed and Breakfast accommodation. All en suite and standard rooms have colour TV, clock radio, hairdryer and tea/coffee making facilities. Owners Geoffrey and Elizabeth are committed to providing a first class service and extend a warm welcome to all guests. Non-smoking throughout.
Single rooms from £30, double from £50, per night, including breakfast.

Geoffrey and Elizabeth Harvey, The Grafton Guest House, 13 Sea Road, Felixstowe IP11 2BB • 01394 284881 • Fax: 01394 279101
e-mail:info@grafton-house.com • www.grafton-house.com

Signposted on B1119, Fiddlers Hall is a 14th century, moated, oak-beamed farmhouse set in a beautiful and secluded position. It is two miles from Framlingham Castle, 20 minutes' drive from Aldeburgh, Snape Maltings, Woodbridge and Southwold. A Grade II Listed building, it has lots of history and character. The bedrooms are spacious; one has en suite shower room, the other has a private bathroom. Use of lounge and colour TV. Plenty of parking space. Lots of farm animals kept. Traditional farmhouse cooking. Bed and Breakfast terms from £65 per room.

Mrs Jennie Mann, Fiddlers Hall, Cransford, Near Framlingham, Woodbridge IP13 9PQ • 01728 663729 • www.fiddlershall.co.uk

High House Farm

Cransford, Framlingham, Woodbridge IP13 9PD
Tel: 01728 663461 * Fax: 01728 663409
e-mail: b&b@highhousefarm.co.uk
www.highhousefarm.co.uk

Exposed oak beams • inglenook fireplaces • one double room, en suite and one large family room with double and twin beds and private adjacent bathroom • children's cots • high chairs • books • toys • outside play equipment • attractive semi-moated gardens • farm and woodland walks.

Explore the heart of rural Suffolk, local vineyards, Easton Farm Park, Framlingham and Orford Castles, Parham Air Museum, Saxtead Windmill, Minsmere, Snape Maltings, Woodland Trust and the Heritage Coast.

Bed and Breakfast from £25. Reductions for children and stays of three nights or more.

134 EAST OF ENGLAND

Norfolk
Hopton, Ipswich, Saxmundham

The Old Rectory is a Listed building dating from the 16th century, well situated to explore East Anglia, being on the Suffolk/Norfolk border. Bury St Edmunds is 12 miles away, the market town of Diss is 8. Cambridge, Ipswich and Norwich are within easy reach. The house is beautifully furnished and many period features add to the charm of this lovely stylish family home.
The luxurious bedrooms have en suite bathrooms.
Sarah and Bobby delight in entertaining guests in their beautifully restored home. A no smoking house.

**Bobby & Sarah Llewellyn, The Old Rectory
Hopton, Suffolk IP22 2QX • Tel: 01953 688135
e-mail: llewellyn.hopton@btinternet.com
www.theoldrectoryhopton.com**

- Continental/English breakfast • dinner available
- licensed • children and pets welcome by arrangement
- closed Christmas, New Year and Easter

*Gold
GOLD AWARD*

A comfortable modernised Edwardian house set in a large secluded garden located four miles south of Ipswich. Ideally situated to explore the Suffolk heritage coast and countryside, within easy reach of "Constable Country", Lavenham, Kersey, the historic market town of Bury St Edmunds plus many other picturesque locations.

Twin, double and single bedrooms; guests' bathroom with shower and toilet, lounge with TV. Good pub meals available in the village.
From £27 per person per night. No smoking.

**Mrs Rosanna Steward, High View,
Back Lane, Washbrook, Ipswich IP8 3JA
Tel: 01473 730494
e-mail: rosanna3@suffolkholidays.com
www.suffolkholidays.com**

Set well back from the main road in a quiet location • Always a warm welcome • Ideal for walking/cycling and the Heritage Coast • Vintage transport available free for longer stays
• One double and one family room with en suite/private bathrooms • Open all year.

**SWEFFLING HALL FARM
Sweffling, Saxmundham IP17 2B
www.swefflinghallfarm.co.uk
Tel & Fax: 01728 663644 • e-mail: stephenmann@suffolkonline.net**

---

symbols

🚭	Totally non-smoking	🐕	Pets Welcome
🐎	Children Welcome	**SB**	Short Breaks
♿	Suitable for Disabled Guests	🍷	Licensed

Norfolk

EAST OF ENGLAND 135

Stowmarket, Woodbridge / Framlingham

A warm welcome and homely atmosphere awaits you at our attractive farmhouse set in the beautiful surroundings of mid-Suffolk. Comfortably furnished bedrooms with en suite shower rooms, tea/coffee making facilities. One double, one twin and two single rooms. Central heating. Guests' own lounge with TV; dining room. Ideal location for exploring, walking, cycling and birdwatching. **Open all year • No smoking • No pets** B&B from £65-£70 per double/twin room; £40 to £45 per single room.

Red House Farm
Haughley • Suffolk

Mrs Mary Noy, Red House Farm, Station Road, Haughley, Near Stowmarket IP14 3QP
Tel: 01449 673323 • Fax: 01449 675413
e-mail: mary@redhousefarmhaughley.co.uk
www.redhousefarmhaughley.co.uk

SB

A warm welcome awaits you at our exceptional moated farmhouse dating from the 13th Century, and set in extensive grounds including Ace all weather tennis court, in a superb spot two and a half miles north of Dennington, 13 miles from Woodbridge. A comfortable base with log fires in winter and plenty of beams. Close to Snape Maltings, the coast, Minsmere and many places of interest.

Accommodation comprises one double and one twin bedroom, or two twins let as singles; guests' own bathroom and sitting room. Good pubs nearby. Bread and marmalade home made.
Parking available • Children welcome • Non-smoking.
B&B from £30 single, £60 double/twin.

SB

Grange Farm, Dennington, Woodbridge IP13 8BT
Tel: 01986 798388 • mobile: 07774 182835 • www.grangefarm.biz

---

Other specialised holiday guides from FHG

PUBS & INNS OF BRITAIN

COUNTRY HOTELS OF BRITAIN

WEEKEND & SHORT BREAKS IN BRITAIN & IRELAND

THE GOLF GUIDE WHERE TO PLAY, WHERE TO STAY

PETS WELCOME!

SELF-CATERING HOLIDAYS IN BRITAIN

500 GREAT PLACES TO STAY IN BRITAIN

CARAVAN & CAMPING HOLIDAYS IN BRITAIN

FAMILY BREAKS IN BRITAIN

Published annually: available in all good bookshops or direct from the publisher:
FHG Guides, Abbey Mill Business Centre, Seedhill, Paisley PA1 1TJ
Tel: 0141 887 0428 • Fax: 0141 889 7204
e-mail: admin@fhguides.co.uk • www.holidayguides.com

Derbyshire

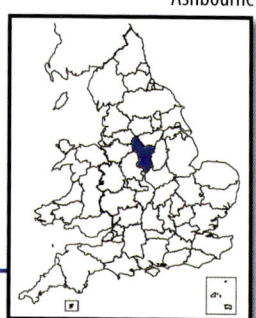

Ashbourne

Stone Cottage

A charming cottage in the quiet village of Clifton, one mile from the Georgian market town of Ashbourne.

Each bedroom is furnished to a high standard with all rooms en suite, with four-poster bed, TV and coffee making facilities. A warm welcome is assured and a hearty breakfast in this delightful cottage. There is a large garden to relax in.

Ideal for visiting Chatsworth House, Haddon Hall, Dovedale, Carsington Water and the theme park of Alton Towers.

B&B from £22.50pp. Good country pubs nearby serving evening meals.

Enquiries to: Mrs A. M. Whittle, Stone Cottage, Green Lane, Clifton, Ashbourne, Derbyshire DE6 2BL
Telephone: 01335 343377
Fax: 01335 347117 • e-mail: info@stone-cottage.fsnet.co.uk

Turlow Bank

Hognaston, Ashbourne, Derbyshire DE6 1PW
Tel & Fax: 01335 370799
e-mail: turlowbank@w3z.co.uk
www.turlowbank.co.uk

Recently renovated early 19th century farmhouse in a quiet location, surrounded by glorious views. Spacious guest lounge with log fire; double bedroom with private bathroom, king-size bedroom en suite, central heating throughout. Full English breakfast, vegetarians catered for. Pub meals available locally, restaurant and cafe nearby. A step away from walking country and Carsington Water is only a short walk, where water sports, bird watching and cycling are available. Convenient for all attractions of the Peak District. *Bed and Breakfast from £35 to £55 pppn.*

Derbyshire

Ashbourne, Burnaston

THE MIDLANDS 137

Near Dovedale and Manifold Valley B&B and Self-catering

SB

On a working farm in quiet countryside, within easy reach of Alton Towers, stately homes and places of historic interest. Ideal touring centre.

- **B&B** – 4 double/twin rooms (3 en suite); dining/sitting room with TV. Tea/coffee making; full central heating; open fire. Terms from £30pppn; reduced rates for children; cot and high chair available.

- **Self-catering** – Cottage (sleeps 7), two farmhouses (sleep 12), River Lodge (sleeps 5). Sitting rooms and dining rooms (kitchen/diner in cottage). Electric cookers, fridges, washing machine and dryer. All have open fires. Car essential; nearest shops 3 miles. Phone. Pets permitted. ETC ★★★★

Details from Mrs M.A. Richardson, Throwley Hall Farm, Ilam, Near Ashbourne, Derbyshire DE6 2BB
Tel: 01538 308202/308243
www.throwleyhallfarm.co.uk • e-mail: throwley@btinternet.com

Small family-run guest house with accent on good food, locally produced where possible, and quality accommodation in a warm and friendly atmosphere.

Originally three terraced cottages, now converted into one rather individual house which has been our home since 1986. Comfortable sitting room, five en suite bedrooms, all with colour TV and well-stocked tea tray. Safe parking in delightful garden at the rear of the house. No smoking.

Bed and Breakfast from £25 per person.

Compton House, 27-31 Compton, Ashbourne DE6 1BX
01335 343100 • e-mail: jane@comptonhouse.co.uk •
www.comptonhouse.co.uk

AA ★★★★ Guest Accommodation

Self contained in Derbyshire

Beautifully renovated Victorian stables providing 7 self-contained en-suite apartments, each sleeping 4-5, with Lounge Area, Gallery Bedroom and Fully Fitted Kitchen.

Grassy Lane, Burnaston,
Derbyshire DE65 6LN
Tel: 01332 510000
www.stableslodge.co.uk

Stables Lodge

Overnight Accommodation
Holiday Accommodation · Weekend Breaks

DERBYSHIRE
Buxton, Chesterfield, Chinley

Braemar

Guests are warmly welcomed into the friendly atmosphere of Braemar, situated in a quiet residential part of this famous spa town. Within five minutes' walk of all the town's many and varied attractions i.e., Pavilion Gardens, Opera House, swimming pool; golf courses, horse riding, walking, fishing, etc are all within easy reach in this area renowned for its scenic beauty. Many of the Peak District's famous beauty spots including Chatsworth, Haddon Hall, Bakewell, Matlock, Dovedale and Castleton are nearby. Accommodation comprises comfortable double and twin bedded rooms fully en suite with colour TV and hospitality trays, etc. Full English Breakfast served and diets catered for. Non-smokers preferred.

Terms from £26.50 inclusive for Bed and Breakfast. Weekly terms available.

Roger and Maria Hyde
10 Compton Road, Buxton SK17 9DN
Tel: 01298 78050 • e-mail: buxtonbraemar@supanet.com
www.cressbrook.co.uk/buxton/braemar

The Clarendon Guest House

Located near the town centre and within easy reach of the Peak District, this Victorian town house offers a warm and cheerful welcome, whether on business or pleasure. Comfortable, cosy rooms, each with TV and tea/coffee facilities. The rear walled garden offers a peaceful summer retreat. Full English breakfast; special diets catered for.

Bed and Breakfast from £23 single, from £45 double/twin room en suite.

Mr & Mrs A. Boardman, The Clarendon Guest House, 32 Clarence Road, Chesterfield S40 1LN (01246 235004)
www.clarendonguesthouse.com

Moseley House Farm
Maynestone Road, Chinley,
High Peak SK23 6AH
Tel: 01663 750240

A stunning location in the Peak District is where you will find this quality farmhouse. Lovely bedrooms, en suite or with private bathrooms, charming ground floor suite with own entrance. Relax in the garden. Village half mile – good pubs and restaurants. Ideal spot for a holiday on a working farm.
Double or twin £27 per person, single £30.
Also self-catering cottage. Farmhouse, sleeps six.

e-mail: goddardbromley@aol.com
www.visitderbyshire.co.uk

Derbyshire

Derby, Glossop

BONEHILL FARM

01332 513553

This 120 acre mixed farm with Georgian farmhouse is set in peaceful rural surroundings, yet offers all the convenience of being only three miles west of Derby, on the A516 between Mickleover and Etwall. Within 10 miles there is a choice of historic houses to visit; Calke Abbey, Kedleston Hall, Sudbury Hall. Peak District 20 miles, Alton Towers 20 miles.

Accommodation in three bedrooms (one twin, one double en suite, one family room with en suite facilities), all with tea/coffee making facilities. Cot and high chair provided. Open all year. Croquet available.

B&B per night: single from £30, double from £52.

A warm and friendly welcome awaits you.

Mrs Catherine Dicken, Bonehill Farm, Etwall Road, Mickleover DE3 0DN

www.bonehillfarm.co.uk

Graham and Julie Caesar

Windy Harbour Farm Hotel

Woodhead Road, Glossop SK13 7QE

01457 853107 • www.peakdistrict-hotel.co.uk

Situated in the heart of the Peak District on the B6105, approximately one mile from Glossop town centre and adjacent to the Pennine Way.

All our bedrooms are en suite, with outstanding views of Woodhead and Snake Passes and the Longdendale Valley is an ideal location for all outdoor activities.

A warm welcome awaits you in our licensed bar and restaurant serving a wide range of excellent home-made food.

Bed and Breakfast from £30 per night

THE MIDLANDS

Derbyshire
Hope Valley, Matlock, Mayfield

Causeway House B&B, Back Street, Castleton, Hope Valley S33 8WE
01433 623291 • email: steynberg@btinternet.com

Causeway House is a 16th Century Cruck Cottage in the heart of Castleton in the beautiful Peak District. The area is renowned for its scenery, history and heritage with amazing walks, cycling and Blue John caves to visit.

The accommodation has three en suite double rooms, a single and a twin room with shared bathroom. One of the rooms has a four-poster bed.

Nick and Janet Steynberg offer you a hearty Full English, Continental or Vegetarian Breakfast.

A piece of Heaven for you and your family.

Glendon
Knowleston Place,
Matlock DE4 3BU
Tel: 01629 584732

Warm hospitality and comfortable accommodation in this Grade II Listed building. Conveniently situated by the Hall Leys Park and River Derwent, it is only a short level walk to Matlock town centre. Large private car park.

Rooms are centrally heated and have washbasin, colour TV and tea/coffee making facilities. En suite available. Totally non-smoking.

An ideal base for exploring the beautiful Peak District of Derbyshire, with easy access to many places of interest including Chatsworth House, Haddon Hall, Crich Tramway Village and Heights of Abraham cable car.

AA ★★★★ Guest House

Contact: Mrs S. Elliott • B&B from £28.50 per person per night

---

MONA VILLAS
Church Lane
Middle Mayfield
Mayfield
Near Ashbourne
DE6 2JS
Tel: 01335 343773

A warm, friendly welcome to our home with purpose-built en suite accommodation. Beautiful views over open countryside. A local pub serves excellent food within a five minute walk. Situated near Alton Towers, Dove Dale, etc. Three en suite rooms available, single supplement applies. Family rooms available. Parking.

Bed and Breakfast from £24.00 to £27.00 per night.

e-mail: info@mona-villas.fsnet.co.uk
www.mona-villas.fsnet.co.uk

AA ★★★★ Bed & Breakfast

---

symbols

- Totally non-smoking
- Children Welcome
- Suitable for Disabled Guests
- Pets Welcome
- **SB** Short Breaks
- Licensed

Derbyshire

THE MIDLANDS

Stanton-by-Bridge, Winster

Ivy House Farm is a small arable working farm. The farmhouse was converted in 2000 and we have also converted our redundant cowsheds into four ground floor bedrooms (2 double, 2 twin) all of which are en suite, with tea/coffee making facilities and TV. The area has lots to do and see, such as Calke Abbey, ski slopes, Alton Towers, motor racing at Donington Park, not forgetting the National Forest. Children are welcome, but we are strictly non-smoking. Ample off-road parking.
Bed and Breakfast from £40 pppn.

Ivy House Farm Guesthouse, Stanton-by-Bridge, Derby DE73 7HT
Tel: 01332 863152
e-mail: mary@guesthouse.fsbusiness.co.uk • www.ivy-house-farm.com

SB

Ample private parking • Non-smoking throughout
Bed and Breakfast from £24 per person

Mrs Jane Ball, Brae Cottage, East Bank, Winster DE4 2DT
Tel: 01629 650375

In one of the most picturesque villages in the Peak District National Park this 300-year-old cottage offers independent accommodation across the paved courtyard. Breakfast is served in the cottage. Rooms are furnished and equipped to a high standard; both having en suite shower rooms, tea/coffee making facilities, TV and heating.

The village has two traditional pubs which provide food. Local attractions include village (National Trust) Market House, Chatsworth, Haddon Hall and many walks from the village in the hills and dales.

Please note

All the information in this book is given in good faith in the belief that it is correct. However, the publishers cannot guarantee the facts given in these pages, neither are they responsible for changes in policy, ownership or terms that may take place after the date of going to press. Readers should always satisfy themselves that the facilities they require are available and that the terms, if quoted, still apply.

Visit the FHG website
www.holidayguides.com
for details of the wide choice of accommodation featured in the full range of FHG titles

142 THE MIDLANDS

Herefordshire

Herefordshire
Burghill, Hereford

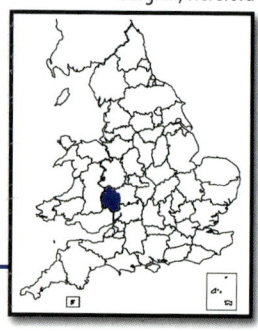

Heron House, Canon Pyon Road, Portway, Burghill, Hereford HR4 8NG
Tel: 01432 761111 • Fax: 01432 760603
e-mail: info@theheronhouse.com • www.theheronhouse.com

Heron House, with its panoramic views of the Malvern Hills, provides friendly and spacious Bed and Breakfast services. Facilities include en suite, twin room, colour TV, tea making equipment.

Situated four miles north of Hereford in a rural location, this is an ideal base for walking, fishing, golf, cycling and bird-watching. Secure off-road parking. Non-smoking.

Bed and full English Breakfast from £25 per person per night.

This detached Victorian villa is situated in a quiet, tree-lined residential road. It offers boutique-style bed and breakfast accommodation, blending the luxury and comfort of a good hotel with warm, friendly service. The house is totally non-smoking. Our contemporary dining room offers an excellent breakfast range including the traditional full English, Continental and vegetarian breakfast, with healthy options available. We have 12 en suite bedrooms, including ground floor accommodation, with a choice of single, double, twin and family rooms. Our beautifully furnished rooms have ironing board and iron, tea and coffee making facilities and colour TV. Our large superior rooms are available with CD and DVD, and have a mini-bar and seating areas. Wi-fi is also available.

Somerville House
12 Bodenham Road, Hereford HR1 2TS
Tel: 01432 273991 • Fax: 01432 268719
e-mail: enquiries@somervillehouse.net • www.somervillehouse.net

easy driving distance from the M5, Ross-on-Wye, Great Malvern, Gloucester and Leominster

Sink Green Farm
Rotherwas, Hereford HR2 6LE • Tel: 01432 870223
e-mail: enquiries@sinkgreenfarm.co.uk
www.sinkgreenfarm.co.uk

A friendly welcome awaits you at this our 16th century farmhouse overlooking the picturesque Wye Valley, yet only three miles from Hereford. Our individually decorated en suite rooms, one four-poster, all have tea/coffee making facilities, colour TV and central heating. Relax in our extensive garden, complete with summer house and hot tub, or enjoy a stroll by the river. Fishing by arrangement.

Prices from £30 per person • Children welcome • Pets by arrangement

Herefordshire
Ledbury

Church Farm
Coddington, Ledbury HR8 1JJ
Tel: 01531 640271
Mobile: 07861 358549

Relax and enjoy our lovely 16th century Listed timber framed farmhouse in the quiet hamlet of Coddington. The market town of Ledbury is 4 miles away, the Malvern Hills, with all their beautiful walks, 4 miles. Hereford, Worcester, Gloucester and Ross-on-Wye are all a half-hour drive, Cheltenham 45 minutes approx.

We are a working farm with a lovely garden and rural views. Immediate access to wonderful walks through peaceful country lanes and farmland.

We offer a combination of en suite and shared bathroom accommodation. Comfortable lounge with TV and log fires on chilly evenings in the inglenook fireplace. Ample car parking space. Aga-cooked breakfast. Everything homemade where possible. Over 25 years' experience caring for guests, with a large number of repeat bookings. A warm welcome is assured in a quiet, relaxed atmosphere. B&B from £35pppn double.

Relax, unwind and enjoy your holiday.
Please phone Jane for further information.

www.dexta.co.uk

AA ★★★★ FARMHOUSE

The Coach House is an 18th century coaching stable providing unique Bed & Breakfast accommodation near Ledbury. All around is wonderful walking country, from the Malvern Hills to the Black Mountains. In the main house, guests have sole use of a lounge and kitchen, with a choice of single, double and twin rooms, all en suite. Newly converted for 2006, the *Tower Suite* of private lounge and en suite double bedroom.

Tariffs for 2009: £27pppn double and twin, £31 single. Reduced by £1.50pppn for 3 nights and more.

Tower Suite: min. 2 nights:
£150 for two nights and £60 per night thereafter.

Mrs S.W. Born, The Coach House, Putley, Near Ledbury HR8 2QP (01531 670684)
e-mail: wendyborn@putley-coachhouse.co.uk   www.putley-coachhouse.co.uk

SB

Hill Farm, Eastnor, Ledbury

HILL FARM is a 300-year-old stone and brick farmhouse surrounded by woodland at the foot of the Malvern Hills, one mile from Ledbury and one mile from Eastnor Castle.

Accommodation comprises one twin room and two family rooms also used as twin/double rooms, all with washbasin, TV and tea/coffee making facilities. Guests' own sittingroom with log fire and the dining room look out onto a large garden and rural views.

Bed and Breakfast from £22.50–£30. Evening Meal by arrangement from £12.
Mrs C. Gladwin, Hill Farm, Eastnor, Ledbury HR8 1EF • 01531 632827

Herefordshire
Leominster, Ross-on-Wye

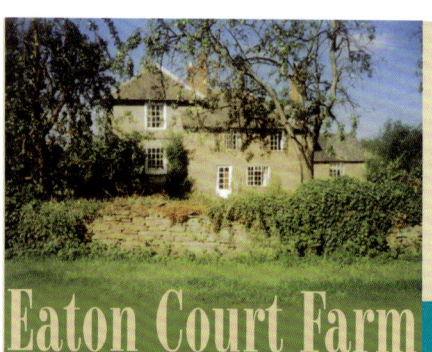

Eaton Court Farm

Bed & Breakfast accommodation in a Listed Georgian farmhouse. In countryside, yet on the outskirts of Leominster town, with many interesting shops including antique markets. An excellent point for just stopping off or as a base for local pursuits of interest. Kingsize, double and twin rooms with bath/shower room en suite. Lounge with TV. Full English Breakfast.

Terms from £30 pppn (minimum two nights). Car parking on site. Children of 10 years and over are welcome. Sorry, no pets. Open from April to end October. Also small caravan and camping site on the farm.

Mrs Pritchard, Stoke Prior Road, Leominster, Hereford HR6 0NA • Tel: 01568 612095

BROOKFIELD HOUSE

This detached Listed building has been awarded four stars and Highly Commended by the AA.
- We have a large private car park and yet we are a minute's walk of the town's shops, restaurants and pubs.
- All rooms are spacious with king size beds.
- Bed and Breakfast from £32pppn.
- For dull details visit our website.

www.brookfield-house.co.uk
Brookfield House,
Overross Street, Ross-on-Wye HR9 7AT
Tel: 01989 562188

Lea House

A 16th century former coaching inn, Lea House has been beautifully refurbished, with exposed oak beams, an inglenook fireplace, antiques and imaginative decor. The spacious bedrooms have kingsize or twin beds and full en suite or private bathrooms. AA award-winning breakfasts are a real treat, with home-made breads and jams, fresh fruit and juice, local butcher's sausages and locally smoked fish. Dinner is also available on request.

On the Hereford/Gloucester border, adjacent to the Royal Forest of Dean and the spectacular Wye Valley, there is a wealth of activities and wonderful walking.

**We accept dogs and children • Free WiFi
Bed and Breakfast from £30 - £37.50 pppn.**

Lea House, Lea, Ross-on-Wye HR9 7JZ • Tel: 01989 750652
enquiries@leahouse.co.uk • www.leahouse.co.uk

Herefordshire

Ross-on-Wye

THE MIDLANDS 145

❖ Thatch Close Bed & Breakfast ❖
Llangrove
Ross-on-Wye HR9 6EL

SB

Situated between the Black Mountains and the Wye Valley, with marvellous views from every angle, Thatch Close is the ideal location for a weekend break or a longer stay.

Secluded, peaceful, comfortable Georgian farmhouse, yet convenient for A40, M4 and M50. Our three lovely bedrooms, all en suite, have magnificent views over the unspoilt countryside. Relax in the visitors' lounge or sit in the shade of mature trees in our garden. You may be greeted by our dog or free flying parrot. Terms from £35 per person (sharing). Please telephone or e-mail for brochure.

Mrs M.E. Drzymalski (01989 770300)
e-mail: info@thatchclose.co.uk • www.thatchclose.co.uk

AA **** Guest Accommodation

Wildlife Action Gold Award

Looking for Holiday Accommodation?

FHG
KUPERARD

for details of hundreds of properties throughout the UK, visit our website

www.holidayguides.com

Leicestershire & Rutland

Belton-in-Rutland, Leicester

THE Old Rectory

Belton-in-Rutland, Oakham LE15 9LE
Tel: 01572 717279 • Fax: 01572 821369

Guest accommodation. Victorian country house and guest annexe in charming village overlooking Eyebrook valley and rolling Rutland countryside. Comfortable and varied selection of rooms, mostly en suite, with direct outside access. Prices from £28 per person per night including breakfast. Small farm environment (horses and sheep) with excellent farmhouse breakfast. Public House 100 yards. Lots to see and do: Rutland Water, castles, stately homes, country parks, forestry and Barnsdale Gardens. Non-smoking. Self catering also available.

e-mail: bb@iepuk.com   www.theoldrectorybelton.co.uk

Abinger Guest House

Situated ¾ mile west of Leicester city centre, Abinger Guest House offers exceptional standards of comfort, cleanliness, cuisine and configuration at bargain basement prices. Refurbished and redecorated to demanding standards, all eight guest rooms offer TV with Freeview, designer glass washbasins, complimentary beverages, luxury sprung mattresses, hairdryers and mini-refrigerators. Ample parking is available, and regular buses to the city stop just outside, with easy access to many attractions. Breakfast fare is regularly complimented by guests, and the best produce available is offered.

Bob, Teresa and Mel will be delighted to welcome you.

175 Hinckley Road, Leicester LE3 0TF • 0116 255 4674
www.leicesterguest.co.uk

Leicestershire & Rutland

THE MIDLANDS 147

Loughborough, Melton Mowbray

Elm Cottage

A friendly B&B situated on the A6, a 10 minute stroll from Loughborough Town Centre. There is ample parking, reasonably priced accommodation and easy access to the M1, East Midlands Airport, Derby, Nottingham or Leicester. Single, double, twin and family rooms available, some en suite. They have central heating, colour TV, and beverage tray. Irons and hairdryers are available upon request.

Single room from £15, Double/Twin room from £45, Family room from £60.

142 Leicester Road, Loughborough LE11 2AQ
Tel: 01509 237422
www.elmcottage.info

SB

Charnwood Lodge

Charnwood Lodge assures you of a warm welcome, offering superior en suite rooms equipped with TV and beverage tray, and a tastefully decorated dining room (with separate tables), serving a full English breakfast, and evening meals on request. Relaxing TV lounge and bar. Ground floor and disabled rooms available; also four-poster and family rooms. Situated on main A6, 10 minutes' walk from the town centre. Set in own gardens with private car park. We are close to all local amenities within the Charnwood area; East Midlands Airport is 12 miles, Derby 18 miles, Donington Park 12 miles, Nottingham 15 miles, Leicester 15 miles.

We hope you enjoy your stay with us and will recommend us to your friends. From £38 to £57 per night.
All major credit cards (except Amex) accepted. Internet access available.

www.charnwoodlodge.com

Liz & Klaus Charwat, Charnwood Lodge, 136 Leicester Road, Loughborough LE11 2AQ
Tel: 01509 211120 • Fax 01509 211121 • e-mail: reservations@charnwoodlodge.com

GUEST HOUSE ★★★★

SB

Hillside House

27 Melton Road, Burton Lazars, Melton Mowbray LE14 2UR

Situated on the edge of the village with views over rolling countryside, Hillside House is a comfortable, converted old farm building, offering one double and one twin room both en suite, and one twin with private bathroom. All have colour TV and tea/coffee making facilities. There is a guests' lounge.

Rutland Water, Geoff Hamilton's Garden and Belvoir Castle are close by. Melton Mowbray with its bustling market is 1½ miles away.

Bed and Breakfast from £25 to £27.50; 10% reduction for 3-night stay (except during special events). Single supplement.

• Children over ten only. • Closed Christmas and New Year. • Off road parking.

BED & BREAKFAST ★★★★

Tel: 01664 566312 • e-mail: hillhs27@aol.com • www.hillside-house.co.uk

SB

Shoby Lodge Farm, Shoby, Melton Mowbray LE14 3PF
Mrs Linda Lomas - 01664 812156

Set in attractive gardens, Shoby Lodge is a spacious, comfortable, tastefully furnished farmhouse. Enjoy an Aga-cooked breakfast and beautiful views of the surrounding countryside. Accommodation comprises two double and one twin en suite rooms. All rooms have tea and coffee making facilities and TV. Close to the market town of Melton Mowbray and ideally situated for Leicester and Nottingham. Coarse fishing available on the farm.

Terms from £26-£30 pppn.
Single occupancy £30-£35.

FARMHOUSE ★★★★ English Garden Council Silver Award

Lincolnshire

Boston, Gainsborough

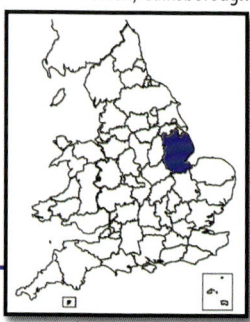

An early 18th century Listed farmhouse with spacious en suite bedrooms and original beamed ceilings. Enjoy a generous farmhouse breakfast using fresh local produce. Centrally located for five 'Bomber Country' museums, championship golf at Woodhall Spa, antiques at Horncastle and local fishing. Historic pubs nearby serving excellent evening meals. Within easy reach of the east coast and the Lincolnshire Wolds. One double and one twin bedroom. Central heating, tea and coffee facilities and colour TV.
Open all year except Christmas • No smoking Children welcome • B&B from £20pp; reductions for three days or more.

Mrs C. Whittington, High House Farm, Tumby Moorside, Near Coningsby, Boston PE22 7ST • Tel: 01526 345408 • e-mail: HighHousefarm@aol.com

---

The Black Swan Guest House
21 High Street, Marton, Gainsborough, Lincs DN21 5AH
Tel: 01427 718878
info@blackswanguesthouse.co.uk • www.blackswanguesthouse.co.uk

As resident proprietors, Judy and John Patrick offer a warm welcome at our delightfully converted former 18th century coaching inn. The property has been fully refurbished, using much of the original materials and retaining many original features. The house and stable block now offer comfortable rooms which are en suite, with digital TV and tea/coffee making facilities. There is a guest lounge where you can enjoy a drink in the evenings, or just relax. Our breakfasts are all freshly cooked to order using locally sourced best quality produce. The local area is steeped in history, from Roman times through to the old airfields of the Second World War, and the city of Lincoln is only 12 miles away, with its stunning cathedral and old city centre in the Bailgate area. For those of you who need to keep in touch, wireless broadband is available.
We are a non-smoking establishment.

Single from £45, double/twin from £68.

Lincolnshire

THE MIDLANDS 149

Horncastle, Louth, Market Rasen, Peterborough

Baumber Park

Spacious elegant farmhouse of character in quiet parkland setting, on a mixed farm. Large plantsman's garden, wildlife pond and grass tennis court. Fine bedrooms with lovely views, period furniture, log fires and books. Central in the county and close to the Lincolnshire Wolds, this rolling countryside is little known, quite unspoilt, and ideal for walking, cycling or riding. Championship golf courses at Woodhall Spa. Well located for historic Lincoln, interesting market towns and many antique shops. Enjoy a relaxing break, excellent breakfasts, and a comfortable, homely atmosphere.

*Two doubles, one twin, all en suite or private bathroom.
Bed and Breakfast from £26.*

**Mrs C.E. Harrison, Baumber Park, Baumber, Near Horncastle LN9 5NE
01507 578235 • Fax: 01507 578417 • mobile: 07977 722776
mail@baumberpark.com • www.baumberpark.com**

SB

KEDDINGTON HOUSE Host Home
**5 Keddington Road, Louth LN11 0AA
Tel: 01507 603973 • Mobile: 0781 8290990**

Tony Moss offers:
- A large Victorian house, set in its own grounds 100 yards back from the road, with extensive parking.
- Double/twin/single and family en suite rooms
- Separate lounges with tea/coffee/biscuits always available
- Heated outdoor swimming pool (summer months only)
- Easy access to Louth town centre – Lincolnshire Wolds

Ideally placed for Lincoln, Grimsby and Market Rasen Racecourse. Within half-an-hour of the seaside at Mablethorpe and Skegness. Cadwell Park 10 minutes away - early breakfasts if required.

e-mail: tony@keddingtonhouse.co.uk • www.keddingtonhouse.co.uk

---

Exchange the noise of city traffic for the birdsong of the countryside whilst staying at Redhurst B&B, set in gardens and orchard in a small village nestling on the edge of the Lincolnshire Wolds. Ideal setting for visiting the many and varied attractions of Lincolnshire.

Two twin en suite (one ground floor). From £24 and £27pppn.
One single with private facilities. From £27pn.
Open all year • Sorry no pets.
Non-smoking • Self-catering also available.

**Mrs Vivienne Klockner, Redhurst,
Holton-cum-Beckering, Market Rasen LN8 5NG
Tel/Fax: 01673 857627 • Mobile: 07804 636 858
www.RedhurstBAndB.co.uk**

SB

Bed & Breakfast at No. 19 West Street
Kings Cliffe, Near Stamford, Peterborough PE8 6XB
Tel: 01780 470365 • Fax: 01780 470623

A beautifully restored 500-year-old Listed stone house, reputedly one of King John's Hunting Lodges, situated in the heart of the stone village of Kings Cliffe on the edge of Rockingham Forest. Both the double and twin rooms have their own private bathrooms, and there is colour TV and a welcome tray in each. There is also an en suite family room. In the summer breakfast can be served on the terrace overlooking a beautiful walled garden. Off-street parking is behind secure gates. Within 10 miles there are seven stately homes, including Burghley House famous for the Horse Trials, Rutland Water, and the beautiful old towns of Stamford and Oundle. Open all year.

A non-smoking house • Bed and Breakfast from £35-£60 per person • Proprietor: Jenny Dixon
e-mail: kjhl_dixon@hotmail.com • www.kingjohnhuntinglodge.co.uk

Lincolnshire

Skegness, Stamford

**Mrs S. Evans, Willow Farm,
Thorpe Fendykes, Wainfleet,
Skegness PE24 4QH
Tel: 01754 830316
e-mail: willowfarmhols@aol.com
www.willowfarmholidays.co.uk**

In the heart of the Lincolnshire Fens, Willow Farm is a working smallholding with free range hens, goats, horses and ponies. Situated in a peaceful hamlet with abundant wildlife, ideal for a quiet retreat – yet only 15 minutes from the Skegness coast, shops, amusements and beaches.

Bed and Breakfast is provided in comfortable en suite rooms from £22 per person per night, reductions for children (suppers and sandwiches can be provided in the evening on request). Rooms have tea and coffee making facilities and a colour TV and are accessible to disabled guests. Friendly hosts! Ring for brochure.

Horse riding available

Park Farm Bed and Breakfast

**Careby, Near Stamford, Lincolnshire PE9 4EA
Tel: 01780 410 515 • Mobile: 07747 047 135
enquiries@parkfarmcareby.co.uk
www.parkfarmcareby.co.uk**

Silver SILVER AWARD

10 minutes to the centre of Stamford, Park Farm offers quality B&B in a peaceful country setting. Spacious en suite bedrooms with comfy beds. Views over open countryside and a friendly welcome. Facilities include full size TV, DAB radio alarms, wireless internet, hairdryer, hospitality tray. Comprehensive breakfast menu with good selection of cold and cooked food. 10% discount for 3 night mid-week breaks. For photos and full details please view our web page.

Other specialised holiday guides from **FHG**

PUBS & INNS OF BRITAIN

COUNTRY HOTELS OF BRITAIN

WEEKEND & SHORT BREAKS IN BRITAIN & IRELAND

THE GOLF GUIDE WHERE TO PLAY, WHERE TO STAY

PETS WELCOME!

SELF-CATERING HOLIDAYS IN BRITAIN

500 GREAT PLACES TO STAY IN BRITAIN

CARAVAN & CAMPING HOLIDAYS IN BRITAIN

FAMILY BREAKS IN BRITAIN

Published annually: available in all good bookshops or direct from the publisher:
FHG Guides, Abbey Mill Business Centre, Seedhill, Paisley PA1 1TJ
Tel: 0141 887 0428 • Fax: 0141 889 7204
e-mail: admin@fhguides.co.uk • www.holidayguides.com

Lincolnshire

THE MIDLANDS

Woodhall Spa

Homely Bed and Breakfast in a traditional, unspoilt Victorian guest house in the centre of Woodhall Spa, Lincolnshire's unique resort.

Off-street parking. Good food close by. Excellent centre for touring, walking and cycling. Golf locally.

En suite rooms. Tea and coffee making facilities and TV in rooms.

Special rates for short breaks.

Mrs Claire Brennan
Claremont
Guest House
9-11 Witham Road,
Woodhall Spa LN10 6RW
Tel: 01526 352000

AA

SB

VILLAGE LIMITS COUNTRY PUB, RESTAURANT & MOTEL
'TASTES OF LINCOLNSHIRE' BEST PUB 2006 • RUNNER UP 2007
'TASTES OF LINCOLNSHIRE' BEST ACCOMMODATION 2007

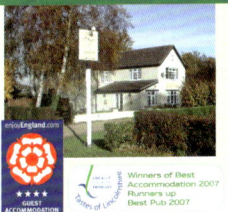

- Award-winning tastes of Lincolnshire
- Food Tues-Sat 12-2pm & 7-9pm
- Popular 3-course Sunday lunch
- Home-made meals
- Local produce

Winners of Best Accommodation 2007
Runners up Best Pub 2007

Stixwould Road, Woodhall Spa LN10 6UJ
01526 353312 • www.villagelimits.co.uk

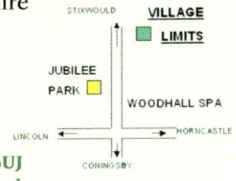

A warm welcome awaits you at this peaceful, sunny, detached house, which is set beside the River Witham on the outskirts of Woodhall Spa, a village which is noted for its 'old world' charm, park with open-air heated swimming pool, Kinema in the woods and championship golf course. A garden, five-acre woodland garden, rowing boat, riverbank walks and membership of a local leisure club are also yours to enjoy, plus seasonal coarse fishing. There are numerous pubs and restaurants locally, or you are welcome to bring back a takeaway. We have a telephone, wireless e-mail, fridge, iron and hairdryer for guests to use, and each of our three en suite guest bedrooms has a TV, DVD, clock radio and hot drinks trolley. A video, piano and open fire help to make the lounge and sun room relaxing areas.

Kirkstead Old Mill Cottage
Tattershall Road, Woodhall Spa LN10 6UQ
Tel: 01526 353637 • Mobile: 07970 040401
Barbara and Tony Hodgkinson • www.woodhallspa.com

A cooked, Gold Award English breakfast is served or you can choose a lighter, healthy option.
Non-smoking.
B&B from £30 per person

---

symbols

🚭	Totally non-smoking	🐕	Pets Welcome
🐎	Children Welcome	**SB**	Short Breaks
♿	Suitable for Disabled Guests	🍷	Licensed

Northamptonshire

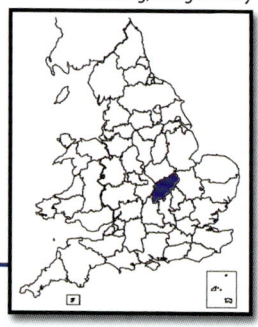

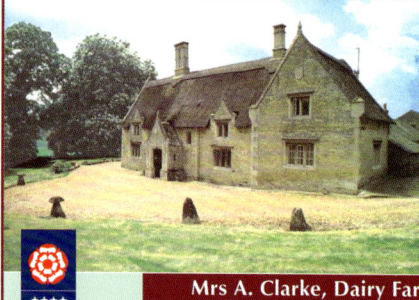

ENJOY A HOLIDAY in our comfortable 17th century farmhouse with oak beams and inglenook fireplaces. Four-poster bed now available. Peaceful surroundings, large garden containing ancient circular dovecote. Dairy Farm is a working farm situated in a beautiful Northamptonshire village just off the A14, within easy reach of many places of interest or ideal for a restful holiday. Good farmhouse food and friendly atmosphere. Open all year, except Christmas. Bed and Breakfast from £28 to £40 (children under 10 half price); Evening Meal £17.

Mrs A. Clarke, Dairy Farm, Cranford St Andrew, Kettering NN14 4AQ
Telephone: 01536 330273

Murcott Mill Farmhouse
Long Buckby NN6 7QR
Tel & Fax: 01327 842236

Imposing Georgian mill house set within a working farm. Large garden and lovely outlook over open countryside. All rooms are en suite with colour TV. Central heating throughout and visitors have their own lounge and dining room with open log fires.

An ideal stopover, close to M1, and good location for touring. Evening meals served by arrangement. Children and pets welcome.

Bed and Breakfast from £35 single; double £60. Open all year.

e-mail: carrie.murcottmill@virgin.net • www.murcottmill.com

Nottinghamshire

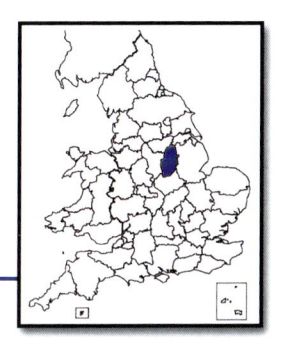

Burton Joyce, Elton

BURTON JOYCE. Mrs V. Baker, Willow House, 12 Willow Wong, Burton Joyce, Nottingham NG14 5FD (0115 931 2070; Mob: 07816 347706).
A large period house (1857) in quiet village two minutes' walk from beautiful river bank, yet only five miles from City. Attractive, interesting accommodation with authentic Victorian ambience. En suite available. Bright, clean rooms with tea/coffee facilities, TV. Off-road parking. Porch for smokers. Ideally situated for Holme Pierrepont International Watersports Centre; golf; National Ice Centre; Trent Bridge (cricket); Sherwood Forest; Nottingham Racecourse; Shelford Pony Trials and the unspoiled historic town of Southwell with its Minster and Racecourse. Good local eating. Please phone first for directions. *Rates: From £26 per person per night.*

SB

The Grange • Elton

The Grange offers traditional farmhouse Bed and Breakfast in a non-smoking environment with full en suite facilities, TV, tea/coffee making and parking.

Owned by Mr and Mrs Don and Brenda Masson – Don is an ex-professional Scottish International Footballer. The Grange is set in the Vale of Belvoir, 100 metres off the A52 between Nottingham and Grantham, 50 metres from an excellent pub serving good food, and five minutes' drive to Bingham and Bottesford.

Free wi-fi at The Grange

An excellent location for walks in the Vale of Belvoir. Please note that we do not accept credit/debit cards.

Terms from £40-£45 single, £65-£69 double/twin.

AA Bed & Breakfast Highly Commended

The Grange Bed & Breakfast, Sutton Lane, Elton NG13 9LA
Mobile: 07887 952181
www.thegrangebedandbreakfastnotts.co.uk

Nottinghamshire

Mansfield, Sutton-in-Ashfield

Boon Hills

This is a stone-built farmhouse, standing 300 yards back from A632 on edge of village. It is on a 120-acre arable farm with dogs, cats, hens and horses. Situated on the edge of Sherwood Forest, six miles from Visitors' Centre, eight miles from M1, 10 miles from A1. Chatsworth House, Newstead Abbey, Hardwick Hall and Creswell Crags all within easy reach. One double en suite, one double and one twin with shared bathroom; toilet; fitted carpets throughout. Open fires. Background central heating for comfort all year round. Large sittingroom/diningroom with colour TV.

Children welcome; babysitting • No pets • Car essential – parking. Tea/coffee making facilities • B&B from £21 per night, Evening Meal available nearby • Non-smokers only. Rates reduced for children. Open all year.

Mrs L. Palmer, Boon Hills Farm, Nether Langwith, Mansfield NG20 9JQ • 01623 743862
e-mail: palmers@boonhills.wanadoo.co.uk
www.bedandbreakfast-nottinghamshire.com

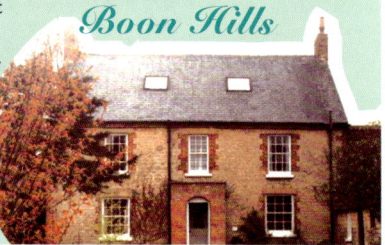

Dalestorth Guest House

is an 18th century Georgian family home converted in the 19th century to become a school for young ladies of the local gentry and a boarding school until the 1930s. In 1976 it was bought by the present owners and has been modernised and converted into a comfortable, clean and pleasant guest house serving the areas of Mansfield and Sutton-in-Ashfield, offering overnight accommodation of Bed and Breakfast or longer stays to businessmen, holidaymakers or friends and relations visiting the area. Please send for further information.

Mr P. Jordan, Dalestorth Guest House,
Skegby Lane, Skegby,
Sutton-in-Ashfield NG17 3DH
01623 551110 • www.dalestorth.co.uk

Please note

All the information in this book is given in good faith in the belief that it is correct. However, the publishers cannot guarantee the facts given in these pages, neither are they responsible for changes in policy, ownership or terms that may take place after the date of going to press. Readers should always satisfy themselves that the facilities they require are available and that the terms, if quoted, still apply.

The FHG Directory of Website Addresses

on pages 347-362 is a useful quick reference guide for
holiday accommodation with e-mail and/or website details

Shropshire

Church Stretton

Shropshire

THE MIDLANDS 155

SB

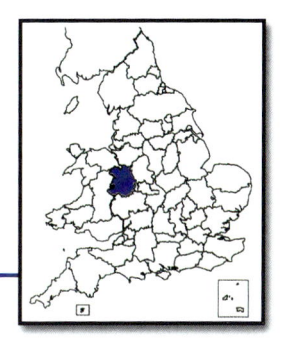

Lovely 17th century farmhouse in peaceful village amidst the beautiful South Shropshire Hills, an Area of Outstanding Natural Beauty. The farmhouse is full of character and all rooms have heating and are comfortable and spacious. The bedrooms are either en suite or private bathroom with hairdryers, tea/coffee making facilities, patchwork quilts and colour TV. There is a lounge with colour TV and inglenook fireplace. Children welcome. We are a working farm, centrally situated for visiting Ironbridge, Shrewsbury and Ludlow, each being easily reached within half an hour. Touring and walking information is available for visitors. Bed and full English Breakfast from £26pppn. Non-smoking. Open all year excluding November, December and January.

Mrs Mary Jones, Acton Scott Farm, Acton Scott, Church Stretton SY6 6QN • Tel: 01694 781260
Fax: 0870-129 4591 • e-mail: fhg@actonscottfarm.co.uk • www.actonscottfarm.co.uk

The Travellers Rest Inn

**Upper Affcot
Church Stretton SY6 6RL
Tel: 01694 781275
Fax: 01694 781555
reception@travellersrestinn.co.uk
www.travellersrestinn.co.uk**

Situated between Church Stretton and Craven Arms, and surrounded by The South Shropshire Hills. We, Fraser and Mauresia Allison, the owners assure you a warm welcome, good food, good beers, good accommodation, and good old fashioned service.

For those wishing to stay overnight with us at The Travellers Rest we have 12 very nice en suite guest bedrooms: six of these being on the ground floor with easy access, and two of these are suitable for accompanied wheel chair users. The bedrooms are away from the main area of the Inn and have their own entrance to the car park and garden, ideal if you have brought your pet with you and a midnight walk is needed.

Our well stocked Bar can satisfy most thirsts throughout the day with cask ales, lagers, stouts, spirits, wines and minerals. The Kitchen takes care of your hunger, be it for a snack or a full satisfying meal, vegetarians no problem. Food is served until 9pm in the evening.

156 THE MIDLANDS — Shropshire

Church Stretton, Clun, Craven Arms, Ironbridge

Court Farm

Court Farm is a Listed farmhouse, sympathetically renovated to provide guests with four-star rated en suite accommodation. One twin and one double room are available with views over the farmhouse garden and are positioned away from the owners' quarters for added privacy and peacefulness. The surrounding countryside is ideal for walking and there are many local attractions and places of interest to visit.

Mrs Alison Norris, Court Farm, Gretton, Church Stretton SY6 7HU • 01694 771219
www.courtfarm.eu

AA ★★★★ Guest Accommodation

Llanhedric

SB

Put your feet up and relax in the recliners as the beauty of the garden and the views of Clun and its surrounding hills provide solace from the stress of modern day life. Receive a warm welcome at this traditional oak-beamed farmhouse set back from the working farm. Two bedrooms, double en suite or double/family with private bathroom, tea/coffee facilities and good home cooking. Visitors' lounge with inglenook fireplace; separate dining room. Walks, history and attractions all close by.

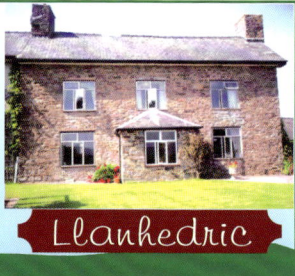

Bed and Breakfast from £26. Reductions for children. Non-smoking household. Regret no dogs in house. Open April to October.

Mrs M. Jones, Llanhedric, Clun, Craven Arms SY7 8NG • 01588 640203
e-mail: llanhedric@btconnect.com • www.llanhedricfarm.co.uk

Ward Farm

SB

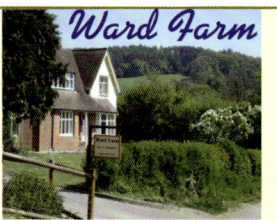

Farmhouse B&B on a traditional, organic working farm with Hereford cattle, sheep, Gloucester Old Spot and Berkshire pigs, and free-range poultry. Located in South Shropshire's AONB. Beautiful countryside, quiet location. Close to Ludlow, Wenlock Edge and the Stretton Hills. Ideal for walkers or just for a peaceful break. Three large rooms all with comfy chairs, TV, clock/radio, hairdryer and hospitality tray. Two doubles and one ground floor twin with en suite wet-floor shower. Wide doorways suitable for wheelchair access. Tea/coffee and home-made cake on arrival.

- Double £28-£34pppn.
- Single £32-£38pppn

We also have a Camping & Caravanning Club Certified site.

★★★★ B&B / Silver Award

Juliet Bateman, Ward Farm B&B,
Westhope, Craven Arms, Shropshire SY7 9JL
Tel: 01584 861601
e-mail: contact@wardfarm.co.uk
www.wardfarm.co.uk

Linley Crest

SB

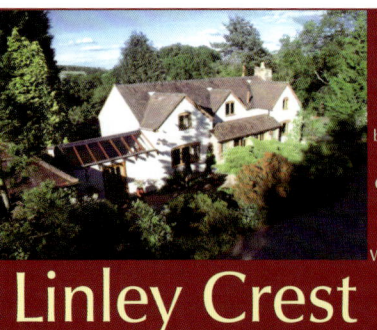

Very convenient for the medieval towns of Shrewsbury, Bridgnorth, Much Wenlock, Ludlow, Ironbridge and the dramatic landscape of the Long Mynd. We offer three generous double rooms with TV, beverage tray, hairdryer – two of which have a shower en suite, guest-controlled heating and EASY ACCESS; additionally, one has a private conservatory. The third bedroom has a private bathroom. Delicious English breakfast provided and special diets catered for. Pub serving food within staggering distance. Open all year; off-road parking; drying facilities. No smoking, no pets, no cards. Children very welcome. From £25.00 per person per night. Seven night's stay for the price of six. Euro payment accepted. Wir sprechen Deutsch – Herzlich willkommen! Warm welcome assured.

Jutta and Alan Ward, Linley Crest
Linley Brook, Near Bridgnorth WV16 4SZ
Tel & Fax: 01746 765527

Shropshire
Ludlow, Market Drayton

THE MIDLANDS 157

Henwick House
Gravel Hill, Ludlow SY8 1QU

A warm and friendly welcome awaits you in this privately owned former coach house Bed and Breakfast.

Delightful en suite rooms, TV, tea/coffee making facilities, comfortable beds and good traditional English Breakfast. Private parking.

Situated approximately half-a-mile from the castle and shops and local inns.

One double room, two twin, and one single room, all en suite.

Terms from £28 per person.

Mr and Mrs R. Cecil-Jones
01584 873338

Ravenscourt Manor

A warm welcome is assured at Ravenscourt, a superb Tudor Manor set in two acres of lovely gardens. Beautifully furnished and equipped bedrooms. Wonderful area for walking or touring. Two miles from Ludlow, famous for its restaurants and architecture, eight miles from Leominster, famous for antiques, and 15 miles from Hereford and Worcester with their historic cathedrals. Close to National Trust properties and only 40 minutes from Ironbridge and Stratford. Excellent home cooked food. All rooms are en suite with remote-control colour TV, tea/coffee facilities and central heating. B&B from £32.50pp

M.A. and E. Purnell, Ravenscourt Manor, Woofferton, Ludlow SY8 4AL
Tel: 01584 711905 • e-mail: elizabeth@ravenscourtmanor.plus.com
www.smoothhound.co.uk or www.virtual-shropshire.co.uk

SB

The Four Alls Inn & Motel
Newport Rd, Woodeaves, Market Drayton TF9 2AG

A warm welcome is assured at the Four Alls, situated in a quiet location of Woodeaves yet only a mile from the town of Market Drayton, and within easy reach of Shropshire's premier attractions.

Relax in our spacious bar, sample our home-cooked food and excellent traditional beers, then enjoy a good night's sleep in one of our nine en suite chalet-style rooms with central heating, TV and tea/coffee making facilities. The function room is available for weddings, celebrations or as a conference venue and can accommodate 50-100. Large car park.

Tel: 01630 652995 • Fax: 01630 653930
e-mail: inn@thefouralls.com • www.thefouralls.com

SB

AA ★★★ Inn

Shropshire
Munslow, Newport

THE Crown COUNTRY INN

Set below the rolling hills of Wenlock Edge, the Crown Country Inn is an ideal place to stay and explore the area. This Grade II Listed Tudor inn retains many historic features, including oak beams and flagstone floors.

Here you can sample traditional ales, fine food and a warm welcome from hosts, Richard and Jane Arnold. The menu offers a tempting variety of traditional and more exotic dishes, plus daily 'specials', all freshly prepared using the finest ingredients. Accommodation is available in three large bedrooms, all en suite, with television and tea/coffee making facilities.

- *Shropshire Good Eating Awards* • *Restaurant of the Year*

www.crowncountryinn.co.uk • info@crowncountryinn.co.uk

**Munslow
Near Craven Arms
Shropshire SY7 9ET
Tel: 01584 841205**

Sambrook Manor
Sambrook, Newport TF10 8AL • www.sambrookmanor.co.uk

Sambrook is a quiet, pretty village set in picturesque countryside close to the Shrops/Staffs border and within easy reach of Lilleshall sports centre, H.A.A.C., Ironbridge, Shrewsbury, Stafford and the Potteries. The charming historic Listed manor house (1702 AD) offers comfortable bedrooms, all en suite with TV and tea tray, and a relaxing lounge and conservatory, which opens on to a large garden. Full English breakfast cooked to your individual taste. Close to the Shropshire Union Canal and the national cycle network and with easy access to the Midlands motorway network. Local pub/restaurant within walking distance, also local fishing and horse riding. Stabling available and many accessible bridle paths. Private on-site parking. Boot room and cycle shelter. B&B Double/Twin £25, Single £30, reduction for children.

**Tel: 01952 550256 • mobile: 07811 915535
e-mail: sambrookmanor@btconnect.com**

Shropshire
Oswestry, Telford

THE MIDLANDS 159

TOP FARM HOUSE — Knockin, Near Oswestry SY10 8HN

Full of charm and character, this beautiful 16th century Grade 1 Listed black and white house is set in the delightful village of Knockin. Enjoy the relaxed atmosphere and elegant surroundings of this special house with its abundance of beams. Sit in the comfortable drawing room where you can read, listen to music, or just relax with a glass of wine (please feel free to bring your own tipple). Hearty breakfasts from our extensive menu are served in the lovely dining room which looks out over the garden. The large bedrooms are all en suite, attractively decorated and furnished. All have tea/coffee making facilities, colour TV, etc. Convenient for the Welsh Border, Shrewsbury, Chester and Oswestry. Friendly hosts and great atmosphere.

Bed and Breakfast from £27.50 to £35.

Telephone: 01691 682582

e-mail: p.a.m@knockin.freeserve.co.uk

The Mill House — Shrewsbury Road, High Ercall, Telford TF6 6BE

Judy and Chris Yates welcome you to The Mill House, an 18th century converted water mill situated beside the River Roden on a 9 acre working small holding. Located in the village of High Ercall, halfway between the historic county town of Shrewsbury and the new town of Telford.

Luxury B&B accommodation in three beautifully decorated, en suite bedrooms. Perfect for exploring Shropshire and the Welsh borderlands. A short distance from the World Heritage Site of the Ironbridge Gorge and the surrounding area offers a wide range of attractions and activities to suit all tastes.

Children welcome. Dogs by prior arrangement. Non-smoking.
Single £35 pppn, Double/Twin £24pppn,
Family room (sleeps 4) from £24 pppn.

01952 770394 • e-mail: cjpy@lineone.net • www.ercallmill.co.uk

Looking for Holiday Accommodation?

FHG KUPERARD

for details of hundreds of properties throughout the UK, visit our website

www.holidayguides.com

Staffordshire

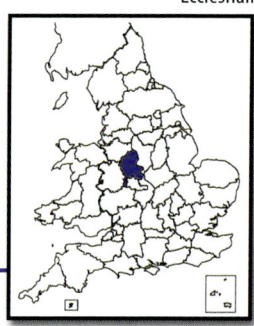

Staffordshire
Eccleshall

Cobbler's Cottage

A five minute walk from the centre of historic Eccleshall and just past the 12th century church is Cobbler's Cottage, in a lane within the conservation area.
We offer two bedrooms: one double and one twin, both with en suite shower, colour TV, and tea/coffee making facilities.
Eccleshall has seven pubs, five with restaurants for your evening meal. Ideally situated midway between Junctions 14 and 15 of the M6; the Potteries, Wedgwood, Ironbridge, Alton Towers and other attractions are within easy reach. Pets welcome. Non-smoking.
£35 for single occupancy, £55 for two sharing, inclusive of full Breakfast.

Mrs Sue Pimble, Cobbler's Cottage, Kerry Lane, Eccleshall ST21 6EJ
Tel: 01785 850116 • E-Mail: cobblerscottage@tinyonline.co.uk

OFFLEY GROVE FARM Adbaston, Eccleshall, Staffs ST20 0QB • Tel/Fax: 01785 280205

You'll consider this a good find! Quality accommodation and excellent breakfasts. Small traditional mixed farm surrounded by beautiful countryside. The house is tastefully furnished and provides all home comforts. Whether you are planning to book here for a break in your journey, stay for a weekend or take your holidays here, you will find something to suit all tastes among the many local attractions. Situated on the Staffordshire/Shropshire borders we are convenient for Alton Towers, Stoke-on-Trent, Ironbridge, etc. Reductions for children. Play area for children. Open all year. Many guests return.
Bed and Breakfast all en suite from £27pp • Self-catering cottages available • Brochure on request.
e-mail: enquiries@offleygrovefarm.co.uk • www.offleygrovefarm.co.uk

symbols

🚭	Totally non-smoking	🐕	Pets Welcome
🐎	Children Welcome	**SB**	Short Breaks
♿	Suitable for Disabled Guests	🍷	Licensed

Staffordshire
Stoke-on-Trent

THE MIDLANDS 161

Sam and Joan would like to invite you to stay in their 17th century stone-built farmhouse nestling in the Staffordshire Moorlands. Hollinhurst Farm is a working farm offering our visitors the opportunity of seeing a variety of free-ranging animals in a beautiful location.

A high standard of facilities is available for the discerning traveller - we offer a selection of rooms to cater to your needs including ground floor accommodation. Twin, double and family rooms available, all equipped with TV and tea/coffee making facilities, most of our rooms are en suite and have panoramic views.

Within easy reach of the M6 and A50.

Hollinhurst Farm Bed & Breakfast
Park Lane, Endon, Stoke-on-Trent ST9 9JB
Tel: 01782 502633
e-mail: joan.hollinhurst@btconnect.com
www.smoothhound.co.uk/hotels/hollinhurst

★★★ FARMHOUSE

Other specialised holiday guides from **FHG**

PUBS & INNS OF BRITAIN

COUNTRY HOTELS OF BRITAIN

WEEKEND & SHORT BREAKS IN BRITAIN & IRELAND

THE GOLF GUIDE WHERE TO PLAY, WHERE TO STAY

PETS WELCOME!

SELF-CATERING HOLIDAYS IN BRITAIN

500 GREAT PLACES TO STAY IN BRITAIN

CARAVAN & CAMPING HOLIDAYS IN BRITAIN

FAMILY BREAKS IN BRITAIN

Published annually: available in all good bookshops or direct from the publisher:
FHG Guides, Abbey Mill Business Centre, Seedhill, Paisley PA1 1TJ
Tel: 0141 887 0428 • Fax: 0141 889 7204
e-mail: admin@fhguides.co.uk • www.holidayguides.com

Warwickshire

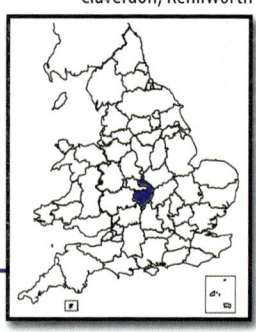

Claverdon, Kenilworth

Austons Down B&B

Austons Down B&B is a family home set in 100 acres of the Arden Special Landscape Area. Situated 25 minutes from the NEC and 10 minutes from Stratford-upon-Avon the accommodation is ideal for visitors to the Midlands area. There are many beautiful walks just a step from the front door, whilst Stratford-upon-Avon, Warwick Castle, Kenilworth Castle and the NEC are only a short drive away. Available for the business traveller as well as the holiday visitor, Austons Down B&B offers a warm welcome in a relaxed family home.

Tel: 01926 842068
www.austonsdown.com

Austons Down
Saddlebow Lane, Claverdon,
Warwickshire CV35 8PQ

Castle Laurels Guest House

Castle Laurels offers cleanliness and comfort, together with wonderful breakfasts prepared using locally sourced ingredients; supper/snack menu available. Set in the heart of the old town, opposite Kenilworth Castle, the guesthouse is within a few minutes walk of a number of pubs and restaurants. We are licensed with 12 en-suite non-smoking rooms, all equipped with TV, telephone and refreshments. Our wifi system means guests also have unlimited broadband internet access free-of-charge.
Prices include breakfast.
Doubles/Twins from £75.00. Singles from £45.00
Doubles/Twins for single occupancy from £60.00.

Tel: 01926 856179
e-mail: dave@castlelaurels.co.uk

Castle Laurels Guest House
22 Castle Road, Kenilworth, Warwickshire CV8 1NG
www.castlelaurels.co.uk

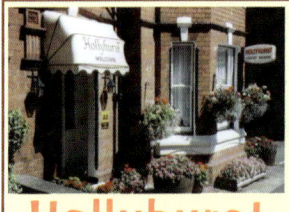

Hollyhurst Guest House

A comfortable Victorian house close to the town centre and a pleasant stroll from Kenilworth Castle. A market town with excellent restaurants, located in the heart of the Warwickshire countryside, Kenilworth is well connected by road and convenient for the NEC, Stoneleigh Park and the University of Warwick. You'll find the Hollyhurst perfect as a business base or holiday stopover. In either case we offer real hospitality and home comforts in our seven-bedroom guest house. Four rooms have en suite/private facilities and there is private parking for up to seven vehicles.

Trudi and Ken Wheat, The Hollyhurst Guest House,
47 Priory Road, Kenilworth CV8 1LL
Tel & Fax: 01926 853882
e-mail: admin@hollyhurstguesthouse.co.uk
www.hollyhurstguesthouse.co.uk

AA ★★★ Guest Accommodation

No pets
Bed and Breakfast from £25 per person

Warwickshire
Leamington Spa, Stratford-Upon-Avon

THE MIDLANDS 163

Hill Farm

Guests are welcome all year round to this comfortable, centrally heated farmhouse on a 350 acre mixed working farm. Ideally situated for Warwick, Coventry, Stratford-upon-Avon, Leamington Spa, Royal Showground, Birmingham, NEC and the Cotswolds.

Three pretty double bedrooms and two twin rooms with washbasins, tea and coffee facilities and TV. Some are en suite. Guests' sittingroom with colour TV; lovely conservatory for breakfast dining and excellent Breakfast Menu. Car preferable, ample parking.

Farm Stay UK member. FHG past Diploma Winner.
Bed and Breakfast from £25-£30pp double, £30-£35 single

Mrs R. Gibbs, Hill Farm, Lewis Road, Radford Semele, Leamington Spa CV31 1UX
Tel: 01926 337571 • www.hillfarm.info

Holly Tree Cottage
Birmingham Road, Pathlow, Stratford-upon-Avon CV37 0ES
Tel & Fax: 01789 204461

SB

Period cottage dating from 17th Century, with antiques, paintings, collection of porcelain, fresh flowers, tasteful furnishings and friendly atmosphere. Picturesque gardens, orchard, paddock and pasture with wildlife and extensive views over open countryside. Situated 3 miles north of Stratford-upon-Avon towards Henley-in-Arden on A3400.

Rooms have television, radio/alarm, hospitality trays and hairdryers. Breakfasts are a speciality. Pubs and restaurants nearby.

Ideally located for Theatre, Shakespeare Country, Heart of England, Cotswolds, Warwick Castle, Blenheim Palace and National Trust Properties. Well situated for National Exhibition Centre, Birmingham and National Agricultural Centre, Stoneleigh.

Children welcome, pets by arrangement. Non-smoking.

Bed and Breakfast from £32.50 per person.

e-mail: john@hollytree-cottage.co.uk • www.hollytree-cottage.co.uk

Warwickshire
Stratford-Upon-Avon

Cadle Pool Farm

This charming oak-panelled and beamed family house is part of an arable farm.

Situated two miles from Stratford-upon-Avon, only eight minutes from the Royal Shakespeare Theatre, it is an ideal touring centre for Warwick, Oxford and the Cotswolds. Family and double bedrooms, one en suite, one with private bathroom, all with central heating, TV and tea/coffee making facilities. There is an antique oak dining room. The grounds and ornamental pool are particularly attractive, with peacocks and ducks roaming freely.

Children over 10 are welcome, sorry no pets.

Tariff: Bed and Breakfast £80 (2 people)
£70 if staying 2 nights or more.

**Mrs M. Turney, Cadle Pool Farm,
The Ridgeway,
Stratford-upon-Avon CV37 9RE
Tel: 01789 292494**

Mil-Mar Guest House
96 Alcester Road, Stratford-upon-Avon CV37 9DP
Tel: 01789 267095 • Fax: 01789 262205

Mil-Mar, a family run Guest House which has been in the Spencer family for many years, is situated 800 metres from the town centre, convenient for the Shakespeare properties, the three Shakespeare Theatres and over 35 pubs, brasseries and restaurants to suit all tastes and pockets. An ideal base from which to explore The Cotswolds, Oxfordshire and Warwickshire. The non-smoking accommodation consists of double rooms, twin rooms and family rooms for three; all rooms en suite.

e-mail: milmar@btinternet.com • www.mil-mar.co.uk

Linhill Guest House   Tel: 01789 292879
35 Evesham Place, Stratford-upon-Avon CV37 6HT
e-mail: enquiries@linhillguesthouse.co.uk • www.linhillguesthouse.co.uk

Linhill is a comfortable Victorian Guest House run by a friendly family. It is situated only five minutes' walk from Stratford's town centre with its wide choice of fine restaurants and world famous Royal Shakespeare Theatre. Every bedroom at Linhill has central heating, colour TV, tea/coffee making facilities and washbasin. En suite facilities are also available, as are packed lunches and evening meals. Bicycle hire and babysitting facilities if desired. Leave the children with us and re-discover the delight of a candlelit dinner in one of Stratford's inviting restaurants.

Forget-Me-Not Guest House
18 Evesham Place, Stratford-upon-Avon CV37 6HT
Tel & Fax: 01789 204907

Forget-Me-Not Guest House is a family-run establishment that offers immaculate en-suite accommodation, delicious hearty breakfasts and a warm welcome right in the middle of Stratford upon Avon. A very enjoyable and unforgettable stay awaits you with Kate and John Morris offering a comfortable and relaxing stay. We are open all year round and are happy to accommodate you and your needs.

Forget-Me-Not offers 5 comfortable en-suite rooms situated within 5 minutes' walking distance of the theatre and town centre - three double rooms, one twin, one luxury super king. Family rooms can be arranged. All bedrooms have colour television, tea and coffee making facilities. Iron and hair dryer are available on request. A babysitting service can be arranged if booked in advance. For your comfort, Forget-Me-Not is totally non-smoking.

www.forgetmenotguesthouse.co.uk

Warwickshire

THE MIDLANDS 165

Stratford-Upon-Avon, Warwick

Whitchurch Farm

Wimpstone, Stratford-upon-Avon CV37 8NS

Bed & Breakfast accommodation on a working farm in a rural setting deep in the heart of South Warwickshire

2 double bedrooms and two family/twin rooms, all en suite, with TV, mini-fridge, tea/coffee making, hairdryer, and clock radio. Guest sitting room, dining room, garden and ample parking space. Non-smoking.

Wide choice of breakfast menu, seasonally changing dinner menu. Vegetarian options.

Tel: 01789 450359 • e-mail: jweeah@aol.com • www.whitchurchfarm.co.uk

THE CROFT

Haseley Knob,
Warwick CV35 7NL
Tel/Fax: 01926 484447

- Friendly family country guesthouse.
- Non-smoking.
- All rooms en suite or private bathroom, TV, hairdryer, tea/coffee.
- Central location for Warwick, Stratford, Coventry and NEC.

e-mail: david@croftguesthouse.co.uk
www.croftguesthouse.co.uk

Please note

All the information in this book is given in good faith in the belief that it is correct. However, the publishers cannot guarantee the facts given in these pages, neither are they responsible for changes in policy, ownership or terms that may take place after the date of going to press. Readers should always satisfy themselves that the facilities they require are available and that the terms, if quoted, still apply.

West Midlands

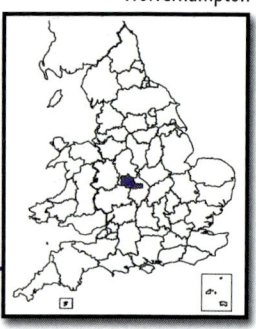

WOLVERHAMPTON. Featherstone Farm Hotel, New Road, Featherstone, Wolverhampton WV10 7NW (01902 725371; Fax: 01902 731741; mobile: 07836 315258).
This is a small, high-class country house hotel set in five acres of unspoiled countryside, only one mile from Junction 11 on the M6 or Junction 1 on the M54. The main house has eight en suite bedrooms with all the facilities one would expect in a hotel of distinction. Kings Repose Indian Restaurant, serving freshly prepared dishes, and licensed bar. Secure car park.
• Self-contained fully furnished cottages with maid service are also available.
ETC ★★★
e-mail: terry396mellor@btinternet.com
www.featherstonefarm.co.uk

Other specialised holiday guides from FHG

PUBS & INNS OF BRITAIN • **COUNTRY HOTELS** OF BRITAIN
WEEKEND & SHORT BREAK HOLIDAYS IN BRITAIN
THE GOLF GUIDE WHERE TO PLAY, WHERE TO STAY
500 GREAT PLACES TO STAY • **SELF-CATERING HOLIDAYS** IN BRITAIN
BED & BREAKFAST STOPS • **CARAVAN & CAMPING HOLIDAYS**
FAMILY BREAKS IN BRITAIN

Published annually: available in all good bookshops or direct from the publisher:
FHG Guides, Abbey Mill Business Centre, Seedhill, Paisley PA1 1TJ
Tel: 0141 887 0428 • Fax: 0141 889 7204
e-mail: admin@fhguides.co.uk • www.holidayguides.com

The FHG Directory of Website Addresses
on pages 347-362 is a useful quick reference guide for holiday accommodation with e-mail and/or website details

Worcestershire

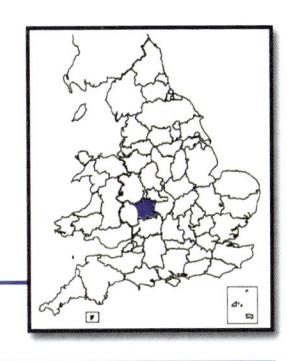

Bromsgrove, Droitwich Spa

Worcestershire

THE MIDLANDS 167

Ladybird Lodge

Ladybird Lodge in Bromsgrove is a magnificent 43-bedroom hotel with panoramic views looking out over the beautiful North Worcestershire countryside. All the rooms are en suite and fitted with imported solid oak furniture, and modern features include state of the art televisions and DVD players.

Rosado's, a very modern and chic Italian restaurant, provides a fresh new experience in dining out, and a menu to spoil any personal taste.

Ladybird Lodge is an ideal place to stay for visitors to the local area, including Birmingham, the NEC, Worcester and Stratford, near to Bromsgrove railway station and links with every major motorway network in the UK.

For reservations please call 01527 889900, book online below or e-mail us at info@ladybirdlodge.co.uk.
Ladybird Lodge, 2 Finstall Road, Aston Fields, Bromsgrove, Worcestershire B60 2DZ • www.ladybirdlodge.co.uk

Phepson Farm

Bed & Breakfast — Rural Escape

In our 17th century oak beamed farmhouse and converted buildings, we offer a warm welcome, award-winning breakfasts and a relaxed and informal atmosphere. All rooms en suite with colour TV, hairdryers and tea/coffee facilities. Situated on a sheep farm with scenic fishing lake; walking on Wychavon Way. Convenient for touring the beautiful Heart of England.

Self-catering also available. Credit cards accepted. Bed & Breakfast from £30 – £40pppn.

Phepson Farm, Himbleton, Droitwich Spa, Worcestershire WR9 7JZ
Tel: 01905 391205 • e-mail: info@phepsonfarm.co.uk

www.phepsonfarm.co.uk

Worcestershire

Great Malvern, Malvern Wells

Croft Guest House
Bransford, Worcester WR6 5JD

16th-18th century part black-and-white cottage-style country house situated in the Teme Valley, four miles from Worcester and Malvern. Croft House is central for visiting numerous attractions in Worcester, Hereford, the Severn Valley and surrounding countryside. River and lake fishing are close by, and an 18-hole golf course opposite. Comfortable, non-smoking house. Three en suite guest rooms (two double, one family) and one with washbasin are available. Rooms are double glazed and have colour TV, radio alarm, hairdryer and courtesy tray. TV lounge, residential licence. Dogs welcome by arrangement.

*B&B from £28 to £39 single
£47 to £65 double*

Full English breakfast is prepared from home-grown/made produce in season.

Ann & Brian Porter • Tel: 01886 832227
e-mail: hols@brianporter.orangehome.co.uk • www.croftguesthouse.com

---

BRICKBARNS, a 200-acre mixed farm, is situated two miles from Great Malvern at the foot of the Malvern Hills, 300 yards from the bus service and one-and-a half miles from the train. The house, which is 300 years old, commands excellent views of the Malvern Hills and guests are accommodated in one double, one single and one family bedrooms with washbasins; two bathrooms, shower room, two toilets; sittingroom and diningroom. Children welcome and cot and babysitting offered. Central heating. Car essential, parking. Open Easter to October for Bed and Breakfast from £22 nightly per person. Reductions for children and Senior Citizens. Birmingham 40 miles, Hereford 20, Gloucester 17, Stratford 35 and the Wye Valley is just 30 miles.

Mrs J.L. Morris, Brickbarns Farm, Hanley Road, Malvern Wells WR14 4HY
Tel: 016845 61775 • Fax: 01886 830037

---

symbols

🚭	Totally non-smoking	🐕	Pets Welcome
🐴	Children Welcome	**SB**	Short Breaks
♿	Suitable for Disabled Guests	🍷	Licensed

East Yorkshire

Aldbrough

East Yorkshire

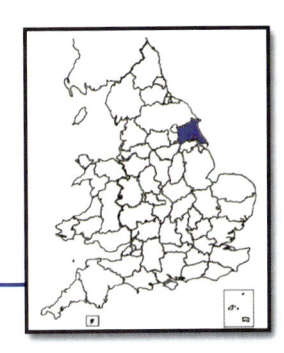

YORKSHIRE 169

Wentworth House Hotel

12 Seaside Road, Aldbrough,
Near Hull HU11 4RX
Tel & Fax: 01964 527246
enquiry@wentworthhousehotel.com
www.wentworthhousehotel.com

Family-run hotel set in spacious gardens, offering delightful accommodation. In the attractive licensed dining room the emphasis is placed on good home cooking, and special/medical diets can be catered for.
Ideal for small exclusive functions, for up to 100 guests (buffet style) or 20 guests at a formal meal, and provide a very personalised service and sole use of the hotel.

- ALL DOUBLE ROOMS EN SUITE, ONE WITH PRIVATE LOUNGE.
- BEDROOMS HAVE COLOUR TV, TELEPHONE AND RADIO ALARM CLOCK.
- BAR AREA WITH SELECTION OF WINES, SPIRITS & BEERS.
- CONFERENCE FUNCTION ROOM.
- GAMES ROOM • CAR PARK

Publisher's note

While every effort is made to ensure accuracy, we regret that FHG Guides cannot accept responsibility for errors, misrepresentations or omissions in our entries or any consequences thereof. Prices in particular should be checked.
We will follow up complaints but cannot act as arbiters or agents for either party.

YORKSHIRE

East Yorkshire
Beverley, Bridlington

ROBEANNE HOUSE
Tel: 01430 873312

Driffield Lane, Shiptonthorpe, York YO43 3PW

AA Guest Accommodation ★★★

A friendly, informal and comfortable guest house, conveniently located for York, the Wolds and the East Coast. The accommodation we offer includes either spacious comfortable suites in the main guest house or luxury log cabins situated within our extensive gardens. All our rooms are non smoking.

Whether here for a holiday, a romantic break or on business, we can offer you a quiet country location whilst still being accessible to the surrounding areas. The local pubs are just a leisurely five to ten minute walk away.

robeannehouse@btconnect.com
www.robeannehouse.co.uk

The rooms in the main house and cottage are either twin bedded or king-size. They are all very pleasantly decorated and equipped, with en suite facilities with shower, welcome pack of tea, coffee, hot chocolate and biscuits, books, colour television/DVD, hairdryer and ironing facilities. Each room also has a breathtaking countryside view.

We also have a family suite, ideal for larger parties or the larger family, equipped with two bedrooms, and a bathroom with shower. Our log cabins are well equipped, with en suite facilities with shower, colour television/DVD, hairdryer and ironing facilities. They also have a balcony with sitting area overlooking the lovely, peaceful, garden.

Rosebery House

1 Belle Vue, Tennyson Avenue, Bridlington YO15 2ET
Telephone: 01262 670336

SB

A Grade II Listed Georgian house with character. It has a long sunny garden and superb views of the gardens and sea. Amenities are close by making it an ideal centre for walking, bird-watching, golfing, wind and sailboarding or touring the historic, rolling Wolds. A high standard of comfort, friendliness and satisfaction guaranteed. All rooms are en suite, centrally heated, have colour TV and tea/coffee facilities. Vegetarian menu available. Some car parking available. Open all year except Christmas and New Year.

Bed and English Breakfast from £27pp, Bed and Continental Breakfast £24.
Senior Supersaver October to June excluding Bank Holidays.

e-mail: info@Rosebery-house.com • www.Rosebery-house.com

THE TENNYSON
19 TENNYSON AVENUE, BRIDLINGTON YO15 2EU
Tel: 01262 604382

SB

Small, non-smoking, family hotel offering all usual amenities. B&B from £24pppn. All rooms en suite. Located within easy walking distance of town centre, North Beach and cliff walks. Dogs £2.50 per dog per stay. AA ★★★

www.thetennysonhotel.co.uk

East Yorkshire **YORKSHIRE 171**

Driffield

The Old Mill
HOTEL & RESTAURANT

Mill Lane, near Driffield YO25 3BQ
Tel: 01377 267284

Friendly country house hotel in tranquil Yorkshire Wolds. Renowned in-house restaurant provides à la carte and bar meal menu.

Beautiful walks, Heritage Coastline, golf, clay pigeon shooting and famous North York Moors all nearby. The hotel is within easy access of Beverley, York, Scarborough and Bridlington.

Why not come and meet our 4 Labradors?!

B&B £55pp, DB&B £75pp

B&B £75 per room - double occupancy

Discount on stays of 3 or more nights

AA ★★ HOTEL

enquiries@old-mill-hotel.co.uk • www.old-mill-hotel.co.uk

Looking for Holiday Accommodation?

FHG
KUPERARD

for details of hundreds of properties throughout the UK, visit our website

www.holidayguides.com

North Yorkshire

North Yorkshire
Coverdale, Danby

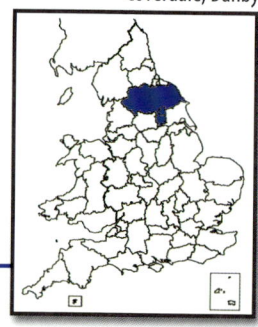

Peacefully situated farmhouse away from the madding crowd.
B&B with optional Evening Meal • Home cooking.
Pets sleep where you prefer.
Ideally positioned for exploring the beautiful Yorkshire Dales.

**Mrs Julie Clarke, Middle Farm,
Woodale, Coverdale, Leyburn,
North Yorkshire DL8 4TY 01969 640271**
e-mail: j-a-clarke@hotmail.co.uk

www.yorkshirenet.co.uk/stayat/middlefarm/index.htm

ROWANTREE FARM is a family-run dairy farm situated in the heart of the North York Moors. Ideal walking and mountain biking area, with panoramic moorland views. Coast easily accessible. Our non-smoking home comprises one family room and one twin-bedded room, with private bathroom and private shower room, also full central heating, beverage tray, CD clock radio and hairdryer. Relax in our residents' lounge with colour TV/video. Ample car parking.

- Children welcome; cot and high chair available.
- Good home cooking (vegetarians catered for), served in our separate dining room. Packed lunches available.
- B&B from £25; Evening Meal by prior arrangement.

Mrs L. Tindall, Rowantree Farm, Ainthorpe, Whitby YO21 2LE • 01287 660396
e-mail: krbsatindall@aol.com • www.rowantreefarm.co.uk

The Fox & Hounds Inn

Residential 16th Century Coaching Inn set amidst the beautiful North York Moors. Freshly prepared dishes served every lunchtime and evening. Quality selected wines and Theakston real ales. Superb en suite accommodation available.
Special Breaks available November to March.
Situated between Castleton and Danby on the Fryup Road.
Ainthorpe, Danby, Whitby, N. Yorkshire YO21 2LD
For bookings please Tel: 01287 660218
e-mail: info@foxandhounds-ainthorpe.com
www.foxandhounds-ainthorpe.com

YORKSHIRE

North Yorkshire

Glaisdale

Hollins Farm
Glaisdale, Whitby, North Yorkshire YO21 2PZ
Tel: 01947 897516

Comfortable accommodation available in 16th century character farmhouse in the beautiful Esk Valley, 9 miles from historic Whitby.

One large family/double room sleeping up to four/five and one family/double room en suite, sleeping up to three. Both rooms have washbasins, colour TV and tea/coffee facilities. Guests' sitting/diningroom with colour TV, and a conservatory. Cot and high chair available.

Full traditional farmhouse breakfast provided, or vegetarian alternative available.

Many historic towns, villages and places of interest to visit and nearby activities include pony trekking and fishing.

Camping facilities also available.

SB

EGTON BANKS FARM
◆Glaisdale, Whitby YO21 2QP◆
Tel: 01947 897289

Beautiful old farmhouse (pre 1750) situated in a lovely valley close to quiet roadside. Working farm set in 120 acres of pastureland and woods. Centre of National Park. Warm and friendly atmosphere. Diningroom/Lounge for guests with TV and books. Close to river, one mile from Glaisdale village and mainline railway, eight miles to Whitby, four miles steam railway and Heartbeat country. Both bedrooms have pretty decor and TV. One double and one family/twin room, both en suite. Full Yorkshire Breakfast. Packed lunches. All diets catered for. B&B from £23-£27. No pets, no smoking.

e-mail: egtonbanksfarm@agriplus.net
www.egtonbanksfarm.agriplus.net

SB

Red House Farm

Listed Georgian farmhouse featured in "Houses of the North York Moors". Completely refurbished to the highest standards, retaining all original features. Bedrooms have bath/shower/toilet, central heating, TV and tea making facilities. Excellent walks straight from the doorstep. Friendly farm animals – a few cows, horses, geese and pretty free-roaming hens. One-and-a-half acres of gardens, sitting-out areas. Magnificent views. Interesting buildings – Listed barns now converted to 3 holiday cottages. Games room with snooker table. Eight miles from seaside/Whitby. Village pub within walking distance. Stabling available for horses/dogs. Non-smoking.

Tom and Sandra Spashett, Red House Farm, Glaisdale, Near Whitby YO21 2PZ • Tel & Fax: 01947 897242
e-mail: spashettredhouse@aol.com
www.redhousefarm.com

SB

North Yorkshire
Harrogate

Central House Farm

A warm welcome awaits you at this traditional farmhouse set in a picturesque valley, 10 minutes from the Spa town of Harrogate with its beautiful gardens. The scenic Yorkshire Dales are only a short drive away, and York and Leeds are also within easy reach. All rooms are en suite with colour TV and drinks making facilities. There is a guest lounge for you to relax and enjoy the peaceful surroundings. Good pubs and restaurants nearby. Open all year. Totally non-smoking.

Bed and Breakfast from £30pp double, £45 single.

Haverah Park, Harrogate HG3 1SQ
Tel: 01423 566050 • Fax: 01423 709152
www.centralhousefarm.co.uk
jayne@centralhousefarm.freeserve.co.uk

The Cavendish Hotel

3 Valley Drive, Harrogate,
North Yorkshire HG2 0JJ

Overlooking the beautiful Valley Gardens, close to Harrogate's Conference Centre and extensive shopping area, the Cavendish Hotel is an ideal location for visitors – be it for business or pleasure.

All rooms, including our four-poster bedroom, have en suite facilities, colour television, tea and coffee tray. We hope to make your stay enjoyable.

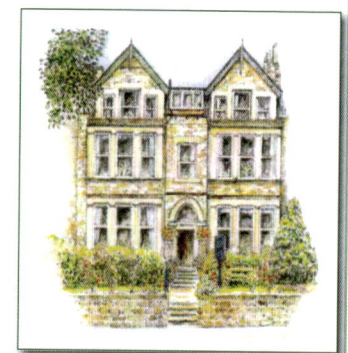

Pay us a visit – you'll be pleased you have!

Tel (Reservations): 01423 509637
Fax: 01423 504434
e-mail: cavendishhotel@gmail.com

North Yorkshire

Harrogate, Helmsley

HARROGATE. Mr Derek and Mrs Carol Vinter, Spring Lodge, 22 Spring Mount, Harrogate HG1 2HX (01423 506036).
Attractive Edwardian guest house situated in a quiet cul-de-sac, yet close to all the amenities of Harrogate, Britain's floral spa town, with its elegant and outstanding architecture and gardens, antique shops and restaurants. Ideal tourist base for visiting the Dales and North York Moors, historic York and bustling Leeds. All year round a warm welcome awaits you from the resident proprietors. Accommodation comprises three double rooms, one twin and one single. En suite rooms available. Coffee and tea making facilities in all rooms.
Rates: Bed and Breakfast from £28 per person.

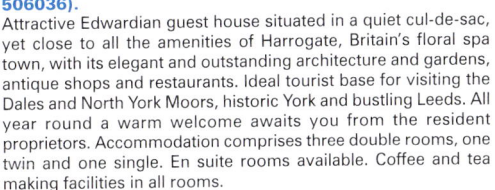

VisitBritain ★★★
e-mail: spring_lodge@btinternet.com
www.spring-lodge.co.uk

The Coppice

A high standard of comfortable accommodation awaits you at The Coppice, with a reputation for excellent food and a warm friendly welcome. All rooms en suite with telephones. Quietly located off Kings Road, five minutes' walk from the elegant shops and gardens of the town centre. Just three minutes' walk from the Conference Centre. Ideal location to explore the natural beauty of the Yorkshire Dales. Midway stop Edinburgh–London.

Free Yorkshire touring map - ask for details.

Bed and Breakfast £45 single, £65 double, twin from £65, family room £78; Snacks available.

★★★★ GUEST HOUSE

9 Studley Road, Harrogate HG1 5JU
Tel: 01423 569626 • Fax: 01423 569005
e-mail: coppice@harrogate.com • www.harrogate.com/coppice

Homely, comfortable, Christian accommodation. Spacious stone built bungalow in beautiful Nidderdale which is very central for touring the Yorkshire Dales; Pateley Bridge two miles, Harrogate 14 miles, Ripon nine miles. Museums, rocks, caves, fishing, bird watching, beautiful quiet walks, etc all nearby. En suite rooms (one twin, two double), TV. Private lounge. Tea making facilities available. Choice of breakfast. Evening meals available one mile away. Ample parking space on this working farm. Open Easter to end of October.

Mrs C.E. Nelson, Nidderdale Lodge Farm, Fellbeck, Pateley Bridge, Harrogate HG3 5DR • Tel: 01423 711677

Helmsley is beautifully situated for touring the North York Moors National Park, East Coast, York, "Herriot" and "Heartbeat" country. There is a wealth of footpaths and bridleways to explore. A warm welcome awaits you in the comfortable relaxed atmosphere of this elegant Georgian town house just off the market square, overlooking All Saints Church to the front and Helmsley Castle to the rear.

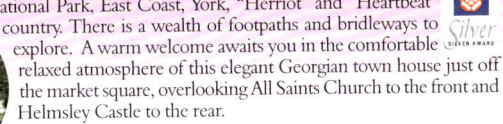

All rooms are en suite, with tea/coffee making facilities, digital colour TV, radio alarm, hairdryer, central heating. Private gardens and car park. Highly recommended for good food. Bed and Breakfast from £28pppn. Please telephone, or write, for colour brochure.

As recommended by the Which? *Good B&B Guide.*

Stilworth House 1 Church Street, Helmsley YO62 5AD • Mrs C. Swift
Tel: 01439 771072 • www.stilworth.co.uk

Barn Close Farm

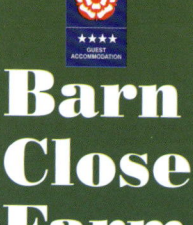

Rievaulx,
Helmsley,
North Yorkshire
YO62 5LH

01439 798321

Mrs J. Milburn

BARN CLOSE FARM is nicely situated in the North York Moors National Park. This family farm in beautiful surroundings offers homely accommodation to holidaymakers all year round. Within easy reach of Rievaulx Abbey and many other places of interest, it is an ideal centre for tourists.

Pony trekking nearby • Good walking terrain!
Highly commended for good food.

Two double rooms, one en suite; bathroom; toilets;
sitting room and dining room.

Bed and Breakfast from £28 to £40, Evening Dinner £18.
"WHICH?" RECOMMENDED. "DAILY TELEGRAPH" RECOMMENDED.

NEWTON HOUSE, KNARESBOROUGH

Delightful Georgian Guest Accommodation. Spacious, tastefully decorated, exceptionally well equipped rooms.
Ideal base for exploring Yorkshire.

- **Genuine warm welcome** • **Comfortable sitting-room** • **DAB radios, TVs, WIFI** • **Molton Brown toiletries** • **Licensed**

- AA 4 Star
- AA Highly Commended
- AA Breakfast Award

Tel: 01423 863539
www.newtonhouseyorkshire.com
e-mail: newtonhouse@btinternet.com

North Yorkshire
Kirkbymoorside

• Brickfields Farm •
Kirkby Mills, Kirkbymoorside YO62 6NS

Brickfields Farm provides spacious, comfortable and stylish bed and breakfast accommodation with a spacious twin room in the farmhouse, and two double rooms and two twin rooms (one of which is wheelchair accessible) in the barn conversion. All rooms are on the ground floor and have TV with Freeview, DVD/CD player, teas/coffees and a fridge with fresh milk and mineral water. A generous Yorkshire breakfast is served in the conservatory.

There is a wide range of restaurants and dining pubs locally, and the farm makes an ideal base for exploring Moors, Dales, Whitby and the East Coast.

Ample parking • No Smoking • No Children • No Pets.

Janet Trousdale
Tel: 01751 433074
e-mail: janet@brickfieldsfarm.co.uk
www.brickfieldsfarm.co.uk

B&B from £45. Open all year.

Golden Lion HOTEL
Market Place, Leyburn, North Yorkshire DL8 5AS

At the gateway to Wensleydale, this splendid hotel dates from 1765, although it has been tastefully modernised. Light meals and afternoon teas are served in the bars, and the restaurant with its picture windows and colourful murals is a popular venue. Excellent accommodation is available in rooms with bathrooms en suite, television, telephone, radio and tea and coffee-makers. A lift operates to all floors. Within easy walking distance is the little town of Middleham on the River Ure which is well known as a racehorse training centre.

Tel: 01969 622161
Fax: 01969 623836
info@goldenlionleyburn.co.uk

THE OLD STAR
West Witton, Leyburn DL8 4LU
Tel: 01969 622949
enquiries@theoldstar.com
www.theoldstar.com

Formerly a 17th century coaching inn, now a family-run guest house. You are always welcome at the Old Star.
The building still retains many original features. Comfortable lounge with oak beams and log fire. Bedrooms mostly en suite with central heating and tea/coffee making facilities.
Two good food pubs in village. In the heart of the Yorkshire Dales National Park we are ideally situated for walking and touring the Dales. Large car park. Open all year except Christmas. En suite Bed and Breakfast from £26pppn.

Sunnyridge •• ARGILL FARM
Harmby, LEYBURN DL8 5HQ • Tel: 01969 622478
Mrs Hilary Richardson • richah@freenet.co.uk
www.sunnyridgeargillfarm.co.uk

Situated on a small sheep farm in Wensleydale, Sunnyridge is a spacious bungalow in an outstanding position. Magnificent views are enjoyed from every room. In the heart of the Yorkshire Dales near The Forbidden Corner, it is an ideal centre for exploring the wide variety of activities and attractions; or a restful stop-over for travellers. Sample Yorkshire hospitality and relax in comfortable ground floor accommodation comprising one double or twin bedroom and one family/double/twin-bedded room, both en suite, each with colour TV, tea/coffee facilities and hairdryer.

Non-smoking • Guest lounge • Children welcome • Pets by arrangement • B&B from £28

symbols

- Totally non-smoking
- Children Welcome
- Suitable for Disabled Guests
- Pets Welcome
- SB — Short Breaks
- Licensed

North Yorkshire

Malham (Yorkshire Dales National Park)

Malham • Miresfield Farm

GUEST HOUSE ★★★

SB

- In beautiful gardens bordering village green and stream.
- Well known for excellent food.
- 11 bedrooms, all with private facilities.

Mr C. Sharp, Miresfield Farm, Malham, Skipton BD23 4DA • Tel: 01729 830414
www.miresfield-farm.com

- Full central heating.
- Two well furnished lounges and conservatory for guests' use.
- B&B from £32pppn.

North Yorkshire
Malham, Northallerton, Pickering

BECK HALL
Malham • North Yorkshire

18th century B&B on the Pennine Way, log fires and huge breakfasts. Midweek and 4-night specials. Ideal for exploring the Yorkshire Dales.

Built in 1710, Beck Hall has been providing accommodation since the 1930s. There are now 13 double en suite rooms and 4 twin rooms; 4 with four-poster. Spacious guest lounge with log fire. Full English breakfast, fish, vegetarian or lighter continental selection.
Malham is one of the most visited villages in the Yorkshire Dales, with plenty of things to do for the walker, cyclist or family. The market towns of Settle and Skipton are nearby and the Settle-Carlisle Railway is a good bet for a day out. If the weather palls there are caves nearby and other indoor attractions. The Lake District, Kendal and Windermere are an hour's drive.

Beck Hall, Cove Rd, Malham, North Yorkshire BD23 4DL
Tel: 01729 830332
e-mail: simon@beckhallmalham.com
www.beckhallmalham.com

Lovesome Hill Farm
Mary & John Pearson • Tel: 01609 772311
Lovesome Hill, Northallerton DL6 2PB

Central location for exploring the Dales and Moors, Durham and York. Enjoy the comfort and welcome we have to offer you at our traditional working farm with en suite bedrooms of various combinations and styles, some on ground floor. Gate Cottage, our luxurious suite, with its antique half-tester bed and its own patio, has views towards the Hambleton Hills. Enjoy home-made produce including our own free-range eggs cooked on the Aga. Brochure available.

"Which?" Recommended 2005, Les Routiers 2006, B&B of the North 2004.
Open all year except Christmas and New Year • B&B from £32-£40 twin/double, £35-£45 single.
Evening Meal available £15-£20.
www.lovesomehillfarm.co.uk • e-mail: mail@lovesomehillfarm.co.uk

---

Tangalwood
Roxby Road,
Thornton-le-Dale,
Pickering
YO18 7TQ

ETC ★★★★

One twin and one double en suite rooms, one single; all with tea/coffee making facilities and TV; alarm clock/radio and hairdryer also provided; diningroom; central heating.

Very clean and comfortable accommodation with good food. Situated in a quiet part of this picturesque village, which is in a good position for Moors, "Heartbeat" country, coast, North York Moors Railway, Flamingo Park Zoo and forest drives, mountain biking and walking. Good facilities for meals provided in the village. Open Easter to October for Bed and Breakfast from £28-£32pp. Private car park. Secure motorbike and cycle storage.

TELEPHONE: 01751 474688 • www.accommodation.uk.net/tangalwood

North Yorkshire

YORKSHIRE 181

Pickering

Banavie

is a large semi-detached house set in a quiet part of the picturesque village of Thornton-le-Dale, one of the prettiest villages in Yorkshire with its famous thatched cottage and bubbling stream flowing through the centre. We offer our guests a quiet night's sleep and rest away from the main road, yet only four minutes' walk from the village centre. One large double or twin bedroom and two double bedrooms, all tastefully decorated with en suite facilities, colour TV, hairdryer, shaver point etc. and tea/coffee making facilities. There is a large guest lounge, tea tray on arrival. A real Yorkshire breakfast is served in the dining room. Places to visit include Castle Howard, Eden Camp, North Yorkshire Moors Railway, Goathland ("Heartbeat"), York etc. There are three pubs, a bistro and a fish and chip shop for meals. Children and dogs welcome. Own keys. Car parking at back of house.

B&B from £27pppn
• SAE please for brochure • Welcome To Excellence •
• Hygiene Certificate held • No Smoking •
Mrs Ella Bowes

SB

BANAVIE, ROXBY ROAD, THORNTON-LE-DALE, PICKERING YO18 7SX
Tel: 01751 474266 • e-mail: info@banavie.uk.com • www.banavie.uk.com

---

Looking for Holiday Accommodation?

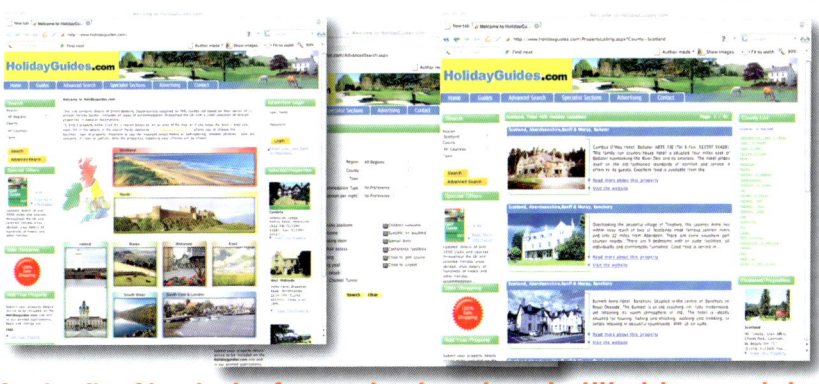

FHG KUPERARD

for details of hundreds of properties throughout the UK, visit our website

www.holidayguides.com

182 YORKSHIRE

North Yorkshire
Richmond, Ripon, Robin Hood's Bay

Stonesthrow, Dalton, Near Richmond DL11 7HS

SB

With a welcoming fire, private garden and conservatory, Stonesthrow offers you a friendly, family atmosphere. Unmistakable Yorkshire hospitality from the moment you arrive – we greet you with a tea or coffee and home-made cakes. Situated midway between the towns of Richmond and Barnard Castle, it offers you an ideal base for exploring the Yorkshire Dales, Teesdale, and York. Stonesthrow, has well appointed bedrooms with TV, tea/coffee facilities and full central heating. Off-road parking. Non-smoking. Sorry, no pets. Children eight and over are welcome.

B&B £25pppn double, £28 single.
Mrs S. Lawson, Stonesthrow, Dalton, Near Richmond DL11 7HS • 01833 621493 • mobile: 07970 655726
e-mail: stonesthrowd@aol.co.uk • www.stonesthrowdalton.co.uk

Browson Bank Farmhouse Accommodation

A newly converted granary set in 300 acres of farmland. The accommodation consists of three very tastefully furnished double/twin rooms all en suite, tea and coffee making facilities, colour TV and central heating. A large, comfortable lounge is available to relax in. Full English breakfast served. Situated six miles West of Scotch Corner (A1). Ideal location to explore the scenic countryside of Teesdale and the Yorkshire Dales and close to the scenic towns of Barnard Castle and Richmond. Terms from £25 per night.

Browson Bank Farmhouse, Browson Bank, Dalton, Richmond DL11 7HE
Tel: (01325) 718504 or Mobile: (07703) 325088 • www.browsonbank.co.nr

Mrs Julie Bailes, CHERRY CROFT, Bedale Lane, Wath, Ripon HG4 5ER

- CHERRY CROFT is situated in the quiet village of Wath, approx. three miles north of the historic market town of Ripon; two miles from A1(M).
- Accommodation comprises two double rooms with TV and tea making facilities.
- All rooms are on the ground floor.
- Ideal location for touring the Dales and Herriot Country.
- £20 per person, Bed & Breakfast.

Tel: 01765 640318

ROBIN HOOD'S BAY. Mrs B. Reynolds, 'South View', Sledgates, Fylingthorpe, Whitby YO22 4TZ (01947 880025). Pleasantly situated, comfortable accommodation in own garden with sea and country views. Ideal for walking and touring. Close to the moors, within easy reach of Whitby, Scarborough and many more places of interest. There are two double rooms, lounge and diningroom. Parking spaces. Phone for further details.
Rates: Bed and Breakfast from £23.

North Yorkshire

Saltburn-by-the-Sea, Scarborough

The Arches
Tel: 01287 677512
www.thearcheshotel.co.uk

- The Arches offers a relaxing environment and overlooks spectacular views of cliffs and golf course.
- All rooms are individually furnished and have en suite bathrooms.
- Ideal location for touring Whitby, Heartbeat Country, North York Moors Railway, golf and horse riding.
- Bed and Breakfast from £35 single, £60 double.
- We pride ourselves on our relaxed, informal atmosphere and good old fashioned food.
- Two self-contained holiday cottages are also available.

The Arches, Manx Lodge, Low Farm, Brotton, Saltburn-by-the-Sea TS12 2QX

Angela & Roland Thompson, THE WINDMILL BED AND BREAKFAST
Mill Street, Off Victoria Road, Scarborough YO11 1SZ • 01723 372735

18th Century Windmill Non-Smoking establishment offering quality accommodation five minutes' walk from town centre, station and Stephen Joseph Theatre. We have 9 en suite rooms, with a mix of double, family, twin and four-poster rooms at varying prices. All our rooms have tea/coffee facilities and remote-control colour TV, and are centrally heated. We also have two lovely apartments in the Windmill itself where you can stay on a bed and breakfast or self-catering basis. There is private parking in the courtyard.

Bed and Breakfast from £32.00 per person per night.
Children aged 2-14 £10.00 when sharing with two adults.

www.scarborough-windmill.co.uk • • • • • e-mail: info@scarborough-windmill.co.uk

HARMONY GUEST HOUSE
www.theharmonyguesthouse.co.uk

The Harmony Guest House is a typical Victorian Terrace on three floors, built in 1890.
We have four family rooms (including the double bedroom with adjoining childrens' room). All rooms are en suite, one with bath.
Child/veggie/doggie friendly Guest House.
Local produce, home-cooked, no "boil in the bag".
Informal atmosphere.

B&B £22pppn, BBEM £32. Open all year.

13 PRINCESS ROYAL TERRACE, SOUTH CLIFF, SCARBOROUGH YO11 2RP
Tel: 01723 373562 • e-mail: harmonyguesthouse@hotmail.com

North Yorkshire

Scarborough, Skipton

Scarborough •• Terrace Hotel

A small family-run Hotel situated between North and South Bays, close to all Scarborough's many attractions and only a short walk from the town centre, rail and bus stations. Private car park. Three double bedrooms (one en suite), three family rooms (one en suite) and one single bedroom, all with colour TV and tea making facilities. Full Fire Certificate. Totally non-smoking.
Bed and full English Breakfast from £19.00. En suite facilities £3 extra pppn. One night supplement £2.00 pp.
Children (sharing room with adults) under 4 years FREE, 4 to 11 years half price.

Sylvia and Chris Kirk, The Terrace Hotel, 69 Westborough, Scarborough YO11 1TS • 01723 374937

www.4hotels.co.uk/uk/hotels/theterrace.html • www.smoothhound.co.uk/hotels/theterrace.html

Distinctively Different

Peaceful and relaxing retreat, octagonal in design and set in two acres of private grounds with 360° panoramic views of the National Park and sea. An ideal centre for walking or touring. Two miles from Scarborough and within easy reach of Whitby, York and the beautiful North Yorkshire countryside. Tastefully decorated en suite centrally heated rooms with colour TV and all with superb views. Attractive dining room, guest lounge and relaxing conservatory. Traditional English breakfast, including vegetarian. Licensed. Private parking facilities. Personal service and warm, friendly Yorkshire hospitality. Bed and Breakfast from £29 to £37. *Non-smoking.*
Children over 7 years welcome • Spacious 5-berth caravan also available for self-catering holidays – £150 to £355.

Sue and Tony Hewitt, Harmony Country Lodge, Limestone Road, Burniston, Scarborough YO13 0DG • 0800 2985840 • Tel & Fax: 01723 870276
e-mail: tony@harmonylodge.net • www.harmonycountrylodge.co.uk

Detached 16th century farmhouse in private grounds. Quiet, with safe parking. One mile east of Skipton, Gateway to the Dales, and close to many places of beauty and interest. Luxury B&B with fireside treats in the lounge. All rooms are quiet and spacious, with panoramic views, washbasin and toilet (some full en suite), tea/coffee facilities and electric overblankets.
Sorry, no smoking, no pets, no children.
Terms: £28-£36pppn; single occupancy £36-£56.
Open all year. Credit cards accepted.
Farm cottage sometimes available.

Tel: 01756 793849
www.yorkshirenet.co.uk/accgde/lowskibeden

LOW SKIBEDEN FARMHOUSE, HARROGATE ROAD, SKIPTON BD23 6AB

Please note

All the information in this book is given in good faith in the belief that it is correct. However, the publishers cannot guarantee the facts given in these pages, neither are they responsible for changes in policy, ownership or terms that may take place after the date of going to press. Readers should always satisfy themselves that the facilities they require are available and that the terms, if quoted, still apply.

Gamekeeper's Inn

Set in the heart of the beautiful Yorkshire Dales

A warm welcome awaits you

When you arrive at the Gamekeeper's Inn you will find a warm and personal welcome. The traditional limestone building, originally a gamekeepers cottage, has a stylish and contemporary interior. Our striking modern conservatory, housing the Poacher's Restaurant, is like the food it serves - new, bold and exciting.

Set in the heart of Wharfedale in the glorious Yorkshire Dales National Park it is ideally situated for exploring North Yorkshire and all that it has to offer including great walks, inspirational views, dramatic limestone scenery, fly fishing and pony trekking. Great for bed and breakfast or for a longer stay, this stylish Inn has all you need. Guests also have free use of the facilities at the adjacent Health and Beauty Club including gym, sauna and swimming pool.

All of our rooms are en-suite with luxurious white bathrobes and Molton Brown toiletries. Everything in your room has been designed to make your stay comfortable and welcoming. You will find a TV, a choice of DVDs and a well stocked hospitality tray complete with home made biscuits and fresh fruit.

For those who like to keep in touch with the outside world Wi-Fi is also available in all rooms free of charge.

Log Cabins

We also have four luxurious solid pine log cabins which are available for self-catering breaks. Designed to provide a comfortable holiday home for short or longer-term breaks. Available in three or four bedroom layouts to suit couples or larger family groups. From the moment you step inside you will be captivated by the space and beauty of your surroundings. The open plan design and impressive vaulted ceilings create a spacious living area while the mellow, natural colour of the solid pine logs complements and enhances the luxurious contemporary furnishings, specially selected by our own interior designer.

Poacher's Restaurant and Bistro

Our AA dining rosette and our certificate from the AA for a superb breakfast, tell you that you will be well fed here.

Our superb Poacher's Restaurant and our Bistro Bar serve only fresh food, cooked to order by our talented head chef Matt Ingham and his team, with an emphasis on flavour and simple yet meticulous presentation.

Gamekeeper's Inn, Long Ashes Park, Threshfield, Nr. Skipton, North Yorkshire, BD23 5PN
Tel: 01756 752434 • email: info@gamekeeperinn.co.uk • www.gamekeeperinn.co.uk

North Yorkshire

Staithes, Stokesley, Whitby

BROOKLYN B & B

Situated on a quiet terrace in the old part of the picturesque, historic village of Staithes, with its artistic and Captain Cook associations, Brooklyn is a solid, red brick house, built in 1921 by a retired sea captain. It has three letting rooms (two doubles, one twin) which are individually decorated with views across the rooftops to Cowbar cliffs. All have a television and tea/coffee making facilities, and although not en suite, do have washbasins. The dining room doubles as a sitting room for guests, and breakfasts are generous, vegetarians catered for, and special diets by arrangement. Pets and children are most welcome.

MS M.J. HEALD, BROOKLYN B&B,
BROWN'S TERRACE, STAITHES,
NORTH YORKSHIRE TS13 5BG
Tel: 01947 841396
m.heald@tesco.net
www.brooklynuk.com

The best B&B in the best village in North Yorkshire

★★★ BED & BREAKFAST

Four Wynds

A warm and friendly welcome awaits you at *Four Wynds*, a smallholding set in beautiful, quiet and tranquil countryside on the edge of the North Yorkshire Moors and within easy commuting distance of Teeside (15 minutes) and only five minutes from the A19. This is the perfect location for visiting York and Whitby, or for touring Herriot, Captain Cook and Heartbeat Country, and an ideal stopover for 'Coast to Coast', 'Cleveland Way' and 'Lykewake' walkers – transport can be arranged from a pick-up point. All bedrooms have tea/coffee making facilities, colour TV and radio alarm, some en suite. Traditional hearty breakfast served at a time to suit and evening meal on request. Ample free and safe parking. Sorry no dogs.

★★★ BED & BREAKFAST

B&B from £26 to £30 en suite pppn.
Tel: 01642 701315

Sue Barnfather, Four Wynds,
Whorl Hill, Faceby, Stokesley TS9 7BZ

Endeavour B&B

Situated in the historic town of Whitby, this luxuriously appointed detached residence is on the West Cliff, with sea views yet close to the centre of town. Recently refurbished, this lovely home offers top class accommodation with three en suite bedrooms, two with fabulous sea views and all having hospitality trays, colour TVs and central heating. There is a chiller for the convenience of guests.

Full English breakfasts are served in the lovely dining room, which has separate tables. Parking for three cars. Heather and John offer friendly and personal service to ensure guests are comfortable and content during their stay. Bed and Breakfast from £30 pppn; special rate midweek short breaks available. Non-smoking.

HEATHER AND JOHN HALL • Endeavour B&B
Upgang Lane, Whitby YO21 3EA
Tel: 01947 821110 • e-mail: hhall49@hotmail.com
www.holidayinwhitby.com

North Yorkshire
Whitby, York

"Come as a Guest - Leave as a Friend"
ASHFORD NON-SMOKING GUEST HOUSE

The Ashford is a family-run guest house providing a relaxed, informal atmosphere and friendly service. Situated on Whitby's West Cliff, the Ashford occupies a superb position in Royal Crescent, overlooking Crescent Gardens and the sea. It is ideally situated for coastal and country walks, and makes an excellent base for exploring the North York Moors. Take a short drive inland and visit "Heartbeat Country", the North York Moors Railway, Rievaulx Abbey, Pickering and a myriad of pretty moorland villages, or take the coast road to discover the attractions of Scarborough, Bridlington and Filey. A little further afield you will find the historic city of York and Harrogate.

- Totally non-smoking • Full central heating
- Comfortable lounge • All bedrooms have en suite facilities, courtesy tray and colour TV
- Good home cooking • Access at all times
- Short breaks available • VisitBritain ★★★

Bed and Breakfast from £26pppn

Janice and Donna Hillier
ASHFORD NON-SMOKING GUEST HOUSE
8 Royal Crescent, Whitby YO21 3EJ
Tel: 01947 602138
e-mail: info@ashfordguesthouse.co.uk
www.ashfordguesthouse.co.uk

Ryedale House

Exclusive to non-smokers, welcoming Yorkshire house of character at the foot of the moors, National Park "Heartbeat" country. Three-and-a-half-miles from Whitby. Magnificent scenery, moors, dales, picturesque harbours, cliffs, beaches, scenic railways, superb walking - it's all here! Highly commended, beautifully appointed rooms with private facilities, many extras. Guest lounge; breakfast room with views over Esk Valley. Enjoy the large south-facing terrace and landscaped gardens. Extensive traditional and vegetarian breakfast choice. Local inns and restaurants - two within a short walk. Parking available, also public transport

Bed and Breakfast: double £29-£31pppn, single £32pppn, minimum stay two nights • Weekly reductions all season.
Monday-Friday 4 night offers available (not high season) • Regret, no pets or children.

Mrs Pat Beale, Ryedale House, 156 Coach Road, Sleights, Near Whitby YO22 5EQ
Tel & Fax: 01947 810534 • www.ryedalehouse.co.uk

Fairthorne

John and Joan Harrison invite you for a restful holiday in a peaceful country setting - a dormer bungalow with central heating, TV, shaver points, tea making facilities and en suite in bedrooms; TV lounge and dining room. Pleasant family atmosphere. Situated three miles north of York, within easy reach of East Coast and Yorkshire Moors and near golf course. Bus stop 50 yards if required.
Private car park and large garden.

B&B from £25pppn (double room), £30 single • Reductions for children • Open all year

Mrs J.W. Harrison, Fairthorne, 356 Strensall Road, Earswick, York YO32 9SW • Tel & Fax: 01904 768609
e-mail: harros@tiscali.co.uk

The Cavalier
city centre accommodation
39 Monkgate, York YO31 7PB • Tel & Fax: 01904 636815

The Cavalier is an early Georgian Listed building, recently refurbished to provide very comfortable accommodation. It is ideally located close to the city centre and yards from the ancient city walls and most of the historic sites. Also convenient for touring North York Moors, Dales and East Coast resorts. Most rooms are en suite, and all have washbasins, colour TV, shaver points, radio alarms, and tea/coffee making facilities. Hairdryer and ironing facilities are available on request. Bed and full English breakfast with vegetarian options. Amenities include sauna, pay phone, garage parking, full central heating.

Full Fire Certificate • Open all year • Non-smoking
Winter/Spring mini-breaks available, details on request.

http://cavalier.yorkwebsites.co.uk

Blossoms York

Set in a Georgian townhouse on a leafy avenue, a warm welcome awaits at our friendly, family-run guest house. Located only minutes' walk from the historic Bar Walls and York Minster, restaurants, bars and shopping, we are in an ideal location for exploring York. We pride ourselves on offering a good service combined with value-for-money prices. All rooms are recently decorated and en suite with WC and shower; TV, tea tray and phone. Family rooms for up to 6 people. Bar and lounge. Free internet access and wi-fi. Free car park. Local information available.

Sun-Thurs from £22.50pp • Fri and Sat from £30pp.
3-night midweek spring and autumn specials from £20pp
See our website for latest prices and offers

Tel: 01904 652391
Fax: 01904 652392
e-mail: fhg@blossomsyork.co.uk

www.blossomsyork.co.uk

ST GEORGE'S

6 St George's Place,
York YO24 1DR
Tel: 01904 625056
Fax: 01904 625009
e-mail: sixstgeorg@aol.com
www.stgeorgesyork.com

St George's is a small and friendly family-run Victorian residence in a quiet cul-de-sac by York's beautiful racecourse.

- All rooms, one of which is on the ground floor, are en suite with tea/coffee tray and TV. • Non-smoking.
- Vegetarians are catered for. • Private enclosed parking.
- The hotel is only a 10-minute walk from the City Walls and many places of historic interest.
- £60 per double or twin room

HALL FARM
Gilling East, York YO62 4JW
e-mail: virginia@hallfarmgilling.co.uk
www.hallfarmgilling.co.uk
01439 788314

Come and stay with us at Hall Farm

A beautifully situated 400 acre working stock farm with extensive views over Ryedale. We offer a friendly, family welcome with home made scones on arrival. A ground floor double en suite room is available and includes hospitality tray with home-made biscuits. Sittingroom with TV and open fire on chilly evenings, diningroom with patio doors to conservatory. You will be the only guests so the breakfast time is up to you. Full English Breakfast includes home-made bread and preserves.

Terms from £30 per person.

Excellent eating places in Helmsley and the nearby villages. York, Castle Howard and the North York Moors within half-an-hour drive.

Church View B&B
Stockton-on-the-Forest, York YO32 9UP

This 200 year-old former farmhouse is located in the pretty village of Stockton on the Forest approximately 4 miles from York. All bedrooms are en suite and have been newly refurbished and decorated, each individually designed, from a romantic four-poster room to our popular large, ground floor family room. Cosy lounge with TV, video, music and real log fire on chilly evenings (you are welcome to bring your own wine). Breakfast of your choice, made with local produce, and home made jams will set you up for the day. The Fox Inn is just a stroll away, serving a good selection of local ales. Forest Park Golf Course lies to the rear of the house. We are ideally located for visiting the North Yorkshire Moors, East Coast (30 minutes by bus) and many more attractions. Many guests return - we hope to see you soon.

Prices from £25pp. **Lynn & Alan Manners**

tel: 01904 400403 • mobile: 07752 273371
e-mail: manners@87churchview.fsnet.co.uk • www.bandbyork.co.uk

HIGH BELTHORPE

Set on an ancient moated site at the foot of the Yorkshire Wolds, this comfortable Victorian farmhouse offers huge breakfasts, private fishing and fabulous walks. With York only 13 miles away, it is a peaceful rural idyll that both dogs and owners will love. Open all year except Christmas. From £25.

Bishop Wilton, York YO42 1SB
Tel: 01759 368238
Mobile: 07786 923330
www.holidayswithdogs.com

Newton House

Diana and John offer all their guests a friendly and warm welcome to their Victorian end town house a few minutes' walk from the city centre, York's beautiful Minster, medieval walls and museums. We are only a 40 mile drive from coastal resorts, the lovely Yorkshire Moors and Dales. Three double/twin en suite rooms, colour TV, tea/coffee tray, central heating. Breakfast menu. Car park. NON-SMOKING. Fire Certificate. Terms from £26pp.

Newton House, Neville Street, Haxby Road, York YO31 8NP • 01904 635627

York House

York's premier Bed & Breakfast

Receive a warm welcome at this family-run guesthouse. Enjoy breakfast in our attractive conservatory or outside on our beautiful patio. York House is approximately 10 minutes' walk from York Minster and is the perfect base for a visit to York or the surrounding areas. Rooms offer all the conveniences you could need for a relaxing and enjoyable stay.

These are just a few of the facilities offered:
- en suite shower or bath facilities
- four-poster • double, twin, family and single rooms
- tea/coffee making facilities
- off-street parking • free wifi access
- full English/vegetarian breakfast.
- No smoking establishment
- Prices from £29pppn.
- Children welcome

David and Katherine Leedham • York House, 62 Heworth Green, York YO31 7TQ
Tel & Fax: 01904 427070
e-mail: yorkhouse.bandb@tiscali.co.uk • www.yorkhouseyork.co.uk

North Yorkshire
York

THE NEW INN MOTEL
Main Street, Huby
York YO61 1HQ
Tel: 01347 810219
AA ★★★ HIGHLY COMMENDED

Nestling behind the New Inn, this modern, motel-style accommodation has a quiet location in the village of Huby, 9 miles north of York. Comfortable bedrooms are spacious and neatly furnished, and breakfast, which makes use of locally sourced produce, is served in the cosy dining room. The reception area hosts an array of tourist information, and the resident owners provide a very friendly and helpful service. Pets by arrangement.

8 en suite non-smoking ground floor rooms of which 3 are family rooms • Parking available
Prices from £35-£50 (single) and £60-£70 (double) • Tea/coffee, central heating and TV

www.newinnmotel.co.uk • enquiries@newinnmotel.freeserve.co.uk

SB

FOURPOSTER LODGE
ETC ★★★

Your hosts, Shirley and Gary, welcome you to their imaginatively named Victorian villa. Enjoy the relaxing atmosphere, the comfort and luxury of our four-poster beds. Start the day with the house speciality "a hearty English breakfast". Take a leisurely 10-minute stroll to York's historic city centre with all its fascinations. Fulford Golf Course, and York University are also invitingly close. We are licensed and have a private car park.
For more information or a brochure, please contact:

68/70 Heslington Road, York YO10 5AU
Tel & Fax: 01904 651170
www.fourposterlodge.co.uk

A warm and friendly welcome awaits you at Cumbria House - an elegant, tastefully decorated Victorian guest house, where comfort and quality are assured. We are convenient for the city, being only 15 minutes' walk from York's historic Minster and yet within minutes of the northern by-pass (A1237). A launderette, bank and children's park are close by. 
All rooms have colour TV, radio alarms and tea/coffee facilities. Most are en suite and all are non-smoking. Central heating. Fire Certificate. Guests' car park.

Full English breakfast or vegetarian alternative • Non-smoking • B&B £27 to £30 per person
Cumbria House, 2 Vyner Street, Haxby Road, York YO31 8HS • 01904 636817
e-mail: candj@cumbriahouse.freeserve.co.uk • www.cumbriahouse.com

SB

Alder Carr House

• A country house, set in its own extensive grounds, offering spacious and comfortable accommodation.
• All bedrooms look towards the rolling hills of the Yorkshire Wolds.
• Only a 10 minute drive to York's Park & Ride enables you to combine city sightseeing with quiet country relaxation.
• A wide range of restaurants and country pubs in a three mile radius gives excellent choice for evening meals.
• An ideal base for exploring the many aspects of Yorkshire.
• Twin/double/family rooms - all en suite or private bathroom. • Prices from £30 per person.

Mr and Mrs G. Steel, Alder Carr House, York Road, Barmby Moor, York YO42 4HT
Tel: 01759 380566 • mobile: 07885 277740 • e-mail: chris.steel@aldercarrhouse.plus.com

Oaklands Guest House

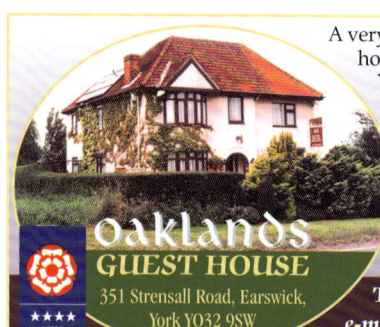

A very warm welcome awaits you at our attractive family home set in open countryside, yet only three miles from York. Ideally situated for City, Coast, Dales and Moors.

Our comfortable bedrooms have central heating
* en suite facilities • colour TV • razor point
* tea & coffee tray • radio alarms • hairdryers

Full breakfast is served in a light airy dining room. Discounts available. Open all year. No pets. Smoking in garden only.

Bed and full English Breakfast from £23.

351 Strensall Road, Earswick, York YO32 9SW
Telephone: 01904 768443
e-mail: mavmo@oaklands5.fsnet.co.uk

ASCOT HOUSE
80 East Parade, York YO31 7YH
Tel: 01904 426826 • Fax: 01904 431077
ETC/AA ★★★★ • ETC SILVER AWARD

An attractive Victorian villa with easy access to the historic city centre by walking or by public transport. Most rooms have four-poster or canopy beds, and family and double rooms are en suite. All rooms have central heating, colour TV and tea/coffee facilities. Sauna available to hire by the hour. Private enclosed car park.

Singles from £30 to £70, doubles £60 to £76 including Traditional English Breakfast and VAT.

e-mail: admin@ascothouseyork.com • www.ascothouseyork.com

Other specialised holiday guides from FHG

PUBS & INNS OF BRITAIN

COUNTRY HOTELS OF BRITAIN

WEEKEND & SHORT BREAKS IN BRITAIN & IRELAND

THE GOLF GUIDE WHERE TO PLAY, WHERE TO STAY

PETS WELCOME!

SELF-CATERING HOLIDAYS IN BRITAIN

500 GREAT PLACES TO STAY IN BRITAIN

CARAVAN & CAMPING HOLIDAYS IN BRITAIN

FAMILY BREAKS IN BRITAIN

Published annually: available in all good bookshops or direct from the publisher:

FHG Guides, Abbey Mill Business Centre, Seedhill, Paisley PA1 1TJ
Tel: 0141 887 0428 • Fax: 0141 889 7204
e-mail: admin@fhguides.co.uk • www.holidayguides.com

South Yorkshire

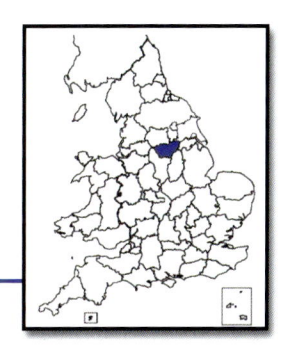

Doncaster

Rock Farm

Rock Farm, Hooton Pagnell,
Doncaster DN5 7BT
Tel/Fax: 01977 642200
Mobile: 07785 916186
e-mail: info@rockfarm.info
www.rockfarm.info

★★★ FARMHOUSE

A warm welcome and a hearty breakfast await guests at this Grade II Listed stone farmhouse on a 200-acre mixed farm. Situated in the picturesque stone-built village of Hooton Pagnell, six miles north-west of Doncaster, 5 minutes from the A1 and Brodsworth Hall, 10 minutes M62, M1 and M18. Open all year.

Single, double or twin rooms and a twin-bedded suite.

Family rooms from £70, Double rooms from £60
Twin from £50, Single from £30

Visit the FHG website
www.holidayguides.com
for details of the wide choice of accommodation featured in the full range of FHG titles

West Yorkshire

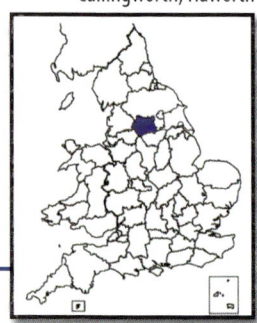

Cullingworth, Haworth

If you are looking for a warm and comfortable environment in which to relax and enjoy your stay whilst visiting Yorkshire then The Manor will be perfect for you. This luxurious 5 Star Silver Award retreat offers a relaxing and refreshing base from which to explore some of the most beautiful countryside in Yorkshire. Lovingly restored, this 18th Century Manor House is enhanced by many original features. Ideally situated for exploring the rugged Pennine moorland or Bronte Country, the Yorkshire Dales and beyond.

The Manor Guest House
Sutton Drive, Cullingworth, Bradford BD13 5BQ
Tel: 01535 274274 • e-mail: michele.cotter@btinternet.com
www.cullingworthmanor.co.uk

Far Laithe Farm, Laycock, Keighley, BD22 0PU
Tel: 01535 661993 • Contact: Mrs Sylvia Lee • e-mail: sylvia@farlaithefarm.co.uk

This traditional 17th century Yorkshire farm is close to Haworth, Skipton and the Dales, in the heart of open countryside. Visitors are warmly welcomed and will enjoy the wonderful cosy and peaceful atmosphere. Tea-making facilities and colour TV in all bedrooms. Luxury en suite facilities. Dinner is served in the licensed oak-furnished diningroom where great pride taken in the quality of the food. Guests are welcome to relax in the comfortable parlour, or spend some time in the peaceful garden, with beautiful views.

www.farlaithefarm.co.uk

symbols

🚭	Totally non-smoking		🐕	Pets Welcome
🎠	Children Welcome		**SB**	Short Breaks
♿	Suitable for Disabled Guests		🍷	Licensed

West Yorkshire
Wakefield

The Bank House Hotel
11 Bank Street, Westgate, Wakefield WF1 1EH
Tel: 01924 368248 • Fax: 01924 363724

We are a small family-run business with a warm and friendly welcome to all our guests. Our staff are always happy to help ensure your stay is a pleasant one. Our rooms are all en suite, with tea/coffee making facilities and Sky TV. All parties are welcome and are catered for.

We are two miles from the M1 and M62 and five miles from the A1.
The main Westgate rail station and bus station are five minutes away. Our location is in the city centre, based near the Ridings shopping complex, the Theatre Royal Opera House, and all the popular Westgate nightlife. We have many local attractions nearby, which our staff will be happy to direct you to.

The FHG Directory of Website Addresses
on pages 347-362 is a useful quick reference guide for holiday accommodation with e-mail and/or website details

Please note
All the information in this book is given in good faith in the belief that it is correct. However, the publishers cannot guarantee the facts given in these pages, neither are they responsible for changes in policy, ownership or terms that may take place after the date of going to press. Readers should always satisfy themselves that the facilities they require are available and that the terms, if quoted, still apply.

Durham

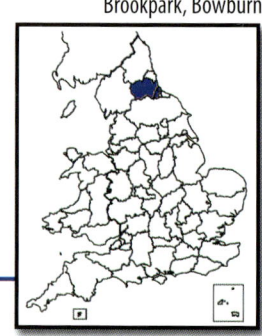

Brookpark, Bowburn

My Way Guest House

is situated in an ideal location just outside Durham City, with easy access to the major road network and well placed for both the business visitor to Durham and tourists visiting the county.

The tastefully furnished conservatory and breakfast room is an ideal place to start your day, with a choice of both continental and Full English breakfast included in the room price.

All our tastefully furnished rooms have en suite or private facilities and private entrance. Each opens onto a decked patio area, an ideal location for those evening drinks overlooking the gardens as the sun sets over the valley beyond.

My Way Guest House provides excellent relaxing facilities with easy access to Durham City.

West Farm, Broompark, Co Durham DH7 7RW
Tel: 0191 375 0874
www.mywayguesthouse.co.uk • e-mail: info@mywayguesthouse.co.uk

---

BOWBURN. The Hillrise Guest House, 13 Durham Road West, Bowburn, Durham DH6 5AU (0191 377 0302; Fax: 0191 377 0898).
Located at Junction 61 of the A1(M). The Hillrise Guest House, Bowburn, is approximately 300 metres down from the roundabout on the left hand side. We are conveniently placed for both the city of Durham and the county, besides being handy for nearby towns such as Chester-le-Street, Washington, Spennymoor, Stockton, Middlesborough and Sunderland. The Guest House offers a very high standard of accommodation and home cooked food. Most of the rooms are en suite with colour TV and hospitality tray. No smoking throughout the building, but there is a small patio area outside the dining room for the convenience of smokers.
enjoyEngland.com ★★★ *GUEST ACCOMMODATION.*
e-mail: enquiries@hill-rise.com   www.hill-rise.com

Terms quoted in this publication may be subject to increase if rises in costs necessitate

Durham

NORTH EAST ENGLAND 197

Castleside, Durham, Frosterley in Weardale

Charming farmhouse with stunning views.
You will be most welcome.
Ideal for Newcastle, Durham, Beamish etc.
Bed and Breakfast; dinner available, licensed.
Great for pets.

IRENE MORDEY AND DAVID BLACKBURN,
BEE COTTAGE FARMHOUSE,
CASTLESIDE, CONSETT DH8 9HW
Tel: 01207 508224

e-mail: beecottage68@aol.com • www.beecottage.co.uk

Hamsteels Hall

Hamsteels Hall is an 18th century Country House, Grade II Listed, tastefully restored but retaining all its original features – inglenook fireplaces, shuttered windows, panelled rooms etc. It is in an elevated position, with fantastic views. Spacious and comfortable en suite rooms with TV/video, hospitality tray etc; all double rooms have four-poster beds. Relax in the gardens, by the pond with its water features, or walk to the nearby garden centre, or the Browney River with its rustic picnic area. Only 10 minutes' drive to Durham City and Beamish Open Air Museum. Ideal for touring Northumbria. Walkers and cyclists welcome.

Contact June Whitfield for details or check out our website.

Hamsteels Hall, Hamsteels Lane, Quebec, Durham DH7 9RS
Tel: 01207 520388
e-mail: june@hamsteelshall.co.uk • www.hamsteelshall.co.uk

Newlands Hall, Frosterley in Weardale, Bishop Auckland DL13 2SH

A warm welcome awaits you on our beef and sheep farm surrounded by beautiful open countryside with its magnificent views of Weardale - an Area of Outstanding Natural Beauty. Rich in wildlife, the farm is at the centre of a network of local footpaths. The area has much to offer visitors, ranging from the high wild fells of Weardale and Teesdale to pretty villages, market towns and the University City of Durham, with its cathedral, castle and medieval streets.
Accommodation comprises a family room with en suite bathroom and a family room with en suite shower. Both rooms have stunning views, tea/coffee making facilities, TV, hairdryer, radio alarm and central heating. Sorry no pets and no smoking indoors. Full English breakfast is served with homemade bread, our own free range eggs and other local produce.

Bed and Breakfast from £27.50 per person per night, reduced rates for children under 10 years old sharing. Open Easter to October.

01388 529233 or 07970 032517
e-mail: carol@newlandshall.co.uk • www.newlandshall.co.uk

198 NORTH EAST ENGLAND **Durham**

Spennymoor, Stanley, Waterhouses

Highview Country House

Set in picturesque countryside, Highview Country House is ideal for peace and tranquillity. The guesthouse is situated on the outskirts of a quiet village, just a short walk to public houses serving food. Only 10 minutes from the A1M motorway, junction 60, and the beautiful historic City of Durham, our location allows easy access to explore the North East of England. All rooms are equipped with en suite shower facility, TV, fridge and hospitality tray. We offer a hearty breakfast of Full English, fresh fruit, cereals and yoghurts. Set in our own grounds we offer plenty of off road parking.
Bed and Breakfast rates from £30 per person per night.

Kirk Merrington, Near Spennymoor DL16 7JT • 01388 811006
e-mail: jayne@highviewcountryhouse.co.uk • www.highviewcountryhouse.co.uk

Bushblades Farm
Harperley, Stanley, County Durham

Comfortable Georgian farmhouse set in large garden. Twin ground floor en suite, and double first floor en suite bedrooms. All rooms have tea/coffee making facilities, colour TV and easy chairs. Ample parking. Children over 12 years welcome. Sorry, no pets.
Bed and Breakfast from £35-£40 single, £60-£65 double.
Self-catering accommodation also available.

Telephone: 01207 232722
e-mail: bushbladesfarm@hotmail.com

Near Durham, Metro Centre, Beamish Museum; Hadrian's Wall, Northumberland Coast under an hour.

Ivesley Equestrian Centre
Ivesley, Waterhouses, Durham DH7 9HB
Tel: 0191 373 4324 • Fax: 0191 373 4757

Ivesley is a comfortable 18th century country house set in its own 220 acres of farmland and countryside. There is a large drawing room and a large dining room. Most bedrooms have private facilities, and all have been decorated and furnished to a very high standard. Excellent food and wine is served; fully licensed.

Contact Mrs P.A. Booth.
Bed and Breakfast
Fully inclusive
Riding Holidays

Situated 7 miles from Durham, this is an ideal base for exploring the North East. Handy for exploring Durham University and Beamish Museum.

e-mail: ivesley@msn.com • www.ridingholidays-ivesley.co.uk

Northumberland
Alnwick

Northumberland

Alndyke Farmhouse B&B

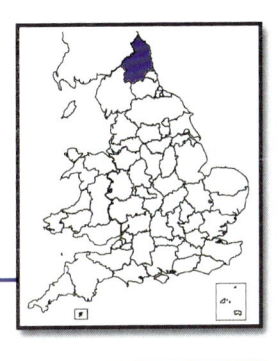

Alndyke Farmhouse is a Georgian Grade II Listed farmhouse set in 500 acres of arable farmland which has been in the Davison family for 3 generations.

All the en suite guest rooms are spacious and tastefully decorated, with colour TV, radio alarm and hairdryer. A hospitality tray is provided on arrival, with tea, coffee and home-made shortbread. Breakfast is served in the south-facing dining room which enjoys great countryside views. The relaxing guest lounge has a wood burning stove - sit back with a good book, enjoy the view or watch TV.

Alndyke is perfect for visiting Northumberland - 10 minutes by car to the beach, and a 30 minute walk to the historic town of Alnwick with its castle and gardens.

Strictly non-smoking. Private car park.

Alnmouth Road, Alnwick NE66 3PB
Tel: 01665 510252 • e-mail: laura@alndyke.co.uk • www.alndyke.co.uk

---

Comfortable farmhouse accommodation on working mixed farm situated on the Heritage Coast between the villages of Craster and Howick. Ideal base for walking, golfing, bird-watching or exploring the coast, moors and historic castles. The Farne Islands, famous for their colonies of seals and seabirds, and Lindisfarne (Holy Island) are within easy driving distance. Accommodation is in two double rooms with washbasins. Guests have their own TV lounge/dining room with full central heating. Bed and Breakfast from £25. Open April to October. Non-smoking.

Howick Scar Farm House
Craster, Alnwick NE66 3SU
Tel & Fax: 01665 576665
e-mail: stay@howickscar.co.uk
www.howickscar.co.uk

Redfoot Lea

Part of a recently converted farmsteading dating back to 1850. On the outskirts of Alnwick (1.5 miles), the house has the advantage of being in the country, while being close to local amenities and attractions, bars and restaurants. There are two cosy, co-ordinated, well equipped bedrooms on the ground floor, a beautiful sitting room with a south-facing aspect, and a spectacular dining hall. Open all year. North Northumberland Local Food 'Gold Award'.

Greensfield Moor Farm, Alnwick NE66 2HH
Tel: 01665 603891 • Fax: 01665 606429 • Mobile: 07870 586214
info@redfootlea.co.uk • www.redfootlea.co.uk

Hawkhill Farmhouse *a place to relax*

This spacious farmhouse is situated in the open countryside of rural Northumberland between the historic market town of Alnwick and the breathtaking coast.

It is an ideal base for exploring this beautiful region, or an ideal retreat for anyone looking to 'get away from it all'. For families there is plenty to see and do - spend all your days exploring the rugged unspoilt Northumberland coast or visiting castles and historic houses.

Hawkhill Farmhouse has an elegant dining room, and a large drawing room with access to the extensive grounds.

The one double and two twin-bedded rooms are en suite, with TV, tea/coffee making facilities and hairdryer. All rooms enjoy extensive views over fields and countryside.
There is plenty of secluded private parking.
Double £35-£40pppn, Single £40-£47.

Mrs Margery Vickers, Hawkhill Farmhouse,
Lesbury, Alnwick NE66 3PG
Tel: 01665 830380 07989 258295 • Fax: 01665 830093
e-mail: stay@hawkhillfarmhouse.com
www.hawkhillfarmhouse.com

Northumberland

NORTH EAST ENGLAND 201

Berwick-Upon-Tweed

Clovelly is a centrally situated town house only minutes away from good golf courses, riverside walks, the Elizabethan Walls, restaurants, shops and the Maltings Art Centre.

A high standard of accommodation is offered, with many thoughtful little extras and a delicious multi-choice breakfast. Single, double and twin rooms, all en suite.

This is a non-smoking house.
Residents' parking tickets supplied.
Open all year.
B&B £27.50 to £35.

Vivienne Lawrence
CLOVELLY HOUSE
58 West Street,
Berwick-upon-Tweed TD15 IAS
Tel: 01289 302337

e-mail: vivroc@clovelly53.freeserve.co.uk
www.clovelly53.freeserve.co.uk

SB

Situated one minute from Berwick-upon-Tweed's main thoroughfare this hotel is surrounded by walls and ramparts built by Queen Elizabeth I to protect Berwick. Accommodation consists of two family rooms, one double, one twin/triple and one single room (can sleep up to 14). All are en suite with colour TV, tea/coffee, central heating, hairdryer, trouser press and ironing facilities. A wide range of attractions and activities are on offer with lots of beaches and picnic areas within easy walking distance. Ideal centre point for visits to Edinburgh and Newcastle. Private parking. Restaurant and bar lounge. Vegetarians also catered for.

Fred and Lynda Miller, Cobbled Yard Hotel,
40 Walkergate, Berwick-upon-Tweed, Northumberland TD15 1DJ
Tel: 01289 308 407 • Fax: 01289 330 623
e-mail: allmail@cobbledyardhotel.onyxnet.co.uk
www.cobbledyardhotel.com

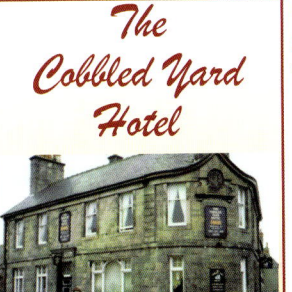

The Cobbled Yard Hotel

Friendly Hound Cottage
Ford Common,
Berwick-upon-Tweed TD15 2QD

Set in a quiet rural location, convenient for Holy Island, Berwick, Bamburgh and the Heritage coastline. Come and enjoy our top quality accommodation, excellent breakfasts, and warm welcome. *Arrive as our guests and leave as our friends.*

Tel: 01289 388554 • www.friendlyhoundcottage.co.uk

NORTHUMBERLAND
Corbridge, Ellingham

Low Fotherley is an impressive Victorian farmhouse built around 1895 situated on the A68 south of Riding Mill in the beautiful Northumbrian countryside with outstanding views. The market towns of Hexham and Corbridge are nearby. Explore Hadrian's Wall, Durham, Beamish, Kielder, the Scottish Borders, Northumberland's coastline, Bamburgh and the Farne Islands. The farmhouse has lots of character, with open fireplaces and beams. The house is spacious and comfortable.

Our rooms are of a high standard. One twin en suite, one double en suite and one double with private facilities, all with full central heating, TV, tea/coffee making facilities, hairdryer and radio. Farmhouse breakfast is cooked on the Aga with toast, home-made jams and marmalade. Families welcome. No smoking. £27.50-£30.00 per person, discounts for children.

ETC ★★★★
FARM STAY UK MEMBER.

Mrs L. Adamson, Low Fotherley Farm, Riding Mill, Corbridge NE44 6BB
Tel: 01434 682277
e-mail: hugh@lowfotherley.fsnet.co.uk • www.westfarm.freeserve.co.uk

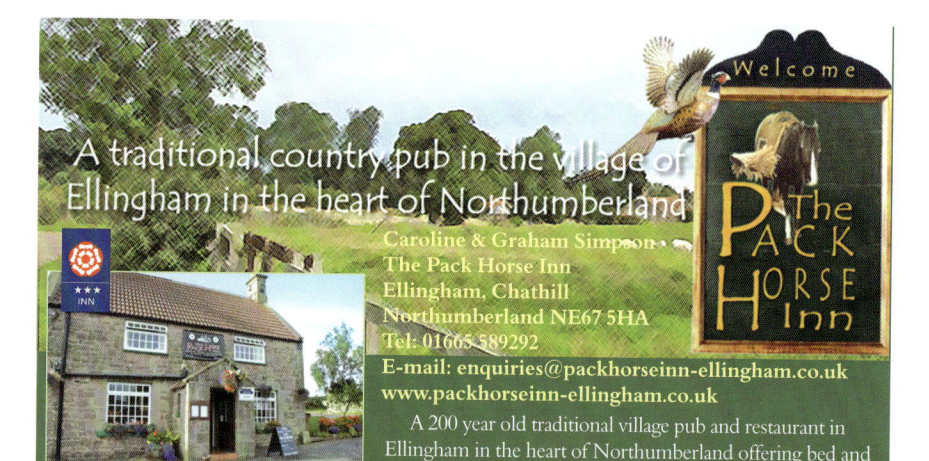

A traditional country pub in the village of Ellingham in the heart of Northumberland

Caroline & Graham Simpson
The Pack Horse Inn
Ellingham, Chathill
Northumberland NE67 5HA
Tel: 01665 589292
E-mail: enquiries@packhorseinn-ellingham.co.uk
www.packhorseinn-ellingham.co.uk

A 200 year old traditional village pub and restaurant in Ellingham in the heart of Northumberland offering bed and breakfast and self catering holiday accommodation"

Ellingham has changed little since the ancient drovers' roads were well-travelled routes, and the Packhorse Inn offers an oasis of rural tranquillity, a superb location for exploring Northumberland or just for a peaceful and enjoyable break from your journey.

Bed & breakfast accommodation in two double and three twin-bedded rooms. Every room has a colour television, tea and coffee making facilities and an en suite shower-room or bathroom. There is also an adjoining self-contained cottage which sleeps four people. Families with children are made very welcome at the Packhorse Inn, whether for a meal or to stay. There's a sunny beer garden to the rear of the Inn looking out across the village field. We also have a comfortable family lounge adjoining our bar.

Northumberland

NORTH EAST ENGLAND 203

Gilsland, Haltwhistle

Hadrian's Wall
Northumberland

Bush Nook

Overlooking Hadrian's Wall, Bush Nook Guest House offers comfortable accommodation in a stunning location.

Featured in *'Cumbria Life'* magazine and on TV's *'Britain's Best Breaks'* Bush Nook has a reputation for quality and hospitality. With a guest lounge and conservatory, many guests return to relax, unwind and enjoy award-winning dinners served in our licensed dining room.

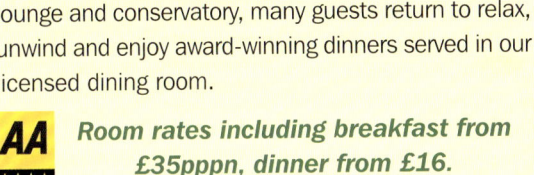

AA — Guest Accommodation ★★★★

Room rates including breakfast from £35pppn, dinner from £16.

Silver SILVER AWARD

Bush Nook, Upper Denton, Gilsland CA8 7AF
Tel: 01697 747194 • www.bushnook.co.uk
info@bushnook.co.uk

SB

Saughy Rigg Farm

info@saughyrigg.co.uk
www.saughyrigg.co.uk

- High quality en suite rooms
- Delicious home-cooked food
- Open to non-residents
- Pets and families welcome

Saughy Rigg Farm, Twice Brewed, Haltwhistle, Northumberland NE49 9PT • Tel: 01434 344120

---

symbols

🚭 Totally non-smoking	🐕 Pets Welcome
🐎 Children Welcome	**SB** Short Breaks
♿ Suitable for Disabled Guests	🍷 Licensed

Struthers Farm
Catton, Allendale, Hexham NE47 9LP

Struthers Farm offers a warm welcome in the heart of England, with many splendid local walks from the farm itself. Panoramic views. Situated in an area of outstanding beauty. Double/twin rooms, en suite bathrooms, central heating. Good farmhouse cooking. Ample safe parking. Come and share our home and enjoy beautiful countryside. Near Hadrian's Wall (½ hour's drive). Children welcome, pets by prior arrangement. Open all year.

Bed and Breakfast from £30; Optional Evening Meal from £12.50.

Contact Mrs Ruby Keenleyside
01434 683580

Carr Edge Farmhouse

Enjoy a warm farmhouse welcome in this skilfully converted late 18thC Granary and Stable block which is attached to the farmhouse. Overlooking the South Tyne Valley, it has spectacular views of the North Pennines and provides an ideal base for walkers and cyclists. We offer a local pick up and drop off service.

There is a choice of traditional farmhouse, continental or vegetarian breakfasts, all served in the stone flagged breakfast room. Lounge for relaxing in, with TV, books and board games. All three guest bedrooms are en suite and centrally heated, with tea and coffee facilities, electric blankets and hair dryers. Boot room. Drying, laundry and ironing facilities are available.

From £35pp single; Double/Twin/Family from £30pp.

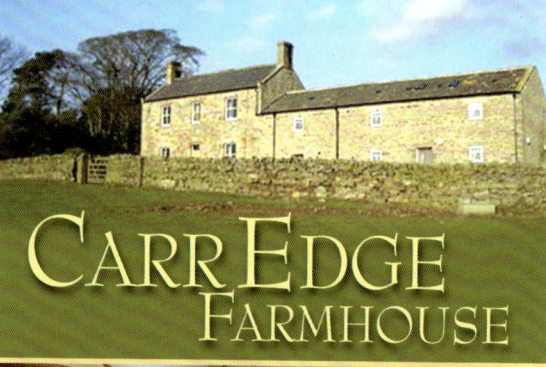

Michael & Sandie Gibson, Carr Edge Farmhouse Newbrough, Hexham, Northumberland NE47 5EA
Tel: 01434 674788 • Mobile: 07789 752517
E-mail: stay@carredge.co.uk • www.carredge.co.uk

Northumberland

NORTH EAST ENGLAND 205

Hexham

Battlesteads Hotel & Restaurant

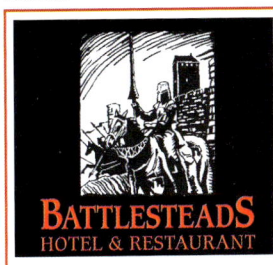

**Wark
Hexham
Northumberland
NE48 3LS
01434 230209**

Silver Award

Dating from 1747, this stone-built inn and restaurant features excellent bar meals and à la carte menus, good choice of wines, and cask and conditioned beers. A friendly, family-run hotel, with 17 en suite bedrooms, including ground floor rooms with disabled access, it is ideally placed for Hadrian's Wall, Kielder and Border Reiver Country.

• Pets are very welcome.

From £50-£60pppn

**e-mail: info@battlesteads.com
www.battlesteads.com**

GREENCARTS FARM
www.greencarts.co.uk

Greencarts is a working farm situated in Roman Wall country, ideally placed for exploring by car, bike or walking. It has magnificent views of the Tyne Valley. It is warm and homely, with central heating and log fires. Home-cooked food is provided. En suite accommodation with safe car/bike parking. Convenient for Hexham Racecourse; fishing available locally. All welcome. Bed and Breakfast from £25 to £40. Open all year. Campsite and bunk barn also available.

Mr & Mrs D Maughan, Greencarts Farm,
Humshaugh, Hexham NE46 4BW
Tel/Fax: 01434 681320
e-mail: sandra@greencarts.co.uk

Publisher's note

While every effort is made to ensure accuracy, we regret that FHG Guides cannot accept responsibility for errors, misrepresentations or omissions in our entries or any consequences thereof. Prices in particular should be checked.

We will follow up complaints but cannot act as arbiters or agents for either party.

NORTH EAST ENGLAND

Northumberland

Longframlingham, Morpeth, Otterburn

The Anglers Arms
A Legend in the very Heart of Northumberland

This traditional Coaching Inn is situated only 6 miles from Morpeth, beside picturesque Weldon Bridge on the River Coquet. Bedrooms are cosy and welcoming, with a touch of olde worlde charm. Be prepared for a hearty Northumbrian breakfast!

Meals can be be enjoyed in the friendly bar, or outdoors on sunny summer days; alternatively dine in style and sophistication in the à la carte Pullman Railway Carriage restaurant. Ideal for exploring both coast and country, the Inn also caters for fishermen, with its own one-mile stretch of the River Coquet available free to residents.

The Anglers Arms
Weldon Bridge, Longframlington,
Northumberland NE65 8AX
Tel: 01665 570271/570655
Fax: 01665 570041
info@anglersarms.fsnet.co.uk
www.anglersarms.com

---

40 Bullers Green, Morpeth
Northumberland NE61 1DE • 01670 503195

Located close to the centre of Morpeth, convenient for shopping, restaurants, pubs and entertainment. Convenient for A1 and with excellent transport links to Newcastle upon Tyne and the rest of Northumberland. All our comfortable bedrooms are well appointed, with TV and tea & coffee making facilities. Hair dryer, iron and ironing board available. Wireless internet hot-spot. Conservatory. No pets.

single rooms • twin rooms • double rooms • some en suite.

enquiries@cottingburnhouse.co.uk
www.cottingburnhouse.co.uk

Cottingburn House
Bed and Breakfast

SB

Welcome to our farmhouse, built in the 1400s in Border Reiver country, on a 960 acre stock farm in an Area of Outstanding Natural Beauty. Panoramic views of the Rede Valley and the Cheviot Hills. Private fishing and stables. Wide range of facilities nearby. Spacious en suite bedrooms and guests' lounge in self contained part of our home. Tasty breakfast. Open all year. Children and pets welcome. Terms from £30 twin/double, £35 single.

Mrs Jane Walton, Dunns Houses, Otterburn,
Newcastle Upon Tyne NE19 1LB • 01830 520677
e-mail: dunnshouses@hotmail.com • www.northumberlandfarmholidays.co.uk

Northumberland
Otterburn, Rothbury

NORTH EAST ENGLAND

COUNTRY SIDE BREAKS

Come to the heart of rural Northumberland and stay in the historic 3 ★★★ Otterburn Tower. Nestling in 32 acres of woodland and terraced gardens, it is the ideal place to get away from it all, with the best of local produce created for you by our team of chefs. All our rooms are en suite, comfortable and unique. Come and have an active weekend – learn Clay Target Shooting, Fishing, go on a Quad Bike safari. Explore Kielder Water, walk Hadrian's Wall or just relax.

THE OTTERBURN TOWER Country House Hotel & Restaurant
01830 520620 email info@otterburntower.com

Glimpse the red squirrel from our splendid 18th century Georgian farmhouse on this 1100 acre livestock farm. Relax in beautifully appointed, spacious en suite bedrooms with superb views over open countryside. Elegant, comfortable lounge with log fire. Delicious Aga cooked breakfasts using local produce, with home-made bread and preserves. Ideally located for visiting Northumberland's many attractions including Alnwick Castle and Gardens and National Trust Cragside.

- *'Pride of Northumbria' Best B&B Award Winner*
- *Open January-December • Children and pets welcome*
- *Terms from £35-£37.50 twin/double, £45-£50 single.*

Lee Farm, Near Rothbury, Longframlington, Morpeth NE65 8JQ
Contact: Mrs Susan Aynsley • Tel & Fax: 01665 570257
e-mail: enqs@leefarm.co.uk • www.leefarm.co.uk

Katerina's Guest House

High Street, Rothbury NE65 7TQ • 01669 620691

Charming old guest house, ideally situated for the amenities of pretty Rothbury village, and to explore Northumberland's hills, coast, Alnwick Castle and gardens. Beautiful bedrooms, each decorated and colour co-ordinated to enhance its individual character; some with original stone fireplaces/beamed ceilings, all en suite, with four-poster beds, TV, and superbly stocked tea tray (with home-made scones!). Wide, interesting choice of breakfasts; licensed evening meals also available – sample Cath's bread, 'whisky porridge', vegetarian nutballs, or Steak Katerina.

Bed and Breakfast from £64-£74 per room per night, depending on number of nights booked.

e-mail: cath@katerinasguesthouse.co.uk www.katerinasguesthouse.co.uk

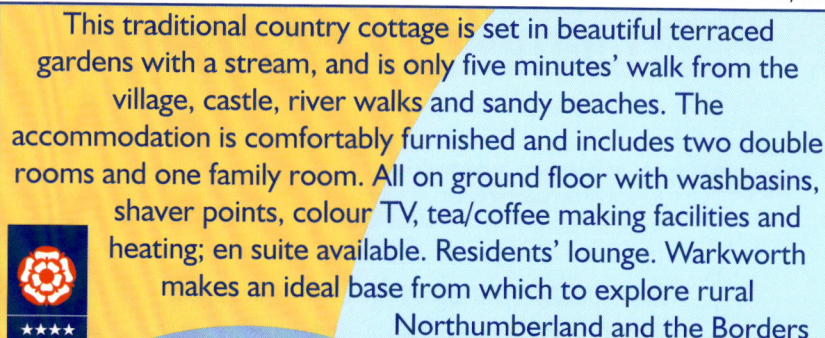

Northumberland

Warkworth, Wooler

This traditional country cottage is set in beautiful terraced gardens with a stream, and is only five minutes' walk from the village, castle, river walks and sandy beaches. The accommodation is comfortably furnished and includes two double rooms and one family room. All on ground floor with washbasins, shaver points, colour TV, tea/coffee making facilities and heating; en suite available. Residents' lounge. Warkworth makes an ideal base from which to explore rural Northumberland and the Borders with their unspoilt beauty and historic interest.

Children welcome, reduced rates
Non-smokers • Private parking
Colour brochure available • Open all year
Terms from £30pppn; en suite from £32pppn.

e-mail: beck-n-call@lineone.net
www.beck-n-call.co.uk
Tel: 01665 711653

Beck'N'Call
Birling West Cottage
Warkworth NE65 0XS

Looking for Holiday Accommodation?

FHG
KUPERARD

for details of hundreds of properties throughout the UK, visit our website

www.holidayguides.com

Tyne & Wear
Heddon-on-the-Wall

Tyne & Wear

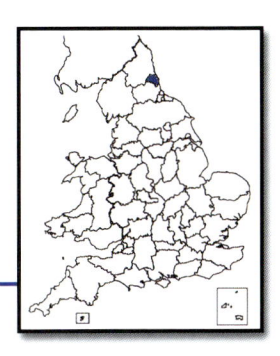

NORTH EAST ENGLAND 209

Ironsign Farm B&B
Country House & Farm Restaurant

Ironsign is a country house, ideally situated for a variety of visitors. Set in the Tyne Valley in beautiful surroundings yet within easy reach of Newcastle and the historic towns of Hexham and Corbridge. Newcastle airport is also easily accessed.

All rooms are en suite and tastefully decorated. One ground floor room has good access for disabled guests. Guests can dine in the farm restaurant where the menu features favourite French and other European dishes, using mainly local produce.

Ironsign Farm B&B
Military Road, Heddon-on-the-Wall, Newcastle-upon-Tyne NE15 0JB
Tel: 01661 853802

symbols

🚭	Totally non-smoking	🐕	Pets Welcome
🎠	Children Welcome	**SB**	Short Breaks
♿	Suitable for Disabled Guests	🍷	Licensed

210　NORTH EAST ENGLAND　　　　　　　　　　Tyne & Wear
Newcastle-Upon-Tyne

New Kent Hotel

127 Osborne Road,
Jesmond,
Newcastle-upon-Tyne
NE2 2TB
Tel: 0191-281 7711
Fax: 0191-281 3369

This privately owned hotel is situated in a quiet location, but only minutes from the city centre. It has built up a reputation for good food and friendly, efficient service in a warm and congenial atmosphere. All bedrooms are en suite, with hospitality tray, direct-dial telephone, colour TV with satellite, and radio. There is a spacious cocktail lounge and a restaurant serving the best of modern and classic cuisine. Local attractions include the Metro Centre, Northumbria National Park, Holy Island and Bamburgh Castle.
Single from £52.50, double from £89.50.

AA ★★★

Other specialised holiday guides from FHG

PUBS & INNS OF BRITAIN

COUNTRY HOTELS OF BRITAIN

WEEKEND & SHORT BREAKS IN BRITAIN & IRELAND

THE GOLF GUIDE WHERE TO PLAY, WHERE TO STAY

PETS WELCOME!

SELF-CATERING HOLIDAYS IN BRITAIN

500 GREAT PLACES TO STAY IN BRITAIN

CARAVAN & CAMPING HOLIDAYS IN BRITAIN

FAMILY BREAKS IN BRITAIN

Published annually: available in all good bookshops or direct from the publisher:
FHG Guides, Abbey Mill Business Centre, Seedhill, Paisley PA1 1TJ
Tel: 0141 887 0428 • Fax: 0141 889 7204
e-mail: admin@fhguides.co.uk • www.holidayguides.com

Cheshire
Balterley, Chester

Cheshire

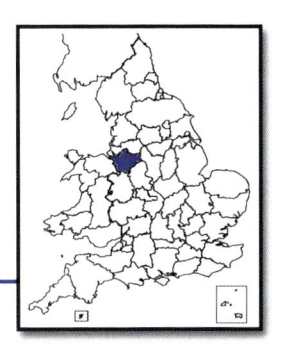

NORTH WEST ENGLAND 211

BALTERLEY (near Crewe). Mrs Joanne Hollins, Balterley Green Farm, Deans Lane, Balterley, Near Crewe CW2 5QJ (01270 820214).
Jo and Pete Hollins offer guests a friendly welcome to their home on a 145-acre working farm in quiet and peaceful surroundings. Green Farm is situated on the Cheshire/Staffordshire border and is within easy reach of Junction 16 on the M6. An excellent stop-over place for travellers journeying between north and south of the country. Two family rooms en suite; two double and two twin en suite in converted cottage can be either B&B or self-catering using the fully equipped kitchen in the cottage; all on ground floor. Tea-making facilities and TV in all rooms. Cot provided. This area offers many attractions; we are within easy reach of historic Chester, Alton Towers and the famous Potteries of Staffordshire.
Rates: Bed and Breakfast from £25 per person.
• Working farm, join in. • Open all year. • Caravans and tents welcome.

Vicarage Lodge
11 Vicarage Road, Hoole, Chester CH2 3HZ

A late Victorian family-run guesthouse offering a warm welcome and peaceful stay. Situated in a quiet residential area just off the main Hoole Road, yet only one mile from the city centre. Double and twin rooms, en suite available.

All rooms have washbasins, central heating, hair dryers, shaver points, remote-control colour TV and tea/coffee facilities. Large selection of breakfast choices.
Private car park on premises.
Good-sized patio garden where guests can relax.

Bed and Breakfast from £25pp single, £45 twin/double. Weekly and winter terms available.

Tel: 01244 319533

212 NORTH WEST ENGLAND — Cheshire

Chester, Crewe, Holmes Chapel

WHITE WALLS a 100 year old converted stables, in the heart of award-winning village of Christleton, two miles from Chester, off the A41, close to A55, M53 and North Wales. Walking distance to village pub and two canalside pub/restaurants, church, Post Office, hairdresser and bus stop. Half-hourly bus service to Chester. The village pond is home to swans, mallards, Aylesbury ducks and moorhens. En suite double bedroom, twin-bedded room with washbasin, all including English Breakfast. Minimum rates from £35 single, £50 double. Colour TV, tea/coffee making facilities, central heating, overlooking garden. Non-smoking. Sorry, no children or pets.

SB

Brian and Hilary Devenport, White Walls,
Village Road, Christleton, Chester CH3 7AS
Tel: 01244 336033 • e-mail: hilary-devenport@supanet.com

Mitchell's of Chester Guest House

28 Hough Green, Chester CH4 8JQ
Tel: 01244 679004
Fax: 01244 659567
e-mail: mitoches@dialstart.net
www.mitchellsofchester.com

SB

AA ★★★★★

Visit Chester & Cheshire Annual Awards 2006 Best B&B - Commended
Silver SILVER AWARD

This elegantly restored Victorian family home is set on the south side of Chester, on a bus route to the city centre. Guest bedrooms have been furnished in period style, with fully equipped shower room and toilet, central heating, TV, refreshment tray and other thoughtful extras. An extensive breakfast menu is served in the elegant dining room, and the guest lounge overlooks the well-maintained garden.

The historic city of Chester is ideally placed for touring Wales and the many attractions of the North West of England.

HIGHER ELMS FARM

Brian and Mary Charlesworth, Higher Elms Farm, Minshull Vernon,
Crewe CW1 4RG • Tel: 01270 522252

400-year old farmhouse situated on a working farm overlooking the Shropshire Union Canal. Oak-beamed comfort in dining and sitting rooms. Double, twin and single rooms, en suite with TV, and tea/coffee. No dinners but there are four pubs within two miles. Vegetarians and Coeliacs catered for. Convenient for M6, Oulton Park, Bridgemere Garden World, Stapeley Water Gardens, Nantwich, Chester, Tatton Park and Jodrell Bank.

Bed and Breakfast from £29.
e-mail: higherelmsfarm1@aol.com
http://members.aol.com/tomsworld/higherelmsfarmhomepage.html

Chris & Anne Massey — Bridge Farm Bed & Breakfast

In the shadow of Jodrell Bank Telescope with its popular visitors centre, Chris and Anne offer quality accommodation in our pretty farm house. Relax in our well appointed rooms with all modern comforts including digital TVs, radio internet etc. We specialise in yummy breakfasts using quality local produce, help yourself to garden fruit compote with creamy yogurt or fresh fruit before enjoying a freshly prepared Cheshire breakfast. Easy to find just 3 miles J 18, M6.

★★★★ GUEST ACCOMMODATION

Bridge Farm • Blackden • Holmes Chapel • Crewe • Cheshire CW4 8BX
Tel 01477 571202 • e-mail: stay@bridgefarm.com www.bridgefarm.com

Cheshire
NORTH WEST ENGLAND 213

Hyde, Middlewich

Needhams Farm
charlotte@needhamsfarm.co.uk
www.needhamsfarm.co.uk

A cosy 16th century farmhouse set in peaceful, picturesque surroundings by Werneth Low Country Park and the Etherow Valley, which lie between Glossop and Manchester. The farm is ideally situated for holidaymakers and businessmen, especially those who enjoy peace and quiet, walking and rambling, golfing and riding, as these activities are all close by. At Needhams Farm everyone, including children and pets, receives a warm welcome. Good wholesome evening meals available Monday to Thursday. Friday/Saturday/Sunday by arrangement.

Fire Certificate held.
Open all year.
Bed and Breakfast from £25 single, £40 double;
Evening Meal £8.

Mrs Charlotte R. Walsh, Needhams Farm, Uplands Road, Werneth Low, Gee Cross, Near Hyde SK14 3AG
Tel: 0161 368 4610

The Harvest Store (formerly Hopley House)
Nantwich Road, Wimboldsley, Middlewich, Cheshire CW10 0LN

Set in the small and pleasant hamlet of Wimboldsley, The Harvest Store is comfortable and homely and there is a warm and friendly welcome to all. There are seven rooms in an old converted barn all either en suite or with private bathroom. Breakfast is served in the Tea Room using the best local fresh produce. Take a look around our Farm Shop which sells local cheese and meats and maybe purchase one of our homemade cakes.

Surrounded by fields, but easy to find on the A530 - come and stay with us while you enjoy what Cheshire has to offer.

Bed and Breakfast
£58 twin/double; £34 single.

A non-smoking establishment.

www.harveststore.co.uk
Tel: 01270 526292 • e-mail: mail@harveststore.co.uk

214 NORTH WEST ENGLAND — Cheshire
Nantwich, Northwich

LEA FARM

Charming farmhouse set in landscaped gardens, where peacocks roam, on 150-acre working family farm. Spacious bedrooms, colour TVs, electric blankets, radio alarm and tea/coffee making facilities. Centrally heated throughout. Family, double and twin bedrooms, en suite facilities. Luxury lounge, dining room overlooking gardens. Pool/snooker; fishing in well stocked pool in beautiful surroundings. Bird watching. Children welcome, also dogs if kept under control. Help feed the birds and animals. Near to Stapeley Water Gardens, Bridgemere Garden World. Also Nantwich, Crewe, Chester, the Potteries and Alton Towers.

Wrinehill Road, Wybunbury, Nantwich CW5 7NS
Tel: 01270 841429
Tel: 01270 841030

B&B from £26pp children half price.

AA/ETC ★★★ Farmhouse

e-mail: leafarm@hotmail.co.uk • www.leafarm.co.uk

Stoke Grange Farm
Chester Road, Hurlstone, Nantwich, Cheshire CW5 6BT
Tel & Fax: 01270 625525

Luxury 4 Star Bed & Breakfast accommodation set in the beautiful rural Cheshire countryside near Nantwich, family owned and run by Lisa & Nick Jones. All rooms are en suite with tea and coffee facilities, colour TV with Freeview & remote control, and hairdryers, one has a four-poster bed, Jacuzzi and balcony overlooking the Shropshire Union Canal. Breakfasts are a delicious feast combining locally sourced products such as our own free-range eggs and award winning sausages, and we also offer Continental and Vegetarian Breakfasts. Packed Lunches and laundry service by arrangement. There is a children's play area and a pet's corner and guests have full use of the grounds.

e-mail: info@stokegrangefarm.co.uk
www.stokegrangefarm.co.uk

ASH HOUSE FARM
Chapel Lane, Acton Bridge, Northwich CW8 3QS
Tel: 01606 852717 • Fax: 01606 853752

A warm welcome, good food and comfort is assured at our Georgian farmhouse on a mixed working farm in scenic countryside. Tastefully furnished, with original period features. Guests' lounge, log fire, excellent views. Also our newly converted accommodation in the courtyard consisting of one double, one king-size and two twin rooms, all furnished and decorated to a very high standard. One twin and one king-size bedroom on the upper floor, and one twin and one double on the ground floor, all en suite, with underfloor heating. Ideal for business and pleasure, Chester, Liverpool, Manchester, NT properties, gardens, Oulton Park etc. Just off A49, 10 minutes M56. Open all year.

sue_schofield40@hotmail.com • www.ashhousefarm.co.uk

Please note

All the information in this book is given in good faith in the belief that it is correct. However, the publishers cannot guarantee the facts given in these pages, neither are they responsible for changes in policy, ownership or terms that may take place after the date of going to press. Readers should always satisfy themselves that the facilities they require are available and that the terms, if quoted, still apply.

Cumbria

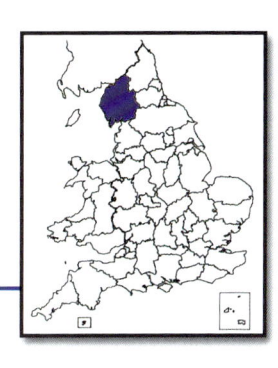

Ambleside

THE GABLES
AMBLESIDE - THE LAKE DISTRICT

A stylish bed and breakfast set in the heart of Ambleside

- Hearty breakfasts
- Secure bike storage
- Drying room
- Private parking
- Free wireless internet
- Winter breaks & special offers

A WARM WELCOME AWAITS YOU

Church Walk, Ambleside, Cumbria LA22 9DJ
Telephone: 015394 33272 www.thegables-ambleside.co.uk
Email: info@thegables-ambleside.co.uk

Melrose Guest House~Ambleside
relax@melrose-guesthouse.co.uk • www.melrose-guesthouse.co.uk

Elegant stone-terraced Victorian Lakeland house set over four floors. Peacefully situated just off the centre of Ambleside, with all shops and restaurants just two minutes' stroll away. Great choice of walks to choose from straight from the door – lakes, fells and waterfalls.

Bed & Breakfast • Single, double, twin and family rooms, all en suite or with private facilities.

Church Street, Ambleside LA22 0BT
015394 32500

CROYDEN HOUSE

Church Street, Ambleside LA22 0BU
Tel: 015394 32209

Croyden House is a non-smoking guest house situated on a quiet street just a minute's walk from the main bus stop and centre of Ambleside, a popular Lakeland village offering a wide range of shops, restaurants and inns catering for all tastes. The en suite rooms have colour TV, tea/ coffee making facilities; some have views of Loughrigg and Fairfield Horseshoe.

A generous home-cooked breakfast is served and special diets catered for by arrangement. Enjoy home baked scones and cakes, light lunches and afternoon teas in our adjacent Tea Rooms. Freshly made packed lunches by arrangement - home made cake included!

Guests have the use of a private car park.

B&B from £25 - £45 pppn.
Spring and Autumn Offers
Groups Welcome

e-mail: sylvia@croydenhouseambleside.co.uk • www.croydenhouseambleside.co.uk

SB

015394 32330
www.smallwoodhotel.co.uk

Smallwood House
Compston Road, Ambleside, Cumbria LA22 9DJ
...where quality and the customer come first

En suite rooms

Car parking

Leisure Club Membership

Cumbria — Ambleside

NORTH WEST ENGLAND 217

ROTHAY MANOR HOTEL & RESTAURANT

AA ★★★

Silver AWARD

Enjoy a Short Break at any time of year at this award-winning Country House Hotel in the heart of the Lake District, just a short walk from the centre of Ambleside and Lake Windermere. Owned and run by the Nixon family for over 40 years, it retains the comfortable, relaxed atmosphere of a private house, and is well known for excellent food and wine. Ideally situated for walking or sightseeing. Families and disabled guests welcome. Free use of nearby leisure centre.

Good Food Guide • Short listed for Cumbria Tourism "Taste" Awards 2008

Non-smoking • All major credit cards accepted

Rothay Bridge, Ambleside LA22 0EH
Tel: (015394) 33605 • Fax: (015394) 33607
e-mail: hotel@rothaymanor.co.uk
www.rothaymanor.co.uk/family

Ferndale Lodge

Ferndale Lodge is a small, family-run guesthouse close to the centre of Ambleside, where you will find a warm and friendly welcome. Offering excellent accommodation at realistic prices with a hearty home cooked English or Vegetarian breakfast. All 10 bedrooms have full en suite facilities, colour television and tea/coffee making tray. Full central heating throughout, rooms available with fell views, including a ground floor bedroom.

The Ferndale is open all year round with a private car park, offers packed lunches, clothes/boot drying and ironing facilities. A wide choice of places to dine are within minutes of a level walk. An ideal walking base. Special offers available, please telephone for more details.

Bed and Breakfast £25-£35pppn. Weekly £175-£210pp. Please phone for brochure.

Ferndale Lodge, Lake Road, Ambleside LA22 0DB
Tel: 015394 32207
e-mail: stay@ferndalelodge.co.uk   www.ferndalelodge.co.uk

★★★ GUEST HOUSE

218 NORTH WEST ENGLAND — Cumbria
Ambleside

The Anchorage Guest House

Rydal Road, Ambleside LA22 9AY
Tel & Fax: 015394 32046

A warm welcome awaits you at the Anchorage in lovely Ambleside, the heart of the Lake District. Helen and Arthur, the resident owners, do their best to make your stay an enjoyable one. High quality accommodation in very comfortably furnished and decorated rooms. Open all year, with wonderful views of Loughrigg Fell and Wansfell Pike, yet only a few minutes' walk from the village centre.

The house offers an ideal base from which to explore the Lake District with fell walking, climbing, mountain biking and water sports all nearby. For the less energetic, Ambleside village has a lot to offer, with The Bridge House, Museum and Cinema, not to mention all the traditional shops and cafes to explore. There are also plenty of restaurants and pubs for a great night out. Ample parking. Non-smoking.

From £26.00pppn to £34.00pppn

WINTER SPECIALS
from November 07-March 08
excluding Bank Holidays
£25pppn for stays of 2 nights or more

e-mail: theanchorageguesthouse@hotmail.com
www.theanchorageguesthouse.co.uk

Ambleside Lodge
Heart of the English Lake District

This elegant Lakeland home, dating from the 19th century, has been sympathetically converted and now offers a high standard of accommodation. All bedrooms are en suite, with colour TV, tea/coffee making facilities and delightful views.

The Premier suites and king-size four-poster rooms with jacuzzi spa baths offer relaxation and indulgence.

Leisure facilities available at a private club just 5 minutes' drive away include swimming pool, sauna, steam room, squash, gym and beauty salon. Free parking.

AMBLESIDE LODGE, ROTHAY ROAD, AMBLESIDE, CUMBRIA LA22 0EJ
015394 31681 • Fax: 015394 34547 • www.ambleside-lodge.com

Cumbria
Ambleside

KENT HOUSE
Lake Road, Ambleside LA22 0AD

Kent House, an elegant Victorian Guest House, retains many original features, with the comfort and convenience of central heating, colour TV, towels, toiletries, complimentary tea/coffee/chocolate making facilities in all the spacious guest rooms. WiFi access is enabled throughout at no extra charge. Kent House is ideally situated for those who wish to enjoy exploring the Lake District, fell walking, visiting the homes of Beatrix Potter and Wordsworth, and other attractions. There is also an excellent choice of eating establishments nearby.

Rooms from £29 per person per night.

Tel: 015394 33279

e-mail: mail@kent-house.com • www.kent-house.com

The Dower House

Lovely old house, quiet and peaceful, stands on an elevation overlooking Lake Windermere, with one of the most beautiful views in all Lakeland. Its setting within the 100-acre Wray Castle estate (National Trust), with direct access to the Lake, makes it an ideal base for walking and touring. Hawkshead and Ambleside are about ten minutes' drive and have numerous old inns and restaurants. Ample car parking; prefer dogs to sleep in the car. Children over five years welcome.

Bed and Breakfast from £33.50pp
Dinner, Bed & Breakfast from £50.50pp
Open all year round

Wray Castle, Ambleside
Cumbria LA22 0JA
Tel: 015394 33211

SB

symbols

⊘	Totally non-smoking	🐕	Pets Welcome
🐎	Children Welcome	**SB**	Short Breaks
♿	Suitable for Disabled Guests	▽	Licensed

Limnerslease,
Bongate, Appleby CA16 6UE

Limnerslease is a family-run guest house five minutes' walk from the town centre. A good half-way stopping place on the way to Scotland. There is a good golf course and an indoor heated swimming pool. Many lovely walks are all part of the charm of Appleby. Two double and one twin bedrooms, all with washbasin, colour TV, tea/coffee making facilities at no extra charge; bathroom, toilet; dining room. Open January to November with gas heating. Ample parking.

Bed and Breakfast from £24 to £26.

Mrs K.M. Coward • Tel & Fax: 017683 51578
e-mail: kathleen@limnerslease63.fsnet.co.uk
http://mysite.freeserve.com/limnerslease

Annisgarth B&B, 48 Craig Walk, Bowness-on-Windermere LA23 2JT
Tel: 015394 43866
www.annisgarth.co.uk
e-mail: sharron@annisgarth.com

B&B from £20 to £35pppn

Exclusively non-smoking.

Sharron Macdonald welcomes you to her friendly and relaxed Victorian home, quietly situated only minutes' walk from Lake Windermere and all the cafes, pubs, restaurants, shops and attractions of Bowness village. Three double bedrooms, one twin, and a de luxe room with a spa bath and lake view. All rooms have TV with DVD and a collection of movies and books to read. All diets are catered for including gluten free, vegetarian and vegan. All produce is local with free range eggs.

Fairfield Garden Guest House

Brantfell Road, Bowness-on-Windermere Cumbria LA23 3AE
Tel: 015394 46565

Situated just above Bowness village and Lake Windermere, The Fairfield is set in peaceful, secluded surroundings and is an ideal base for exploring this lovely area, being just a short walk to the waterfront at Lake Windermere, as well as all restaurants and shops.

Tony and Liz Blaney provide a high standard of genuine hospitality in a homely atmosphere. Single, twin, double, four-poster, de luxe and family rooms.
Residents' lounge and licensed bar • Free internet access - wifi hotspot

tonyandliz@the-fairfield.co.uk • www.the-fairfield.co.uk

Cumbria
NORTH WEST ENGLAND 221
Bowness-on-Windermere, Brampton

Holly Cottages
GUEST HOUSE

Holly Cottage dates back to the 17th century and is situated within the conservation area in the oldest part of the village of Bowness. We offer four double en suite rooms each with tea/coffee making facilities and colour television. Most rooms overlook the garden. Access to the house is available for your use at all times. Private parking.

Centrally situated to all shops and restaurants. Lake Windermere and boat trips five minutes away. Excellent position for exploring the Lake District. If you enjoy walking, cycling, shopping, steam power, visiting houses and gardens, viewing wonderful scenery or simply pottering about, there is something here for any age or ability. We have a large organic cottage garden which is wildlife friendly. Holistic therapies including aromatherapy massage, homeopathy, luxury facials and pampering are available to residents and non residents.

We look forward to welcoming you soon

Jan & Jim Bebbington, 2 Holly Cottages, Rayrigg Road, Bowness-on-Windermere LA23 3BZ
Tel: 015394 44250 • hollycottages@hotmail.com • www.hollycottagesguesthouse.co.uk

SB

The Blacksmiths Arms

The Blacksmith's Arms offers all the hospitality and comforts of a traditional country inn. Enjoy tasty meals served in the bar lounges, or linger over dinner in the well-appointed restaurant. The inn is personally managed by the proprietors, Anne and Donald Jackson, who guarantee the hospitality one would expect from a family concern. Guests are assured of a pleasant and comfortable stay. There are eight lovely bedrooms, all en suite. Peacefully situated in the beautiful village of Talkin, the inn is convenient for the Borders, Hadrian's Wall and the Lake District. There is a good golf course, walking and other country pursuits nearby.

**Talkin Village, Brampton,
Cumbria
CA8 1LE
Tel: 016977 3452
Fax: 016977 3396**

e-mail: blacksmithsarmstalkin@yahoo.co.uk • www.blacksmithstalkin.co.uk

222 NORTH WEST ENGLAND — Cumbria

Brampton, Brough

Walton High Rigg
Walton, Brampton, Cumbria CA8 2AZ

Enjoy peace, comfort and warm hospitality at this 18th century Listed working dairy/sheep farm with spectacular views of the Lakes and Pennines. Explore Scotland, Hadrian's Wall or the Lakes. Many lovely walks, golf, fishing, riding available nearby. Children can help to feed the animals, follow the farm trail to the waterfall or relax in the garden. Excellent home cooking. Evening meal by arrangement. Non-smoking. Open March to October. Guest Lounge. Bed and Breakfast from £25.

★★★ FARMHOUSE

Contact: Mrs Margaret Mounsey • Tel: 01697 72117 • Fax: 01697 741697
e-mail: mounsey_highrigg@hotmail.com • www.waltonhighrigg.co.uk

River View • Brough • Cumbria

River View is a converted stone barn in a pleasant riverside location in the village of Brough which has public houses and shops, close to the market towns of Kirkby-Stephen and Appleby in Westmorland. Being just off the A66 makes us an ideal North / South stop over. Convenient for visiting the Lake District, Yorkshire Dales, and North Pennines.

A warm, friendly atmosphere awaits and we will try to do our best to make you feel at home. Accommodation in one double and one twin bedrooms, both en suite.

Prices from £25 per person per night (from £50 per double room).

★★★★ BED & BREAKFAST

Brough, Cumbria CA17 4BZ • Tel: 017683 41894
E-mail: riverviewbb@btinternet.com • www.riverviewbb.co.uk

symbols

- 🚭 Totally non-smoking
- 🎠 Children Welcome
- ♿ Suitable for Disabled Guests
- 🐕 Pets Welcome
- **SB** Short Breaks
- 🍷 Licensed

Cumbria

NORTH WEST ENGLAND 223

Burton-in-Kendal, Caldbeck, Carlisle

RUSSELL FARM
Burton-in-Kendal, Carnforth, Lancs LA6 1NN
Tel: 01524 781334
email: miktaylor@farming.co.uk

- Bed, Breakfast and Evening Meal offered
- Ideal centre for touring Lakes and Yorkshire Dales, or as a stopover for Scotland or the South 
- Good food, friendly atmosphere on working dairy farm
- Modernised farmhouse
- Guests' own lounge

Contact Anne Taylor for details.

Swaledale Watch, Whelpo, Caldbeck CA7 8HQ
Tel & Fax: 016974 78409

Mixed farm of 300 acres situated in beautiful countryside within the Lake District National Park. Central for Scottish Borders, Roman Wall, Eden Valley and the Lakes. Primarily a sheep farm (everyone loves lambing time). Visitors are welcome to see farm animals and activities. Many interesting walks nearby or roam the peaceful Northern fells. Enjoyed by many Cumbrian Way walkers. Very comfortable accommodation with excellent breakfasts. All rooms have private facilities. Central heating. Tea making facilities. We are a friendly Cumbrian family and make you very welcome. Bed and Breakfast from £25 to £31. Contact: **Mr and Mrs A. Savage**

e-mail: nan.savage@talk21.com
www.swaledale-watch.co.uk

CORNERWAYS Guest House • Carlisle
107 Warwick Road, Carlisle CA1 1EA • 01228 521733

Cornerways is a large Grade II Listed Victorian property, recently extensively refurbished and situated within a conservation area in the heart of historic Carlisle. Just five minutes' walk to the city centre for most amenities and attractions, including the Cathedral, Castle, Tullie House Museum and Hadrian's Wall National Trail. An ideal base for exploring the Eden Valley, the Scottish Borders and the Lake District National Park. Off-street parking. Located 1¼ miles from M6 Junction 43. Bus and rail stations are just a five minute walk away. Standard and en suite rooms. Children over 5 years welcome.

SB

e-mail: info@cornerwaysbandb.co.uk • www.cornerwaysbandb.co.uk

Cumbria

Carlisle

Mrs Dorothy Nicholson, Gill Farm, Blackford, Carlisle, Cumbria CA6 4EL

Gill Farm

In a delightful setting on a beef and sheep farm, this Georgian-style farmhouse, dated 1740, offers a friendly welcome to all guests.

- Near Hadrian's Wall • Gretna Green • Lake District
- Golf • Fishing • Swimming • Large agricultural auction markets
- Cycle path passes our entrance.

Accommodation is in one double room en suite, one double and one twin bedrooms. All rooms have washbasins, shaver points and tea/coffee making facilities. Two bathrooms, shower; lounge with colour TV; separate diningroom. Central heating. Car essential, good parking.

B&B from £25 to £30 • Telephone for further details or directions.

Tel: 01228 675326 • mobile: 07808 571586

ABBERLEY HOUSE
33 Victoria Place, Carlisle CA1 1HP

An imposing town house offering informal, comfortable high standard en suite rooms with TV, tea and coffee facilities and private parking. We are only a short walk from the excellent town centre with its fine variety of shops, restaurants, pubs and of course the cathedral, castle and award-winning Tullie House museum. Also close by are Stoney Holme and Swift golf courses, the Sands sports and leisure centre and the splendid River Eden. A short drive takes you to historic Hadrian's Wall, the magnificent Lake District and romantic Gretna Green.

Tel: 01228 521645

Our rates start from only £25 per person which includes English breakfast and taxes.

e-mail: bbs@abberleyhouse.co.uk • www.abberleyhouse.co.uk

Visit the FHG website
www.holidayguides.com

for details of the wide choice of accommodation featured in the full range of FHG titles

Cumbria
Cockermouth

THE MANOR HOUSE
Oughterside, Aspatria, Cumbria CA7 2PT

Our lovely manor farmhouse dates from the 18th century and retains many original features as well as several acres of land. Rooms are spacious with large en suite bathrooms, tea and coffee making facilities, full size TVs, views and lots of little extras. Our double rooms have kingsize beds and our twin room has double beds. The grounds are home to many species of birds, including barn owls. Set in peaceful surroundings we enjoy easy access to the magnificent scenery of the Western Lakes and Solway Coast.
Pets and children welcome.
Bed & Breakfast from £25. Evening meals by arrangement.
Self-catering caravans available (adults only).
Tel & Fax: 016973 22420
e-mail: richardandjudy@themanorhouse.net
www.themanorhouse.net

The Rook Guesthouse
9 Castlegate
Cockermouth
CA13 9EU

Interesting 17th century town house, adjacent to historic castle. We offer comfortable accommodation with full English, vegetarian or Continental breakfast. All rooms are en suite with colour TV, beverage tray and central heating.

Cockermouth is an unspoilt market town located at the North Western edge of the Lake District within easy reach of the Lakes, Cumbrian Coast and Border country.
We are ideally situated as a base for walkers, cyclists and holidaymakers. Open all year, except Christmas.

B&B Double £45, Single £25.
www.therookguesthouse.gbr.cc/
Mrs V. A. Waters
Tel: 01900 828496

Mosser Heights
Mosser, Cockermouth, Cumbria CA13 0SS

Tel: 01900 822644
e-mail: AmandaVickers1@aol.com
www.stayonacumbrianfarm.co.uk

Expect a warm welcome at our family-run farm, just off the beaten track, yet near to the fells and lakes of Loweswater (two miles) and Cockermouth (four miles). Comfortable spacious en suite bedroom, cosy lounge and dining room with log fires. A hearty breakfast to set you up for the day. An ideal base for walking, cycling, touring and bird watching. Arrive as guests and leave as friends.
We are a hidden jewel awaiting your discovery!

SB

Rose Cottage
Lorton Road, Cockermouth CA13 9DX

Family-run guest house on the outskirts of Cockermouth. Warm, friendly atmosphere. Ample off-road parking. All rooms en suite with colour TV, tea/coffee, central heating and all have double glazing.

Pets most welcome in the house (excluding dining room), and there are short walks nearby. Ideal base for visiting both Lakes and coast.

Tel & Fax: 01900 822189
www.rosecottageguest.co.uk

Sun Hotel & 16th Century Inn

A superbly located 10-bedroom hotel designed to overlook the village and enjoy panoramic mountain views. With a large private garden, patio, comfortable lounge, and extensive restaurant menu and wine list, the hotel offers comfortable en suite accommodation in a peaceful and informal setting.

All bedrooms have been recently refurbished, with a relaxing night's sleep as good as promised! Better still, when built (in 1902), the hotel was attached to the end of a 16th century pub! It is now a freehouse with real ales and real fires in a classic Lakeland setting of beamed ceiling, flagged floor and an old range.

Coniston LA21 8HQ • Tel: 015394 41248
Fax: 015394 41219 • info@thesunconiston.com
www.thesunconiston.com

Cumbria

NORTH WEST ENGLAND 227

Crosby-on-Eden, Ennerdale Bridge, Gilsland

The Wallfoot
Park Broom, Crosby-on-Eden, Carlisle CA6 4QH
Tel: 01228 573696 • Fax: 01228 573240
www.wallfoot.co.uk

- The Wallfoot Hotel & Restaurant is a popular hotel just 3 miles east of Carlisle, conveniently located for Carlisle, Brampton, Carlisle Airport and the Hadrian's Wall National Trail.
- We are surrounded by fabulous scenery and lovely walks; the Eden Golf Course is on our doorstep. We are a fantastic base for visiting the Lake District and South West Scotland.
- The hotel boasts a newly refurbished bar and restaurant and offers a traditional bar menu and exciting new restaurant menu.
- Cycle shed and drying facilities available.

The Shepherds Arms Hotel

A gem of a country house hotel and inn, offering first-rate en suite accommodation, an extensive bar menu of home-cooked dishes, and a fine selection of real ales. Ennerdale Bridge is situated on one of the most beautiful stretches of Wainwright's Coast to Coast Walk and very popular with walkers.

The hotel has eight double/twin rooms (6 en suite, 2 with private bathrooms). All are non-smoking and have telephone, digital TV, radio alarm, and tea/coffee making facilities. Breakfast is served in the Georgian panelled dining room.
Complement your meal with a selection of fine wines and relax afterwards in the comfortable lounge with its open log fire.

The Shepherds Arms bar is open to the public and is included in *The Good Pub Guide* and CAMRA *Good Beer Guide*. Specialities are real ales and home-cooked locally sourced produce from the extensive bar menu.

Ennerdale Bridge, Lake District National Park CA23 3AR
Tel: 01946 861249
e-mail: shepherdsarms@btconnect.com
www.shepherdsarmshotel.co.uk

The Hill on the Wall,
Gilsland CA8 7DA

In an outstanding hill top location overlooking the Irthing Valley and Hadrian's Wall at Birdoswald, this 16th century fortified farmhouse or "bastle" has three bedrooms. One double en suite, one twin en suite (ground floor) and one twin with private bathroom. A lounge is also provided for guests. One acre of garden and private parking.
We provide the greatest of comfort, delicious food and a warm welcome to all who visit this historic and beautiful area. With the introduction of the Hadrian's National Trail in May 2003, The Hill is ideally situated for walkers, being about half a mile from the Wall.

Bed and Breakfast from £34 to £37.50 per person based on two people sharing.
£50 single occupancy of a double room.

Mrs E Packer - 016977 47214 • www.hadrians-wallbedandbreakfast.com
e-mail: info@bed-breakfast-hadrianswall.com

Cumbria

Grasmere, Hawkshead, Helton

DUNMAIL HOUSE
KESWICK ROAD, GRASMERE LA22 9RE
015394 35256

A few minutes' walk from the centre of Grasmere and the Lake, Dunmail House is an elegant, 5-Star Bed & Breakfast set in beautiful gardens with stunning views of the nearby fells.

Our reputation is one of high standards and personal attention to detail in a warm and friendly atmosphere. We have tried to think of everything you might need - Egyptian cotton sheets, fluffy towels, luxury toiletries, flat screen TV, dvd, and hairdryer as well as complimentary hot drinks tray.

Our extensive breakfast catering for all tastes is guaranteed to set you up for the day.

e-mail: info@dunmailhouse.com • www.dunmailhouse.com

Paul and Fran Townsend
Pepper House
Satterthwaite LA12 8LS • Tel: 01229 860206

A warm welcome awaits in 16th century cruck-frame farmhouse with elevated position in tranquil valley on edge of Grizedale Forest (abundant wildlife), four miles from Hawkshead. Peaceful base for exploring the Lakes, close to Beatrix Potter's Hilltop and Ruskin's Brantwood. Miles of forest trails for walking and cycling. Sympathetically updated, all bedrooms have en suite facilities. Two comfortable lounges. Central heating, log fires; dining room and terraces with wonderful views. Licensed bar, generous home cooking. Non-smoking. Bed and Breakfast from £35; Dinner from £16. See all details at **www.pepper-house.co.uk**

Also ask us about two self-catering cottages, stunningly located on traditional Lakeland working farm, or go to
www.hartsophallcottages.com

Beckfoot Country House,
Helton, Penrith CA10 2QB
Tel: 01931 713241 • Fax: 01931 713391
e-mail: info@beckfoot.co.uk • www.beckfoot.co.uk

A beautiful Victorian country house set in three acres of gardens, with wonderful views of the Lowther valley, a tranquil and unspoilt corner of the Lake District National Park.

All rooms are en suite, spacious and well appointed with TV, hospitality tray and complimentary toiletries; luxurious executive suite with four-poster. Ironing facilities available. Cumbrian breakfast served in the oak-panelled diningroom.

Activities nearby include walking, cycling, horse riding, fishing, golf, swimming and paragliding, or visit Hadrian's Wall and the Scottish Borders, Eden Valley, historic Carlisle city, historic castles and gardens.

Special three-night breaks available.   AA ★★★★ *Guest Accommodation*

Please note

All the information in this book is given in good faith in the belief that it is correct. However, the publishers cannot guarantee the facts given in these pages, neither are they responsible for changes in policy, ownership or terms that may take place after the date of going to press. Readers should always satisfy themselves that the facilities they require are available and that the terms, if quoted, still apply.

Cumbria

NORTH WEST ENGLAND 229

Howgill, Kendal

Bramaskew Farmhouse

Mrs J Postlethwaite,
Bramaskew, Howgill,
Sedbergh LA10 5HX
Tel: 015396 21529
stay@drawellcottage.co.uk
www.drawellcottage.co.uk

Bramaskew Farmhouse Bed & Breakfast

Farmhouse en suite acccommodation on family-run farm with panoramic views of the Lune Valley and the Howgill Fells.

10 minutes from J37 of M6 and within Yorkshire Dales National Park. 5 minutes' drive from the book town of
Sedbergh and on the Dalesway footpath.

A great location for walking or touring the Lakes and the Dales. Many footpaths from the farmhouse.

Two en suite rooms, both with TV and tea/coffee facilities.

Pre-booked evening meals available.

Highly Commended with the English Tourism Council for excellent standards of comfort and quality. Recommended by *Which? Good Bed & Breakfast Guide*. Tranthwaite Hall is said to date back to 1186. A charming olde world farmhouse with beautiful oak beams, doors and rare black iron fire range. This working dairy/sheep farm has an idyllic setting half-a-mile up an unspoilt country lane where deer can be seen, herons fishing in the stream and lots of wild flowers. This is a very peaceful and quiet retreat yet only minutes from all Lakes and local attractions. Attractive bedrooms, all are en suite and have TV, tea/coffee making facilities, hair dryer, radio and full central heating. Guest lounge. Full English breakfast is served with eggs from our farm and home-made jam and marmalade. We like guests to enjoy our home and garden as much as we do. Walking, pony trekking, golf and many good country pubs and inns nearby. Bed and Breakfast £28 to £30.

Tranthwaite Hall
Underbarrow, Near Kendal LA8 8HG
Tel:015395 68285
e-mail: tranthwaitehall@aol.com
www.tranthwaitehall.co.uk

Hollin Root Farm
Garth Row, Skelsmergh,
Kendal LA8 9AW (01539 823638)

Dating from 1844, Hollin Root Farm is a typical Lakeland farmhouse set in beautiful open countryside with land down to the river. Situated 3 miles north of Kendal on the edge of the Lake District National Park, it is a good base from which to explore the Lake District or the Yorkshire Dales (Lake Windermere is only 8 miles away) and popular as a stopover between England and Scotland.
On the ground floor we have a flexible Double/Twin/Family room with en suite facilities. The room has tea/coffee making facilities and colour TV with freeview channels.
There are excellent eating out venues in nearby Kendal and surrounding areas.
We serve excellent full English or Continental breakfasts with our own fresh free-range eggs and home- made preserves. Packed lunches are available. Vegetarians are welcome. Children and pets are welcome. We are open all year round and are a non smoking establishment.

e-mail: b-and-b@hollin-root-farm.freeserve.co.uk
www.hollinrootfarm.co.uk

SB

Cumbria
Keswick

Location! Location! Location!

Bassenthwaite
❖ Hall Farm ❖

Bassenthwaite Village, Near Keswick Cumbria CA12 4QP

Bed and Breakfast - Good accommodation at sensible prices. A friendly welcome awaits you at our lovely 17th century farmhouse which is fully modernised whilst retaining its olde worlde character. A charming lounge/dining room furnished with antiques is available for guests' use any time. Delightful bedrooms with individual period furnishings. Hand basin in rooms, two bathrooms close by. Excellent Cumbrian breakfast, with healthy options. Switch off and unwind in this beautiful corner of England. Small dogs welcome.

Bed and Breakfast from £25-£35 pppn.

Tel & Fax: 017687 76393
www.bedandbreakfast-lakedistrict.co.uk
e-mail: stay@amtrafford.co.uk

Littletown Farm

Littletown Farm, Newlands,
Keswick, Cumbria CA12 5TV
Tel: 017687 78353
E-mail: info@littletownfarm.co.uk
www.littletownfarm.co.uk

Littletown Farm is a traditional working Lakeland farm offering bed & breakfast accommodation in the beautiful, unspoilt Newlands valley, in the heart of the Lake District National Park.

In a unique location nestled at the foot of Catbells, the farm was the inspiration behind Beatrix Potter's Mrs Tiggywinkle stories. The beautiful Northern fells surround the accommodation, providing spectacular scenery and remarkable tranquillity, an ideal retreat to get away from it all.

Licensed bar, large dining room, comfortable TV lounge, wi-fi access and large enclosed garden. Each bedroom has its own stunning view looking directly onto the fells.
Traditional Farmhouse breakfast, packed lunches arranged if required.

*8 rooms in total, 6 of which have private facilities, each room with tea & coffee making facilities. 2 family rooms available.
Double/twin rooms from £36pppn including Full Lakeland Breakfast.*

Cumbria
Keswick

NORTH WEST ENGLAND

Lane Head Farm
Country Guest House

A warm welcome awaits you upon your arrival at Lane Head Farm, located in glorious countryside in the foothills of Blencathra, close to Keswick. This is a marvellous place to relax, explore and enjoy the spectacular beauty of the Lake District National Park.

There is a peaceful garden where you may be lucky enough to glimpse our resident red squirrel on one of the feeders or playing on the lawn. We have a number of different bird feeders as well which attract Greater Spotted Woodpeckers, Siskins and Goldfinches to name a few.

There are many interesting places to visit in the locality and after a day's exploring you can be sure to return to a freshly cooked two or three course dinner. Enjoy a pre-dinner drink in the lounge while you browse the wine list and meet new friends. After dinner tea and coffee can be served in the lounge or you may prefer to sample one of our malt whiskeys, a Cognac or an Armagnac.

There are seven individually designed en-suite rooms, including four-posters. All our rooms have complimentary tea and coffee making facilities (fair-trade coffee, hot chocolate, sugar and the tea is ethically sourced Lakeland Tea), TVs, radio alarm clocks, hairdryers, complimentary toiletries and complimentary mineral water on day of arrival.

**Lane Head Farm Country Guest House,
Troutbeck, Near Keswick CA11 0SY**
info@laneheadfarm.co.uk • www.laneheadfarm.co.uk
Tel: 017687 79220

SB

AA ★★★★ Guest House

Cumbria
Keswick

Badgers Wood
Bed and Breakfast Accommodation in Keswick

30 Stanger Street, Keswick, Cumbria CA12 5JU
Tel/Fax: 017687 72621
E-mail: enquiries@badgers-wood.co.uk
www.badgers-wood.co.uk

Badgers Wood guest house has been awarded the prestigious *Visit Britain 'Silver Award'* to reflect the quality of its bedroom and en suite facilities following completion of a full refurbishment. A traditional Victorian slate fronted house in a quiet cul-de-sac just two minutes walk from the market square, restaurants and bus station. Our six fully en suite bedrooms have co-ordinated bedroom furniture, soft furnishings by Dorma and Sanderson and an HD ready flatscreen colour TV, individual room controlled central heating and views towards the fells.

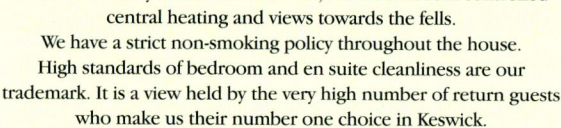

We have a strict non-smoking policy throughout the house. High standards of bedroom and en suite cleanliness are our trademark. It is a view held by the very high number of return guests who make us their number one choice in Keswick.

Enjoy our delicious full English breakfast or a lighter breakfast option and we gladly cater for vegetarians, coeliac and dairy free diets.

Lindisfarne Guest House
21 Church Street, Keswick CA12 4DX
Tel: 017687 73218

A cosy, friendly guest house with home cooking and hearty breakfasts. Situated within a residential area close to the town centre of Keswick and within easy walking distance of Lake Derwentwater and Fitz Park. We have some en suite rooms and all bedrooms have colour TV, tea/coffee facilities, central heating and washbasin.

Bed and Breakfast from £28.00pp; Evening Meal optional. Chris and Alison Burns look forward to welcoming you.

e-mail: alison230@btinternet.com
www.lindisfarnehouse.com

Keswick

Maple Bank Country Guest House

Rhona and Tommy extend a warm welcome to guests both old and new at Maple Bank Country Guest House, a magnificent Edwardian residence set in an acre of beautiful gardens near the town of Keswick, right in the heart of the Lake District National Park and close to all of its many facilities. The House commands uninterrupted views across the Derwent valley towards the lofty Skiddaw and the smaller Latrigg, and is ideally placed for walking, climbing, water sports, and other less strenuous activities like fishing or visiting local pubs and eateries! We pride ourselves on the service we offer to guests and will try our utmost to make your stay as comfortable and enjoyable as possible. We have plentiful free and secure parking, secure cycle storage and a drying room

There are 5 spacious double rooms and two twin rooms, all en suite with colour TV, plentiful wardrobe space, tea & coffee making facilities, iron and ironing board (on request), and hairdryer. Our spacious yet cosy family room is en suite, with one double bed, one single bed, colour TV, plentiful wardrobe space, tea & coffee making facilities, iron and ironing board (on request), and hairdryer

**Maple Bank, Braithwaite, Keswick, Cumbria CA12 5RY
Tel: 01768 778229 • Fax: 01768 778000
e-mail: enquiries@maplebank.co.uk • www.maplebank.co.uk**

Keswick Park Hotel • Cumbria

The Keswick Park Hotel is family-owned and personally run with an excellent team of staff committed to helping you have a relaxed and enjoyable stay in Keswick and the Lake District. A fine Victorian house set in the heart of Keswick close to all local shops, restaurants and pubs, but still close to the parks and mountains. All our 16 bedrooms have good quality pine or mahogany furniture, and there are also all fully en-suite with bath or shower rooms. Despite being near the centre of town many rooms boast fine views of Skiddaw, Walla Crag, or the Grisedale Range.
Lounge bar/café with award-winning garden. Small private car park.
We offer three-night mid-week out-of-season breaks. Please call us for details.

**33 Station Road, Keswick, Cumbria, CA12 4NA
Telephone: (017687) 72072 • Fax: (017687) 74816
e-mail: info@KeswickParkHotel.com • www.KeswickParkHotel.com**

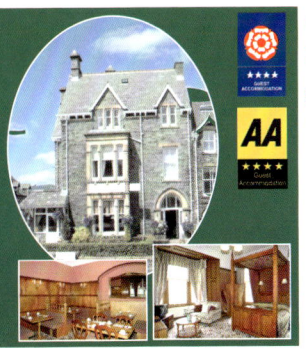

SB

Woodside

Ideally situated away from the busy town centre yet only a short walk down the C2C bridle path to the town. This is a family-run establishment with a friendly reception guaranteed. After a good night's sleep you will be ready for a hearty English breakfast together with cereal, fruit and yoghurt, vegetarian option available. Ample private parking. Dogs welcome by arrangement. Minimum child age 6 years.
B&B from £30.

**Ann & Norman Pretswell, Woodside, Penrith Road,
Keswick CA12 4LJ • 017687 73522
www.woodsideguesthouse.co.uk**

234 **NORTH WEST ENGLAND** **Cumbria**

Kirkby-in-Furness, Kirkby Lonsdale

Low Hall

Low Hall is a Victorian farmhouse on a working beef and sheep farm, with land running from the Duddon estuary to Kirkby Moor. It is set in peaceful countryside, offering spectacular views of the Duddon estuary and Lakeland fells. The farmhouse itself is nestled into a hill with a mature wood running alongside.

There are three extremely spacious guest rooms; two double rooms and one twin room, all with en suite shower. All rooms have colour TV and videos, radio, full central heating, hospitality trays and toiletries. Hairdryers and ironing facilities are available. We also have a sofa bed available in one of the double rooms to accommodate children. We very much regret that we are unable to accept children under 10 years. A traditional farmhouse breakfast is our speciality.

Bed & Breakfast per person, per night: £29.00
(single room supplement applies)
Minimum 2 night stay at Bank Holidays
All major credit and debit cards accepted.

**Low Hall Farm, Kirkby-in-Furness
CUMBRIA LA17 7TR • Tel: 01229 889220**

E-mail: enquiries@low-hall.co.uk • www.low-hall.co.uk

Barbon Inn

**Barbon,
Near Kirkby Lonsdale
Cumbria LA6 2LJ
Tel & Fax: 015242 76233**

If you are torn between the scenic delights of the Lake District and the Yorkshire Dales, then you can have the best of both worlds by making your base this friendly 17th century coaching inn nestling in the pretty village of Barbon.

Individually furnished bedrooms provide cosy accommodation, and for that extra touch of luxury enquire about the elegant mini-suite with its mahogany four-poster bed.

Fresh local produce is featured on the good value menus presented in the bar and restaurant, and the Sunday roast lunch with all the trimmings attracts patrons from near and far. A wide range of country pursuits can be enjoyed in the immediate area

Bedrooms, dining room and lounge non-smoking.

www.barbon-inn.co.uk

Cumbria
NORTH WEST ENGLAND 235

Kirkby Lonsdale, Kirkby Stephen

WYCK HOUSE - KIRKBY LONSDALE

Quality accommodation in Victorian town house, close to local pubs and restaurants. Double and twin rooms with en suite facilities; all rooms have TV and hospitality trays. The famous Ruskin's View and Devil's Bridge are only a short walk away. We are situated on the Cumbrian, Lancashire and Land's End to John O'Groats cycle ways. Safe storage for cycles. There are also two golf courses close by for keen golfers. Ideally situated between the Lakes and Dales. No smoking. B&B from £30 to £39pppn.

Pat & Brian Bradley, Wyck House,
4 Main Street, Kirkby Lonsdale LA6 2AE • Tel & Fax: 015242 71953
e-mail: wyckhouse@studioarts.co.uk • www.studioarts.co.uk/wyckhouse.htm

Cocklake House
MALLERSTANG CUMBRIA CA17 4JT
017683 72080

Charming, High Pennine Country House B&B in unique position above Pendragon Castle in Upper Mallerstang Dale, offering good food and exceptional comfort to a small number of guests. Two double rooms with large private bathrooms. Three acres riverside grounds. Dogs welcome.

symbols

- Totally non-smoking
- Children Welcome
- Suitable for Disabled Guests
- Pets Welcome
- **SB** Short Breaks
- Licensed

Cumbria

Lake District, Langdale, Maryport

GRIZEDALE LODGE

Licensed Luxury Bed & Breakfast

Set in the heart of Grizedale Forest National Park, in a beautiful location, and within easy reach of Beatrix Potter country, Windermere and Coniston. All visitors to Grizedale Lodge can be assured of a warm welcome, friendly attention and of every effort being made to ensure that their stay is enjoyable. All rooms en suite, some with four-posters. Central heating. Residents' licence. Open all year, from £30pppn.

Hawkshead, Ambleside LA22 0QL
Tel 015394 36532 • Fax: 015394 36572
enquiries@grizedale-lodge.com
www.grizedale-lodge.com

Book with this advert and claim a FREE dessert

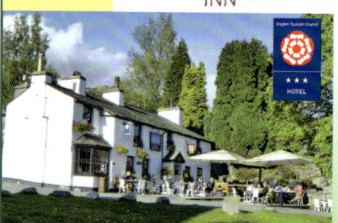

THE BRITANNIA INN

Elterwater, Langdale, Cumbria LA22 9HP
Tel: 015394 37210

A 500 year-old quintessential Lakeland Inn nestled in the centre of the picturesque village of Elterwater amidst the imposing fells of the Langdale Valley. Comfortable, high quality en suite double and twin-bedded rooms. Dogs welcome. Enquire about our Mid-Week Special Offer of three nights B&B for the price of two. Relax in the oak-beamed Bars or Dining Room whilst sampling local real ales and dishes from our extensive menu of fresh, home-cooked food using lots of Cumbrian produce. *Quiz Night most Sundays.*

www.britinn.co.uk • e-mail: info@britinn.co.uk

Riverside B&B

10 Selby Terrace, Maryport CA15 6NF
Tel: 01900 813595

Clean, welcoming Victorian townhouse, family-run. Many original features including stained glass entrance, staircase, fireplaces, coving etc. No smoking. Ideal base for the Lake District and Coastal Route. Cyclists and Walkers Welcome. Fishing available (sea and river). Delicious full English breakfast and towels provided. Colour TV and tea/coffee facilities in all rooms. Packed lunch available.

Standard rooms: one single, one double and one family (double and two single beds also used as a twin/double/triple), from £20pppn.
One double en suite room available from £23pppn.

Contact: Mrs L. Renac.

Cumbria — NORTH WEST ENGLAND 237

Newbiggin on Lune, Penrith

Tranna Hill
B&B Accommodation in Cumbria

Tranna Hill offers a relaxing and friendly atmosphere in a great location. Five miles from M6 Junction 38, ideal base for all activities with Howgill Fells, nature reserve, fish farm and golf course only minutes away.
Well placed for breaking your journey or touring the Lakes and Dales.
En suite rooms furnished to a high standard with TV, refreshment trays, central heating and beautiful views. Private parking and large gardens. Delicious breakfasts. All for £27.00 per person per night.

Mrs Brenda Boustead, Tranna Hill
Newbiggin on Lune, Kirkby Stephen CA17 4NY
Tel: 015396 23207 • e-mail: enquiries@trannahill.co.uk
mobile: 07989 892368 • www.trannahill.co.uk

Silver Award

SB

Peter & Cynthia Barry, Blue Swallow Guest House,
11 Victoria Road, Penrith CA11 8HR • Tel: 01768 866335

Comfortable Victorian house set in the attractive market town of Penrith, ideally situated to explore the Eden Valley, the Lake District, Hadrian's Wall and the Yorkshire Dales. For Golf enthusiasts Penrith boasts an 18 hole Golf Course and a Driving Range. Peter and Cynthia look forward to welcoming you whether you are on holiday, breaking a long journey or in the area for business, you will be made to feel at home. Seven rooms, twin/double or family (four en suite), one private bathroom, two single en suite rooms. All rooms have Freeview/DVD TVs, hospitality trays and WiFi access.
Full English breakfast using local produce.
Credit/Debit Cards accepted.

Bed and Breakfast from £30 to £45 pppn.

e-mail: blueswallow@tiscali.co.uk • www.blueswallow.co.uk

BLUE Swallow GUEST HOUSE

Brooklands

Charming and elegant, Brooklands Guest House is situated in the heart of historic Perth. This beautiful, recently refurbished Victorian terraced house is an excellent base for exploring the many delights of the Lake District National Park while convenient for the attractive Eden Valley.

Our beautifuuly furnished rooms have fans, fridges, radio alarms, bottled water and hospitality tray with chocolates and biscuits, a selection of teas, coffee and hot chocolate. All our bathrooms come complete with dressing gowns, fluffy white towels and luxury toiletries for all your needs.

We have been invited into the famous Michelin Guide and gained AA 4 Star Highly Commended Award for the past five years, putting Brooklands Guest House in the top 10% of Guest Accommodation for overall quality

Leon and Debbie Kirk, Brooklands Guest House,
2 Portland Place, Penrith CA11 7QN (01768 863395)
e-mail: enquiries@brooklandsguesthouse.com   www.brooklandsguesthouse.com

AA Highly Commended Guest House 2007 - 2008

Albany House   5 Portland Place, Penrith CA11 7QN
e-mail: info@albany-house.org.uk • www.albany-house.org.uk

Close to the town centre, Albany House is a lovely mid-Victorian terraced property. Fine, spacious rooms (two double, two multi, one family), en suite facilities, central heating, colour TV, tea/coffee. Situated close to M6, A6 and A66, an ideal base for touring the Lake District, Eden Valley, Hadrian's Wall and Scottish Borders. An excellent stopover, with the warmest welcome and hearty breakfasts. B&B from £25pp.

Contact: Mrs Bell (01768 863072).

SB

AA Guest House Highly Commended

The Sun Inn
Newton Reigny
Near Penrith
Cumbria CA11 0AP

A 17th century coaching inn, located in the picturesque village of Newton Reigny. Why not enjoy lunch in the beer garden with a glass of Thwaites real ale, German lager or chilled wine? If you visit in the winter months you can be sure to find the welcoming sight of a real open log fire to keep the chill out, setting the scene for a hearty home-cooked meal or a lighter dish from our extensive locally sourced menus. The Sun Inn boasts three comfortable en suite rooms and one family room where you'll find TV, toiletries & tea/coffee facilities available. Lunch and evening meals can be taken in the restaurant or in the beer garden (weather permitting).

Tel: 01768 867055
info@thesuninn-newtonreigny.co.uk
www.thesuninn-newtonreigny.co.uk

Greenah Crag,
Troutbeck, Penrith CA11 0SQ (017684 83233)

Enjoy a relaxing break at Greenah Crag, a 17th century former farmhouse peacefully located in the Lake District National Park, 10 miles Keswick, eight miles from M6.
Ideal for exploring Northern Lakes and Western Pennines.
Two doubles en suite, and one twin with washbasin. 
Guests' sittingroom with woodburning stove
Full breakfast.
Excellent choice of pubs within three miles
Regret no pets, no smoking.
Please telephone for brochure.
Bed and Breakfast from £25 per person.

greenahcrag@lineone.net
www.greenahcrag.co.uk

Cumbria

NORTH WEST ENGLAND 239

Penrith, Ullswater

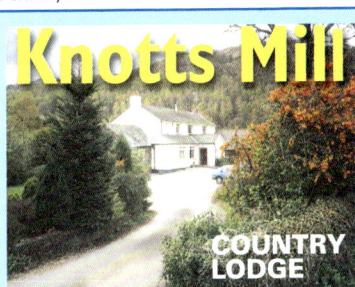

Knotts Mill COUNTRY LODGE

Spacious guesthouse close to magical Ullswater, in peaceful, scenic surroundings. Ideal for walking, boating or touring the Lake District. Nine en suite bedrooms with stunning views, including family rooms and facilities for the disabled. Our large dining room and lounge have picture windows that overlook the fells. Big breakfasts; fully licensed. 10 minutes from Junction 40 M6 with private grounds and parking. Enjoy the beautiful Lake District. Have a relaxing holiday at Knotts Mill Country Lodge.

★★★ GUEST HOUSE

Watermillock, Penrith CA11 0JN • Tel: 017684 86699 • www.knottsmill.com

---

NORCROFT GUEST HOUSE, Graham Street, Penrith CA11 9LQ
Paul Lamb – 01768 862365 • Fax: 01768 210425
e-mail: reservations@norcroft-guesthouse.co.uk • www.norcroft-guesthouse.co.uk

Conveniently situated for the M6, just five minutes' walk from town centre, our large Victorian house boasts an ideal location. We are able to welcome up to 22 guests in newly refurbished, spacious and comfortable en suite rooms, including two family suites with separate connecting children's accommodation. A ground floor/accessible room is also available. All rooms have colour TV and tea/coffee making facilities. We are non-smoking and have a private off-street car park. Cyclists welcome. The guest house is fully licensed. Internet access. B&B £33 to £55.

Elm House GUEST HOUSE

Whether you're a couple, family or single traveller you can be assured of a warm and friendly welcome at Elm House. This family-run guest house is located just 400 metres from Lake Ullswater, and makes an ideal base for touring the Lakes or for a relaxing break away from it all. Eight rooms, including a family suite, 7 en suite and one with a private bathroom. All rooms have lovely views of the surrounding countryside. There is a choice of a hearty Cumbrian breakfast or vegetarian option. The beautifully presented rooms, cleanliness and attention to detail mean a wonderful stay is guaranteed.

**Anne & Mark Vause
Elm House Guest House,
Pooley Bridge, Penrith, Cumbria CA10 2NH
Tel: 017684 86334
e-mail: enquiries@stayullswater.co.uk
www.stayullswater.co.uk**

The FHG Directory of Website Addresses
on pages 347-362 is a useful quick reference guide for holiday accommodation with e-mail and/or website details

Cumbria

Wasdale, Windermere

Bridge Inn

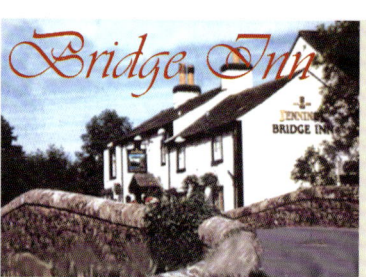

The Bridge Inn, once a coach halt, is now a fine, comfortable, award-winning country inn, offering hospitality to all travellers and visitors.

The Inn has an excellent reputation for good food, with "real" food served in the Dalesman Bar, or in the Eskdale Room.

We serve an excellent selection of Jennings real ales. 16 bedrooms. Weddings and other private and business functions catered for in our function room. Licensed for civil ceremonies, partnerships, naming ceremonies and renewal of vows.

10 minute drive to "Britain's favourite view – Wastwater"

This unspoiled area of the Lake District offers superb walking and climbing.

Features in the 'Good Beer & Pub Guide' 2008.

Bridge Inn, Santon Bridge, Wasdale CA19 1UX
Tel: 019467 26221 • Fax: 019467 26026
e-mail: info@santonbridgeinn.com
www.santonbridgeinn.com

Beaumont House

Beaumont House is an elegant Victorian Villa occupying an enviable position for all amenities of Windermere/Bowness, and is an ideal base from which to explore Lakeland. The highest standards prevail and the en suite bedrooms are immaculate.

We provide all modern comforts, superb breakfasts, genuine hospitality, excellent value. Private car park. Bed and Breakfast from £50 single, £80 double. Please ring or e-mail for details of special offers. Free leisure facilities at nearby country club.

Holly Road, Windermere LA23 2AF
Tel: 015394 47075 • Fax: 015394 88311
e-mail: beaumonthotel@btinternet.com
www.lakesbeaumont.co.uk

Briardene Guest House

4 Ellerthwaite Road, Windermere LA23 2AH • 015394 43571

The delightful Briardene Guesthouse was built in 1888 from local Lakeland stone and slate and retains much of it's original character. We offer a high standard of comfort and a warm friendly atmosphere with three tastefully decorated en suite double bedrooms, furnished with either a kingsize 4-poster or wrought iron/brass bed, and including reclaimed pine furniture. All rooms have a flat screen TV with DVD player, fridge, iron and ironing board, tea/coffee making facilities with complimentary biscuits, hot chocolate, bottled water and a bottle of wine (for 3-night stays or more). Fresh fluffy towels, bathrobes and toiletries are provided too. We offer superb breakfasts with an excellent menu choice, private off-road parking for all our guests and genuine hospitality.
We are exclusively non-smoking. Sorry we do not take children or pets.

e-mail: enquiries@briardene.com • www.briardene.com

Cumbria
Windermere

NORTH WEST ENGLAND 241

GREEN GABLES
37 Broad Street, Windermere LA23 2AB

AA
★★★
Guest House

A family-owned and run licensed guesthouse in Windermere centrally situated one-minute's walk from village centre with shops, banks and pubs and only five minutes from the station or bus stop. Accommodation comprises two doubles, one family triple/twin and one single room, all en suite; one family (four) and two family triple/twin rooms with private facilities; all with central heating, colour TV, hairdryers, kettles, tea & coffee. Comfortable lounge bar on the ground floor. No smoking in bedrooms. We can book tours and trips for guests and can advise on activities and special interests. B&B from £23 to £30 pppn. Special Winter offers available.
Open just about all year round.
Contact **Carole Vernon and Alex Tchumak**.

Tel: 015394 43886
e-mail: greengables@FSBdial.co.uk
e-mail: info@greengablesguesthouse.co.uk

Firgarth Guest House

★★★
GUEST HOUSE

This elegant Victorian house, built in Lakeland stone around 1875, offers views to the rear over Wynlass Beck, along with comfortable en suite rooms, a residents' lounge and private parking.

Firgarth Guest House is conveniently situated just 12 minutes' walk from the centre of Windermere, which offers a range of shops, pubs and restaurants. The guest house has a great location between the busy villages of Windermere and Bowness. It is a clean, comfortable and reasonably priced bed and breakfast situated in the number one location within the English Lake District National Park: Windermere.

The guest lounge is comfortable, with plenty of books and information on local walks, as well as a selection of games to keep you amused in the evenings. The traditional breakfast menu is all freshly prepared. There is a choice of orange juice, grapefruit, fresh fruit salad, cereals, yoghurt and a variety of cooked-to-order breakfasts.

The guest house is regretfully unable to accept arrivals after 20.00hrs.

Room from £28.00pppn • Children over 10 years old welcome

Ambleside Road, Windermere LA23 1EU
Tel: 015394 46974
e-mail: enquiries@firgarth.com • www.firgarth.com

Holly-Wood Guest House

Holly Road, Windermere LA23 2AF
Tel: 015394 42219

Holly-Wood is a beautiful, family-run Victorian house offering clean comfortable accommodation, set in a quiet position 3 minutes' walk from Windermere village amenities. It is the perfect place to unwind after a day exploring the Lakes.
• All rooms en suite • Private car park • Hearty traditional/vegetarian breakfasts • Non-smoking throughout • Help with walk planning available • All major credit cards accepted.

Bed & Breakfast from £35pppn.
Please contact Ian or Yana for more information
We look forward to welcoming you to Holly-Wood

e-mail: info@hollywoodguesthouse.co.uk
www.hollywoodguesthouse.co.uk

Beckmead House

A small, family-run guest house with quality accommodation, delicious breakfasts and a relaxed friendly atmosphere. Single, double or family rooms, with en suite or private showers, all decorated to a high standard with central heating, electric blankets, tea/coffee making facilities, colour TV and hairdryers. Comfortable residents' lounge.

Walking, climbing, sailing, water skiing, pony trekking, golf nearby, or visit historic houses, gardens and museums.

Mrs Dorothy Heighton, Beckmead House,
5 Park Avenue, Windermere LA23 2AR
Tel & Fax: 015394 42757
e-mail: beckmead_house@yahoo.com
www.beckmead.co.uk

St John's Lodge

Lake Road, Windermere, Cumbria LA23 2EQ
Tel: 015394 43078 • Fax: 015394 88054
e-mail: mail@st-johns-lodge.co.uk • www.st-johns-lodge.co.uk

This pretty Lakeland B&B is ideally situated between Windermere village and the lake (10 minutes' walk) and close to all amenities. The guesthouse caters exclusively for non-smokers and has been awarded 3 AA Yellow Stars Highly Commended. The choice of breakfast menu is probably the largest in the area. From a touring visitor's point of view, or if you prefer healthier alternatives, this is a refreshing change. There is the usual choice of cereals and fresh fruit and a good selection of traditional English breakfasts, but there are also over 20 other tasty dishes, including vegetarian/vegan/gluten free, fresh fish, and a number of house specialities. All guests are offered free access to a nearby local luxury leisure club (about 2 minutes by car). Free internet access is provided via a dedicated computer. For laptop owners, 24 hour Wi-Fi is available.

Cumbria

NORTH WEST ENGLAND 243

Windermere

LANGDALE CHASE
Hotel

Windermere,
Cumbria LA23 1LW
Tel: 015394 32201
www.langdalechase.co.uk
e-mail: sales@langdalechase.co.uk

AA ★★★

English Tourism Council ★★★ HOTEL

SB

Magnificent country house hotel with over six acres of beautifully landscaped grounds sloping to the edge of Lake Windermere. Panoramic views of lake and fells, log fires, excellent food, and friendly, professional staff all ensure a memorable stay. Short Break details on request. 29 bedrooms, all with private bathrooms. Completely Non-Smoking. Children and pets welcome. Open all year.

**Cumbria Tourist Board - Hotel of the Year 2005 Silver Award
Website of the Year Award 2005 • Taste of England Award 2005**

Beautiful, spacious farmhouse dating from the 16th century, with oak beams and old oak panelling in guest lounge. The poet, William Wordsworth, used to visit here. Working farm. Magnificent scenery abounds, handy for Beatrix Potter attractions. Conveniently situated between Kendal and Lake Windermere, half-a-mile up a pretty country lane. A warm welcome awaits you.

SB

Bed and Breakfast £32per person per night.
Two double and one triple/twin en suite rooms. No smoking. No pets.
Open February to December. Approximately 15 minutes from Junction 36 M6.
'Bed & Breakfast Nationwide' Inspected & Approved.

**Mrs Pat Metcalfe, Crook Hall,
Crook, Near Kendal LA8 8LF
Tel: 01539 821352**
E-mail: metcalfe@croockhallfarm.co.uk
www.crookhallfarm.co.uk

NORTH WEST ENGLAND — Cumbria

Windermere

Hawksmoor Guest House

The Hawksmoor is a lovely spacious Lakeland guest house, ideally situated between the villages of Windermere and Bowness-on-Windermere, where you can find many shops, restaurants and of course the lake itself.

Whether you simply want to relax, visit Beatrix Potter's Hill Top or put on your boots and explore the fells, you'll discover the best of both worlds at The Hawksmoor. Guests are also entitled to complimentary use of the leisure facilities at Parklands Country Club in Bowness.

There is a choice of 9 bedrooms, with double, twin and family rooms available. Each bedroom is fully en suite, with colour television, tea/coffee making facilities, wine glasses & bottle opener, hairdryer, clock/radio and fully fitted wardrobes. Every room has views of either the gardens or woodland.

Lake Road, Windermere LA23 2EQ • Tel/Fax: 015394 42110
e-mail: enquiries@hawksmoor.com • www.hawksmoor.com

Brook House — 30 Ellerthwaite Road, Windermere LA23 2AH

A friendly welcome awaits you at Brook House which is convenient for village and lake. Ideal touring centre. Personal service and excellent English cooking, under the personal supervision of the proprietors.

All rooms are decorated to a high standard; residents' lounge with colour TV; full central heating. All bedrooms have colour TV, tea/coffee tray. Four bedrooms full ensuite, one bedroom with private facilities. Children over 8 years welcome. Access to rooms at all times. Guests' parking.

Full Fire Certificate. Open all year. Bed and Breakfast from £25 to £35.

Mrs J. Seal - 015394 44932
e-mail: stay@brookhouselakes.co.uk
www.brookhouselakes.co.uk

Meadfoot Guest House

A warm welcome and a memorable holiday experience await you at Meadfoot, with your hosts, Sandra and Tim Shaw. Meadfoot is a detached house set in its own grounds on the edge of Windermere village. There is a large garden with patio for guests' use. The bedrooms, all en suite, are tastefully furnished with pine furniture - some are on the ground floor, some are four-poster and one is a self-contained family suite with two separate rooms and direct access to the garden. Private car park.

Free Leisure Club facilities available nearby.

B&B £25-£40pppn

New Road, Windermere LA23 2LA
Tel: 015394 42610
e-mail: enquiries@meadfoot-guesthouse.co.uk • www.meadfoot-guesthouse.co.uk

---

symbols

- Totally non-smoking
- Children Welcome
- Suitable for Disabled Guests
- Pets Welcome
- **SB** Short Breaks
- Licensed

Lancashire

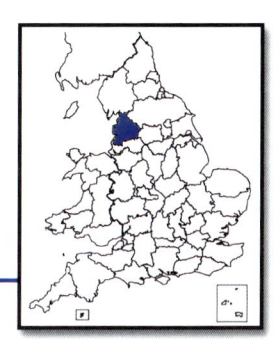

Blackburn, Blackpool

THE BROWN LEAVES COUNTRY HOTEL

LONGSIGHT ROAD, COPSTER GREEN, NEAR BLACKBURN BB1 9EU
01254 249523 • Fax: 01254 245240

Situated on the A59 halfway between Preston and Clitheroe, five miles from Junction 31 on M6 in beautiful Ribble Valley. All rooms ground floor, en suite facilities, satellite TV, tea-making and hairdryer. Guests' lounge and bar lounge. Car parking. Pets by arrangement. All credit cards welcome.

www.brownleavescountryhotel.co.uk

The Berwick

2nd Place in the Lancashire and Blackpool Tourism Awards Guest Accommodation of the Year 2007/8

The multi award-winning Berwick offers a warm and friendly welcome. Small and family-run, we offer a relaxing break and one of the best holiday experiences in Blackpool. Beautifully decorated en suite guest bedrooms, comfortable TV lounge and spacious dining room. Extensive choice of home made food at breakfast and dinner.

B&B from £23.00pppn, based on two people sharing a room. Evening meal available

**23 King Edward Avenue
Blackpool FY2 9TA
Tel: 01253 351496**
theberwickhotel@btconnect.com
www.theberwickhotel.co.uk

Sunnyside & Holmsdale Hotel

A warm friendly welcome awaits you at...

Bed & Breakfast - two minutes from North Station, five minutes from Promenade, all shows and amenities.
- Colour TV lounge. • Central heating. • No smoking.
- Children welcome. • Reductions for children sharing.
- Senior Citizens' reductions May and June, always welcome. Stairlift available.
- Special diets catered for, good food and warm friendly atmosphere awaits you.
- **Bed and Breakfast from £20.**

Overnight guests welcome when available. Small parties catered for.

**Proprietors: Elsie and Ron Platt
25-27 High Street, Blackpool FY1 2BN
Tel: 01253 623781**
e-mail: elsieplatt@btinternet.com

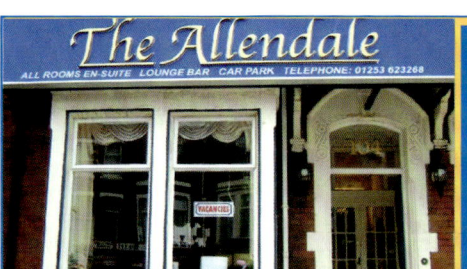

The Allendale

ALL ROOMS EN-SUITE   LOUNGE BAR   CAR PARK   TELEPHONE: 01253 623268

**104 Albert Road
Blackpool FY1 4PR
Tel: 01253 623268**
www.allendalehotelblackpool.co.uk

Ideally situated in the heart of town, close to the Winter Gardens, clubs, the Tower and shopping centre. Free car parking.
Resident proprietors, the Johnson Family, assure you of a pleasant and comfortable stay, whether for business or pleasure.
9 double, 3 twin and 3 family bedrooms, all en suite.
Evening meals available.

The Allendale

Lancashire

NORTH WEST ENGLAND 247

Blackpool, Chorley, Clitheroe

The Berkswell Hotel is a family-run licensed hotel near to Blackpool's Pleasure Beach, South Pier, Sandcastle, Lido and Airport. There are seven double, one twin, one family and one single bedrooms.

**Berkswell Hotel
8 Withnell Road, South Shore,
Blackpool FY4 1HF
Tel: 01253 341374
     0800 977 4723
www.berkswellhotel.co.uk**

- All rooms en-suite
- Colour TV/DVDs (library of DVDs to borrow).
- Hairdryers
- Tea & coffee facilities
- Good home cooking
- Tables for two
- Special diets catered for
- Car park • Late keys
- Full central heating
- Double glazed throughout
- Comfortable bar

Parr Hall Farm ETC/AA ★★★★

Within an hour of the Lake District, Yorkshire Dales, Peak District, Chester and North Wales, Parr Hall Farm is an ideal base for touring the local area. Attractions nearby include Camelot Theme Park, Martin Mere, Southport, Blackpool and antiques at Bygone Times, Heskin Hall, Park Hall and Botany Bay. All rooms are en suite, with central heating. Good food nearby. Ground floor rooms. Off-road parking.

From M6 take A5209 for Parbold, then immediately take B5250 right turn for Eccleston. After five miles, Parr Lane is on the right, the house is first on the left.

B&B from £35 per person, reductions for children.

**Parr Hall Farm, Eccleston, Chorley PR7 5SL
01257 451917 • Fax: 01257 453749
enquiries@parrhallfarm.com • www.parrhallfarm.com**

Rakefoot Farm
Chaigley, Near Clitheroe BB7 3LY
Tel: (Chipping) 01995 61332 or 07889 279063 • Fax: 01995 61296
e-mail: info@rakefootfarm.co.uk • website: www.rakefootfarm.co.uk

VisitBritain ★★★★
VisitBritain ★★★/★★★★★

Family farm in the beautiful countryside of the Ribble Valley in the peaceful Forest of Bowland, with panoramic views. Ideally placed for touring Coast, Dales and Lakes. 9 miles M6 Junction 31a. Superb walks, golf and horse riding nearby, or visit pretty villages and factory shops. Warm welcome whether on holiday or business, refreshments on arrival.

BED AND BREAKFAST or SELF-CATERING in 17th century farmhouse and traditional stone barn conversion. Wood-burning stoves, central heating, exposed beams and stonework. Most bedrooms en suite, some ground floor. Excellent home cooked meals, pubs/restaurants nearby. Garden and patios. Dogs by arrangement. Laundry.
Past winner of NWTB Silver Award for Self-catering Holiday of the Year.

**B&B £25 - £32.50pppn sharing, £25 - £37.50pn single
S/C four properties (3 can be internally interlinked)
£111 - £695 per property per week. Short breaks available.**

Lancashire

Clitheroe, Lancaster, Morecambe,

Rose Cottage

A warm welcome awaits in our exclusively non-smoking 200-year-old cottage. At the gateway to the Ribble Valley, an ideal stop when visiting Scotland, only 30 minutes' drive to Blackpool and the 5 miles from the M6 J31, ideal for walkers and cyclists, also business persons wanting a friendly, homely environment. Each well equipped room offers guests a comfortable, relaxing stay; all have private facilities, welcome tray, flat-screen TV with Freeview, wifi and fridge for guests' use.

Off-road parking, including covered parking for motorbikes and cycle lock. Pets welcome.

e-mail: bbrose.cott@talk21.com • www.rosecottagebandb.com
Tel: 01254 813223 • Fax: 01254 813831
LONGSIGHT ROAD (A59), CLAYTON-LE-DALE, NEAR MELLOR, RIBBLE VALLEY, LANCASHIRE BB1 9EX

A large detached bungalow, three miles south of Lancaster and 400 yards from Lancaster University. Access from M6 Junction 33 and A6 in Galgate village. Two double bedrooms each with shower, toilet, colour TV and tea/coffee making facilities. One bedroom also has a private TV lounge. Full central heating. Spacious parking. A good location for visiting Blackpool, Morecambe, the Lake District and Yorkshire Dales. You will be sure of a friendly welcome and a homely atmosphere.

• Bed and Breakfast from £25 per person. • Sorry, no pets. • Non-smokers only please. • Open all year.

Roy and Helen Domville, Three Gables, Chapel Lane, Galgate, Lancaster LA2 0PN • 01524 752222

Broadwater House

Bed and Breakfast from £24

The Broadwater is a small friendly guest house, situated on the select East Promenade with glorious views of Morecambe Bay and Lakeland Mountains.

Only five minutes' walk from the town centre, shops and amusements. We offer every comfort and the very best of foods, varied and plentiful with choice of menu. All rooms en suite with heating, colour TV and tea making facilities.

A perfect base for touring, the Broadwater is only 45 minutes' drive away from Blackpool, Yorkshire Dales and the Lake District, and 10 minutes from the historic city of Lancaster.

**Mrs R. Holdsworth, Broadwater House,
356 Marine Road, East Promenade, Morecambe LA4 5AQ
Tel: 01524 411333 • www.thebroadwaterhotel.co.uk**

Lancashire / Merseyside   **NORTH WEST ENGLAND** 249

Preston

BELL FARM

Beryl and Peter welcome you to their 18th century farmhouse in the quiet village of Pilling. The area has many footpaths and is ideal for cycling. Easy access to Blackpool, Lancaster, the Forest of Bowland and the Lake District. One family room, one double and one twin. All en suite. Tea and coffee making facilities. Lounge and dining room. All centrally heated.
Full English breakfast.
Children and pets welcome.
Open all year except Christmas and New Year.
Bed and Breakfast from £27.50.
Peter Richardson, Bell Farm, Bradshaw Lane, Scronkey, Pilling, Preston PR3 6SN

Tel: 01253 790324
www.bellfarm.co.uk

Merseyside

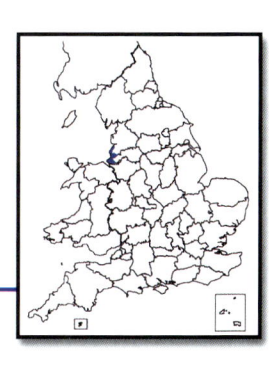

Bebington, Liverpool

The Bebington Hotel
24 Town Lane, Bebington, Wirral CH63 5JG • 0151-645 0608

A family business which guarantees a warm and friendly welcome within a professional atmosphere.
Close to Bebington station and within easy reach of Birkenhead, Liverpool and Chester. All rooms en suite, colour TV, tea/coffee facilities. Car park. WiFi. Family rooms available.

e-mail: enquiries@bebingtonaccom.co.uk
www.bebbingtonaccom.co.uk

Holme Leigh Guest House
93 Woodcroft Road, Wavertree, Liverpool L15 2HG

Recently fully refurbished • All rooms comfortably furnished complete with TV, tea and coffee and en suite facilities • Full central heating • Award-winning breakfast room • Close to Sefton Park, just two miles from the M62 and 20 minutes from the airport, 2½ miles from city centre.

En suite rooms: single from £25,
twin/double from £48, family from £65.
All rates include VAT and Continental breakfast.

Tel: 0151-734 2216
e-mail: info@holmeleigh.com
www.holmeleigh.com

SB

Merseyside
Southport

THE LEICESTER • SOUTHPORT

Lorraine and Louise welcome you to The Leicester, located in the heart of Southport, about 20 miles north of Liverpool.

- 10 individually designed en suite bedrooms (single, double, twin), all with hospitality tray, ironing facilities, hairdryer, toiletries, fresh towels and room safe.
- Modern, spacious dining room serving choice of breakfast menu. Evening meals by arrangement.
- Lounge/bar area with comfortable sofas and 42" plasma TV.

The Leicester
24 Leicester Street, Southport PR9 0EZ
Tel: 01704 530049
Fax: 01704 545561
www.theleicester.com

Looking for Holiday Accommodation?

FHG KUPERARD

for details of hundreds of properties throughout the UK, visit our website

www.holidayguides.com

Scotland

Castle Park Guest House, Edinburgh, page 284

Enverdale House Hotel, Couper Angus, Perthshire, page 304

'Sunnyside', Isle of Arran, Ayrshire & Arran, page 271

Clachan Cottage Hotel, Lochearnhead, page 307

Scotland · Regions

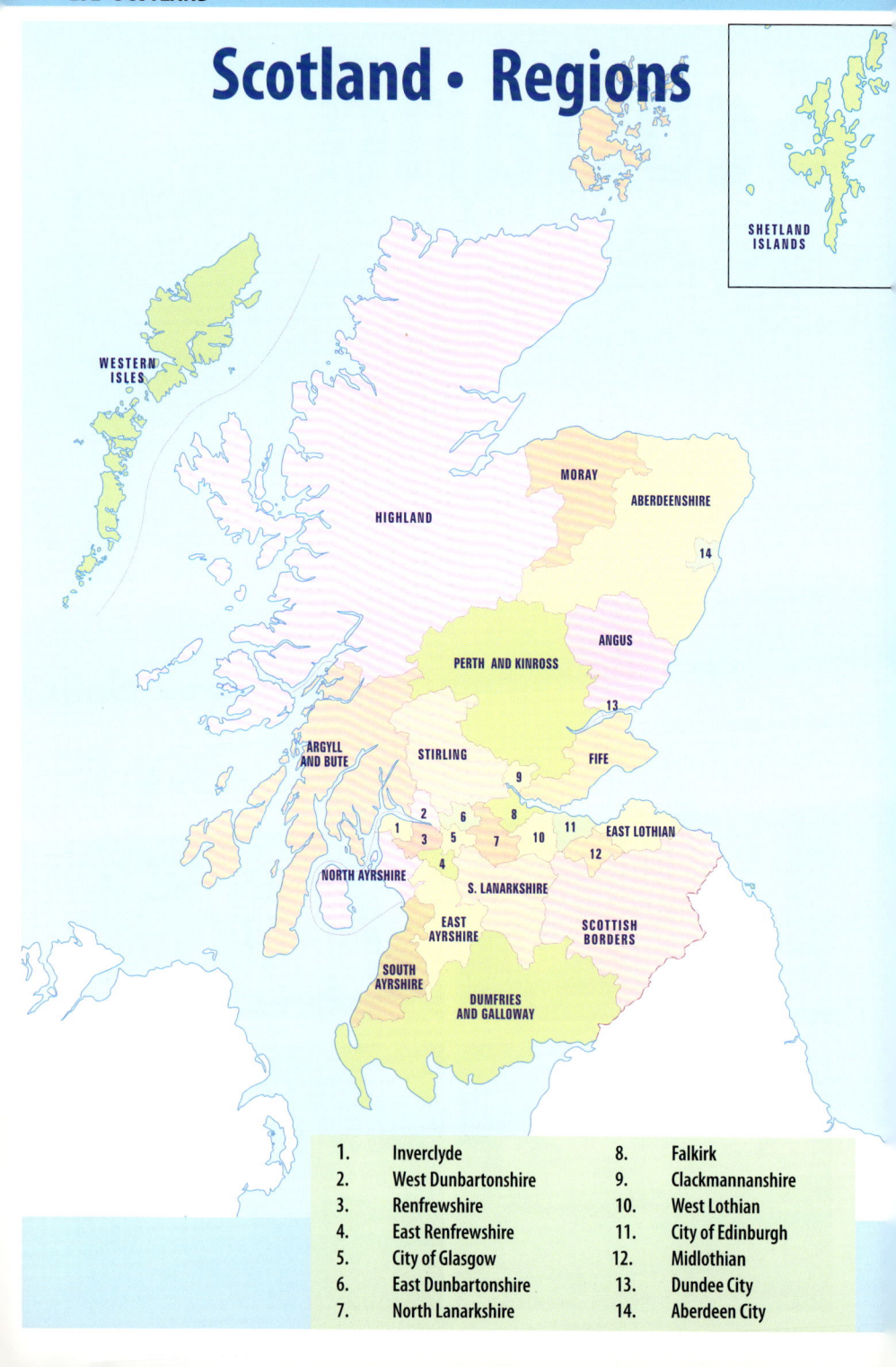

1. Inverclyde
2. West Dunbartonshire
3. Renfrewshire
4. East Renfrewshire
5. City of Glasgow
6. East Dunbartonshire
7. North Lanarkshire
8. Falkirk
9. Clackmannanshire
10. West Lothian
11. City of Edinburgh
12. Midlothian
13. Dundee City
14. Aberdeen City

Aberdeen, Banff & Moray

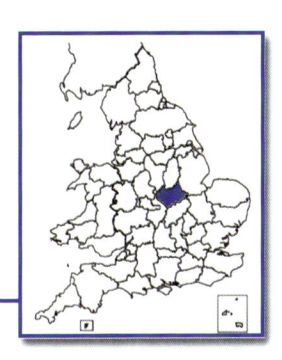

Ballater, Banchory

Aberdeen, Banff & Moray

CAMBUS O'MAY HOTEL
Ballater
Aberdeenshire AB35 5SE
Tel & Fax: 013397 55428
www.cambusomayhotel.co.uk

This family-run country house hotel is situated four miles east of Ballater overlooking the River Dee and its environs. The hotel prides itself on the old-fashioned standards of comfort and service it offers to its guests. Excellent food is available from the table d'hôte menu which changes daily and can be complemented by fine wines from the cellar. The 12 bedrooms have en suite facilities and the hotel is centrally heated throughout.

The area affords a wealth of interests such as hill walking, golf, fishing, and shooting, and there are many historic sites including Balmoral Castle.

Ardconnel

Home from home bungalow in a quiet location, yet just a three minute walk from the High Street and all amenities. Ideal base for walking, fishing, golfing and sightseeing or exploring the Castle and Whisky Trails nearby. All guest accommodation overlooks Banchory Golf Course and to the hills beyond.

One double/twin room en suite, one double/twin with private bathroom. Guest lounge and sun lounge.

Bed & Breakfast from £22pppn (sharing), single £36-£40. Open March - October.

Mrs Jean Robb, Ardconnel, 6 Kinneskie Road, Banchory AB31 5TA • 01330 822478

SB

Aberdeen, Banff & Moray

Banchory, Crathie

Best Western The Burnett Arms Hotel

- Banchory town centre on Royal Deeside
- 20 courses within 45 minutes' drive
- 16 en suite rooms with satellite TV
- Drying room and storage for clubs
- Bar Lunches/Suppers, High Teas, Dinner
- Two bars cater for all tastes
- Special rates for golfers on request

25 High Street, Banchory AB31 5TD
Tel: 01330 824944 • Fax: 01330 825553
e-mail: theburnett@btconnect.com
www.burnettarms.co.uk

The Inver Hotel
Crathie, Ballater, Aberdeenshire AB35 5XN
013397 42345

Built in 1760, and situated between Ballater and Braemar. You will receive a warm Deeside welcome, and enjoy good home cooking with a choice of many fine wines. Or drink your favourite dram beside an open log fire. All bedrooms en suite. Open to non-residents

e-mail: info@inverhotel.com
www.inverhotel.com

symbols

🚭	Totally non-smoking	
🐎	Children Welcome	
♿	Suitable for Disabled Guests	
🐕	Pets Welcome	
SB	Short Breaks	
🍷	Licensed	

Aberdeen, Banff & Moray

Dufftown, Forres

SCOTLAND 255

DAVAAR

**Church Street, Dufftown
AB55 4AR
Tel: 01340 820464**

Davaar is a traditional Victorian stone Scottish villa. It is situated adjacent to the main square in Dufftown, which although only a village, is the Malt Whisky capital of Scotland, with seven distilleries. All bedrooms are en suite, and have TV and tea/coffee facilities. For the energetic we have two mountain cycles for hire to explore the local cycleways. Details from Mrs Susan Cameron.

Double or twin-bedded rooms from £55, family from £65

Davaar@ClunieCameron.co.uk • www.davaardufftown.co.uk

Sherston House
**Hillhead, Forres IV36 2QT
01309 671087 • Fax: 01343 850535**

Tastefully restored stone built house one mile from Forres and beside main A96. Large, comfortable, en suite rooms with TV, tea/coffee making facilities, hairdryers and trouser press. Garden area available. Home-cooked dinners available "highly recommended". Wonderful gardens in Forres and Findhorn Village and Foundation also nearby. Excellent location for golf, pony trekking, walking and fishing.

B&B from £25-£30 pppn.

Publisher's note

While every effort is made to ensure accuracy, we regret that FHG Guides cannot accept responsibility for errors, misrepresentations or omissions in our entries or any consequences thereof. Prices in particular should be checked.

We will follow up complaints but cannot act as arbiters or agents for either party.

Inverurie

GRANT ARMS HOTEL
The Square, Monymusk, Inverurie AB51 7HJ
Tel: 01467 651226 • Fax: 01467 651494
e-mail: grantarmshotel@btconnect.com

SB

This splendid former coaching inn of the 18th century has its own exclusive fishing rights on ten miles of the River Don, so it is hardly surprising that fresh salmon and trout are considered specialities of the restaurant, which is open nightly. Bar food is available at lunchtimes and in the evenings, and a pleasing range of fare caters for all tastes.

Double and twin rooms, all with private facilities, accommodate overnight visitors, and some ground floor bedrooms are available, two of which have been specifically designed for wheelchair users.

A traditional Scottish welcome and a real interest in the welfare of guests makes a stay here a particular pleasure.

£80pppn; £90 for 2 persons. Bargain Weekends available.

Other specialised holiday guides from FHG

PUBS & INNS OF BRITAIN

COUNTRY HOTELS OF BRITAIN

WEEKEND & SHORT BREAKS IN BRITAIN & IRELAND

THE GOLF GUIDE WHERE TO PLAY, WHERE TO STAY

PETS WELCOME!

SELF-CATERING HOLIDAYS IN BRITAIN

500 GREAT PLACES TO STAY IN BRITAIN

CARAVAN & CAMPING HOLIDAYS IN BRITAIN

FAMILY BREAKS IN BRITAIN

Published annually: available in all good bookshops or direct from the publisher:
FHG Guides, Abbey Mill Business Centre, Seedhill, Paisley PA1 1TJ
Tel: 0141 887 0428 • Fax: 0141 889 7204
e-mail: admin@fhguides.co.uk • www.holidayguides.com

Angus & Dundee SCOTLAND 257
Brechin, Kirriemuir

Angus & Dundee

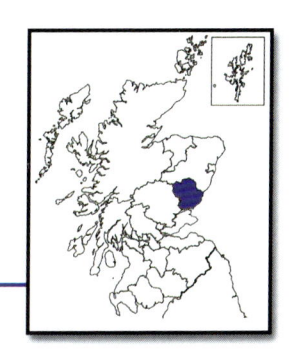

Brathinch is an 18th century farmhouse on a family-run working arable farm, with a large garden, situated off the B966 between Brechin and Edzell.
Rooms have private or en suite bathroom, TV and tea/coffee making facilities. Shooting, fishing, golf, castles, stately homes, wildlife, swimming and other attractions are all located nearby. Easy access to Angus Glens and other country walks. Open all year.
Double £25pppn, twin £26pppn, single £30pn.
We look forward to welcoming you.

Brathinch Farm
By Brechin DD9 7QZ
01356 648292 • Fax: 01356 648003
brathinch@tesco.net

SB

Muirhouses Farm

Muirhouses is a livestock and arable farm set amidst beautiful Angus countryside, close to the Cairngorm National Park.

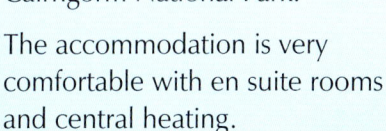

The accommodation is very comfortable with en suite rooms and central heating.

Every comfort is assured, from the homely welcome on arrival to the delicious breakfast. An excellent base for golf, walking and cycling.

SB

Cortachy, Kirriemuir,
Angus DD8 4QG
Tel: 01575 573128 • *Mrs S. McLaren*
e-mail: muirhousesfarm@farming.co.uk
www.muirhousesfarm.co.uk

Argyll & Bute

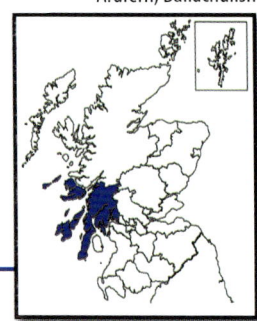

Ardfern, Ballachulish

The Galley of Lorne Inn
Ardfern, By Lochgilphead PA31 8QN
Tel: 01852 500284   Fax: 01852 500578
Web: www.galleyoflorne.co.uk   Email: enquiries@galleyoflorne.co.uk

- 17th Century Grade C listed Drovers Inn with stunning views across Loch Craignish out to Jura and Scarba
- Ideal location for leisure activities • Walking, Fishing, Sailing, Boat Trips, Horse Riding, Diving, Cycling, Golf etc.
- Six Ensuite Bedrooms • Central heating, Colour Satellite LCD TV, Tea and Coffee making facilities
- Dining available in Restaurant, Lounge Bar and Public Bar • Restaurant, Bar and Kids menus • Local Produce
- Food available Monday to Sunday lunchtimes and evenings • Seafood our speciality with mussels from our Loch
- Functions & Weddings catered for • Real Ales • Wine List • Fine collection of Malt Whiskies

view our website for more details

Lyn-Leven, a superior, award-winning licensed guest house overlooking Loch Leven, with every comfort, in the beautiful Highlands of Scotland, is situated one mile from historic Glencoe village.
Four double, two twin and two family bedrooms, all rooms en suite; sittingroom and diningroom.
Central heating. Excellent and varied home cooking served daily. Children welcome at reduced rates. An ideal location for touring. Fishing, walking and climbing in the vicinity.
The house is open all year except Christmas.
Car not essential but private car park provided. 
Bed and Breakfast from £25 • Dinner, Bed and Breakfast from £220 to £255 per person per week
Credit and debit cards accepted
**Mr & Mrs J.A. MacLeod, Lyn-Leven Guest House, Ballachulish PH49 4JP
Tel: 01855 811392 • Fax: 01855 811600 • www.lynleven.co.uk**

Looking for holiday accommodation?
for details of hundreds of properties
throughout the UK visit:
www.holidayguides.com

Argyll & Bute
Cairndow

SCOTLAND 259

Cairndow Stagecoach Inn

A Warm Scottish Welcome on the Shores of Loch Fyne

Cairndow, Argyll PA26 8BN
Tel: 01499 600286
Fax: 01499 600220

AA ★★★ HOTEL

Across the Arrochar Alps at the head of Loch Fyne, this historic coaching inn enjoys a perfect position. All bedrooms are en suite with TV, radio, central heating, tea/coffee and direct-dial phone. Seven de luxe bedrooms with king-size beds and five new lochside rooms are available. Dine by candlelight in our Stables Restaurant; lounge meals and drinks served all day. Ideal centre for touring Western Highlands and Trossachs.

www.cairndowinn.com

Amenities include a loch-side beer garden, sauna, solarium; tee times are available at Loch Lomond.

SHORT BREAKS AVAILABLE

Other specialised holiday guides from **FHG**

PUBS & INNS OF BRITAIN
COUNTRY HOTELS OF BRITAIN
WEEKEND & SHORT BREAKS IN BRITAIN & IRELAND
THE GOLF GUIDE WHERE TO PLAY, WHERE TO STAY
PETS WELCOME!
SELF-CATERING HOLIDAYS IN BRITAIN
500 GREAT PLACES TO STAY IN BRITAIN
CARAVAN & CAMPING HOLIDAYS IN BRITAIN
FAMILY BREAKS IN BRITAIN

Published annually: available in all good bookshops or direct from the publisher:
FHG Guides, Abbey Mill Business Centre, Seedhill, Paisley PA1 1TJ
Tel: 0141 887 0428 • Fax: 0141 889 7204
e-mail: admin@fhguides.co.uk • www.holidayguides.com

260 **SCOTLAND** Argyll & Bute
Dunoon, Glencoe, Inveraray

SB
🍷

West End Hotel
West Bay, Dunoon PA23 7HU
www.westendhotel.com

Tel: 01369 702907 • Fax: 01369 706266
e-mail: mike@westendhotel.com

Situated on the traffic-free West Bay, with private parking, the West End enjoys magnificent views of the Clyde Estuary, yet is only minutes' walk from the town centre.

- All family, twin and double rooms have en suite facilities
- Varied menus • Licensed bar
- Live entertainment most weekends • Games room

Families welcome.

2-nights Dinner, Bed & Breakfast from £76
4-nights Dinner, Bed and breakfast from £140.

Strathassynt

- We are a family-run, licensed Guest House in the beautiful village of Ballachulish, right next to the spectacular scenery of Glencoe and situated ideally for exploring the Scottish Highlands and Islands.
- All of our rooms have en suite facilities, colour TV, DVD player, hospitality tray and individually controlled room heaters.
- We have a comfortable guest lounge, mini bar facilities, separate diningroom, drying room, bike store and large car park.
- We can also offer our guests access to leisure facilities including a swimming pool, jacuzzi, sauna and gym. Easy to find, next door to the Tourist Information Centre. Bed and Breakfast from £20.

Mike and Christine Richardson, Strathassynt Guest House,
Loanfern, Ballachulish, Near Glencoe PH49 4JB • 01855 811261
Fax: 01855 811914 • e-mail: info@strathassynt.com • www.strathassynt.com

Killean Farmhouse

Killean Farmhouse is located just a few miles outside Inveraray. Ideally situated for walking, climbing, pony trekking or just touring. There is fishing for trout, pike or salmon, and opportunities to enjoy boating, water skiing or windsurfing. The whole area is steeped in history and the town of Inveraray itself is a classic example of 18th century Scottish town planning. With all this in mind, the cottages provide high quality accommodation for family holidays.

Mrs Semple, Killean Farmhouse, Inveraray PA32 8XT • Tel: 01499 302474

Argyll & Bute

SCOTLAND 261

Inveraray, Isle of Gigha, Oban

Minard Castle, Inveraray

Stay in style in our 19th Century Scottish castle which stands in its own grounds in beautiful countryside beside Loch Fyne, three-quarters-of-a-mile from the A83 Inveraray to Lochgilphead road.

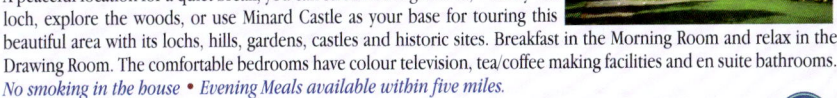

A peaceful location for a quiet break, you can stroll in the grounds, walk by the loch, explore the woods, or use Minard Castle as your base for touring this beautiful area with its lochs, hills, gardens, castles and historic sites. Breakfast in the Morning Room and relax in the Drawing Room. The comfortable bedrooms have colour television, tea/coffee making facilities and en suite bathrooms. *No smoking in the house • Evening Meals available within five miles.*

Bed and Breakfast £55-£60 per person, children half price • Open April to October • We offer a warm welcome in a family home • Self-catering property also available, £150 to £370 per week.

Reinold & Anne Gayre, Minard Castle, Minard PA32 8YB • Tel & Fax: 01546 886272
e-mail: reinoldgayre@minardcastle.com • www.minardcastle.com

Gigha Hotel

The community-owned Isle of Gigha (Gaelic: God's Island) is known as The Jewel of the Inner Hebrides. The Atlantic's crystal clear waters surround this six-mile long magical isle, and lap gently on to its white sandy beaches - creating an aura of peace and tranquillity.

The Gigha Hotel caters admirably for the discerning holidaymaker with comfortable accommodation and first class cuisine, including fresh local seafood. There are also holiday cottages available.

A must for any visitor is a wander around the famous sub-tropical Achamore Gardens, where palm trees and many other exotic plants flourish in Gigha's mild climatic conditions.

The Isle of Gigha Heritage Trust retails quality island-related craft products, some of which have utilised the Trust's own tartan. Other activities on offer include organised walks, bird watching, sea fishing, a nine-hole golf course and alternative therapies.

Call us on 01583 505254 Fax: 01583 505244
www.gigha.org.uk

The Barriemore

Corran Esplanade, Oban PA34 5AQ
Tel: 01631 566356 • Fax: 01631 571084

The Barriemore enjoys a splendid location on the Oban seafront. Built in 1895, the house exudes an opulence in keeping with its late Victorian origins.

All bedrooms are beautifully and individually styled and have en suite facilities. The elegant lounge is an ideal spot for quiet relaxation, while the attractive dining room, overlooking Oban Bay, is the perfect place to enjoy full Scottish breakfasts including locally produced smoked haddock and kippers.

reception@barriemore-hotel.co.uk
www.barriemore-hotel.co.uk

The Palace Hotel
Oban

A small, family hotel offering personal supervision, located on Oban's sea front, with wonderful views over the bay, and less than five minutes' walk from the ferry terminal, train and bus station.

Oban, the "Gateway to the Isles", is the ideal base for a West Highland holiday. By boat you can visit the islands of Kerrera, Coll, Tiree, Lismore, Mull and Iona, and by road Glencoe, Ben Nevis and Inveraray. Fishing, golf, horse riding, sailing, tennis and bowls all nearby.

Built nearly 100 years ago, the hotel has been tastefully modernised and redecorated, while keeping as many of the original features as possible.

All the individually decorated bedrooms are en suite, with TV and coffee/tea making, all non-smoking.

Bed and Breakfast is served in the dining room overlooking the bay. Packed lunches available when requested in advance.

Well behaved pets welcome. Reductions for children.

The Palace Hotel
George Street, Oban, Argyll PA34 5SB
Tel: 01631 562294 • Fax: 01631 562863

www.rentalsystems.com/book/glenavon

"The best view in the Bay"

Argyll & Bute
Oban

SCOTLAND 263

Alltavona House

This very attractive Victorian building is situated on the Esplanade, with spectacular views over to the islands of the West Coast. Restaurants and shops are within 10 minutes' walk, and Alltavona is ideally placed for day trips to Mull, Staffa and Iona, as well as activities such as hill walking, bird watching, fishing, canoeing, sailing, and horse-riding. Aonach Mhor and the White Corries are approximately one hour's drive, for some of the best skiing in Scotland. Accommodation is available in two twin rooms and eight double rooms, all en suite. Special rates available out of season, and discounts for longer booking.

**Carol Harris, Alltavona Guest House,
Corran Esplanade, Oban PA34 5AQ
Tel: 01631 565067 • Mobile: 07771 708301
carol@alltavona.co.uk • www.alltavona.co.uk**

Small, family-run guest house where we aim to make your stay as comfortable as possible. All rooms have central heating, colour TV and hospitality trays; some en suite. A full Scottish breakfast is served, although Continental is available if preferred. We have ample private parking at the rear of the house. Situated 10 minutes' walk from the town centre, train, boat and bus terminals. Oban boasts regular sailings to the Islands, and an excellent golf course, as well as walking, cycling, fishing, or just letting the world go by.

A warm welcome awaits you all year round.

**MRS STEWART, GLENVIEW, SOROBA ROAD,
OBAN PA34 4JF • Tel: 01631 562267**

Argyll & Bute
Oban, Tarbert

Kings Knoll Hotel

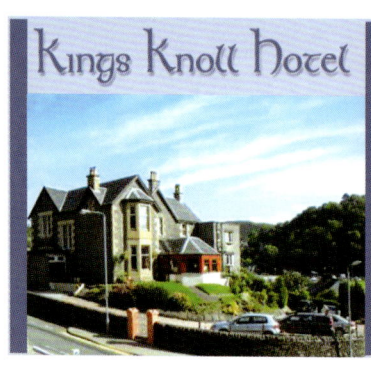

The hotel enjoys magnificent views standing in its own grounds overlooking Oban Bay and is the first hotel that visitors meet when entering on the A85. Most bedrooms are en suite with colour TV and hospitality tray. The elegant Kings Rest lounge bar has a Highland theme and is ideal for a cosy dram before dinner in the Knoll restaurant, which specialises in fresh local produce. Oban is ideally located for visiting the Western Isles and exploring the spectacular local scenery.

Dunollie Road, Oban PA34 5JH
Tel: 01631 562536 • Fax: 01631 566101
e-mail: info@kingsknollhotel.co.uk
www.kingsknollhotel.co.uk

A warm welcome awaits you in this delightful bungalow set in 20 acres of farmland where we breed our own Highland cattle which graze at the front. It is a peaceful location as we are set back from the road, and an ideal spot for touring, with the main ferry terminal at Oban just 10 minutes away. Our luxurious rooms have their own special sitting room attached where you can enjoy your coffee or a glass of wine in peace, and we also have our own restaurant where you can dine.

Mrs J. Currie, Hawthorn, 5 Keil Crofts, Benderloch, Oban PA37 1QS • 01631 720452
e-mail: june@hawthorncottages.com • www.hawthorncottages.com

Rhu House • Tarbert

Rhu House is found in a quiet rural location, set in mature gardens, on the shore of West Loch Tarbert. Situated four miles south of Tarbert on the Campbeltown Road, close to Kennacraig Ferry Terminal. Ideal base for exploring the Kintyre Peninsula or making day trips to the Southerly Hebrides. This is a non-smoking establishment. En suite facilities available, all rooms have scenic views, tea/coffee making facilities and TV. There is a spacious residents' lounge with television. Ample parking, but sorry no dogs in the house.
Prices from £27 per person per night.

Mrs Linda Whyatt, Rhu House, Tarbert PA29 6YF
Tel & Fax: 01880 820231
e-mail: rhuhouse@ukonline.co.uk
www.rhu-house.co.uk

The FHG Directory of Website Addresses
on pages xxx-xxx is a useful quick reference guide for holiday accommodation with e-mail and/or website details

Ayrshire & Arran

Ayr

Ayrshire & Arran

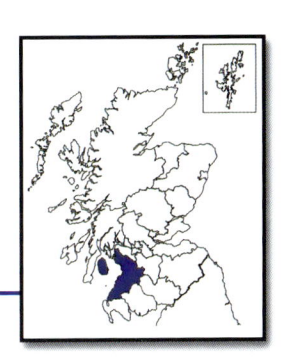

SCOTLAND 265

Traditional 3 Star stone-built farmhouse on working mixed farm with extensive sea views to Arran. Convenient for golf, walking and Burns Country. Also convenient for Culzean Castle and Prestwick Airport.

From Ayr take A719 coast road past Haven Craig Tara; farm is five miles south of Ayr.

Accommodation comprises one double and one twin en suite, ground floor bedrooms with TV and tea/coffee making facilities. Central heating throughout. Children welcome. Pets by arrangement.

Please write, telephone or fax for further information. WELCOME HOST.

Prices from £25. Also self catering.

Mrs L. Wilcox, Fisherton Farm,
Dunure, Ayr KA7 4LF
Tel & Fax: 01292 500223
lesleywilcox@hotmail.com
www.fishertonfarm.homestead.com

MILLER HOUSE
36 Miller Road,
Ayr KA7 2AY
Tel: 01292 282016

A large Victorian B&B with 10 bedrooms, situated close to both the town centre and the seafront, and just 4 miles from Prestwick Airport. Delicious breakfasts served, using local produce; vegetarian and special diets available. Golf is extremely popular in the area, with courses such as Royal Troon and Turnberry. Golf on municipal courses can be booked at a discounted price.

B&B from £25.00pppn

millerhouseayr@hotmail.com
www.millerhouseayr.co.uk

Langley Bank Guest House

39 Carrick Road, Ayr KA7 2RD • 01292 264246

A well appointed Victorian house offering high standards of acccommodation at affordable prices. Centrally located and within walking distance of the town centre, local attractions and golf courses. Double/twin en suite rooms and an en suite family room.
4* luxury accommodation   •   See website for visual tour

Also available for self-catering - a brand new 3-bedroom penthouse apartment offering spectacular views over Arran.
Ideal for golfing parties. Secure underground parking.

e-mail: langleybank@ukonline.co.uk • www.langleybank.co.uk

Craggallan

Craggallan is superbly located in Queen's Terrace, where sea captains and merchants used to live, just 100 yards from Ayr's scenic shore and close to the harbour, now being reborn.

It is just five minutes from the centre of Ayr, where winding streets and monuments make for a fascinating historical walk. Who would guess, for example, that the fine statue of Burns opposite the railway station has an identical copy in Stanley Park, Vancouver.

Ayr's attractions include cinema, live theatre and ten-pin bowling. Craggallan is a 15 minute taxi ride for passengers from Prestwick Airport. We have lots of suggestions for keeping you busy and are well connected in the golf world.

**Craggallan Guest House
8 Queen's Terrace, Ayr KA7 1DU
Tel: 01292 264998
www.craggallan.com**

Ayrshire & Arran

Ayr

SCOTLAND 267

e-mail: eglintonguesthouse@yahoo.co.uk
www.eglintonguesthouse.com

Situated within a part of Ayr steeped in history, within a few minutes' walk of the beach, town centre and many other amenities and entertainment for which Ayr is popular. There are sea and fishing trips available from Ayr Harbour, or a cruise "Doon the Water" on the "Waverley"; golf, swimming pool, cycling, tennis, sailing, windsurfing, walking, etc all available nearby; Prestwick Airport only three miles away.

We have family, double and single rooms, all with washbasins, colour TV and tea/coffee making facilities. En suite facilities and cots available on request. We are open all year round.

Bed and Breakfast from £25. Please send for our brochure for further information.

Peter & Julia Clark, Eglinton Guest House, 23 Eglinton Terrace, Ayr KA7 1JJ • Tel/Fax: 01292 264623

Jacmar B&B @ 23 • Ayr

Welcome to this quality, friendly B&B in a very central location, ideal for all local amenities including the Gaiety Theatre, beach, promenade, racecourse and Burns Country attractions. There is an excellent selection of shops, bars, restaurants and golf courses to cater for all interests. All rooms are tastefully decorated and well appointed, with TV, hospitality tray and hairdryer.
5 minute walk from bus and rail stations, 15 minutes from Prestwick International Airport and 20 minutes from Troon Ferry link.
One double en suite, one family en suite, one single with private facilities.

Mr & Mrs Bolte
Jacmar B&B @ 23
23 Dalblair Road
Ayr KA7 1UF
Tel: 01292 264798
info@jacmar-bandb23.co.uk
www.jacmar-bandb23.co.uk

Leslie Anne
GUEST HOUSE
13 Castlehill Road, Ayr KA7 2HX

Chris and Jennifer extend a warm welcome to their comfortable Victorian guest house, situated close to Ayr town centre and railway station, with links to Prestwick Airport (5 miles) and Glasgow Airport (30 miles).

- All bedrooms are en suite • Ground floor rooms available
- Full cooked Scottish breakfast or continental breakfast • Private parking
- Internet facilities

Ideally positioned for guests to enjoy Ayr's shopping centre and wide variety of bars and restaurants. An excellent base to explore Ayrshire, South West Scotland and the Clyde Coast. Glasgow city centre is only an hour away by train. Ayrshire's famous golf courses are all near by.

Phone: 01292 265646
e-mail: leslieanne2@btinternet.com
www.leslieanne.org.uk

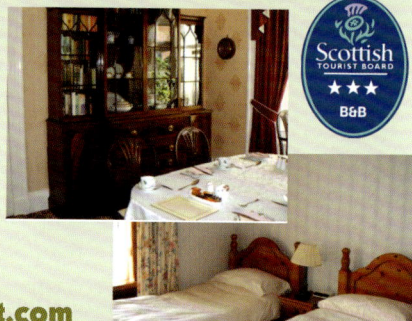

Sunnyside
BED AND BREAKFAST
26 Dunure Road, Alloway, Ayr KA7 4HR

4-Star accommodation close to Burns Cottage, Alloway, birthplace of Robert Burns. We are praised for our **superb service**, **spacious, well furnished double, twin or family bedrooms** and **excellent breakfasts** using **local produce**. Just 5 minutes' walk from the beach and the River Doon. Good bar restaurant 5 minutes' walk, or we can provide home-made soup and sandwiches. Whatever your requirements, we will be pleased to cater for them. *Mrs Helen R Malcolm*

helen@ayrbandb.co.uk
sunnysideayr@aol.com
www.ayrbandb.co.uk
Tel: 01292 441234 • Mobile 07801 556 594

Ayrshire & Arran

Beith, Brodick

SCOTLAND 269

Comfortable friendly accommodation is offered on this 200 acre dairy farm well situated for the A736 Glasgow to Irvine road and for the A737; well placed to visit golf courses, country parks, or leisure centre, also ideal for the ferry to Arran or Millport and for many good shopping centres all around.

A high standard of cleanliness is assured by Mrs Gillan who is a first class cook holding many awards, food being served in the diningroom with its beautiful picture windows.

Three comfortable bedrooms (double en suite, family and twin), all with tea-making facilities, central heating and electric blankets. Two bathrooms with shower; sittingroom with colour TV. Children welcome.

Bed and Breakfast from £18 double room; en suite from £23. Dinner can be arranged.

Mrs Jane Gillan, Shotts Farm, Beith KA15 1LB
Tel & Fax: 01505 502273 • e-mail: shotts.farm@btinternet.com

The Ormidale

is a lively pub with seven bedrooms, famous for its home cooked bar meals, real ale and weekend discos. Set in 7 acres of wooded grounds, 5 minutes from beach and shops.
- 15 minutes from the ferry terminal
- Magnificent views to Goat Fell
- All bedrooms en suite with colour TV, tea/coffee
- Outstanding bar lunches & suppers • Children's menu
- Fully licensed • CAMRA recommended • Beer garden
- Large car park • Children's play area

Room rate from £40 per person per night bed and full Scottish breakfast.

Ormidale is centrally situated on the island and is convenient for mountain access. Pony trekking, putting, swimming, tennis, bowling and golf (Arran has 7 courses) are other activities easily accessible from the Ormidale.

The pub attracts all ages to the regular weekend discos and midweek quiz nights.

Resident Proprietors: Tommy & Barbara Gilmore
Ormidale Hotel, Brodick, Isle of Arran KA27 8BY
e-mail: reception@ormidale-hotel.co.uk
www.ormidale-hotel.co.uk • Tel: 01770 302293

symbols

⊘	Totally non-smoking	🐕	Pets Welcome
🐎	Children Welcome	**SB**	Short Breaks
♿	Suitable for Disabled Guests	🍷	Licensed

Ayrshire & Arran
Brodick, Dalry

Carrick Lodge

Carrick Lodge Guest House, a beautiful, sandstone building situated in an elevated position within attractive mature gardens, enjoys enviable views of Brodick Castle, Brodick Bay and Goatfell.

A relaxed and friendly guest house with spacious accommodation, large dining room and residents' lounge offering panoramic views of the Arran hills.

We provide a warm, friendly welcome to all our guests and can cater for speciality diets in our dining room.

All bedrooms are en suite and come complete with full amenities including television, ironing facilities, hair dryers and tea and coffee making facilities. Free wi-fi internet access. Off-road parking if travelling by car, but Brodick is only a 10 minute walk if on foot.

Arran has something to offer everyone. It is a delight for hillwalkers and climbers and with 7 golf courses, golfers too. Horse riding and trekking are available from two centres on the island and for more of a challenge there is paragliding and quad biking.

Double, twin and single rooms from £32pppn.

Carrick Lodge, Brodick, Isle of Arran KA27 8BH
Tel: 01770 302 550 • Mobile: 07766 074762 • www.carricklodge.co.uk

Langside Farm

Nick and Elise Quick invite you to enjoy a *Superb Bed & Fantastic Breakfast* in a beautiful, spacious 18th century farmhouse in the heart of the Ayrshire countryside. From rustic farmhouse kitchen to sumptuous four-poster bed, Langside Farm is a special place to stay. We welcome you with afternoon tea in the lounge round the log fire, and locally source the best ingredients for your breakfast. Each bedroom has been lovingly designed by us - with little extras everywhere. Langside is an ideal base for leisure and business trips to Ayrshire, and is close to award-winning restaurants. Easy access by car or train to Glasgow, the Clyde coast, ferries to Arran and Ireland, and both airports.

Children are welcome • Strictly no smoking • Fully centrally heated
Each bedroom is en suite • Free off-road parking.
Cyclists, golfers and walkers are welcome • Secure storage available
Babysitting can be arranged • Cot and high chair available.
We welcome your pets and guide dogs (advance notice required)
Laundry and clothes drying facilities available • Wifi access
Garden is available for residents' use • English and French spoken.
Open March until end October + December
Twin/Double £79 per room, Family Room from £79, plus £20 per additional adult and £10 per additional child

By Dalry, Ayrshire KA24 5JZ
Tel: 01294 834402 • Fax: 0870 056 9380
e-mail: mail@langsidefarm.co.uk • www.langsidefarm.co.uk

Ayrshire & Arran　　　　　　　　　　　　　　　　　　　　**SCOTLAND**

Dunlop, King's Cross, Mauchline

East Langton Farm • Near Kilmarnock

A warm welcome in peaceful surroundings, close to all amenities. Twenty minutes to Glasgow or Prestwick Airport, also 20 minutes from the coast with spectacular views overlooking the Isle of Arran, Dalry and the Kilbirnie hills, and Ben Lomond in the distance. Very quiet, peaceful countryside. One double and two twin rooms, all with private bathroom/shower, TV with Teletext, radio alarm, tea/coffee making facilities and hairdryer. Open all year.

£25 per person double, £30 per person single.

Dunlop, Kilmarnock KA3 4DS
Tel: 01560 482978 • Mrs Wilma Burns

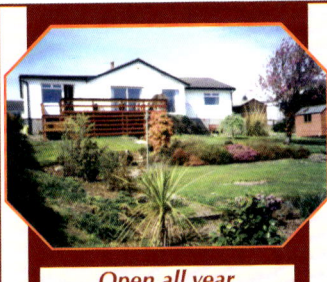

SB

Open all year
Terms from £22pppn

A friendly welcome to Sunnyside, a comfortably furnished bungalow, with one double en suite and one twin-bedded B&B accommodation. Enjoy a wholesome cooked breakfast, or lighter alternatives, and drink in the beautiful unrestricted views over the suntrap garden and across the bonny Clyde.

The peaceful hamlet of King's Cross - off the beaten track, yet easily accessible - is just 15 minutes away from the ferry terminal at Brodick. Natural beauty and history combine to make it an ideal base for exploring Arran: some 56 miles round by road, and aptly described as 'Scotland in miniature'. Sunnyside has full central heating, washbasin, tea/coffee making facilities and colour TV in both rooms, and each having bath and shower. It is fully non-smoking, with private parking.

Mrs Evelyn Coles, "Sunnyside", King's Cross,
Isle of Arran KA27 8RG
Tel: 01770 700422 or 0771 880 5688

SB

Mrs J Clark, Auchenlongford, Ms C. Anglis
Sorn, Mauchline KA5 6JF
01290 550761 or 01290 551331

A warm welcome awaits you at our working sheep farm situated in the hills above the picturesque village of Sorn, only 19 miles from the M74, and 20 miles inland from Ayr. The accommodation is all on the level and comprises three attractive, well appointed bedrooms, with washbasins, tea/coffee making facilities, hair dryer and central heating. There is a large residents' lounge to relax in and soak up the atmosphere of this early 18th century building. A full Scottish breakfast is served with home made jams and marmalades. **B&B from £20.**
Please call for more information.

Please note

All the information in this book is given in good faith in the belief that it is correct. However, the publishers cannot guarantee the facts given in these pages, neither are they responsible for changes in policy, ownership or terms that may take place after the date of going to press. Readers should always satisfy themselves that the facilities they require are available and that the terms, if quoted, still apply.

Ayrshire & Arran
Muirkirk, Patna

The Old Church Bed & Breakfast

is situated in the heart of a quaint historic Ayrshire village surrounded by the Ayrshire Uplands. A former Victorian church, it was converted 4½ years ago to provide a very high standard of accommodation.

- **Cairn Table Suite**: en suite room with king size bed
- **Glenbuck Room**: twin room with private bathroom
- **Glespin Room**: double room with shared bathroom (on request)

All meals, locally sourced and freshly prepared for you, are served in the kitchen which is the heart of our home. We are sure you will find that ALL dining at the Old Church is FINE DINING, from our home baking on arrival to the superb five-course dinners, more casual suppers, full Scottish breakfasts and picnic lunches. Part of Ayrshire Food Network - all food locally produced

Ayr 26 miles, Kilmarnock 26 miles, J12 of M74 15 miles

spacious guest lounge
garden with outdoor seating
off-street parking
laundry facilities
lockable storage for anglers/golfers etc

The Old Church, Glasgow Road, Muirkirk, Ayrshire KA18 3RN
Contact Lesley on: Phone: +44 (0)1290 660045
Mobile: +44 (0)7503001842
e-mail: info@bedandbreakfastayrshire.co.uk
www.bedandbreakfastayrshire.co.uk

A warm welcome awaits you at our family farm situated in the beautiful Doon Valley. An ideal base for touring Ayrshire or Galloway on the Galloway Tourist Route (A713), 6 miles south of Ayr.

Our spacious farmhouse offers en suite twin/double and family rooms with king size beds and all facilities, lounge, dining room and large garden. We serve a delicious varied farmhouse breakfast, with homebaking and farm produce in season. Enjoy a bedtime tea/coffee or hot chocolate with a home baked cookie. Prestwick Airport guests welcome (whatever the time!).

Self catering available from 2009.
Children and pets welcome. B&B from £22.50 pppn, children half price.

Smithston Farm, Patna, By Ayr KA6 7EZ
Mrs Joyce Bothwell - 01292 531211
e-mail: bothwellfarming@onetel.com
www.smithstonfarmhouse.co.uk

Borders
Biggar, Hawick

Borders

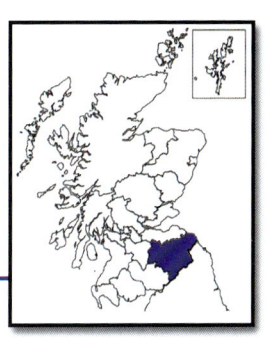

SCOTLAND 273

South Mains Farm is a working family farm, situated in an elevated position with good views, on the B7016 between Biggar and Broughton. An ideal place to take a break on a North/South journey. Edinburgh 29 miles, Peebles 11 miles. Well situated for touring the Border regions in general.

A comfortable bed and excellent breakfast provided in this centrally heated farmhouse. The lounge has a log fire and the bedrooms, two double and one single, have hand-basins, electric blankets and tea/coffee making facilities. Guest bathroom. Open all year. Car essential, parking.

Terms £23 pppn.
If you are interested just ring,
write or call in.
Warm welcome assured.

Mrs Rosemary Harper,
South Mains Farm,
Biggar ML12 6HF
Tel: 01899 860226

SB

Hizzy's Guesthouse

A totally refurbished former hotel, named after Steven Hislop, who won eleven Isle of Man TT victories before his tragic accidental death in 2003. Various rooms available, including two family rooms and a four-poster bedroom. Contact Frankie or Amanda, or visit our website for more information. We guarantee a warm welcome and personal service.

23B North Bridge Street, Hawick TD9 9BD
Tel: 01450 372 101
e-mail: frankie@hizzys.co.uk
www.hizzys.co.uk

SB

274 **SCOTLAND** **Borders**
Jedburgh

Hundalee House

Large historic Manor House set in 15 acres of secluded gardens and woodland near Jedburgh, decorated in a charming Victorian style. All rooms are en suite, one with four-poster, and all with the expected luxuries including TV, tea/coffee making facilities, hairdryer, central heating, wireless internet.

Bed and Breakfast from £26 to £30 per person per night. Single £30 to £45. Reductions for children.

Sheila Whittaker, Hundalee House, Jedburgh TD8 6PA • Tel & Fax: 01835 863011
e-mail: sheila.whittaker@btinternet.com • www.accommodation-scotland.org

The Spinney, Langlee, Jedburgh TD8 6PB

SB

- Spacious rooms with many extra touches to enhance your stay.
- A varied breakfast menu served at separate tables.
- Situated two miles south of Jedburgh on the A68
- One double en suite, one twin en suite and one double with private bathroom
- Open March-November

Tel: 01835 863525
e-mail: thespinney@btinternet.com
www.thespinney-jedburgh.co.uk

Scottish Tourist Board ★★★★ B&B

Ferniehirst Mill Lodge
Jedburgh TD8 6PQ • Tel: 01835 863279

Built in 1980, Ferniehirst Mill Lodge has all the amenities required for your comfort whilst blending with the existing mill buildings and stables.

Just south of Jedburgh, situated in a secluded valley, the Lodge is a haven for bird life. Ideal for walking, fishing and horse riding.

8 bedrooms, all with en suite bathroom or shower, and tea/coffee making facilities. Central heating throughout and the spacious lounge has a log fire for chillier evenings. Full cooked breakfast and dinner are served in the attractive pine dining room. The emphasis is on home cooking using local produce. There is a small bar for residents.

Personal service and warm hospitality from owners Alan and Christine.

AA ★★★

ferniehirstmill@aol.com • www.ferniehirstmill.co.uk

Borders
Jedburgh, Kelso, Melrose

SCOTLAND 275

Early 19th century converted sawmill in one acre of garden, 500 metres off A68 and eight miles south of the border town of Jedburgh. Owned by Jean and Robert Lyle and their little dog Millie, the mill was converted in 1990 into a charming house in a very peaceful and tranquil setting and furnished in a rustic style. Jedburgh has many historical features, as have Melrose, Kelso and Dryburgh, all close at hand.

The mill has one double room en suite and a twin en suite. It lies within the foothills of the Cheviot Hills with many lovely walks with Roman remains all within easy distance. It is also a very handy stopping off point en route to Edinburgh and the Highlands. Fishing available locally.
B&B Single £30pn, Double £25pppn • DB&B £42.50pppn • Open all year.

Mrs Jean Lyle, Edgerston Mill, Jedburgh TD8 6NF • Tel/Fax: 01835 840343
e-mail: jean@edgerston-mill.co.uk • www.edgerston-mill.co.uk

Edenbank House • By Kelso
www.edenbank.co.uk

Enjoy a warm welcome and relax in comfort. Lovely Victorian country house within two miles of Kelso, with magnificent views in all directions. 3 spacious bedrooms, with en suite/private facilities. Open all year.

Tel: 01573 226734 • christina.moffatt@btopenworld.com
Edenbank House, Edenbank, By Kelso TD5 7SX

George & Abbotsford Hotel, Melrose

30 bedrooms (single, twin, double, triple and family) en suite;
also a four-poster for that touch of luxury
Bar lounge, a relaxing environment for light meals and refreshments
Scott's Restaurant provides a quiet and intimate atmosphere
to enjoy our à la carte menu
Open all year • B&B from £35pppn

George & Abbotsford Hotel, High Street, Melrose,
Scottish Borders TD6 9PD
Tel: 01896 822308 • Fax: 01896 823363
www.georgeandabbotsford.co.uk
enquiries@georgeandabbotsford.co.uk

Borders

Peebles, St Boswells

Winkston Farmhouse

Well established, welcoming and comfortably furnished Georgian country house. Situated close to Peebles in the centre of lovely Borders countryside. Very central for all local amenities. Mountain biking, golfing, fishing, walking and much more. Central situation 23 miles from Edinburgh on the bus route. Three rooms: one double/twin en suite, one double and one twin. Non-smoking. Selection of self-catering cottages also available.

Mrs Haydock, Winkston Farmhouse, Peebles EH45 8PH • 01721 721264
e-mail: holidayatwinkston@btinternet.com
www.winkstonholidays.co.uk

Clint Lodge Country Guest House

St Boswells, Melrose TD6 0DZ
Tel: 01835 822027 • Fax: 01835 822656

Enjoy a warm welcome and excellent Bed & Breakfast at this traditional Scottish guest house. The bright and spacious drawing room has an open log fire; small adjoining sun lounge. Residents can enjoy a meal in the atmospheric dining room or a stroll in the large garden. Traditional features have been enhanced, with the old wooden and tiled floors, original fireplaces and wood surrounds adding to Clint Lodge's appealing and relaxing atmosphere. There are five bedrooms - four are en suite, one of the twin rooms has a private bathroom. All have twin or super king size double beds, tea and coffee making facilities, TV, wifi access.

www.clintlodge.co.uk • e-mail: clintlodge@aol.com

Ideally located in the heart of the Scottish Borders

Other specialised holiday guides from **FHG**

PUBS & INNS OF BRITAIN

COUNTRY HOTELS OF BRITAIN

WEEKEND & SHORT BREAKS IN BRITAIN & IRELAND

THE GOLF GUIDE WHERE TO PLAY, WHERE TO STAY

PETS WELCOME!

SELF-CATERING HOLIDAYS IN BRITAIN

500 GREAT PLACES TO STAY IN BRITAIN

CARAVAN & CAMPING HOLIDAYS IN BRITAIN

FAMILY BREAKS IN BRITAIN

Published annually: available in all good bookshops or direct from the publisher:
FHG Guides, Abbey Mill Business Centre, Seedhill, Paisley PA1 1TJ
Tel: 0141 887 0428 • Fax: 0141 889 7204
e-mail: admin@fhguides.co.uk • www.holidayguides.com

Borders   **SCOTLAND** 277

Selkirk, West Linton

THE GARDEN HOUSE
Whitmuir, Selkirk TD7 4PZ
Tel: 01750 721728
e-mail: whitmuir@btconnect.com
www.whitmuirfarm.co.uk

This Scottish Bed and Breakfast offers guests a peaceful stay in a comfortable, warm, modern farm house set in 400 acres with cattle, sheep, crops and woodland. Located between Selkirk and St Boswells, just off the A699, in the heart of the Scottish Borders. Our own loch makes a perfect spot for a picnic or swim, and fishing for perch and pike is allowed; grazing for horses. Walkers are close to both the Southern Upland Way and St Cuthberts Way. There are four bedroom suites available, all with private bath/shower room, TV, tea/coffee facilities, etc. Large south-facing garden with patio area, barbecue and furniture. Ample parking. Pets welcome by arrangement. Terms from £22 to £32 pppn depending on season, room and number of nights stay. Packed lunches and evening meals available.

SB

The Meadows is a modern four bedroom detached house located in a quiet situation near the centre of the conservation village of West Linton, which is on the A702, the main Edinburgh to Carlisle road, with handy access to Edinburgh and central Scotland. All bedrooms have tea/coffee making facilities, TV and hairdryer. Full range of quality breakfasts available including traditional English or scrambled egg with smoked salmon and oatcakes. Evening meals available by prior arrangement. Pets welcome. Parking.
Terms from £23pppn twin, £25pppn single, £25pppn double/twin en suite.

**Mrs M. Thain, The Meadows Bed and Breakfast,
4 Robinsland Drive, West Linton EH46 7JD
01968 661798 • e-mail: mwthain@btinternet.com
www.themeadowsbandb.co.uk**

Visit the FHG website
www.holidayguides.com

for details of the wide choice of accommodation featured in the full range of FHG titles

Dumfries & Galloway

Dumfries & Galloway
Castle Douglas, Dumfries, Gatehouse of Fleet

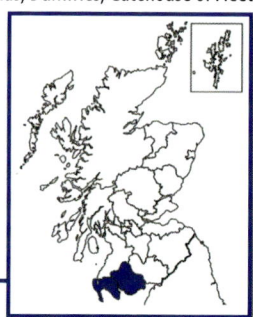

Albion House
49 Ernespie Road, Castle Douglas, Kirkcudbrightshire DG7 1LD

A warm Galloway welcome awaits you at Albion House, which was built around 1860. Well-positioned on the outskirts of town within an acre of private grounds with ample private parking, yet only a few minutes' walk to all amenities. We have a variety of rooms/suites with individual decor providing a high standard of accommodation. Castle Douglas is an ideal location to experience all that Galloway has to offer – stunning scenery, historic buildings, gardens, fishing, golfing and interesting walks. Excellent cycling facilities in the region.

Bed and Breakfast from £30-£32 sharing twin/double Single £40-£42.

Tel/Fax: 01556 502360
e-mail: pikoe007@aol.com

Hamilton House
12 Moffat Road, Dumfries DG1 1NJ
Telephone: 01387 266606 • Fax 01387 262060
Email: bookings@hamiltonhousedumfries.co.uk
www.hamiltonhousedumfries.co.uk

Hamilton House is a four star family-run guest house, centrally located in Dumfries, which has recently been fully refurbished to the highest standard and offers six comfortable, spacious, en suite bedrooms. Private car park to the rear. Close to railway station and DGOne Leisure Centre and approximately 10 minutes' walk from the town centre. Dumfries has a variety of excellent restaurants, bars, cafes and shops. Whether your visit is long or short you will experience a warm welcome at Hamilton House. *Winter Breaks available.*

The Bobbin Guest House • Gatehouse of Fleet

The family-run Bobbin Guest House is located on the High Street within easy walking distance of pubs, cafes and restaurants. Spacious en suite bedrooms equipped with bath/shower, tea/coffee making facilities and colour TV. Guest lounge and dining room. Front door keys allow you to come and go as you please, with private off-road parking to the rear. Bed & Breakfast from £25pppn.

36 High Street, Gatehouse of Fleet, Castle Douglas DG7 2HP • 01557 814229
Contact Helen Findlay for details

Dumfries & Galloway

Kirkton, Moffat

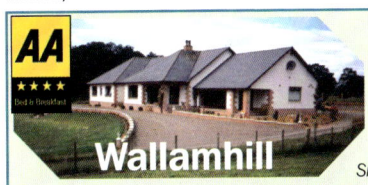

SCOTLAND 279

Wallamhill

A charming country house, tastefully furnished, with a warm, friendly, welcoming atmosphere. The spacious en suite bedrooms (two double/family and one twin) have lovely views over garden and countryside. Beautifully appointed, each room has colour satellite TV plus video, tea/coffee making facilities, shower and toilet, and full central heating. Small health suite, steam room and sauna available for guests' use.

Situated in peaceful countryside only three miles from Dumfries town centre with excellent shopping, swimming pool, ice bowl for curling, green bowling, fishing and golf. Hill and forest walks, birdwatching, cycling and mountain bike trails all nearby.

Bed and Breakfast from £28 per person.

Mr & Mrs G. Hood, Wallamhill House, Kirkton, Dumfries DG1 1SL
Tel: 01387 248249 • e-mail: wallamhill@aol.com • www.wallamhill.co.uk

Hartfell House & The Limetree Restaurant

A country guest house and award-winning restaurant set in the magnificent scenery of Moffat. Located in peaceful surroundings, it is a perfect retreat and an ideal base for exploring Dumfries and Galloway and the Borders. There are seven spacious bedroooms, each with en suite facilities, and a large guest lounge with stunning views. Enjoy a memorable meal in the critically acclaimed Limetree Restaurant. A full Scottish breakfast is cooked to order and a continental buffet is also provided.

B&B from £35 pppn.

Hartfell Crescent, Moffat DG10 9AL • Tel: 01683 220153
www.hartfellhouse.co.uk • enquiries@hartfellhouse.co.uk

Bridge House

A beautiful Victorian property, Bridge House lies in attractive gardens in a quiet residential area on the fringe of the town. The atmosphere is friendly and relaxed. The proprietor is an award winning chef and he provides excellent dinners for both residents and non-residents.

The Master Bedroom boasts a traditional four-poster bed along with delightful views from the large bay window. Double and Twin rooms and a large family room are also available. All rooms are en suite and have tea/coffee making facilities and televisions.

For the comfort and safety of all guests Bridge House is non-smoking throughout. Prices start at £35 per person for B&B. Listed in The Guardian Best Bed & Breakfast Directory.

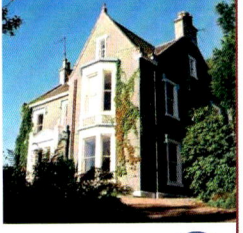

Bridge House, Well Road, Moffat DG10 9JT
Telephone: 01683 220558 • e-mail: info@bridgehousemoffat.co.uk
www.bridgehousemoffat.co.uk

BARNHILL SPRINGS
Country Guest House, Moffat DG10 9QS

Barnhill Springs is an early Victorian country house standing in its own grounds and overlooking some of the finest views of Upper Annandale. Situated on the Southern Upland Way, half-a-mile from the A74/M, the house and its surroundings retain an air of remote peacefulness. Comfortable accommodation, residents' lounge with open fire, all decorated and furnished to an exceptionally high standard of comfort. Ideal centre for touring South-West Scotland and the Borders, or for an overnight stop. Pets free of charge. Bed & Breakfast from £29; Evening Meal (optional) from £18.

Mr & Mrs W. Gray • 01683 220580

The Lagganmore Hotel and Golf Club
Lagganmore, Portpatrick, Dumfriesshire DG9 9AB

Situated just ten yards from the first tee, The Lagganmore Hotel combines traditional Scottish cuisine with comfortable, attractively furnished accommodation. The popular lounge bar remains open all day, serving lunches and suppers. The Lagganmore course provides a great test for every golfer, combining natural valleys and contours with streams and water features. Our feature hole, the Par 5 7th, is the best in South West Scotland.

Tel: 01776 810499 or 01776 810262
info@lagganmoregolf.co.uk
www.lagganmoregolf.co.uk

Special packages combining golf, dinner, full Scottish breakfast and accommodation: two nights £130pp, three nights £150pp.

Looking for Holiday Accommodation?

FHG
KUPERARD

for details of hundreds of properties throughout the UK, visit our website

www.holidayguides.com

Dumfries & Galloway

Sanquhar, Wigtown

SCOTLAND 281

Blackaddie
COUNTRY HOUSE HOTEL

Set in 2 acres of gardens on the banks of the River Nith, by Sanquhar

AWARD WINNING FOOD AND A WARM WELCOME AWAITS

9 bedrooms &
3 self-catering cottages

tel: 01659 50270
www.blackaddiehotel.co.uk

CRAIGLEMINE COTTAGE STB ★★

With a rural location and peaceful atmosphere it's a wonderful place to unwind for a short break or a longer holiday. We have one double/family room, one single/twin room and dining room/lounge. Prices from £23. Evening meals available on request, including vegetarian or other dietary needs. Non- smoking. Off-road parking. Children welcome (under six years free). Pets welcome. An ideal base for walkers, cyclists, golf or touring. We also cater for amateur astronomers - call for details. Whether exploring the history, countryside or unspoilt beaches there is something for everyone. You can be sure of a friendly welcome all year round. Contact us for more details, or visit our website.

Glasserton, Near Whithorn DG8 8NE
Tel: 01988 500594
e-mail: cottage@fireflyuk.net
www.startravel.fireflyinternet.co.uk

SB

Please note

All the information in this book is given in good faith in the belief that it is correct. However, the publishers cannot guarantee the facts given in these pages, neither are they responsible for changes in policy, ownership or terms that may take place after the date of going to press. Readers should always satisfy themselves that the facilities they require are available and that the terms, if quoted, still apply.

282 SCOTLAND   Edinburgh & Lothians
Bathgate, Blackburn, Edinburgh

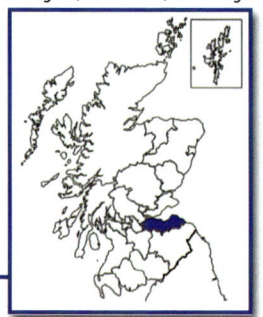

Edinburgh & Lothians

SB

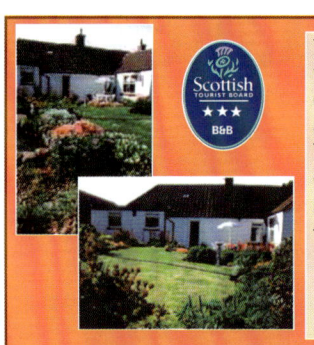

This 17th century farmhouse is situated two miles from M8 Junction 4, which is midway between Glasgow and Edinburgh. This peaceful location overlooks panoramic views of the countryside. All rooms are on the ground floor, ideal for disabled visitors, and have central heating, colour TV and tea/coffee making facilities. We are within easy reach of golf, fishing, cycling (15 mile cycle track runs along back of property). Ample security parking. Open January to December. Pets and children by arrangement.

Terms from £18 to £25 per person per night, single £25 to £30.

Mrs F. Gibb, Tarrareoch Farm, Station Road, Armadale, Near Bathgate EH48 3BJ • 01501 730404
e-mail: nicola@gibb0209.fsnet.co.uk

Cruachan B&B

A relaxed and friendly base is provided at Cruachan from which to explore central Scotland. The centre of Edinburgh can be reached easily by train or by 'park & ride' bus service, and Glasgow is only 35 minutes by car. All rooms en suite/private facilities, full hospitality tray, fresh towels daily, colour TV and central heating. Hosts Kenneth and Jacqueline ensure you receive the utmost in quality of service, meticulously presented accommodation and of course a full Scottish breakfast. They look forward to having the pleasure of your company. All major Credit Cards welcome.

Bed and Breakfast from £29 per person per night.

78 East Main Street, Blackburn EH47 7QS
Tel: 01506 655221 • Fax: 01506 652795
e-mail: enquiries@cruachan.co.uk • www.cruachan.co.uk

AA ★★★ Guest Accommodation

SB

EDINBURGH. International Guest House, 37 Mayfield Gardens, Edinburgh EH9 2BX (0131 667 2511; Fax: 0131 667 1112).
Conveniently situated one and a half miles south of Princes Street on the main A701, on the main bus route. Private parking. All bedrooms en suite, with direct-dial telephone, colour television and tea/coffee making facilities. Some rooms enjoy magnificent views across to the extinct volcano of Arthur's Seat. The full Scottish breakfasts served on the finest bone chine are a delight.
Rates: Bed and Breakfast from £35 to £75 single; £60 to £130 double.
AA ★★★★
e-mail: intergh1@yahoo.co.uk
www.accommodation-edinburgh.com

A useful index of towns/counties appears on pages 363-366

Edinburgh & Lothians

SCOTLAND 283

Edinburgh

Spylaw Bank House

Elegant Georgian Country House built around 1790, situated within the city of Edinburgh. It has a secluded position in walled gardens close to Colinton village and three miles from the city centre. Luxuriously appointed en suite bedrooms with many personal touches. Relax in the original drawing room with its open fire and antique furnishings and take breakfast in the period dining room.

Ideally situated for sightseeing in Edinburgh and touring the Borders, Fife and Perthshire. Five miles from airport, one from city by-pass. Ample parking. Frequent buses to city centre - a 15 minute journey.

Bed and Breakfast from £35 per person.

www.spylawbankhouse.com

David Martin, Spylaw Bank House, 2 Spylaw Avenue, Colinton, Edinburgh EH13 0LR • 0131-441 5022 • mobile: 07981 923017
e-mail: davidsmartin@blueyonder.co.uk

Aaron Lodge,
128 Old Dalkeith Road,
Edinburgh EH16 4SD
Tel: 0131 664 2755
Fax: 0131 672 2236
e-mail: Dot@Baigan.freeserve.co.uk
www.aaronlodgeedinburgh.co.uk

Welcome to Aaron Lodge!

This is a 200 year old former coach house which has been extensively modernised and refurbished.

Every room has:
• 37" LCD TV • Large walk- in shower • Safe • Hairdryer
• Wireless Internet Access • Freeview TV with Sports Channels

Services include:
• Complimentary Tea and Coffee served in conservatory lounge
• Free Parking • Nearest Guest House to new Royal Infirmary

284 **SCOTLAND**　　　　　　　　　　　　　　　　　　　　　　　**Edinburgh & Lothians**

Edinburgh

Blossom House is a traditional stone-built town house attractively situated within the Newington district of Edinburgh, less than one mile from the City Centre and on a main bus route.

All bedrooms are tastefully furnished, with colour TV and tea/coffee hospitality tray; most have en suite facilities. Some rooms enjoy attractive views towards the extinct volcano of Arthur's Seat. Full Scottish breakfasts are served in the spacious dining room. Many fine restaurants are situated nearby, providing a wide range of cuisine to suit everyone's taste and pocket. Central heating. Private car park. B&B from £20 per person per night.

Mrs Kay, Blossom House, 8 Minto Street, Edinburgh EH9 1RG
Tel: 0131-667 5353 • Fax: 0131-667 2813
e-mail: blossom_house@hotmail.com • www.blossomguesthouse.co.uk

CASTLE PARK GUEST HOUSE
75 Gilmore Place, Edinburgh EH3 9NU • Tel: 0131 229 1215 • e-mail: castlepark@btconnect.com

A warm and friendly welcome awaits you at Castle Park Guest House, a charming Victorian Guest House ideally situated close to King's Theatre and city centre. Travel along the Royal Mile with Edinburgh Castle at one end and the Palace of Holyrood House, the Official Scottish Residence of the Queen, at the other end.

Centrally heated throughout, colour TV in all rooms, en suite facilities available, tea/coffee hospitality tray, full Scottish/Continental breakfast. Children welcome – special prices. Off-street car parking.

www.castleparkguesthouse.co.uk

Only 3 miles from Edinburgh Airport and 4 miles from the city centre, this detached bungalow is in an ideal location. There is a good bus service into the centre of Edinburgh and we have free off-street parking available. We are a non-smoking establishment. We can provide single, twin, double and family accommodation. All rooms have a private entrance; en suite facilities; television; hospitality tray; fridge; hairdryer; iron; etc. Breakfast is served in your room (cooked or Continental). Rates from £30 per person.

Ingleneuk Tel: 0131 317 1743
31 Drum Brae North, Edinburgh EH4 8AT
e-mail: ingleneukbnb@btinternet.com • www.ingleneukbandb.co.uk

KENVIE GUEST HOUSE 16 Kilmaurs Road, Edinburgh EH16 5DA

A charming and comfortable Victorian town house situated in a quiet and pleasant residential part of the city, approximately one mile south of the centre and one small block from Main Road (A7) leading to the City and Bypass to all routes. Excellent bus service.

We offer for your comfort, complimentary tea/coffee, central heating, colour TV and No Smoking rooms. En suite rooms available. Lovely breakfasts and lots of additional caring touches.

A warm and friendly welcome is guaranteed from Richard and Dorothy.

Tel: 0131-668 1964 • Fax: 0131-668 1926 • e-mail: dorothy@kenvie.co.uk

Edinburgh & Lothians

Linlithgow, Pathhead

A large Victorian villa with modern spacious accommodation overlooking historic Linlithgow Palace – centrally located for easy access to all local amenities.

With the Town Centre only a few minutes' walk away the house is within easy reach of the Canal Basin, the main bus and rail terminals, and the motorway network to Glasgow, Edinburgh and Stirling.

Open all year. Credit Cards accepted. B&B available from £35 per night.

**Mr & Mrs J Caddle, Strawberry Bank House,
13 Avon Place, Strawberry Bank, Linlithgow EH49 6BL • Tel & Fax: 01506 848 372
e-mail: gillian@strawberrybank-scotland.co.uk
www.strawberrybank-scotland.co.uk**

SB

We are situated on the A68, three miles south of Pathhead at the picturesque village of Fala. The house is an 18th century coaching inn (Listed building). All bedrooms have washbasins and tea/coffee making facilities; two are en suite. All the rooms are comfortably furnished. We are within easy reach of Edinburgh and the Scottish Borders. A warm welcome is extended to all our guests – our aim is to make your stay a pleasant one.

Cost is from £23 per person; children under 12 years £16.

**Mrs Anne Gordon, "Fairshiels",
Blackshiels, Pathhead EH37 5SX
Tel: 01875 833665
e-mail: anne@fairshiels.fsnet.co.uk**

Other specialised holiday guides from FHG

PUBS & INNS OF BRITAIN

COUNTRY HOTELS OF BRITAIN

WEEKEND & SHORT BREAKS IN BRITAIN & IRELAND

THE GOLF GUIDE WHERE TO PLAY, WHERE TO STAY

PETS WELCOME!

SELF-CATERING HOLIDAYS IN BRITAIN

500 GREAT PLACES TO STAY IN BRITAIN

CARAVAN & CAMPING HOLIDAYS IN BRITAIN

FAMILY BREAKS IN BRITAIN

Published annually: available in all good bookshops or direct from the publisher:

FHG Guides, Abbey Mill Business Centre, Seedhill, Paisley PA1 1TJ
Tel: 0141 887 0428 • Fax: 0141 889 7204
e-mail: admin@fhguides.co.uk • www.holidayguides.com

Fife

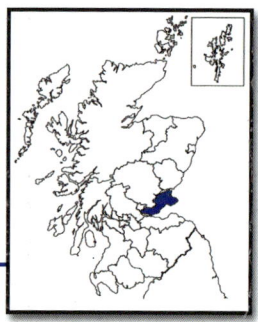

LOMOND GUEST HOUSE inc. Food@Lomonds
Tel: 01333 300511

Situated in the conservation of area of Leven, 150 yards from the beach, and with two golf courses only 5 minutes' walk away. 20 other courses within easy reach.

All rooms are testefully decorated to include digital TV, free internet connection, hospitality tray including mineral water, hairdryer and toiletries, some are also en suite.

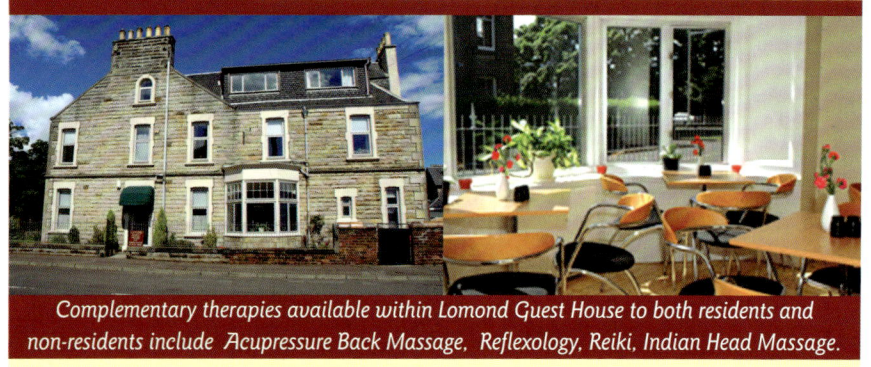

Complementary therapies available within Lomond Guest House to both residents and non-residents include Acupressure Back Massage, Reflexology, Reiki, Indian Head Massage.

Church Road, Leven KY8 4JE • Tel: 01333 300511
www.lomondguesthouse.co.uk • info@lomondguesthouse.co.uk

This quiet Victorian former rectory provides the ideal location for touring. Ideal base for golf enthusiasts, within easy reach of 46 golf courses and only 14 miles from St Andrews. 40 minutes from Edinburgh Airport, Perth and 30-35 minutes from Dundee.

**Mrs Pam MacDonald, Dunclutha Guest House, 16 Victoria Road, Leven KY8 4EX
Tel: 01333 425515 • Fax: 01333 422311
e-mail: pam.leven@blueyonder.co.uk
www.dunclutha.myby.co.uk**

Facilities include three en suite rooms – one double, one twin, one family (sleeps three to four), one family (sleeps three) with private bathroom. Colour TV and tea/coffee facilities in all rooms, cot available. Visitors' lounge with TV. Most credit cards accepted. Open all year. Terms from £30pppn. Non-smoking.

Fife
Culross, St Andrews

St Mungo's B&B

17th century Listed building on the outskirts of the best preserved medieval village in Scotland. Culross has a range of National Trust buildings and an historic abbey. It is an ideal location for touring central Scotland – Edinburgh, Glasgow, Stirling, Perth, St Andrews and the Trossachs are all within easy reach.

Both rooms have views over the Forth Estuary and have TV, hairdryer etc. One family room (sleeps two or three) and one double room, both with en suite.
Full central heating. Extensive mature gardens.

Off-street parking • All rooms non-smoking
Bed and Breakfast from £27.50pp.

Judith Jackson, St Mungo's B&B, Low Causeway, Culross KY12 8HJ
Tel: 01383 882102 e-mail: martinpjackson@hotmail.com
www.milford.co.uk/scotland/accom/h-a-1763.html

Spinkstown Farmhouse

Only two miles from St Andrews on the picturesque A917 road to Crail, Spinkstown is a uniquely designed farmhouse with views of the sea and surrounding countryside. Bright and spacious, it is furnished to a high standard.

Accommodation consists of double and twin rooms, all en suite, with tea/coffee making facilities and colour TV; diningroom and lounge. Substantial farmhouse breakfast to set you up for the day.

The famous Old Course, historic St Andrews and several National Trust properties are all within easy reach, as well as swimming, tennis, putting, bowls, horse riding, country parks, nature reserves, beaches and coastal walks.

Plenty of parking available. Bed and Breakfast from £30.

Mrs Anne Duncan,
Spinkstown Farmhouse,
St Andrews KY16 8PN
Tel & Fax: 01334 473475
e-mail: anne@spinkstown.com
www.spinkstown.com

Glasgow & District

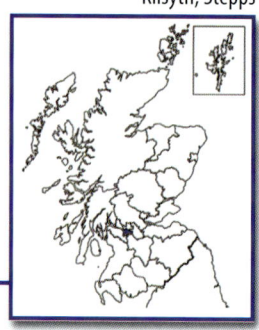

Kilsyth, Stepps

A working family farm situated close to the town of Kilsyth at the foot of the Kilsyth Hills, a great base to explore central Scotland. Glasgow, Stirling 20 minutes. Croy Station is just five minutes' drive away, where a short train journey will take you into the centre of Edinburgh. Golf, fishing, hill walking and a swimming pool are all within half a mile.

One triple/family room, one single room, both with TV and tea/coffee facilities. B&B from £22-£25. Open all year.

Libby MacGregor, Allanfauld Farm, Kilsyth, Glasgow G65 9DF • Tel & Fax: 01236 822155
e-mail: allanfauld@hotmail.com

Stepps village is situated north-east of Glasgow just off the A80. This self-built family home nestles down a quiet leafy lane offering the ideal location for an overnight stay or touring base with the main routes to Edinburgh, Stirling and the North on our doorstep. Easy commuting to Loch Lomond, the Trossachs or Clyde Valley. M8 exit 12 from the south, or A80 Cumbernauld Road from the north. Glasgow only ten minutes away, Glasgow Airport 12 miles. Ample parking.
All rooms offer colour TV, tea/coffee tray and en suite or private facilities. Generous Continental-style breakfast incl. Home from Home – warm welcome assured!
Self-catering also available.
From £25 to £35 per person per night.
Mrs P. Wells • 0141-779 1990 • Fax: 0141-779 1951
e-mail: phyl@avenueend.co.uk • www.avenueend.co.uk

"Avenue End" B&B
21 West Avenue, Stepps, Glasgow G33 6ES

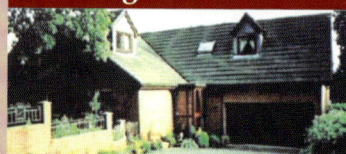

Highlands
Aviemore, Carrbridge

Highlands

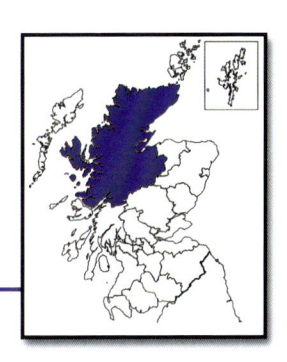

SCOTLAND 289

RAVENSCRAIG

Scottish Tourist Board ★★★★ Guest House — *AA ★★★★ Guest House*

A 12-bedroom Victorian house situated on the main street in Aviemore, right in the centre of Cairngorm National Park. An ideal base for exploring the Highlands. Six en suite rooms available in the main house, some with views towards the Cairngorm Mountains and ski area, others overlook Craigellachie Nature Reserve. Six en suite rooms available in the newly-built garden annexe; large, spacious rooms, each with its own porch and front door onto the garden and parking area. Traditional Scottish breakfast served using locally produced ingredients.

Bed and Breakfast £25 to £40.

Jill and Jonathan Gatenby,
Ravenscraig Guest House,
141 Grampian Road,
Aviemore PH22 1RP
Tel: 01479 810278
Fax: 01479 810210
info@aviemoreonline.com
www.aviemoreonline.com

SB

AA Guest Accommodation

The Pines COUNTRY GUESTHOUSE
DUTHIL, CARRBRIDGE PH23 3ND • 01479 841220

Relax and enjoy our Highland hospitality, woodland setting; all rooms en suite. Traditional or vegetarian home cooking.

B&B from £25 daily; DB&B from £236 weekly. Children and pets welcome.

www.thepines-duthil.co.uk

SB

Highlands

Dornoch, Drumnadrochit, Fort William

A friendly, family-run B&B located alongside Royal Dornoch's Struie Course, close to the beach and all other attractions. All bedrooms are on the ground floor, are comfortably furnished and have en suite shower rooms with washbasin and wc, TV with freeview, wi-fi internet access, hairdryer and complimentary hostess tray.

One room is either twin or super-kingsize and the other has a kingsize and single bed. There is private off-street parking and a garden for your enjoyment.

Rates from £25 pppn.
e-mail: EMackayAmalfi@aol.com
www.amalfidornoch.com

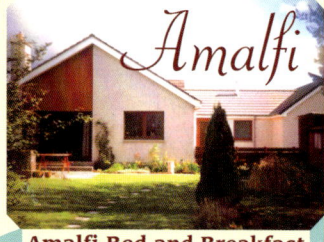

Amalfi Bed and Breakfast
River Street, Dornoch
IV25 3LY
Tel: 01862 810015

Escape to the Scottish Highlands for peace and tranquillity and stay in our comfortable, friendly hotel with fantastic views of Loch Meiklie and Glen Urquhart. The hotel nestles in six acres of wooded grounds close to Loch Ness and Glen Affric nature reserve and is ideally suited for touring the Highlands. Most rooms are en suite and all have tea/coffee making facilities, hairdryer, colour TV, plus video in family rooms. There is a residents' lounge warmed by a log fire, restaurant serving freshly cooked meals and a cosy bar with ample supply of malt whiskies. Bikes can be hired and there is fishing available.

Carol and Ewan Macleod, Glenurquhart House Hotel,
Balnain, Drumnadrochit IV63 6TJ
Tel: 01456 476234
e-mail: info@glenurquhart-house-hotel.co.uk
www.glenurquhart-house-hotel.co.uk

Peacefully located in the heart of 'Nessie' country and with panoramic views of the surrounding hills, Woodlands provides a perfect base from which to explore the history and romance of the beautiful Highlands and Islands. Offering a wide range of tastefully appointed accommodation, comprising two superior en suite rooms (one king/twin suite with private lounge, one large ground floor king/twin equipped to suit the disabled) and two luxury double rooms with en suite facilities.

The STB awards we have received reflect the standard of service and facilities provided • Children over six years welcome • No smoking

Bed and Breakfast from £26 per person per night

Woodlands Guest House

East Lewiston, Drumnadrochit IV63 6UJ • 01456 450356
e-mail: stay@woodlands-lochness.co.uk
www.woodlands-lochness.co.uk

Innishfree Lochyside, Fort William PH33 7NX

Set against the background of Ben Nevis, this spacious Bed and Breakfast house offers a high level of service. Just two miles from the town centre and three miles from Glen Nevis. Visitors are guaranteed a warm friendly welcome and excellent accommodation. All rooms have en suite facilities and also offer remote-control colour TV and tea/coffee making facilities. Breakfast is served in the conservatory, which is overlooked by panoramic views. Enthusiastic advice on pursuits and activities are given. Access to private car park is available. This house has a non-smoking policy and pets are not allowed. Open all year.

Prices from £25 per person per night.

e-mail: mburnsmaclean@aol.com
www.innishfree.co.uk
Mrs Mary MacLean • Tel: 01397 705471

Highlands
Fort William

SCOTLAND 291

Stronchreggan View, Achintore Road, Fort William PH33 6RW

Stronchreggan View is a family-run guest house situated on the shores of Loch Linnhe overlooking the Ardgour Hills. An ideal base for touring the Highlands, being situated one mile south of Fort William on the A82. Fort William, also known as the Outdoor Capital of the Highlands, offers cycling, canoeing, walking, Ben Nevis, the highest mountain in Britain, and much more.

All bedrooms en suite/private bathroom.
Children Welcome. Non-smoking.
Bed and Breakfast from £20 to £30.
See our website for full details.

www.stronchreggan.co.uk
e-mail: graeme@graememcqueen.wanadoo.co.uk
Tel: 01397 704 644

Melantee
Achintore Road, Fort William PH33 6RW

Melantee is a bungalow situated 1½ miles south of the town on the A82 with views of Loch Linnhe. Ideal centre for touring the Highlands, Inverness, Aviemore, Oban, Mallaig, Kyle of Lochalsh, Skye or walk to the top of Britain's highest mountain, Ben Nevis, via the tourist path.

One double, one twin, one triple and one single room, two shared bathrooms with showers. Tea and coffee facilities in all bedrooms. Access to house at all times. Ample parking. Open all year round. Fire Certificate held. Non-smoking.

Storage for bicycles, skis etc
Terms from £21-£23pp.
Welcome Host.
Mrs F. Cook

Tel: 01397 705329 • Fax: 01397 700453 • e-mail: melanteeftwm@aol.com • www.melantee.co.uk

---

Set in the extensive grounds of the former Glenlochy Distillery with its fine distinctive distillery buildings forming a backdrop to one of the most attractive areas in Fort William. The house is situated on the banks of the River Nevis, at the entrance to Glen Nevis and the West Highland Way, but only five minutes' walk from the town centre, railway and bus stations. Seven very well equipped guest rooms, all with en suite facilities, TV, central heating, tea/coffee facilities and hairdryer. Lovely home cooked traditional breakfast. Full fire certificate. Car parking. We look forward to welcoming you. Non-smoking policy in bedrooms. Open all year. Self-catering accommodation also available.

B&B from £22.50 to £38.00 per person per night.

Mrs Linda Allan,
Distillery Guest House & Cottages,
North Road, Nevis Bridge, Fort William PH33 6LR
Tel: 01397 700103 • Fax: 01397 702980
e-mail: DistHouse@aol.com • www.stayinfortwilliam.co.uk

Bed and Breakfast establishment located adjacent to the Caledonian Canal basin on the outskirts of Fort William, affording superb views across the water to Ben Nevis. Providing all the modern comforts for today's traveller, Ben Nevis View caters for two to six people in one double and one family room (one double and two single beds), both en suite with colour TV, hairdryer and tea/coffee making facilities. Enjoy a hearty cooked breakfast in our bright, cheery dining room in true Scottish style. *Terms from £24 to £26 per person per night, subject to season. Family room prices available on request.* Open from February to October. Non-smoking. Sorry, no dogs.

John and Jeanette Mooney,
Ben Nevis View Bed and Breakfast,
Station Road, Corpach, Fort William PH33 7JH
01397 772131
e-mail: info@bennevisview.co.uk
www.bennevisview.co.uk

Highlands
Fort William

LOCH LEVEN HOTEL

John & Hilary would like to welcome you to the lovely Loch Leven Hotel, a small, informal, family-run hotel with excellent food and an ideal base to explore this beautiful region. Enjoy the spectacular scenery from the Lochview Restaurant, garden and new decking, or toast yourself by the log fire in the Public Bar, with its inexpensive menu and wonderful selection of malts. Children and pets always welcome. B&B from £40pp with discounts for Short Breaks.

Tel: 01855 821236
reception@lochlevenhotel.co.uk • www.lochlevenhotel.co.uk
Old Ferry Road, North Ballachulish, Near Fort William PH33 6SA

Stobahn B&B
Fassifern Road, Fort William PH33 6BD
Tel & Fax: 01397 702790
e-mail: boggi@supanet.com

Detached house situated close to the town centre and just a few minutes' walk from the High Street and the railway station. Guest rooms overlook Loch Linnhe. Accommodation consists of one family room, two double and one single, all en suite.

- Bed and Breakfast from £25 to £32 per person.
- Room only from £22 to £26.
- Open all year.

AA ★★★ Bed & Breakfast

Highlands
Fort William

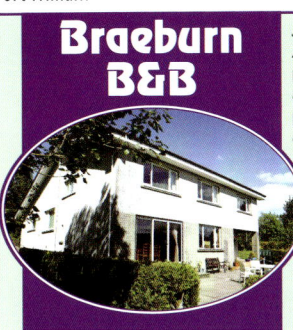

SCOTLAND 293

Braeburn B&B

Stunning views over Loch Linnhe and the Ardgour Hills. A warm welcome awaits you in this spacious, family-run house with panoramic views of the surrounding area. Ben Nevis is only four miles away and can be clearly seen from the house. Situated in its own private grounds with ample off-road parking and storage for bikes and skiiing equipment. Relax in our comfortable residents' lounge or on our sunny patio. Enjoy a hearty breakfast to set you up for the day. We are 3 miles from the town centre and we have a hotel and bars nearby, all serving good food and drink. Ideally situated for touring the West Highlands of Scotland.

En suite rooms ✣ TV ✣ Hospitality tray ✣ Hairdryer
Prices range from £28.00 per person. Open all year

Badabrie, Fort William PH33 7LX • 01397 772047
e-mail: enquiries@braeburnfortwilliam.co.uk
www.braeburnfortwilliam.co.uk

SB

Ossians Hotel — FORT WILLIAM

Situated in the centre of the Fort William's High Street, Ossians Hotel is a friendly and informal base for your holiday, everything is on your doorstep. Shops, restaurants, pubs, museum, library, internet café, bus and railway station, swimming pool, leisure centre, the Old Fort, Loch Linnhe…..all within a 5 minute walk of the hotel.

Whether you are walking the West Highland Way, or the Great Glen Way, climbing Ben Nevis, or just enjoying some of the most spectacular scenery without being energetic, then this is the perfect place to stay. Our restaurant serves traditional Scottish home cooking, with many of your favourite dishes. Meals are served all day. The lounge bar is open all day and evening, for drinks, coffees and snacks.

Ossians Hotel, High Street, Fort William, Inverness-shire PH33 6DH
Tel: 01397 700857 • E-mail: ossiansfw@aol.com • www.ossians.com

Torlinnhe

Relax, unwind and enjoy Torlinnhe hospitality

Andy and Sue Keen promise you a truly memorable stay at our guest house on the shores of Loch Linnhe. We have two double, two twin, one triple and one single room, all with en suite showers, 26" digital TV, DVD player and tea/coffee making facilities – so, make yourself at home !. In nearby picturesque Fort William you'll find plenty of excellent restaurants for you to try out for dinner.
Admire the spectacular view across the loch while you indulge in a delicious breakfast from an extensive menu.

Rates from £25 to £40 including breakfast.
Achintore Road, Fort William PH33 6RW   01397 702583
info@torlinnhe.co.uk   www.torlinnhe.co.uk

SB

Highlands

Gairloch, Grantown-on-Spey, Inverness

A warm welcome awaits at Heatherdale, situated on the outskirts of Gairloch, overlooking the harbour and bay beyond. Within easy walking distance of the golf course and sandy beaches. Ideal base for hill walking. All rooms have en suite facilities, some with sea view. Excellent eating out facilities nearby. Ample parking. Residents' lounge with open fire.

Bed and Breakfast prices from £26 per person per night.

Mrs A. MacIver, Heatherdale, Charleston, Gairloch IV21 2AH
Tel: 01445 712388 • e-mail: BrochoD1@aol.com

An Cala is a lovely Victorian house set in half an acre and offers comfort in a friendly and cosy atmosphere, only a ten minute walk from the town centre. Four delightful en suite guest bedrooms with tea/coffee tray and colour Freeview TV, hairdryers. Doubles have king-size beds. Ideally situated for Spey walks, Munros, RSPB Reserves at Boat of Garten and Loch Insh, the Whisky Trail and as a base for visiting castles and most places in the Highlands. Excellent local golf and tennis clubs. On-site parking. Non smoking. Free wifi access.

B&B from £35 to £38 per person.

Mrs Val Dickinson, An Cala Guest House, Woodlands Terrace, Grantown-on-Spey PH26 3JU
Tel: 01479 873293
e-mail: ancala@globalnet.co.uk • www.ancala.info

Castle View GUESTHOUSE

A late 19th century Victorian house situated on the bank of the River Ness, ideally situated in the centre of Inverness. The High Street and station are only five minutes' walk away and the guest house is in close proximity to good restaurants.

The rooms are spacious, warm and comfortable with high ceilings and central heating; all have shower; family room en suite. All rooms have tea/ coffee making facilities, remote-control video/colour TV. The dining room is particularly well appointed with large windows overlooking the river. Daily newspapers are supplied free and hairdryers, ironing facilities, drying room and trouser presssing can be arranged. Free WiFi.

Traditional Scottish, vegetarian and Continental-style breakfast can be provided. Contact Mr J. Munro.

Castle View Guesthouse, 2a Ness Walk, Inverness IV3 5NE • Tel & Fax: 01463 241443
e-mail: jmunro4161@aol.com   www.castleviewinverness.co.uk

Bay View is set in a rural area on famous Culloden Moor, offering comfortable homely accommodation in one twin-bedded room with en suite shower, one double room with en suite bathroom, and one double room with private bathroom.

An excellent touring base for the Highlands of Scotland and many famous historic sites.
All home made food, local produce used.
Choice of Breakfast.

Bed and Breakfast from £25.

Mrs Margaret Campbell, Bay View, Westhill, By Inverness IV2 5BP
01463 790386 • www.bayviewguest.com

Highlands

SCOTLAND 295

Inverness, Kingussie

The Whins

114 Kenneth Street, Inverness IV3 5QG
Tel: 01463 236215

Comfortable, small, homely, non-smoking accommodation awaits you here. Ten minutes bus and railway stations, with easy access to many golf courses, walking and cycling areas, and a great base for touring North, East and West by car, rail or bus. Two double/twin rooms with TV, tea making, washbasins and heating off season. Bathroom, shared toilet and shower. From £20 per person. Write or phone for full details.

Sunnyholm

Sunnyholm is situated in a large mature, secluded garden in a pleasant residential area within six or seven minutes walking distance of the town centre, tourist information office and all essential holiday amenities. The front of the house overlooks the garden, with the rear allowing easy access to guests' private parking. All rooms are ground floor level and bedrooms are all en suite with colour TV, tea/coffee making facilities, hairdryers, central heating and double glazing. The lounge is a spacious tastefully furnished room with bay window overlooking the garden, as is the diningroom which overlooks the conservatory and garden beyond. **Double/Twin from £25pppn, single from £35pppn.**

Mrs A. Gordon, Sunnyholm Guest House, 12 Mayfield Road, Inverness IV2 4AE
01463 231336 • e-mail: sunnyholm@aol.com • www.invernessguesthouse.com

Ardselma

A former hunting lodge situated within two acres of private grounds, Ardselma has magnificent views of the Cairngorm Mountains. Accommodation comprises two family and one double en suite rooms, one twin room with private facilities, and one single and one twin room with shared facilities. TV lounge available with tea/coffee making facilities; central heating. A three minute walk to the high street or to the golf course. 
• Groups catered for, discounts available
• Children and pets welcome • Safe cycle storage • Bed and Breakfast from £23pppn.

Valerie J. Johnston, Ardselma, The Crescent, Kingussie PH21 1JZ
Mobile: 07786 696384 • e-mail: valerieardselma@aol.com
www.kingussiebedandbreakfast.co.uk

symbols

🚭	Totally non-smoking
🐎	Children Welcome
♿	Suitable for Disabled Guests
🐕	Pets Welcome
SB	Short Breaks
🍷	Licensed

SCOTLAND

Highlands

Kinlochbervie, Kinlochleven

The Kinlochbervie Hotel

An inviting and friendly family-run hotel situated in one of the most stunning areas on the North West coast of Scotland, with views of open seas, surrounding majestic hills and unforgettable sunsets.

Supremely comfortable guest rooms from £30 per person for bed & breakfast.

Kinlochbervie, By Lairg, Sutherland IV27 4RP
Tel: 01971 521275 • Fax: 01971 521438
e-mail: klbhotel@aol.com
www.kinlochberviehotel.com

Scottish Tourist Board ★★ SMALL HOTEL

MACDONALD HOTEL
FORT WILLIAM ROAD,
KINLOCHLEVEN
PH50 4QL
TEL: 01855 831539
FAX: 01855 831416

Ideally located between Glencoe and Ben Nevis at the foot of the Mamores, 50 metres from the West Highland Way, this family-run hotel has all en suite bedrooms with 8-channel digital TV.

The Bothy Bar has great mountain and loch views and serves over 40 malt whiskies, local real ale and fine wines. A pool table, big screen tv and internet access are also available. Food is served in the bar or the restaurant and fresh local produce is used when available. Dogs are welcome! Also, there is a small campsite and nine climbers' cabins - see our website for more details and for very special offers during winter.

e-mail: enquiries@macdonaldhotel.co.uk
www.macdonaldhotel.co.uk

Scottish Tourist Board ★★★ HOTEL

WELCOME WALKERS

Publisher's note

While every effort is made to ensure accuracy, we regret that FHG Guides cannot accept responsibility for errors, misrepresentations or omissions in our entries or any consequences thereof. Prices in particular should be checked.
We will follow up complaints but cannot act as arbiters or agents for either party.

Highlands

SCOTLAND 297

Lairg, Lochinver

Lairg Highland Hotel

Lying in the centre of the village, Lairg Highland Hotel is an ideal base from which to tour the North of Scotland. Superb, home-cooked food, using the best local ingredients, is served in the elegant restaurant and in the attractive setting of the lounge bar. All meals can be complemented by a bottle of wine from a comprehensive list. All bedrooms are individual in character, and furnished to a high standard, with en suite facilities, colour TV and tea/coffee hospitality tray. The popular lounge bar, boasting some fine malt whiskies and good draught beers, is just the place to unwind and relax.

Among the many attractions of this scenic area are fishing, boating, sailing and golf, including Royal Dornoch nearby. Local places of interest include the Falls of Shin, Dunrobin Castle and Clynelish Distillery.

Scottish Tourist Board ★★★ SMALL HOTEL

Main Street, Lairg, Sutherland IV27 4DB
Tel: 01549 402243
Fax: 01549 402593
www.highland-hotel.co.uk
info@highland-hotel.co.uk

Polcraig Guest House nestles on the hillside, centrally in Lochinver village. Family-run, with six very comfortable en suite bedrooms (three twin and three double). Each room is equipped with tea/coffee tray, colour TV, hairdryer and shaving point. Wireless Internet access available.

Enjoy hearty breakfasts in our dining room, with local produce used whenever possible. Generous helpings of fresh salmon, smoked haddock, sausage, bacon, eggs and black pudding will set you up nicely for the day ahead. The area is a paradise for anglers (permits available), climbers, walkers, birdwatchers and photographers. Drying area. Car park.

Mr C. MacLeod, Polcraig Guest House, Lochinver IV27 4LD
Tel & Fax: 01571 844429 • e-mail: cathelmac@aol.com
www.smoothhound.co.uk/hotels/polcraig.html

Scottish Tourist Board ★★★★ GUEST HOUSE

Looking for holiday accommodation?
for details of hundreds of properties throughout the UK visit:

www.holidayguides.com

Highlands
Nairn, Plockton

Aurora Hotel and Italian Restaurant
Nairn, Scotland

The seaside town of Nairn nestles on the south shore of the Moray Firth, with unique views of the mysterious Black Isle, and enjoys some of the sunniest weather in Britain.

At the Aurora Hotel we aim to ensure that all our guests can relax and feel at home, whether staying on business or pleasure.

You can be assured of a warm welcome and comfortable surroundings, with the personal attention of the resident owners. All en suite bedrooms are tastefully decorated, with tea/coffee making facilities, colour TV and central heating.

The hotel is close to all local amenities as well as the beach, harbour, championship golf courses and leisure centre. Nairn is an ideal base for exploring the delights of the Highlands. Historic Culloden Moor and Cawdor Castle and Gardens is close by, with legendary Loch Ness and Urquhart Castle a little further away. It is also ideally placed for following The Whisky Trail.

Why not dine in our restaurant, renowned for its extensive menu of traditional Italian dishes and wide variety of wines.

Aurora Hotel and Italian Restaurant
2 Academy Street, Nairn IV12 4RJ • Tel: 01667 453551 • Fax: 01667 456577
e-mail: aurorahotelnairn@aol.com • www.aurorahotel.co.uk

Bed and Breakfast from £30 per person per night
Dinner, Bed and Breakfast from £40 per person per night

Hill View

Family-run Bed and Breakfast situated in a quiet area with views looking across to the Applecross Hills. Three minute walk to the village, and railway station is nearby. We have two double rooms and one twin room, all en suite/private bathroom. Lovely walks in the area and boat trips available daily. Hotels are a five minute walk away.

Mrs Sybil Cameron, Hill View, 2 Frithard Road, Plockton IV52 8TQ • Tel & Fax: 01599 544226
e-mail: cameron_sybil@yahoo.co.uk

Soluis Mu Thuath Guest House

A warm welcome awaits guests at this family-run guesthouse. All rooms are spacious with lovely views over mountain and forest, en suite facilities, central heating, televisions and hospitality trays. Two of the ground floor rooms are suitable for disabled visitors. Situated about ten miles north of Kyle of Lochalsh, we offer traditional Scottish hospitality.

Margaret & Gerry Arscott
SOLUIS MU THUATH GUEST HOUSE
Braeintra, by Achmore, Lochalsh IV53 8UP
Tel: 01599 577219

Whether you are touring, biking, walking or just soaking up the atmosphere, Soluis Mu Thuath is in the ideal location for exploring some of the most dramatic scenery in the Western Highlands. Visit Skye, Plockton, Torridon, Applecross and Glenelg or enjoy some of the many challenging (and less challenging) walks.

B&B from £25 • Non-smoking
e-mail: soluismuthuath@btopenworld.com
www.highlandsaccommodation.co.uk

Highlands

Plockton, Thurso, Whitebridge

SCOTLAND 299

Tomacs

Fine views overlooking Loch Carron and Applecross Hills. Double and twin bedrooms. One room has en suite facilities and one has private facilities; all have washbasin, central heating, TV and tea/coffee making facilities. Bed and Breakfast from £25.

Mrs Janet MacKenzie Jones, "Tomacs",
Frithard Road, Plockton IV52 8TQ
Tel & Fax: 01599 544321
e-mail: janet@tomacs.freeserve.co.uk

Scottish Tourist Board ★★★ GUEST HOUSE

The family-run Northern Sands Hotel is situated on the shores of the beautiful Dunnet Bay Sands, only three miles away from mainland Britain's most northerly point of Dunnet Head. We are conveniently situated for ferries to the Orkney Isles at Gills Bay and Scrabster. The Castle of Mey and John O' Groats are also close by.

The Hotel has 9 comfortable en suite rooms, and public and lounge bars as well as our restaurant, which is known for being one of the finest in the north, featuring finest local produce cooked fresh for you.

The Northern Sands Hotel
Dunnet, Caithness KW14 8XD
Tel: 01847 851270 • Fax: 01847 851626
www.northernsands.co.uk
e-mail: info@northernsands.co.uk

WHITEBRIDGE HOTEL

Proprietors David & Sarah welcome you to Whitebridge Hotel, where an atmosphere of comfort and quiet goes hand in hand with traditional character. The hotel has stunning views of the Monadhliath Mountains. 12 en suite bedrooms, all with colour TV and tea/coffee making. • Excellent home-prepared food served in the cosy dining room. Comfortable residents' lounge. • Two bars.

Excellent brown trout fishing in the area.

Whitebridge, Loch Ness South
IV2 6UN • 01456 486226

AA ★★ HOTEL

e-mail: info@whitebridgehotel.co.uk • www.whitebridgehotel.co.uk

Borgie Lodge Hotel

Skerray, Tongue, Sutherland KW14 7TH

Set in a secluded Highland glen by the stunning River Borgie lies Borgie Lodge, where mouthwatering food, fine wine, roaring log fires and a very warm welcome awaits after a day's fishing, hill walking, pony trekking or walking on the beach. Relax after dinner with a good malt and tales of salmon, trout and deer.

Tel: 01641 521 332
e-mail: info@borgielodgehotel.co.uk
www.borgielodgehotel.co.uk

Lanarkshire

Lanark

Lanarkshire

Craigend Bed & Breakfast

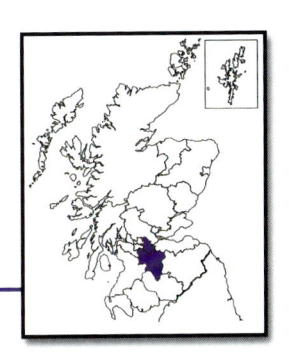

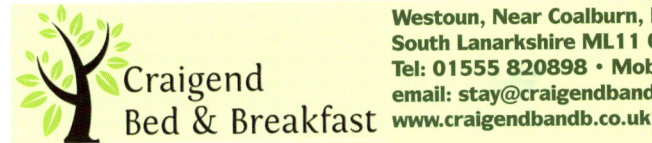

Westoun, Near Coalburn, Lanark,
South Lanarkshire ML11 0NH
Tel: 01555 820898 • Mobile: 07889 174152
email: stay@craigendbandb.co.uk
www.craigendbandb.co.uk

SB

Set in the beautiful Lanarkshire countryside, Craigend Bed and Breakfast offers the perfect peaceful retreat for those wanting to enjoy a picturesque location, whilst being able to easily reach all Central Scotland has to offer. Tucked away at the end of a quiet lane, Craigend Bed and Breakfast is perfectly situated for holiday makers and business travellers alike.

3 double bedrooms, fully en suite, with multi jet power showers
LCD TV with Freeview • DVD player • Wifi internet access • Alarm clock radio
Hairdryer • Complimentary toiletries • Beverage tray
All the produce used in our breakfasts is locally sourced and free-range where possible. Packed lunches available
Pets welcome by arrangement • Pet sitting available
Children over 16 years only
Garaging for Classic Cars and cyclists
One-acre garden with pond and wildlife

Please note

All the information in this book is given in good faith in the belief that it is correct. However, the publishers cannot guarantee the facts given in these pages, neither are they responsible for changes in policy, ownership or terms that may take place after the date of going to press. Readers should always satisfy themselves that the facilities they require are available and that the terms, if quoted, still apply.

Lanarkshire
Lanark, Lesmahagow

St Catherines Bed & Breakfast

Contact: Mrs B. McMillan
1 Kenilworth Road,
Lanark ML11 7BL
Tel/Fax: 01555 662295
Mobile: 07963 779501

At St Catherines you will be assured of a warm welcome and hearty breakfast, whether it be cooked, Continental or vegetarian. The rooms are tastefully decorated and are en suite; all with TV, radio, hairdryer, and complimentary tea tray with snacks etc. We are in a central position a few minutes walk from both bus and train stations, and shops and restaurants.

Lanark has historic links with William Wallace and is a good touring base for Glasgow, Edinburgh and the surrounding area which has many golf courses. Near the New Lanark World Heritage Village. Prices are from £25pp.
Please note there is no smoking anywhere in the house.

e-mail: stcatherinesbb@yahoo.co.uk   www.st-catherines.co.uk

Dykecroft Farm

A modern farmhouse bungalow on Dykecroft Farm, set in lovely surroundings in a rural area on the B7086 (old A726) and within easy reach of the M74, making it the ideal stop between north and south; also convenient for Glasgow and Prestwick airports. Centrally situated for touring Glasgow, Edinburgh, Ayr, Stirling and New Lanark - all within one hour's drive. Nearby is Strathclyde Country Park with all watersports activities; other sporting facilities within two miles include sports centre, golf, fishing, quad bikes, rifle and clay pigeon shooting, and swimming. Guests will enjoy the open fires in our TV lounge and the good breakfasts; TV and tea making facilities in all rooms. A warm and friendly welcome awaits all guests.

Kirkmuirhill, Lesmahagow ML11 0JQ
e-mail: Dykecroft.bandb@tiscali.co.uk
Tel & Fax: 01555 892226
www.DykecroftFarm.co.uk

symbols

	Totally non-smoking		Pets Welcome
	Children Welcome	SB	Short Breaks
	Suitable for Disabled Guests		Licensed

Perth & Kinross
Blairgowrie

Perth & Kinross

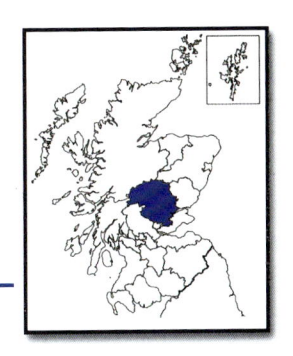

SCOTLAND 303

Glenkilrie Bed & Breakfast is a family-run house where everyone is welcome. It is set in its own grounds on a real working farm approx. 13 miles north of the town of Blairgowrie on the main A93 Perth to Braemar road. Accommodation consists of two double rooms and one twin room, all with en suite facilities. There is a guest lounge with TV, open log fire and tea/coffee making facilities.

For further details contact: Mrs Morag Houstoun, Glenkilrie, Blacklunans, Blairgowrie, Perthshire PH10 7LR • Tel: 01250 882241
e-mail: glenkilrie@btinternet.com or visit www.glenkilrie.co.uk

Scottish Tourist Board ★★★ B&B

BLAIRGOWRIE. Rosalind Young, Holmrigg, Wester Essendy, Blairgowrie PH10 6RD (Tel & Fax: 01250 884309).
One double/twin, one double four-poster and one twin on ground floor. All rooms en suite with tea/coffee making facilities, radio and TV; ironing and hair drying facilities. Comfortable lounge with open fire and colour TV; diningroom. Heating throughout. Vegetarian meals; home cooking and baking; full cooked breakfast. Places of interest range from Scott's 'Discovery' in Dundee to Edinburgh Castle. Also golf, fishing and walking. Parking.
Rates: Bed and Breakfast from £27.50 to £30 per person, discounts for Senior Citizens.
• Pets by arrangement.
www.holmrigg-bnb.co.uk

STB ★★★ *B&B*
e-mail: info@holmrigg.co.uk

Visit the FHG website
www.holidayguides.com
for details of the wide choice of accommodation featured in the full range of FHG titles

Perth & Kinross
Coupar Angus, Crianlarich, Crieff

Enverdale House Hotel

Enverdale House Hotel is a welcoming, family run hotel located in the town of Coupar Angus, in the heart of the beautiful county of Perthshire. Situated in woodland and set in lovely gardens, with ample parking.

Five en suite bedrooms, each with their own individual charm. Enjoy a wide selection of wines and champagnes combined with quality food prepared by our chefs. The ideal retreat for those wanting activity breaks, whether it be climbing, walking cycling or fishing - with the local rivers and lochs providing some of the best fishing in the country. It is also a perfect place for a relaxing holiday just taking in the picturesque scenery.

For reservations contact 01828 627606 • Fax: 01828 627239
Pleasance Road, Coupar Angus, Perthshire PH13 9JB
www.enverdalehotel.co.uk
e-mail: info@enverdalehotel.co.uk or sueenverdale@yahoo.co.uk

AA ★★★ Guest Accommodation

Set just outside the village of Crianlarich, Inverardran House is sited in an elevated position with views across Strathfillan to Ben Challum. This property offers excellent fishing, walking and touring prospects.

We can offer you Bed and Breakfast accommodation for up to nine people in two double rooms and one twin (all en suite) and one triple room with a private bathroom. Tea/coffee making facilities in the rooms. Self-catering also available.

Open all year • Prices from £20 to £25 per person per night based on two sharing, £8 surcharge for a single person. Discounts for longer stays • Evening meals and packed lunches on request.

John and Janice Christie, Inverardran House, Crianlarich FK20 8QS
01838 300240 • e-mail: janice@inverardran.demon.co.uk
www.inverardran.demon.co.uk

Well placed for those travelling north and south, at the edge of the Highlands, near Gleneagles, yet only one hour from Edinburgh and Glasgow.

Situated in beautiful Perthshire, this charming family-run hotel offers comfortable en suite bedrooms and freshly prepared, excellent food, served in our stone-walled restaurant.

BARLEY BREE
restaurant with rooms

Sip a malt whisky by the log fire in the lounge after dinner. There are plenty of local attractions and activities – golf, walking, hunting and fishing in season.

6 Willoughby Street
Muthill
Crieff PH5 2AB

Tel: 01764 681 451   e-mail: info@barleybree.com   www.barleybree.com

Perth & Kinross

Crieff

SCOTLAND 305

Yann's at Glenearn House

is a family-owned business, with Yannick and Shari Grospellier as your hosts.

Glenearn is a large Victorian house in the picturesque town of Crieff, in Perthshire. It has recently been refurbished and now features a restaurant with rooms with a great relaxed atmosphere where you can eat, drink and sleep.

Crieff is known as the Gateway to the Highlands and is a perfect, central location for discovering Scotland, only an hour's drive from Edinburgh and Glasgow. Golf courses are plentiful, ranging from Crieff's two 18-hole courses to the renowned Gleneagles courses, only 8 miles away.

At Yann's, cooking is a passion, The emphasis is on good food, kept simple and traditional, and we aim to make you feel at home in our relaxed and convivial bistro. A relaxed and welcoming lounge awaits you for pre-dinner drinks and coffee or digestifs.

We have five spacious bedrooms (double or twin), all decorated in their own unique style and each with an en suite shower room or adjoining bathroom.

Each bedroom features home-from-home luxuries such as digital television, hi-fi, DVD, tea and coffee-making facilities and quality toiletries.

Yann's at Glenearn House
Glenearn House, Perth Road, Crieff, Perthshire PH7 3EQ
Tel: 01764 650111
e-mail: info@yannsatglenearnhouse.com
www.yannsatglenearnhouse.com

Perth & Kinross

Crieff, Killin

Merlindale

Merlindale is a luxurious Georgian house situated close to the town centre. All bedrooms are en suite, two with sunken bathrooms. Jacuzzi, garden, satellite television and off-road parking all available. There is a large library available for you to browse in. Merlindale is Michelin rated, multi AA Red Diamond, and multi Glenturret Tourism Award winner. A sumptuous family home waits to welcome you.

Merlindale, Perth Road, Crieff PH7 3EQ

Enquiries: please call 01764 655205 or
e-mail: merlin.dale@virgin.net • www.merlindale.co.uk

Drumfinn Guest House
Discover mountains, lochs, rivers and glens

B&B accommodation in the heart of Scotland, ideal for exploring Perthshire, the Trossachs and the Highlands. Drumfinn sits 200 yards from the Falls of Dochart in the centre of Killin which is located on the beautiful Loch Tay. Built in 1837, the house was previously used as a bank and the vault has been retained as a feature in the breakfast room. Five bright, airy and comfortable bedrooms are available, most en suite with spectacular views of the mountains. Full Scottish breakfast served and/or help yourself to the buffet - special dietary requirements are catered for. Terms from £30 pppn double, £35 single.

**Phil & Carol Jones, Drumfinn Guest House,
Manse Road, Killin FK21 8UY • 01567 820900**
e-mail: drumfinnhouse@aol.com • www.drumfinn.co.uk

Please note

All the information in this book is given in good faith in the belief that it is correct. However, the publishers cannot guarantee the facts given in these pages, neither are they responsible for changes in policy, ownership or terms that may take place after the date of going to press. Readers should always satisfy themselves that the facilities they require are available and that the terms, if quoted, still apply.

Perth & Kinross
Lochearnhead, Perth, Pitlochry

CLACHAN COTTAGE HOTEL
Lochearnhead, Perthshire FK19 8PU

- Friendly, family-run hotel in spectacular lochside setting.
- Well placed in Central Scotland for touring.
- Many golf courses within an hour's drive.
- 30 Munroes within 30 minutes.
- Water-sports available from the hotel.

AWARD-WINNING TASTE OF SCOTLAND RESTAURANT • GROUP/SOCIETY RATES

• **PETS WELCOME** •

Tel: 01567 830247
Fax: 01567 830300
info@clachancottagehotel.co.uk
www.clachancottagehotel.co.uk

Lorne Villa Guest House

Ceud Mile Failte
"A hundred thousand welcomes"
await at Lorne Villa.
Three single, four double/twin,
one family room, all en suite.
Open all year. Tricia and Jonathan Whitaker.

65 Dunkeld Road, Perth PH1 5RP • Tel: 01738 628043
e-mail: lorne-villa@hotmail.com

Ashbank House is a traditional stone and slate built Victorian villa providing comfortable guest accommodation within easy reach of local services and amenities, but with a private rural feel. Two double bedrooms and one twin room, all with en suite/private bathroom facilities. A large mature garden offers you privacy, with beautiful views over woodland and mountains. Relax on the patio or take a stroll along the burn. Private off-road parking, secure storage and drying facilities. This area offers a wide range of recreational pursuits including walking, golf, climbing, cycling, motor biking, water sports, fishing, whisky tasting and many more. Other attractions: dam with fish ladder, Pitlochry Festival Theatre.

B&B from £25pppn.

Ashbank House, 14 Tomcroy Terrace, Pitlochry PH16 5JA • 01796 472711
e-mail: ashbankhouse@btinternet.com • www.ashbankhouse.co.uk

Perth & Kinross / Renfrewshire

Stanley

A family-run farm on the A9, 6 miles north of Perth. Accommodation comprises double and twin en suite rooms and a family room (sleeps 4), with private bathroom. The centrally heated farmhouse has a real coal fire in the lounge. There is a large garden and free secure parking. Situated in the area known as "The Gateway to the Highlands", the farm is ideally placed for those seeking some of the best unspoilt scenery in Western Europe. The numerous castles and historic ruins are testimony to Scotland's turbulent past. There are many famous golf courses and salmon and trout rivers in the Perth area, and it is only one hour's drive to both Edinburgh and Glasgow. B&B from £25.

Newmill Farm, Stanley PH1 4PS
Mrs Ann Guthrie • 01738 828281
e-mail: guthrienewmill@sol.co.uk
www.newmillfarm.co.uk

Renfrewshire

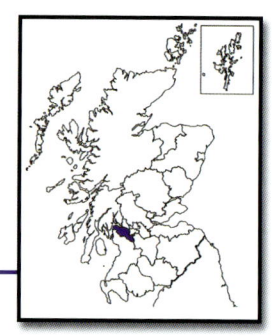

Paisley

Ardgowan House
Tel & Fax: 0141-889 4763

David and Gail welcome you to their two adjacent, family-run guesthouses in the heart of Paisley, Scotland's largest town. Enjoy a drink from our licensed bar in the secluded, peaceful gardens or relax in our delightful summer house. We have two levels of accommodation available, so there is something for everyone, from the two-star Ardgowan guest house to the more upmarket Townhouse Hotel. Both have secure storage facilities for cyclists and hikers and free off-street parking. Situated within one mile of Glasgow International Airport, and only ten minutes from Glasgow City Centre, the excellent transport links allow easy access to Loch Lomond, Robert Burns country, Edinburgh and the Highlands and Islands.
Please see our website for further details.

92-94 Renfrew Road, Paisley, Renfrewshire PA3 4BJ
www.ardgowanhouse.com

Stirling & The Trossachs
Callander, Crianlarich

Stirling
& The Trossachs

SCOTLAND 309

Riverview

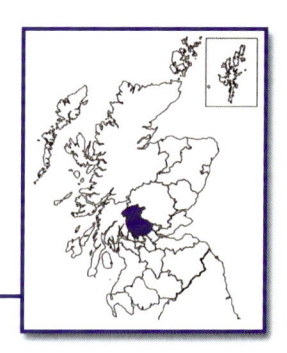

Riverview Guest House, Leny Road, Callander FK17 8AL
Tel: 01877 330635

Excellent accommodation in the Trossachs area which forms the most beautiful part of Scotland's first National Park. Ideal centre for walking and cycling holidays, with cycle storage available. In the guest house all rooms are en suite, with TV and tea-making. Private parking. Also available self-catering stone cottages, sleep 3 or 4. Sorry, no smoking and no pets.
Call Drew or Kathleen Little for details.

e-mail: drew@visitcallander.co.uk
www.visitcallander.co.uk

B&B from £27.50 to £30.00. Low season and long stay discounts available.
Self-catering cottages from £150 to £400 per week (STB 3 & 4 Stars).

SB

Phil and Wendy welcome you to **GLENARDRAN HOUSE** where you can expect a warm welcome and a comfortable and pleasurable stay. Bed and Breakfast accommodation is provided in this late Victorian villa, situated within the village, close to restaurant, pub and shop. Crianlarich is an ideal touring base for visiting many of Scotland's tourist attractions, from the spendid Highlands scenery to the more cultural attractions in Glasgow, Edinburgh and Stirling, as well as plenty to do close at hand. Five spacious and well appointed en suite bedrooms available, including two family rooms.
Terms from £28 per person per night, reductions for children and longer stays. Packed lunches available. 
Glenardran House, Crianlarich FK20 8QS
01838 300236
e-mail: phil@glenardran.co.uk
www.glenardran.co.uk

SB

SCOTLAND

Stirling & The Trossachs
Loch Lomond, Strathyre

Balmaha, Loch Lomond
Enjoy the quiet shore of the loch

Discover a real Scottish welcome at **The Oak Tree Inn** in a picturesque village on the quieter eastern side of Loch Lomond, the perfect base from which to explore the stunning surrounding countryside.

This unique inn, constructed from locally quarried slate, offers an escape from the rush of modern-day life.

The comfortable en suite bedrooms have all modern comforts, with a bunkroom ideal for those wishing more simple accommodation.

The mouthwatering menus cater for all appetites, with an excellent range of ales and spirits available in the friendly bar.

Oak Tree Inn, Balmaha, Loch Lomond G63 0JQ
Tel: 01360 870357 • Fax: 01360 870350
e-mail: info@oak-tree-inn.co.uk • www.oak-tree-inn.co.uk

Coire Buidhe, Strathyre FK18 8NA
Tel: +44 (0)1877 384288
email: coirebuidhe@yahoo.co.uk

Coire Buidhe sits in the beautiful valley of Strathyre, 8 miles north of Callander and an excellent base for touring the Loch Lomond and Trossachs National Park and the country beyond. All double/twin rooms are en suite and full Scottish or Continental style breakfast is offered using local produce where possible. Bar and restaurant meals are available within 'bonnie' Strathyre. Hillwalking, fishing, watersports, cycling and golf are available within the area. Dogs are permitted and a warm and friendly welcome is always assured at Coire Buidhe.

---

symbols

- Totally non-smoking
- Children Welcome
- Suitable for Disabled Guests
- Pets Welcome
- **SB** Short Breaks
- Licensed

Port Ellen

Scottish Islands

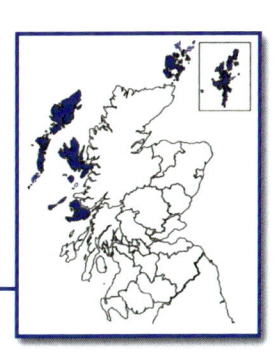

Islay

On the beautiful Hebridean island of Islay - a famous classic links course perched above the golden sands of Laggan Bay, and a hotel run with the warmth and informality that brings people back time and again.

**Machrie Hotel & Golf Links,
Port Ellen, Isle of Islay,
Argyll PA42 7AN
Tel: 01496 302310
Fax: 01496 302404
e-mail: machrie@machrie.com
www.machrie.com**

Publisher's note

While every effort is made to ensure accuracy, we regret that FHG Guides cannot accept responsibility for errors, misrepresentations or omissions in our entries or any consequences thereof. Prices in particular should be checked.
We will follow up complaints but cannot act as arbiters or agents for either party.

Mull

ARGYLL ARMS

01681 700240
Bunessan, Isle of Mull

e-mail: argyllarms@isleofmull.co.uk • www.isleofmull.co.uk

The Argyll Arms Hotel, located on the waterfront of the village of Bunessan, and close to the famous Isle of Iona, provides accommodation, bar and restaurant facilities on the beautiful Isle of Mull.

With spectacular sea and island views, the hotel is the perfect base from which to explore, either by car or on foot if walking is your forte, or by bike. We can arrange bike hire or why not bring your own? Secure storage is available and bikers are most welcome. The new owners invite you to enjoy their friendly and relaxed Scottish hospitality in comfortable accommodation, value-for-money bistro-style food and the unique atmosphere of the Isle of Mull. All rooms en suite.

Open all day 365 days of the year catering for residents and non residents.

symbols

- Totally non-smoking
- Children Welcome
- Suitable for Disabled Guests
- Pets Welcome
- **SB** Short Breaks
- Licensed

Scottish Islands - Orkney / Shetland SCOTLAND 313

Kirkwall

Orkney

Pierowall Hotel
Accommodation in the heart of Westray

Enjoy the friendly atmosphere of a family run hotel with views over Pierowall Bay with Papa Westray visible in the near distance. Ideally situated for visitors wishing to explore the island, we can arrange for a guided tour to pick you up from the hotel and return you for your meals here, or you could take a packed lunch with you.
Why not take a flight on the plane to Papay for the world's shortest scheduled flight, as recorded in the Guinness Book of Records.
We offer freshly cooked meals daily, including locally caught seafood and a variety of fresh fish. Takeaway food available. Small private parties and conferences welcome.

Pierowall Hotel, Pierowall, Westray, Isle of Orkney KW17 2BZ
Tel: 01857 677472 or 677208 • www.pierowallhotel.co.uk

Situated a short walk from the Highland Park Distillery and Visitor Centre, and within reach of all local amenities. Lav'rockha is the perfect base for exploring and discovering Orkney. We offer high quality accommodation at affordable rates. All our rooms have en suite WC and power shower, tea/coffee tray, minibar, hairdryer, radio alarm clock and remote-control colour TV.

We have facilities for the disabled, with full unassisted wheelchair access from our private car park.
All our meals are prepared to a high standard using fresh, local produce as much as possible.
Bed and Breakfast from £28 per person. Special winter break prices available.
WINNER OF BEST B&B ORKNEY; FOOD AWARDS, TASTE OF SCOTLAND ACCREDITED.
Lav'rockha Guest House, Inganess Road, Kirkwall KW15 1SP • Tel & Fax: 01856 876103
e-mail: lavrockha@orkney.com • www.lavrockha.co.uk

SB

Shetland

Brae

Westayre Bed and Breakfast, Muckle Roe, Brae ZE2 9QW

A warm welcome awaits you at our working croft on the picturesque island of Muckle Roe, where we have breeding sheep, pet lambs, ducks and cats. The island is joined to the mainland by a small bridge and is an ideal place for children. The accommodation is of a high standard and has en suite facilities. Guests can enjoy good home cooking and baking. Spectacular cliff scenery and clean safe sandy beaches, bird watching and hill walking and also central for touring North Mainland and North Isles.

Terms: Double/twin rooms en suite £30pppn
Single £28 to £35.

e-mail:westayre@btinternet.com • www.westayre.shetland.co.uk

Skye

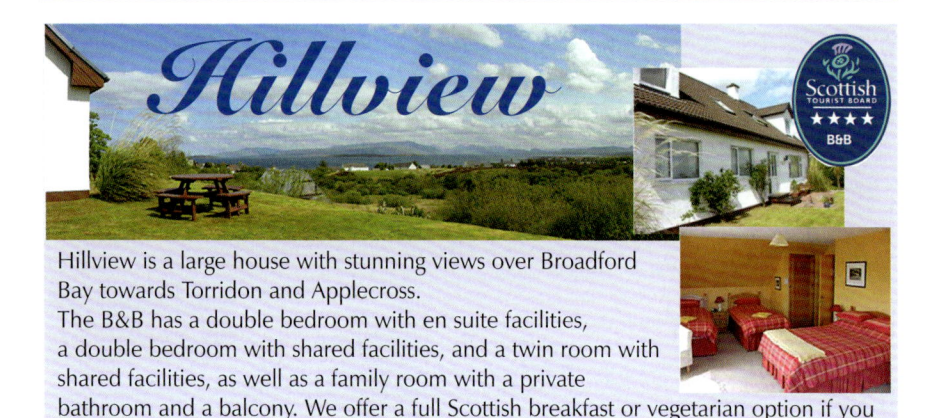

Hillview is a large house with stunning views over Broadford Bay towards Torridon and Applecross.
The B&B has a double bedroom with en suite facilities, a double bedroom with shared facilities, and a twin room with shared facilities, as well as a family room with a private bathroom and a balcony. We offer a full Scottish breakfast or vegetarian option if you prefer. Our rooms are very comfortable and most have stunning sea views.

Hillview B&B is an ideal base for exploring surrounding area. The scenery is wild and dramatic, with the Cuillin range being the island's most famous feature. The landscape varies from the strange rock formations of the Quirang to the lushness of the Garden of Skye in the south of the island. Around Broadford there are numerous mountain and coastal walks for all abilities.

**Isabel MacLeod, Hillview, Blackpark, Broadford, Isle of Skye IV49 9DE
e-mail: isabel@hillview-skye.co.uk • Telephone: 01471 822 083
www.hillview-skye.co.uk**

The FHG Directory of Website Addresses
on pages xxx-xxx is a useful quick reference guide for holiday accommodation with e-mail and/or website details

---

symbols

⊘	Totally non-smoking	🐕 Pets Welcome
🐎	Children Welcome	**SB** Short Breaks
♿	Suitable for Disabled Guests	🍷 Licensed

South Uist

Croft House Bed & Breakfast

3 Milton,
Isle of South Uist HS8 5RY
Tel/Fax: 01878 710224
Mobile: 07748 637995

Croft House is located 10 minutes' walk from Flora MacDonald's birthplace, 5 minutes' walk from the beach and 20 minutes' walk from the Museum and hillwalking. 5 minutes' drive to Askernish golf course.
Two double rooms en suite
One twin-bedded room with private bathroom
Bed & Breakfast £22-£25pppn

Other specialised holiday guides from FHG

PUBS & INNS OF BRITAIN • **COUNTRY HOTELS** OF BRITAIN
WEEKEND & SHORT BREAK HOLIDAYS IN BRITAIN
THE GOLF GUIDE WHERE TO PLAY, WHERE TO STAY
PETS WELCOME • **SELF-CATERING HOLIDAYS** IN BRITAIN
BED & BREAKFAST STOPS • **CARAVAN & CAMPING HOLIDAYS**
FAMILY BREAKS IN BRITAIN

Published annually: available in all good bookshops or direct from the publisher:
FHG Guides, Abbey Mill Business Centre, Seedhill, Paisley PA1 1TJ
Tel: 0141 887 0428 • Fax: 0141 889 7204
e-mail: admin@fhguides.co.uk • www.holidayguides.com

Ratings & Awards

For the first time ever the AA, VisitBritain, VisitScotland, and the Wales Tourist Board will use a single method of assessing and rating serviced accommodation. Irrespective of which organisation inspects an establishment the rating awarded will be the same, using a common set of standards, giving a clear guide of what to expect. The RAC is no longer operating an Hotel inspection and accreditation business.

Accommodation Standards: Star Grading Scheme

Using a scale of 1-5 stars the objective quality ratings give a clear indication of accommodation standard, cleanliness, ambience, hospitality, service and food, This shows the full range of standards suitable for every budget and preference, and allows visitors to distinguish between the quality of accommodation and facilities on offer in different establishments. All types of board and self-catering accommodation are covered, including hotels, B&Bs, holiday parks, campus accommodation, hostels, caravans and camping, and boats.

VisitBritain and the regional tourist boards, enjoyEngland.com, VisitScotland and VisitWales, and the AA have full details of the grading system on their websites

The more stars, the higher level of quality

★★★★★
exceptional quality, with a degree of luxury

★★★★
excellent standard throughout

★★★
very good level of quality and comfort

★★
good quality, well presented and well run

★
acceptable quality; simple, practical, no frills

National Accessible Scheme

If you have particular mobility, visual or hearing needs, look out for the National Accessible Scheme. You can be confident of finding accommodation or attractions that meet your needs by looking for the following symbols.

Typically suitable for a person with sufficient mobility to climb a flight of steps but would benefit from fixtures and fittings to aid balance

Typically suitable for a person with restricted walking ability and for those that may need to use a wheelchair some of the time and can negotiate a maximum of three steps

Typically suitable for a person who depends on the use of a wheelchair and transfers unaided to and from the wheelchair in a seated position. This person may be an independent traveller

Typically suitable for a person who depends on the use of a wheelchair in a seated position. This person also requires personal or mechanical assistance (eg carer, hoist).

Wales

Gellifawr Hotel & Cottages, Newport, Pembrokeshire, page 328

Bron Eifion Country House Hotel, Criccieth, Gwynedd, page 320

Tycam Farm, Aberystwyth, Ceredigion, page 325

Caebetran Farm, Brecon, Powys, page 330

318 WALES

FHG KUPERARD

Looking for Holiday Accommodation?

for details of hundreds of properties throughout the UK, visit our website

www.holidayguides.com

Anglesey & Gwynedd
Criccieth

Anglesey & Gwynedd

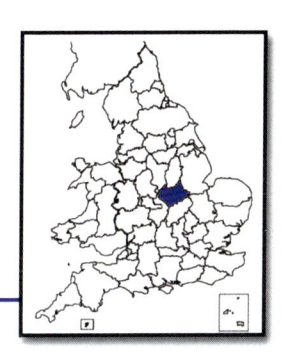

Seaspray

Seaspray is a large, non-smoking Victorian terrace house, situated on the sea front, on the west side of Criccieth Castle on the Lleyn Peninsula. Some rooms are en suite, others have private facilities. Sea views across Cardigan Bay. Criccieth is only a short distance away from the Snowdonia National Park, which boasts some of the most beautiful and spectacular scenery in the country. Ample facilities are available for golfers, sailors, fishermen and ramblers.

Open 10 months of the year • B&B from £25pppn.

Mrs Parker, Seaspray, 4 Marine Terrace, Criccieth LL52 0EF • Tel: 01766 522373
www.seasprayguesthouse.co.uk

Visit the FHG website
www.holidayguides.com
for details of the wide choice of accommodation featured in the full range of FHG titles

WALES — Anglesey & Gwynedd
Criccieth, Dolgellau

Bron Eifion
COUNTRY HOUSE HOTEL

The Grade II Listed house overlooks beautiful gardens, with breathtaking views of the sea. All 19 bedrooms are superbly appointed to ensure your stay is memorable and enjoyable. The Restaurant offers fine food, excellent service and attention to detail. An ideal destination for all golfers who enjoy luxurious accommodation and fine golf. Whether you are looking for a weekend break with a couple of gentle rounds, or a challenging range of courses to test the most experienced golfer, there is a wonderful choice of courses within a 20-minute drive of the hotel. The Hotel is open all year round.

Criccieth, Gwynedd LL52 0SA • Tel: 01766 522385 • Fax: 01766 523796
enquiries@broneifion.co.uk • www.broneifion.co.uk

AA ★★★ HOTEL

Ivy House

FINSBURY SQUARE, DOLGELLAU LL40 1RF
Tel: 01341 422535 • Fax: 01341 422689
e-mail: marg.bamford@btconnect.co.uk
www.ivyhouse-dolgellau.co.uk

A country town guesthouse offering a welcoming atmosphere and good homemade food. Guest accommodation consists of six double rooms, four with en suite toilet facilities, all with colour TV, tea/coffee making facilities and hair dryer. The diningroom has a choice of menu, including vegetarian dishes. The lounge has tourist information literature and there are maps available to borrow. Dolgellau is an ideal touring, walking and mountain biking region in the southern area of the Snowdonia National Park.

Bed and Breakfast from £27.50, en suite from £32.50
WTB ★★★ • AA ★★★

Please note

All the information in this book is given in good faith in the belief that it is correct. However, the publishers cannot guarantee the facts given in these pages, neither are they responsible for changes in policy, ownership or terms that may take place after the date of going to press. Readers should always satisfy themselves that the facilities they require are available and that the terms, if quoted, still apply.

Anglesey & Gwynedd

WALES 321

Talyllyn, Tywyn

Gwesty Minffordd Hotel

Talyllyn, Tywyn, Gwynedd LL36 9AJ

This 17th century Drovers' Inn offers today's traveller all modern comforts. There is a mixture of old and new style centrally heated bedrooms, and three lounges with log fires for relaxation. The delicious meals on offer use local Welsh produce, organic vegetables, Welsh flavourings and are cooked on an Aga. With the Cader Idris Path starting from the door, this Hotel is ideal for walking, touring or sightseeing. The Talyllyn Lake, Dolgoch Falls and the Centre for Alternative Technology are within five miles. Further afield there are beaches and fishing ports, but whatever your taste you will find a real welcome (or Croeso in Welsh) upon your return.

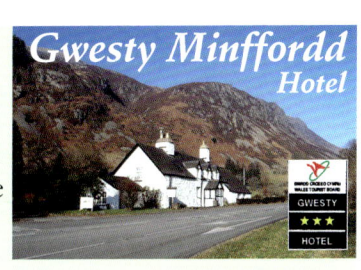

Perhaps that is why guests return year after year.

Tel: 01654 761665 Fax: 01654 761517
e-mail: hotel@minffordd.com • www.minffordd.com

Eisteddfa
Abergynolwyn, Tywyn LL36 9UP

Eisteddfa offers you the comfort of a newly-built bungalow on the Tan-y-coed Ucha Farm, situated adjacent to the farmhouse but with all the benefits of Bed and Breakfast accommodation. The bungalow, which has been designed to accommodate disabled guests, is conveniently situated between Abergynolwyn and Dolgoch Falls with Talyllyn Narrow Gauge Railway running through the farmland. Three bedrooms, two en suite and the third with a shower and washbasin suitable for a disabled person. The toilet is located in the adjacent bathroom. Tea/coffee tray and TV are provided in the bedrooms as are many other extras. We also cater for Coeliac Diets.

Mrs Gweniona Pugh • 01654 782385 • e-mail: hugh.pugh01@btinternet.com

---

symbols

- 🚭 Totally non-smoking
- 🎠 Children Welcome
- ♿ Suitable for Disabled Guests
- 🐕 Pets Welcome
- **SB** Short Breaks
- 🍷 Licensed

North Wales

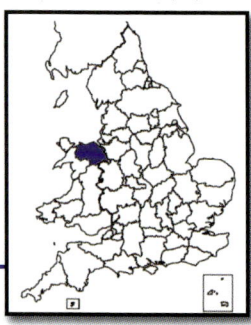

Fairy Glen Hotel offers you a warm and friendly welcome, comfortable accommodation and excellent home-cooked food, in a relaxed and convivial atmosphere. All our rooms are well equipped with central heating, colour TV, alarm clock-radio, hairdryer and tea/ coffee making facilities. We have a TV lounge, and cosy licensed bar for our residents to relax in. Private hotel car park for guests. Four course evening meals £17.50 per person. Bed and Breakfast from £30.00 per person per night.

Brian and Enid Youe, Fairy Glen Hotel, Beaver Bridge, Betws-y-Coed LL24 0SH • 01690 710269
e-mail: fairyglenho@sky.com
www.fairyglenhotel.co.uk

TY COCH FARM-TREKKING CENTRE
PENMACHNO, BETWS-Y-COED LL25 0HJ
Tel: 01690 760248 • e-mail: cindymorris@tiscali.co.uk

Ty Coch is a sheep farm and trekking centre for horse and pony riding.
- Double room with bath etc en suite
- Large room with a double, a single and a sofa bed; shower etc en suite
- Double and a single bed with shower room en suite

All bedrooms have colour TV, tea/coffee making facilities and central heating.
There is a comfortable lounge with colour TV, DVD and video.

Situated in a beautiful valley in the hills, well off the beaten track, in a very quiet and peaceful area. Near National Trust property "Ty Mawr" and 5 to 6 miles to well known tourist village of Betws-y-Coed. We are an easy drive to sandy beaches or Snowdon mountain range. Narrow gauge railways, woollen mills, slate mines, waterfalls, mountain bike tracks, castles, golf and many more attractions nearby.

North Wales

WALES 323

Betwys-y-Coed, Conwy

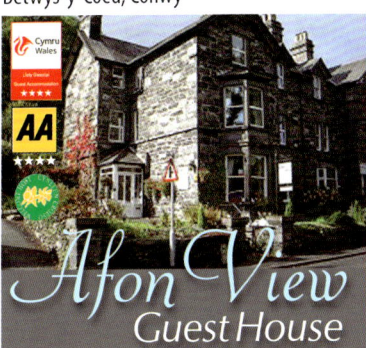

Afon View Guest House

Afon View Guest House is located in the village of Betws-y-Coed in the Snowdonia National Park in North Wales, close to the shops, restaurants and the train station.
- Bed and Breakfast accommodation
- All rooms en-suite • Drying room facilities
- Non-smoking • Car park • Free Wi-Fi internet access

Offering comfortable bed and breakfast (B&B) accommodation, this is an ideal holiday location from which to explore Betws-y-Coed, the Snowdonia National Park, and the rest of North Wales.

Holyhead Road, Betws-y-Coed, Snowdonia, North Wales LL24 0AN
Tel: 01690 710526 • E-mail: welcome@afon-view.co.uk
www.afon-view.co.uk

Bron Celyn Guest House, Lôn Muriau, Llanrwst Road,
Betws-y-Coed LL24 0HD • Tel: 01690 710333 • Fax: 01690 710111

A warm welcome awaits you at this delightful guest house overlooking the Gwydyr Forest and Llugwy/Conwy Valleys and village of Betws-y-Coed in Snowdonia National Park. Ideal centre for touring, walking, climbing, fishing and golf. Also excellent overnight stop en route for Holyhead ferries. Easy walk into village and close to Conwy/Swallow Falls and Fairy Glen.
Most rooms en suite, all with colour TV and beverage makers. Lounge. Full central heating. Garden. Car park. Open all year. Full hearty breakfast, packed meals, evening meals - special diets catered for. Walkers and Cyclists Welcome.
B&B from £24 to £35, reduced rates for children under 12 years. Special out of season breaks.
Jim and Lilian Boughton
e-mail: welcome@broncelyn.co.uk • www.broncelyn.co.uk

SB

Glan Heulog Guest House
Llanrwst Road, Conwy LL32 8LT

Spacious Victorian house, tastefully decorated. With off-road parking. Short walk from historic castle and town walls of Conwy. Ideally situated for touring Snowdonia and North Wales with its many attractions. We have a selection of twin, double and family rooms with en suite facilities, TV and tea/coffee making facilities. There is a large garden with seating to enjoy the far-reaching views. Children welcome. Pets by arrangement. Vegetarians catered for. Strictly non-smoking.
Bed and Breakfast from £25–£35 per person per night.

www.walesbandb.co.uk

Tel: 01492 593845 • e-mail: glanheulog@no1guesthouse.freeserve.co.uk

The Park Hill / Gwesty Bryn Parc
Llanrwst Road, Betws-y-Coed, Conwy LL24 0HD

OUR HOME IS YOUR CASTLE. Family-run country guest house. Ideally situated in Snowdonia National Park. Breathtaking views of Conwy/Llugwy Valleys. Renowned for its excellent service and teddy bear collection. Indoor heated swimming pool with sauna free and exclusively for our guests. Secluded free car park. Golf course and village within six minutes' walking distance. Walkers welcome; guided walks on request. Free shuttle service to nearest railway stations. All our rooms with en suite bathroom facilities, coffee/tea tray, CTV etc. Full cooked English Breakfast. Multilingual staff.

Tel: 01690 710540
e-mail: welcome@park-hill.co.uk
www.park-hill.co.uk

Bed and Breakfast from £30pppn

SB

North Wales / Carmarthenshire

Corwen (Denbighshire)

Situated on the main A5, this converted old police station and courthouse has six prisoners' cells turned into single bedrooms. Washbasins in each, with a bathroom to service three on the first floor and a shower room for three on the ground floor. All double bedrooms have bathrooms en suite. The dining room is where magistrates presided, and the comfortable lounge spreads over the rest of the court. Central heating throughout and TV in the lounge. Bed and Breakfast from £20. Convenient base for touring North Wales.

**Bob and Kit Buckland, Corwen Court Private Hotel,
London Road, Corwen LL21 0DP • 01490 412854**

Carmarthenshire

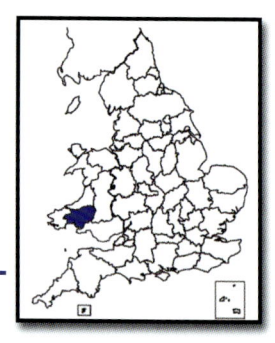

Carmarthen

Plas Farm B&B • Llangynog, Carmarthen

Plas Farm B&B, run by the Thomas family for the past 100 years, offers guests peaceful accommodation on a family-run dairy farm, in a quiet location, ideal as a touring base. Very spacious, comfortable farmhouse with colour TV and welcome tray in all bedrooms. All rooms en suite or with private shower room. TV lounge. Full central heating. Evening meals available at local country inn nearby.
Warm welcome assured.

En route to Fishguard and Pembroke Ferries. Ample safe parking. Good golf course minutes away.

*B&B from £25 per person.
Children under 16 years sharing
family room half price.
A warm welcome awaits.
"Welcome Host"*

**Mrs Margaret Thomas, Plas Farm,
Llangynog, Carmarthen SA33 5DB
Tel & Fax: 01267 211492
www.plasfarm.co.uk
e-mil: plasfarm@hotmail.co.uk**

Ceredigion

Aberystwyth

Ceredigion

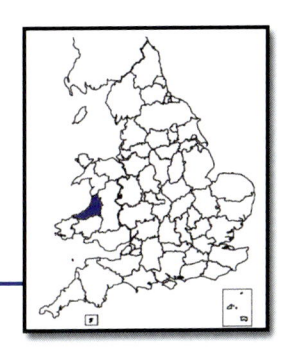

The Farmhouse overlooks the picturesque Rheidol Valley, which is situated 7.5 miles east of Aberystwyth, accessible via the A44 trunk road. Tycam is ideal for a quiet holiday, for walking, birdwatching, fishing, golf and pony trekking or for visiting the many places of interest in the area including the Aberystwyth and Devil's Bridge narrow gauge railway.

Two rooms are available, both en suite and centrally heated. One twin bedded and one double bedroom, lounge/dining room, colour TV. Children over six are welcome and there is a reduction for children under ten years. Sorry no pets. A car is essential and there is ample parking. Bed and Breakfast terms on request.

**Mrs F.J. Rowlands,
Tycam Farm,
Capel Bangor, Aberystwyth
SY23 3NA
01970 880662**

Marine Hotel • Aberystwyth

The Promenade, Marine Terrace, Aberystwyth SY23 2BX

Large seafront hotel with a lift to all floors. Bars, restaurant, bistro and lounges all on ground level. This family-run hotel is highly recommended for its warm, friendly atmosphere, good home cooking, and attention to guests' comfort.

The 52 en suite refurbished bedrooms have TV and tea/coffee making facilities, and most have magnificent views of Cardigan Bay. Complimentary use of leisure suite with sauna, steam room, jacuzzi and gym • The hotel has facilities for disabled guests • Bargain breaks and mini-holidays offer excellent value • Golf parties welcome.

e-mail: marinehotel1@btconnect.com • www.marinehotelaberystwyth.co.uk
Freephone: 0800 0190020 • Tel: 01970 612444 • Fax: 01970 617435

Ceredigion
Aberystwyth

Queensbridge Hotel
The Promenade, Aberystwyth, Ceredigion SY23 2DH
Tel: 01970 612343 • Fax: 01970 617452

Aberystwyth, with its award-winning beach, is one of Wales's favourite traditional seaside towns. With many visitor attractions it is the ideal venue for touring North, Mid and South Wales.

Situated at the quieter end of Aberystwyth's historic Victorian promenade, overlooking the panoramic sweep of Cardigan Bay, the Queensbridge Hotel offers guests superior comfort in fifteen spacious en suite bedrooms, all with colour TV, hospitality tray and telephone. A hearty Welsh breakfast is served in the welcoming Breakfast Room where we pride ourselves on our prompt, efficient service and excellent menu choice.

Established 1972 – "Our reputation for comfort and good service remains steadfast"
www.queensbridgehotelaberystwyth.co.uk

Pembrokeshire

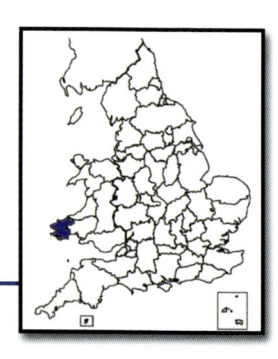

Fishguard

Heathfield Mansion
Letterston, Near Fishguard SA62 5EG
Tel: 01348 840263
e-mail: angelica.rees@virgin.net

A Georgian country house in 16 acres of pasture and woodland, Heathfield is an ideal location for the appreciation of Pembrokeshire's many natural attractions. There is excellent golf, riding and fishing in the vicinity and the coast is only a few minutes' drive away. The accommodation is very comfortable and two of the three bedrooms have en suite bathrooms. The cuisine and wines are well above average. This is a most refreshing venue for a tranquil and wholesome holiday. *Welcome Host Gold*

Pets welcome by prior arrangement only • Cyclists and Coastal Path walkers welcome
Bed & Breakfast from £30 per person • Dinner by arrangement • Discounts for weekly stays

symbols

	Totally non-smoking		Pets Welcome
	Children Welcome	**SB**	Short Breaks
	Suitable for Disabled Guests		Licensed

Pembrokeshire
Goodwick

Ivybridge

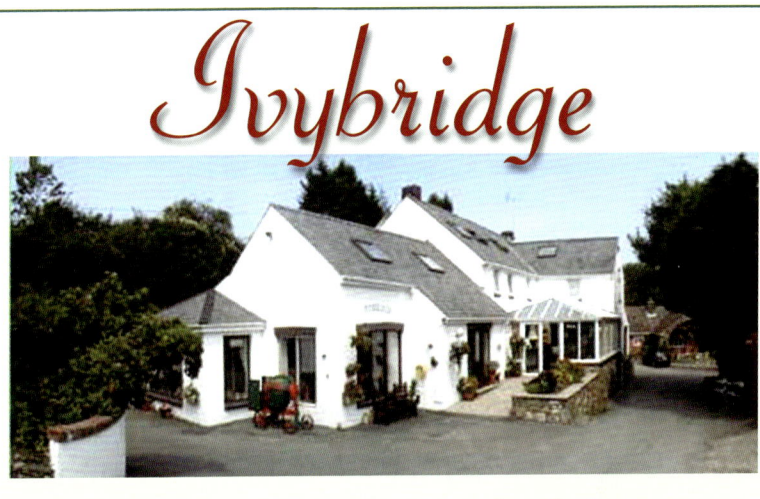

Welcome to Ivybridge

Situated down a leafy lane, Ivybridge is a friendly, family-run guest house offering comfortable accommodation in Fishguard, a picturesque area of Pembrokeshire, within easy reach of the Pembrokeshire coastal paths and the historic City of St Davids.

Try our heated indoor swimming pool or whirlpool, relax in our conservatory or put your feet up in front of a roaring fire and enjoy the company and atmosphere at Ivybridge.

All rooms are e-suite with colour television, hairdryers and hot drink facilities. Wake up to a Full Welsh Breakfast or a Continental Breakfast if preferred. Vegetarian guests are welcome.

At Ivybridge we can offer a set three-course evening meal including tea/coffee, (please book before 12 noon). Snacks and pre-packed lunches can be prepared to your requirements.

Why not indulge in a little pampering at our new spa?

For further information please contact us

Ivybridge, Drim Mill, Dyffryn, Goodwick SA64 0JT
Tel: 01348 875366 • Fax: 01348 872338
e-mail: ivybridge5366@aol.com
www.ivybridgeleisure.co.uk

Wales Cymru
★★★

Pembrokeshire

Haverfordwest, Lamphey, Newport

Haroldston Hall
Portfield Gate, Haverfordwest SA62 3LZ
Tel: 01437 781549

Wales Cymru ★★★★

Far from the madding crowd. A delightful country house set in spacious grounds amid serene rolling countryside just a mile from St Bride's Bay, Coastal Path and sandy beaches. Ideally situated to explore the beauty of Pembrokeshire's National Park. Relax and enjoy the warm, friendly atmosphere, large, comfortable, fully-equipped bedrooms and bathrooms (en suite available). Delicious legendary traditional Aga-cooked breakfast. Non-smoking. No children. Pets must be kept in cars; not allowed in bedrooms. Parking available. Open all year.

e-mail: bstewartthomas@aol.com
www.haroldstonhall.co.uk

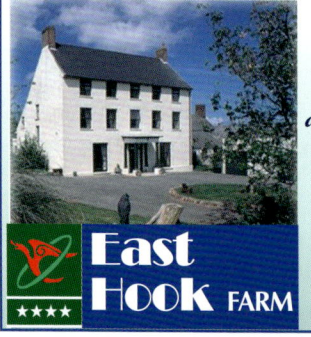

East Hook FARM

Howard and Jen welcome you to their Georgian Farmhouse surrounded by beautiful countryside, four miles from the coastline and three miles from Haverfordwest. Double, twin and family suite available, all en suite. Ground floor rooms available. Pembrokeshire produce used for breakfast.

Bed and Breakfast from £32.50 to £37.50 pp.

Self-Catering cottage available.

Mr and Mrs Patrick, East Hook Farm,
Portfield Gate, Haverfordwest, Pembroke SA62 3LN
01437 762211 • www.easthookfarmhouse.co.uk

THE DIAL INN
Ridgeway Road, Lamphey, Pembroke,
Pembrokeshire SA71 5NU
Tel: 01646 672426 • e-mail: info@dialinn.co.uk

The Dial Inn is situated in Lamphey village, two miles east of Pembroke, and only a stone's throw from the Bishop's Palace. This elegant, interesting and deceptively large village pub has excellent bar food, a daily blackboard menu, and an imaginative dining room menu. All food is freshly prepared and cooked. Also available are fine wines and cask-conditioned ales, and the inn is open for coffee, lunch, dinner and bar meals. Accommodation is available in five luxury en suite bedrooms. Open all year.
It is listed in all the best food and beer guides including 'Which?' and the AA. CAMRA.

GELLIFAWR HOTEL & COTTAGES

This 19th century stone farmhouse has been lovingly restored, ensuring a warm welcome to this family-run hotel. The seven en suite bedrooms are spacious, and have tea/coffee making facilities and colour TV. The non-smoking restaurant offers varied à la carte and bistro menus, and is open to non-residents. There is also a well-stocked bar, where a log-burning fire and friendly staff will ensure an enjoyable visit.

Self-catering **accommodation** is available in double glazed, centrally heated cottages (one to three bedrooms), set around a landscaped courtyard, with modern kitchens and all the comforts of home. This scenic area is ideal for walking, birdwatching, cycling, or just relaxing.

Pontfaen, Newport SA65 9TX
Tel: 01239 820343
e-mail: reservations@gellifawr.co.uk
www.gellifawr.co.uk

Pembrokeshire
Saundersfoot

WALES 329

LANGDON FARM GUEST HOUSE
Saundersfoot & Tenby

Beautifully appointed, idyllic farm guesthouse on working farm overlooking two small lakes in a perfect location close to Saundersfoot and Tenby. All bedrooms en suite with central heating, colour TV and tea/coffee/hot chocolate making facilities. Separate guest sitting room with colour TV. Conservatory/breakfast room overlooking pretty gardens and rolling countryside where horses and sheep leisurely graze while you enjoy your delicious breakfast. Local fresh farm produce used when available. Vegetarians catered for. Perfect base for walking and touring the beautiful beaches, countryside and attractions of Pembrokeshire. Many excellent eating establishments within a short distance, from local Welsh Inns to specialist fish restaurants. Ample parking. No children under 4 years. Open January 15th - November 15th.

Bed and Breakfast £28 - £33pppn (based on two sharing). Welcome Host Gold Award.

KILGETTY, NEAR SAUNDERSFOOT SA68 ONJ • TEL: 01834 814803
E-MAIL: MAIL@STAYINPEMBROKESHIRE.CO.UK
WWW.STAYINPEMBROKESHIRE.CO.UK

Wales Cymru ★★★★

SB

Looking for Holiday Accommodation?

FHG
KUPERARD

for details of hundreds of properties throughout the UK, visit our website

www.holidayguides.com

Powys

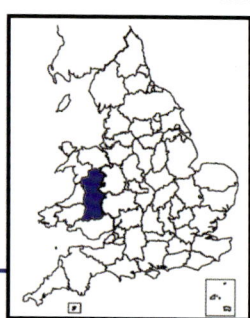

Caebetran Farm

A warm welcome...

a cup of tea and home-made cakes await you when you arrive at Caebetran. Well off the beaten track, where there are breathtaking views of the Brecon Beacons and the Black Mountains, and just across a field is a 400 acre common, ideal for walking, bird-watching or just relaxing. The rooms are all en suite and have colour TV and tea making facilities. The dining room has separate tables, there is also a comfortable lounge with colour TV, DVD and video. Caebetran is an ideal base for exploring this beautiful, unspoilt part of the country, with pony trekking, walking, birdwatching, wildlife, hang-gliding and so much more. Awaiting you are our friendly, beautiful natured collies - Meg and Lad, also Scamp the terrier will play ball, retrieve a stick and walk with you. For a brochure and terms please write or telephone.

"Arrive as visitors and leave as our friends".

**Gwyn and Hazel Davies Caebetran Farm, Felinfach,
Brecon, Powys LD3 0UL
Tel: 01874 754460 • Mob: 0789 1118594
e-mail: hazelcaebetran@aol.com • www.farmbandbinwales.com**

Llanbrynean is a fine, traditional, Victorian farmhouse peacefully situated on the edge of the picturesque village of Llanfrynach, three miles south-east of Brecon. We are in an ideal spot for exploring the area - the Brecon Beacons rise behind the farm and the Brecon/Monmouth canal flows through the fields below.
We are a working family sheep farm with wonderful pastoral views and a large garden. The house is spacious and comfortable with a friendly, relaxed atmosphere. We have two double en suite bedrooms and one twin with private bathroom. All have tea/coffee facilities. There is a sitting room with TV. Excellent pub food within easy walking distance.

Bed and Breakfast from £25pp

**Mrs A. Harpur, Llanbrynean Farm,
Llanfrynach, Brecon LD3 7BQ
Tel: 01874 665222
e-mail: simon.harpur@tiscali.co.uk**

Llanbrynean

Powys

Llanidloes, Newtown

LLANIDLOES. Mrs L. Rees, Esgairmaen, Y Fan, Llanidloes SY18 6NT (01686 430272).
"Croeso Cynnes" a warm welcome awaits you at Esgairmaen, a working farm one mile from Clyweddog reservoir where fishing and sailing can be enjoyed, an ideal base for walking, bird watching and exploring nearby forests. The house commands magnificent views of unspoilt countryside, only 29 miles from the coast. One double and one family room, both en suite with tea/coffee making facilities. Central heating. We offer peace and tranquillity.
- Working farm. • Open April to October.

The Forest
COUNTRY GUEST HOUSE
Wales Cymru ★★★★

Hidden in the beautiful Vale of Kerry, The Forest offers 4-star luxury bed and breakfast in 5 charming en suite rooms. Four acres of gardens, tennis court, games room, kennels and stables, Secluded and peaceful location, perfect to explore many attractions of Mid-Wales.

Paul & Michelle Martin, The Forest, Gilfach Lane, Kerry, Newtown, Powys SY16 4DW
Tel: 01686 621 821 • e-mail: info@theforestkerry.co.uk
www.bedandbreakfastnewtown.co.uk

A warm welcome awaits you at Greenfields

Wales Cymru ★★★

All rooms are tastefully decorated and are spacious in size, each having panoramic views of the rolling Kerry hills. There is a good choice of breakfast menu and evening meals can be provided by prior arrangement; packed lunches are also available. Licensed for residents. Accommodation available in twin, double, family and single rooms, all en suite (twin rooms let as singles if required). Hostess tray and TV in all rooms. The dining room has individual tables. A good place for stopping for one night, a short break or longer holiday. Excellent off-road parking. Brochure available.

B&B from £45 double or twin room, from £26 single and £70 family room.

Mrs Vi Madeley, Greenfields, Kerry, Newtown SY16 4LH
Tel: 01686 670596 • Mobile: 07971 075687 • Fax: 01686 670354
e-mail: info@greenfields-bb.co.uk • www.greenfields-bb.co.uk

symbols

Totally non-smoking	Pets Welcome
Children Welcome	SB Short Breaks
Suitable for Disabled Guests	Licensed

South Wales

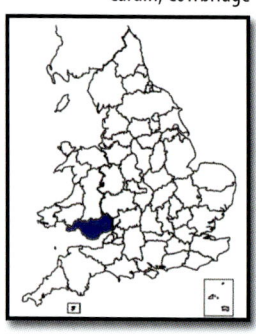

South Wales
Cardiff, Cowbridge

CARDIFF. Mrs Sarah Nicholls, Preste Gaarden Hotel, 181 Cathedral Road, Cardiff CF11 9PN (029 2022 8607; Fax: 029 2037 4805).
This spacious Victorian family home offers olde worlde charm with modern amenities, including en suite facilities in most rooms. You will immediately feel relaxed by the warm welcome given by Sarah. Situated in the heart of the City, close to the Castle, museums, shops and an international array of restaurants and only 100 yards from Sophia Gardens offering walking, fishing and horse riding. Bed and Breakfast includes tea/coffee and biscuits in your room. Well established and independently recommended.
Rates: Bed and Breakfast from £25 to £39 per person includes tea and coffee in your room.

- Self catering apartment also available.
WTB ★★★ *B&B*
e-mail: stay@cosycardiffhotel.co.uk   **www.cosycardiffhotel.co.uk**

Plas Llanmihangel is the finest medieval manor house in the beautiful Vale of Glamorgan. We offer a genuine warmth of welcome, delightful accommodation, first-class food and service in our wonderful home. The baronial hall, great log fires, the ancient tower and acres of beautiful historic gardens intrigue all who stay in this fascinating Grade 1 Listed house. Its long history and continuous occupation have created a spectacular building in romantic surroundings, unchanged since the sixteenth century. A great opportunity to experience the ambience and charm of a past age (selected by the Consumer Association's 'Which?' as one of the Top 20 B&Bs in Great Britain for 2004). Three double rooms. High quality home-cooked evening meal on request. B&B from £33pp.
Independent operator highly commended by www.tripadvisor.co.uk

**PLAS LLANMIHANGEL, Llanmihangel,
Near Cowbridge CF71 7LQ • 01446 774610
e-mail: plasllanmihangel@ukonline.co.uk**

Please note

All the information in this book is given in good faith in the belief that it is correct. However, the publishers cannot guarantee the facts given in these pages, neither are they responsible for changes in policy, ownership or terms that may take place after the date of going to press. Readers should always satisfy themselves that the facilities they require are available and that the terms, if quoted, still apply.

Monmouth

CHURCH FARM GUEST HOUSE

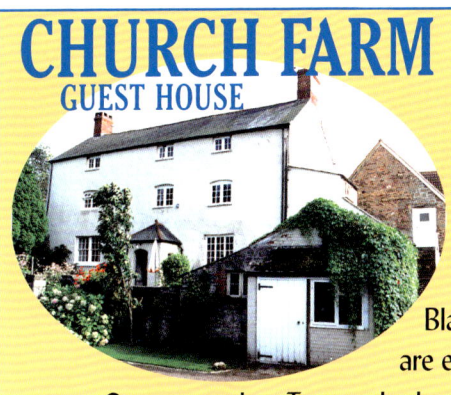

A spacious and homely 16th century (Grade II Listed) former farmhouse with oak beams and inglenook fireplaces, set in large attractive garden with stream. An excellent base for visiting the Wye Valley, Forest of Dean and Black Mountains. All nine bedrooms are en suite or have private facilities.

Own car park • Terrace, barbecue • Colour TV • Non-smoking.
Bed and Breakfast from £30 to £32 per person,
Evening Meals by arrangement.

AA ★★★ Guest Accommodation

Rosemary and Derek Ringer, Church Farm Guest House,
Mitchel Troy, Monmouth NP25 4HZ • 01600 712176
www.churchfarmmitcheltroy.co.uk
info@churchfarmguesthouse.eclipse.co.uk

Tresco Guest House

Redbrook, Near Monmouth
Monmouthshire NP25 4LY
Tel & Fax: 01600 712325
Mobile: 07833 514250

Props: Margery & Arthur Evans

- Situated near River Wye on main road through village
- Well established gardens and views of the river • Canoeing/fishing can be arranged
- Good choice of breakfast - vegetarians catered for • Packed lunches available
- All rooms on ground floor with TV, central heating and tea/coffee making facilities
- En suite double/twin £30pp • Single £25, double £25pp (shared facilities)
- Rates for children on request.
- No smoking inside house • Ample parking
- We provide a friendly welcome and comfortable accommodation

South Wales
Neath, Swansea

18th Century luxury Guest House where our aim is to ensure a peaceful, comfortable and relaxing stay. Our guest rooms are all en suite and spacious, and have central heating, colour TV, tea and coffee making facilities, and panoramic views over the Vale of Neath. Licensed bar and restaurant • Vegetarian & other diets catered for Children welcome • Parking • Non-smoking rooms • Major credit cards accepted • Pets welcome by arrangement

Green Lanterns

www.greenlanterns.co.uk

Mrs C. Jones, Green Lanterns Guest House, Hawdref Ganol Farm, Cimla, Neath SA12 9SL • 01639 631884 • WTB ★★★★

The Alexander

Privately-owned Guest House one mile from city centre, with a good range of amenities nearby. All bedrooms are light and spacious with en suite bath/shower and toilet facilities, colour televisions, radio alarm clocks, generous welcome trays and additional bedding if required. Some rooms have views over Swansea Bay. There are also direct dial telephones in all rooms with internet access.

Wales Cymru ★★★

3 Sketty Road, Uplands, Swansea SA2 0EU
Tel: 01792 470045 • Fax: 01792 476012
E-mail: reception@alexander-hotel.co.uk
www.alexander-hotel.co.uk

Other specialised holiday guides from FHG

PUBS & INNS OF BRITAIN

COUNTRY HOTELS OF BRITAIN

WEEKEND & SHORT BREAKS IN BRITAIN & IRELAND

THE GOLF GUIDE WHERE TO PLAY, WHERE TO STAY

PETS WELCOME!

SELF-CATERING HOLIDAYS IN BRITAIN

500 GREAT PLACES TO STAY IN BRITAIN

CARAVAN & CAMPING HOLIDAYS IN BRITAIN

FAMILY BREAKS IN BRITAIN

Published annually: available in all good bookshops or direct from the publisher:
FHG Guides, Abbey Mill Business Centre, Seedhill, Paisley PA1 1TJ
Tel: 0141 887 0428 • Fax: 0141 889 7204
e-mail: admin@fhguides.co.uk • www.holidayguides.com

Country Inns

Cornwall

Bodmin Moor

Colliford Tavern
"AN OASIS ON BODMIN MOOR"
Colliford Lake, Near St Neot, Liskeard, Cornwall PL14 6PZ • Tel: 01208 821335
e-mail: info@colliford.com • www.colliford.com

Set in attractive grounds which include a children's play area, ponds and a working waterwheel, this delightfully furnished free house offers good food and bar snacks. Sprucely-appointed guest rooms are spacious and have en suite shower, colour television, radio alarm, beverage maker and numerous thoughtful extras. An unusual feature of the tavern is a 37' deep granite well. In the midst of the scenic splendour of Bodmin Moor, this is a relaxing country retreat only a few minutes' walk from Colliford Lake, so popular with fly fishermen. Both north and south coasts are within easy driving distance and terms are most reasonable.

SB

Campsite for touring caravans, motorhomes and tents - full electric hook-up etc available.

Cumbria

Brampton, Coniston

The Blacksmiths Arms

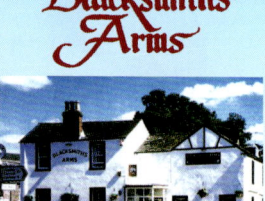

Talkin Village, Brampton, Cumbria CA8 1LE
Tel: 016977 3452 • Fax: 016977 3396
e-mail: blacksmithsarmstalkin@yahoo.co.uk
www.blacksmithstalkin.co.uk

The Blacksmith's Arms offers all the hospitality and comforts of a traditional country inn. Enjoy tasty meals served in the bar lounges, or linger over dinner in the well-appointed restaurant. The inn is personally managed by the proprietors, Anne and Donald Jackson, who guarantee the hospitality one would expect from a family concern. Guests are assured of a pleasant and comfortable stay. There are eight lovely bedrooms, all en suite. Peacefully situated in the beautiful village of Talkin, the inn is convenient for the Borders, Hadrian's Wall and the Lake District. There is a good golf course, walking and other country pursuits nearby.

Sun Hotel & 16th Century Inn

A superbly located 10-bedroom hotel designed to overlook the village and enjoy panoramic mountain views. With a large private garden, patio, comfortable lounge, and extensive restaurant menu and wine list, the hotel offers comfortable en suite accommodation in a peaceful and informal setting. All bedrooms have been recently refurbished, with a relaxing night's sleep as good as promised! Better still, when built (in 1902), the hotel was attached to the end of a 16th century pub! It is now a freehouse with real ales and real fires in a classic Lakeland setting of beamed ceiling, flagged floor and an old range.

Coniston LA21 8HQ • Tel: 015394 41248
Fax: 015394 41219 • info@thesunconiston.com
www.thesunconiston.com

Gloucestershire

Parkend

The Fountain Inn & Lodge

Parkend, Royal Forest of Dean, Gloucestershire GL15 4JD.

Traditional village inn, well known locally for its excellent meals and real ales. A Forest Fayre menu offers such delicious main courses as Lamb Shank In Redcurrant & Rosemary Sauce and Gloucester Sausage in Onion Gravy, together with a large selection of curries and vegetarian dishes.
Centrally situated in one of England's foremost wooded areas, the inn makes an ideal base for sightseeing, or for exploring some of the many peaceful forest walks nearby.
All bedrooms (including two specially adapted for the less able) are en suite, decorated and furnished to an excellent standard, and have television and tea/coffee making facilities. Various half-board breaks are available throughout the year.

Tel: 01594 562189 • Fax: 01594 564378 • e-mail: thefountaininn@aol.com • www.thefountaininnandlodge.com

Shropshire

Bishop's Castle

The Travellers Rest Inn

Upper Affcot
Church Stretton SY6 6RL
Tel: 01694 781275
Fax: 01694 781555
reception@travellersrestinn.co.uk
www.travellersrestinn.co.uk

Situated between Church Stretton and Craven Arms, and surrounded by The South Shropshire Hills. We, Fraser and Mauresia Allison, the owners assure you a warm welcome, good food, good beers, good accommodation, and good old fashioned service.

For those wishing to stay overnight with us at The Travellers Rest we have 12 very nice en suite guest bedrooms: six of these being on the ground floor with easy access, and two of these are suitable for accompanied wheel chair users. The bedrooms are away from the main area of the Inn and have their own entrance to the car park and garden, ideal if you have brought your pet with you and a midnight walk is needed.

Our well stocked Bar can satisfy most thirsts; cask ales, lagers, stouts, spirits, wines and minerals, throughout the day and the Kitchen takes care of your hunger; be it for a snack or a full satisfying meal, vegetarians no problem, food being served until 9pm in the evening.

Publisher's note

While every effort is made to ensure accuracy, we regret that FHG Guides cannot accept responsibility for errors, misrepresentations or omissions in our entries or any consequences thereof. Prices in particular should be checked.
We will follow up complaints but cannot act as arbiters or agents for either party.

symbols

- Totally non-smoking
- Children Welcome
- Suitable for Disabled Guests
- Pets Welcome
- SB Short Breaks
- Licensed

Suffolk

Bury St Edmunds

The Bull Inn & Restaurant

The Street,
Woolpit
Bury St Edmunds
IP30 9SA
Tel: 01359 240393

A family-run pub, ideal for touring the beautiful county of Suffolk

- Traditional food and daily specials lunchtime and evenings (not Sunday pm).
- Good choice of real ales and wines
- Excellent en suite accommodation (single, double and family)
- Large garden and car park

www.bullinnwoolpit.co.uk • info@bullinnwoolpit.co.uk

Please note

All the information in this book is given in good faith in the belief that it is correct. However, the publishers cannot guarantee the facts given in these pages, neither are they responsible for changes in policy, ownership or terms that may take place after the date of going to press. Readers should always satisfy themselves that the facilities they require are available and that the terms, if quoted, still apply.

East Yorkshire

See opposite

THE WOLDS INN
Driffield Road, Huggate, East Yorkshire YO42 1YH
Tel: 01377 288217
huggate@woldsinn.freeserve.co.uk

A peaceful country inn in farming country high in the Wolds, the hostelry exudes an atmosphere well in keeping with its 16th century origins. Panelling, brassware and crackling fires all contribute to a mood of contentment, well supported in practical terms by splendid food served either in the convivial bar, where meals are served daily at lunchtimes and in the evenings, or in the award-winning restaurant where choice may be made from a mouth-watering à la carte menu. Sunday roasts are also very popular.

Huggate lies on the Wolds Way and the inn is justly popular with walkers, whilst historic York and Beverley and their racecourses and the resorts of Bridlington, Hornsea and Scarborough are within easy reach.

First-rate overnight accommodation is available, all rooms having en suite facilities, central heating, colour television and tea and coffee tray.

North Yorkshire

Danby

The Fox & Hounds Inn

- Residential 16th Century Coaching Inn set amidst the beautiful North York Moors.
- Freshly prepared dishes served every lunchtime and evening.
- Quality selected wines and Theakston real ales.
- Superb en suite accommodation available.

Special Breaks available November to March. Situated between Castleton and Danby on the Fryup Road.

Ainthorpe, Danby, Whitby, North Yorkshire YO21 2LD
For bookings please Tel: 01287 660218
e-mail: info@foxandhounds-ainthorpe.com
www.foxandhounds–ainthorpe.com

Other specialised holiday guides from FHG

PUBS & INNS OF BRITAIN • **COUNTRY HOTELS** OF BRITAIN
WEEKEND & SHORT BREAK HOLIDAYS IN BRITAIN
THE GOLF GUIDE WHERE TO PLAY, WHERE TO STAY
500 GREAT PLACES TO STAY • **SELF-CATERING HOLIDAYS** IN BRITAIN
BED & BREAKFAST STOPS • **CARAVAN & CAMPING HOLIDAYS**
FAMILY BREAKS IN BRITAIN

Published annually: available in all good bookshops or direct from the publisher:
FHG Guides, Abbey Mill Business Centre, Seedhill, Paisley PA1 1TJ
Tel: 0141 887 0428 • Fax: 0141 889 7204
e-mail: admin@fhguides.co.uk • www.holidayguides.com

Argyll & Bute

Ardfern

The Galley of Lorne Inn
Ardfern, By Lochgilphead PA31 8QN
Tel : 01852 500284   Fax : 01852 500578
Web : www.galleyoflorne.co.uk   Email : enquiries@galleyoflorne.co.uk

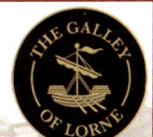

- 17th Century Grade C listed Drovers Inn with stunning views across Loch Craignish out to Jura and Scarba
- Ideal location for leisure activities • Walking, Fishing, Sailing, Boat Trips, Horse Riding, Diving, Cycling, Golf etc.
- Six Ensuite Bedrooms • Central heating, Colour Satellite LCD TV, Tea and Coffee making facilities
- Dining available in Restaurant, Lounge Bar and Public Bar • Restaurant, Bar and Kids menus • Local Produce
- Food available Monday to Sunday lunchtimes and evenings • Seafood our speciality with mussels from our Loch
- Functions & Weddings catered for • Real Ales • Wine List • Fine collection of Malt Whiskies

view our website for more details

Highlands

Fort William

LOCH LEVEN HOTEL

John & Hilary would like to welcome you to the lovely Loch Leven Hotel, a small, informal, family-run hotel with excellent food and an ideal base to explore this beautiful region. Enjoy the spectacular scenery from the Lochview Restaurant, garden and new decking, or toast yourself by the log fire in the Public Bar, with its inexpensive menu and wonderful selection of malts. Children and pets always welcome. B&B from £40pp with discounts for Short Breaks.

Tel: 01855 821236
reception@lochlevenhotel.co.uk • www.lochlevenhotel.co.uk
Old Ferry Road, North Ballachulish, Near Fort William PH33 6SA

Visit the FHG website
www.holidayguides.com

for details of the wide choice of accommodation

featured in the full range of FHG titles

Ratings & Awards

For the first time ever the AA, VisitBritain, VisitScotland, and the Wales Tourist Board will use a single method of assessing and rating serviced accommodation. Irrespective of which organisation inspects an establishment the rating awarded will be the same, using a common set of standards, giving a clear guide of what to expect. The RAC is no longer operating an Hotel inspection and accreditation business.

Accommodation Standards: Star Grading Scheme

Using a scale of 1-5 stars the objective quality ratings give a clear indication of accommodation standard, cleanliness, ambience, hospitality, service and food, This shows the full range of standards suitable for every budget and preference, and allows visitors to distinguish between the quality of accommodation and facilities on offer in different establishments. All types of board and self-catering accommodation are covered, including hotels,
B&Bs, holiday parks, campus accommodation, hostels, caravans and camping, and boats.

VisitBritain and the regional tourist boards, enjoyEngland.com, VisitScotland and VisitWales, and the AA have full details of the grading system on their websites

The more stars, the higher level of quality

★★★★★
exceptional quality, with a degree of luxury

★★★★
excellent standard throughout

★★★
very good level of quality and comfort

★★
good quality, well presented and well run

★
acceptable quality; simple, practical, no frills

National Accessible Scheme

If you have particular mobility, visual or hearing needs, look out for the National Accessible Scheme. You can be confident of finding accommodation or attractions that meet your needs by looking for the following symbols.

Typically suitable for a person with sufficient mobility to climb a flight of steps but would benefit from fixtures and fittings to aid balance

Typically suitable for a person with restricted walking ability and for those that may need to use a wheelchair some of the time and can negotiate a maximum of three steps

Typically suitable for a person who depends on the use of a wheelchair and transfers unaided to and from the wheelchair in a seated position. This person may be an independent traveller

Typically suitable for a person who depends on the use of a wheelchair in a seated position. This person also requires personal or mechanical assistance (eg carer, hoist).

SPECIAL WELCOME SUPPLEMENT

Are you looking for a guest house where smoking is banned, a farmhouse that is equipped for the disabled, or a hotel that will cater for your special diet? If so, you should find this supplement useful. Its three sections, NON-SMOKERS, DISABLED, and SPECIAL DIETS, list accommodation where these particular needs are served. Brief details of the accommodation are provided in this section; for a fuller description you should turn to the appropriate place in the main section of the book.

Non-smoking

CORNWALL, BOSCASTLE. Mrs P. Perfili, Trefoil Farm, Camelford Road, Boscastle PL35 0AD (01840 250606). En suite accommodation with tea/coffee, TV. Overlooking Boscastle village, close to sandy beaches. Open Easter to end October. Short walk to local 16thC inn with good food and real ales. **ETC ★★★**

CUMBRIA, WINDERMERE. Holly-Wood Guest House, Holly Road, Windermere LA23 2AF (015394 42219). Family-run Victorian house 3 minutes from amenities, ideal for exploring Lakes. All rooms en suite. Hearty traditional/vegetarian breakfasts. Non-smoking throughout. **ETC/AA ★★★★**

DEVON, SIDMOUTH. Lower Pinn Farm, Peak Hill, Sidmouth EX10 0NN (01395 513733). 19thC farmhouse on Jurassic Coast with comfortable en suite rooms. Good hearty breakfasts. Children and pets welcome. No-smoking establishment. Open all year. **ETC ★★★★**

DEVON, TORQUAY. Aveland House, Aveland Road, Babbacombe, Torquay TQ1 3PT (Tel: 01803 326622; Fax: 01803 328940). Quietly situated a short walk to Babbacombe sea front, licensed bar, all rooms en suite, free wi-fi access, car park and garden. Special diets catered for. Non-Smoking Silver Award, Green Tourism Gold Award. **AA ★★★★**

GLOUCESTERSHIRE, TEWKESBURY. Mrs Bernadette Williams, Abbots Court, Church End, Twyning, Tewkesbury GL20 6DA (Tel & Fax: 01684 292515). Large farmhouse on working farm, half a mile from M5/M50 junction. 6 en suite bedrooms, large lounge. Cot and high chair available. Reduced rates children and Senior Citizens. Non-smoking. **ETC ★★★**

LINCOLNSHIRE, WOODHALL SPA. Barbara & Tony Hodgkinson, Kirkstead Old Mill Cottage, Tattershall Road, Woodhall Spa LN10 6UQ (01526 353637; Mobile: 07970 040401). Peaceful detached house beside River Witham, with three en suite guest bedrooms and five-acre woodland garden. Cooked Gold Award breakfast served, or lighter, healthy option. Non-smoking.

SUSSEX (EAST), HASTINGS. Peter Mann, Grand Hotel, Grand Parade, St Leonards, Hastings TN38 0DD (Tel & Fax: 01424 428510). Seafront family-run hotel; all rooms with Freeview/DVD player/TV, radio; some en suite. Wi-fi broadband throughout. Unrestricted/disabled parking. Non-smoking throughout. Restaurant and licensed bar. **VB ★** *HOTEL*

Please note

All the information in this book is given in good faith in the belief that it is correct. However, the publishers cannot guarantee the facts given in these pages, neither are they responsible for changes in policy, ownership or terms that may take place after the date of going to press. Readers should always satisfy themselves that the facilities they require are available and that the terms, if quoted, still apply.

Special Diets

CORNWALL, BOSCASTLE. Mrs P. Perfili, Trefoil Farm, Camelford Road, Boscastle PL35 0AD (01840 250606). En suite accommodation with tea/coffee, TV. Overlooking Boscastle village, close to sandy beaches. Open Easter to end October. Short walk to local 16thC inn with good food and real ales. **ETC** ★★★

CUMBRIA, WINDERMERE. Holly-Wood Guest House, Holly Road, Windermere LA23 2AF (015394 42219). Family-run Victorian house 3 minutes from amenities, ideal for exploring Lakes. All rooms en suite. Hearty traditional/vegetarian breakfasts. Non-smoking throughout. **ETC/AA** ★★★★

DEVON, TORQUAY. Aveland House, Aveland Road, Babbacombe, Torquay TQ1 3PT (Tel: 01803 326622; Fax: 01803 328940). Quietly situated a short walk to Babbacombe sea front, licensed bar, all rooms en suite, free wi-fi access, car park and garden. Special diets catered for. Non-Smoking Silver Award, Green Tourism Gold Award. **AA** ★★★★

GLOUCESTERSHIRE, TEWKESBURY. Mrs Bernadette Williams, Abbots Court, Church End, Twyning, Tewkesbury GL20 6DA (Tel & Fax: 01684 292515). Large farmhouse on working farm, half a mile from M5/M50 junction. 6 en suite bedrooms, large lounge. Cot and high chair available. Reduced rates children and Senior Citizens. Non-smoking. **ETC** ★★★

LINCOLNSHIRE, WOODHALL SPA. Barbara & Tony Hodgkinson, Kirkstead Old Mill Cottage, Tattershall Road, Woodhall Spa LN10 6UQ (01526 353637; Mobile: 07970 040401). Peaceful detached house beside River Witham, with three en suite guest bedrooms and five-acre woodland garden. Cooked Gold Award breakfast served, or lighter, healthy option. Non-smoking.

SUSSEX (EAST), HASTINGS. Peter Mann, Grand Hotel, Grand Parade, St Leonards, Hastings TN38 0DD (Tel & Fax: 01424 428510). Seafront family-run hotel; all rooms with Freeview/DVD player/TV, radio; some en suite. Wi-fi broadband throughout. Unrestricted/disabled parking. Non-smoking throughout. Restaurant and licensed bar. **VB** ★ *HOTEL*

Other specialised holiday guides from **FHG**

PUBS & INNS OF BRITAIN

COUNTRY HOTELS OF BRITAIN

WEEKEND & SHORT BREAKS IN BRITAIN & IRELAND

THE GOLF GUIDE WHERE TO PLAY, WHERE TO STAY

PETS WELCOME!

SELF-CATERING HOLIDAYS IN BRITAIN

500 GREAT PLACES TO STAY IN BRITAIN

CARAVAN & CAMPING HOLIDAYS IN BRITAIN

FAMILY BREAKS IN BRITAIN

Published annually: available in all good bookshops or direct from the publisher:

FHG Guides, Abbey Mill Business Centre, Seedhill, Paisley PA1 1TJ

Tel: 0141 887 0428 • Fax: 0141 889 7204

e-mail: admin@fhguides.co.uk • www.holidayguides.com

Accessible Holidays

For many years FHG Guides have highlighted where properties have facilities for disabled visitors. It has however become apparent that the demand for such properties is ever increasing with the Disability Discrimination Act taking effect and the National Accessibility Scheme coming into force.

More proprietors are finding that catering for disabled visitors is rewarding not only from a financial point but also for the satisfaction and pleasure it brings.

The following section features a selection of properties that have met the National Accessible Scheme criteria. Details of the scheme are shown below:

The National Accessible Scheme (NAS) aims to help service providers within the tourism industry make their services more accessible - to encourage more disabled people to use them.

The scheme's standards provide guidelines on how to make reasonable adjustments to services to meet the needs of disabled people. They are split into three category standards, for:

- physically disabled people
- blind or visually impaired people
- deaf or hearing impaired people

National Accessible Scheme

If you have particular mobility, visual or hearing needs, look out for our National Accessible Scheme. You can be confident of finding accommodation that meets your needs by looking for the following symbols. Properties displaying these symbols will have met the National Accessible Scheme criteria.

Typically suitable for guests with sufficient mobility to climb a flight of steps, but who would benefit from fixtures and fittings to aid balance.

Typically suitable for guests with restricted walking ability and for those that may need to use a wheelchair some of the time, and who can negotiate a maximum of three steps.

Typically suitable for guests who depend on the use of a wheelchair, but transfer unaided to and from the wheelchair in a seated position. This person may be an independent traveller.

Typically suitable for guests who depend on the use of a wheelchair in a seated position. This person also requires personal/mechanical assistance (e.g. carer, hoist).

Access Exceptional – Achieves the standards for either independent wheelchair users or assisted wheelchair users and fulfils additional, more demanding requirements providing for several levels of mobility impairment (listed above) and with reference to the British Standard BS 8300:2001

346 SPECIAL WELCOME

Typically provides key additional services and facilities to meet the needs of visually impaired guests.

Typically provides a higher level of additional services and facilities to meet the needs of guests with visual impairment

Typically provides key additional services and facilities to meet the needs of hearing impaired guests

Typically provides a higher level of additional services and facilities to meet the needs of hearing impaired guests

Action for blind people

Action for Blind People is an expert national organisation, ensuring blind and partially sighted people receive practical support in all aspects of their lives. Our mission is to inspire change and create opportunities to enable blind and partially sighted people to have equal voice and equal choice.

Call our National Freephone Helpline on 0800 915 4666 Monday - Friday, 9am - 5pm
Write to us at: Action for Blind People, 14-16 Verney Road, London SE16 3DZ
www.actionforblindpeople.org.uk

NATIONAL FEDERATION OF Shopmobility

The National Federation of Shopmobility UK (NFSUK)

The National Federation of Shopmobility UK (NFSUK) is an independent registered charity, which aims to achieve equal access and independence for disabled people.
Shopmobility is a scheme which lends manual wheelchairs, powered wheelchairs and powered scooters to members of the public with limited mobility, to shop and to visit leisure and commercial facilities.
Shopmobility is for anyone, young or old, whether their disability is temporary or permanent.
It is available for those with injuries, long or short-term disabilities – anyone who needs help with mobility.
Shopmobility is about the freedom to get around. You do not need to be registered disabled to use it.

PO Box 6641, Christchurch BH23 9DQ
Tel: 08456 442 446 • Fax: 08456 444 442
e-mail: info@shopmobilityuk.org • www.shopmobilityuk.org

Accessible Holidays

LINCOLNSHIRE, WOODHALL SPA. Barbara & Tony Hodgkinson, Kirkstead Old Mill Cottage, Tattershall Road, Woodhall Spa LN10 6UQ (01526 353637; Mobile: 07970 040401). Peaceful detached house beside River Witham, with three en suite guest bedrooms and five-acre woodland garden. Cooked Gold Award breakfast served, or lighter, healthy option. Non-smoking.

SUSSEX (EAST), HASTINGS. Peter Mann, Grand Hotel, Grand Parade, St Leonards, Hastings TN38 0DD (Tel & Fax: 01424 428510). Seafront family-run hotel; all rooms with Freeview/DVD player/TV, radio; some en suite. Wi-fi broadband throughout. Unrestricted/disabled parking. Non-smoking throughout. Restaurant and licensed bar. **VB** ★ *HOTEL*

DIRECTORY OF WEBSITE AND E-MAIL ADDRESSES

A quick-reference guide to holiday accommodation with an e-mail address and/or website, conveniently arranged by country and county, with full contact details.

Self-Catering
Hoseasons Holidays Ltd, Lowestoft, Suffolk NR32 2LW
Tel: 01502 502628
- e-mail: louise.thacker@hoseasons.co.uk
- website: www.hoseasons.co.uk

• LONDON

Hotel
Athena Hotel, 110-114 Sussex Gardens, Hyde Park, LONDON W2 1UA
Tel: 020 7706 3866
- e-mail: athena@stavrouhotels.co.uk
- website: www.stavrouhotels.co.uk

Hotel
Gower Hotel, 129 Sussex Gardens, Hyde Park, LONDON W2 2RX
Tel: 020 7262 2262
- e-mail: gower@stavrouhotels.co.uk
- website: www.stavrouhotels.co.uk

B & B
Hanwell B & B, 110a Grove Avenue, Hanwell, LONDON W7 3ES
Tel: 020 8567 5015
- e-mail: tassanimation@ad.com
- website: www.ealing-hanwell-bed-and-breakfast.co.uk/new/index

Hotel
Queens Hotel, 33 Anson Road, Tufnell Park, LONDON N7
Tel: 020 7607 4725
- e-mail: queens@stavrouhotels.co.uk
- website: www.stavrouhotels.co.uk

B & B
S. Armanios, 67 Rannoch Road, Hammersmith, LONDON W6 9SS
Tel: 020 7385 4904
- website: www.thewaytostay.co.uk

• CAMBRIDGESHIRE

B&B
Mrs H. Marsh, The Meadow House, 2A High Street, BURWELL, Cambridgeshire CB25 0HB
Tel: 01638 741926
- e-mail: hilary@themeadowhouse.co.uk
- website: www.themeadowhouse.co.uk

B & B
Mrs Hatley, Manor Farm, Landbeach, CAMBRIDGE, Cambridgeshire CB4 8ED
Tel: 01223 860165
- e-mail: vhatley@btinternet.com
- website: www.smoothhound.co.uk/hotels/manorfarm4

• CHESHIRE

Guest House / Self-Catering
Mrs Joanne Hollins, Balterley Green Farm, Deans Lane, BALTERLEY, Near Crewe, Cheshire CW2 5QJ
Tel: 01270 820 214
- e-mail: greenfarm@balterley.fsnet.co.uk
- website: www.greenfarm.freeserve.co.uk

Country Hotel
Higher Huxley Hall, Huxley, CHESTER, Cheshire CH3 9BZ
Tel: 01829 781 484
- e-mail: info@huxleyhall.co.uk
- website: www.huxleyhall.co.uk

• CORNWALL

Self-Catering
Cornish Traditional Cottages, Blisland, BODMIN, Cornwall PL30 4HS
Tel: 01208 821666
- e-mail: info@corncott.com
- website: www.corncott.com

Self-Catering
Penrose Burden Holiday Cottages, St Breward, BODMIN, Cornwall PL30 4LZ
Tel: 01208 850277 or 01208 850617
- website: www.penroseburden.co.uk

www.holidayguides.com

WEBSITE DIRECTORY

Hotel
Stratton Gardens Hotel, Cot Hill, Stratton,
BUDE, Cornwall EX23 9DN
Tel: 01288 352500
* e-mail: moira@stratton-gardens.co.uk
* website: www.stratton-gardens.co.uk

Hotel
Hampton Manor Country House Hotel,
Alston, CALLINGTON, Cornwall PL17 8LX
Tel: 01579 370494
* e-mail: hamptonmanor@supanet.com
* website: www.hamptonmanor.co.uk

Hotel / Self-Catering
Wringford Down, Hat Lane, CAWSAND,
Cornwall PL10 1LE
Tel: 01752 822287
* e-mail: accommodation@wringforddown.co.uk
* website: www.cornwallholidays.co.uk
         www.wringforddown.co.uk

Self-Catering
Mineshop Holiday Cottages, CRACKINGTON
HAVEN, Bude, Cornwall EX23 0NR
Tel: 01840 230338
* e-mail: tippett@mineshop.freeserve.co.uk
* website: www.mineshop.co.uk

Self-Catering
Delamere Holiday Bungalows, DELABOLE
Contact: Mrs J. Snowden, 8 Warren Road,
Ickenham, Uxbridge, Middlesex UB10 8AA
Tel: 01895 234144
* e-mail: info@delamere-bungalows.com
* website: www.delamerebungalows.com

Self-Catering
Mr P. Watson, Creekside Holiday Houses,
Restronguet, FALMOUTH, Cornwall
Tel: 01326 372722
* website: www.creeksideholidayhouses.co.uk

Self-Catering
Mrs Terry, "Shasta", Carwinion Road, Mawnan
Smith, FALMOUTH, Cornwall TR11 5JD
Tel: 01326 250755
* e-mail: katerry@btopenworld.com

Self-Catering
Simon & Clare Hirsh, Bamham Farm
Cottages, Higher Bamham Farm,
LAUNCESTON, Cornwall PL15 9LD
Tel: 01566 772141
* website: www.bamhamfarm.co.uk

Self-Catering
Mrs A. E. Moore, Hollyvagg Farm,
Lewannick, LAUNCESTON,
Cornwall PL15 7QH
Tel: 01566 782309
* website: www.hollyvaggfarm.co.uk

Self-Catering
Celia Hutchinson,
Caradon Country Cottages, East Taphouse,
LISKEARD, Cornwall PL14 4NH
Tel: 01579 320355
* e-mail: celia@caradoncottages.co.uk
* website: www.caradoncottages.co.uk

Self- Catering
Mr Lowman, Cutkive Wood Holiday Lodges,
St Ive, LISKEARD, Cornwall PL14 3ND
Tel: 01579 362216
* e-mail: holidays@cutkivewood.co.uk
* website: www.cutkivewood.co.uk

Self- Catering
Mrs B. A. Higgins, Trewith Holiday Cottages,
Trewith, Duloe, Liskeard, LOOE,
Cornwall PL14 4PR
Tel: 01503 262184
* e-mail: info@trewith.co.uk
* website: www.trewith.co.uk

Self-Catering
Valleybrook Holidays, Peakswater, Lansallos,
LOOE, Cornwall PL13 2QE
Tel: 01503 220493
* website: www.valleybrookholidays.com

Self-Catering
Tracy Dennett, Talehay Holiday Cottages,
Pelynt, Near LOOE, Cornwall PL13 2LT
Tel: 01503 220252
* e-mail: infobookings@talehay.co.uk
* website: www.talehay.co.uk

Self-catering Lodges
Blue Bay Lodge, Trenance, MAWGAN
PORTH, Cornwall TR8 4DA
Tel: 01637 860324
* e-mail: hotel@bluebaycornwall.co.uk
* website: www.bluebaycornwall.co.uk

Guest House
Mrs Dewolfreys, Dewolf Guest House, 100
Henver Road, NEWQUAY, Cornwall TR7 3BL
Tel: 01637 874746
* e-mail: holidays@dewolfguesthouse.com
* website: www.dewolfguesthouse.com

Self-Catering
Raintree House Holidays, The Old Airfield,
St Merryn, PADSTOW, Cornwall PL28 8PU
Tel: 01841 520228
* e-mail: gill@raintreehouse.co.uk
* website: www.raintreehouse.co.uk

FHG Guides

WEBSITE DIRECTORY 349

Hotel
Torwood Hotel, Alexandra Road,
PENZANCE, Cornwall TR18 4LZ
Tel: 01736 360063
- e-mail: lyndasowerby@aol.com
- website: www.torwoodhousehotel.co.uk

Hotel / Inn
Driftwood Spars Hotel, Trevaunance Cove,
ST AGNES, Cornwall TR5 0RT
Tel: 01872 552428
- website: www.driftwoodspars.com

Guest House
Mr Gardener, The Elms, 14 Penwinnick
Road, ST AUSTELL, Cornwall PL25 5DW
Tel: 01726 74981
- e-mail: pete@edenbb.co.uk
- website: www.edenbb.co.uk

Self-Catering
Mr & Mrs C.W. Pestell, Hockadays,
Tregenna, Near Blisland, ST TUDY,
Cornwall PL30 4QJ
Tel: 01208 850146
- website: www.hockadays.co.uk

Self-Catering
Mrs R. Reeves, Polstraul, Trewalder,
Delabole, ST TUDY, Cornwall PL33 9ET
Tel: 01840 213 120
- e-mail: ruth.reeves@hotmail.co.uk
- website: www.maymear.co.uk

•CUMBRIA

Self- Catering
Kirkstone Foot Apartments Ltd, Kirkstone
Pass Road, AMBLESIDE, Cumbria LA22 9EH
Tel: 015394 32232
- e-mail: enquiries@kirkstonefoot.co.uk
- website: www.kirkstonefoot.co.uk

Guest House / Self- Catering
Cuckoo's Nest & Smallwood House, Compston
Road, AMBLESIDE, Cumbria LA22 9DJ
Tel: 015394 32330
- e-mail: enq@cottagesambleside.co.uk
          enq@smallwoodhotel.co.uk
- website: www.cottagesambleside.co.uk
           www.smallwoodhotel.co.uk

Guest House
Mr A. Welch, The Anchorage Guest House,
Rydal Road, AMBLESIDE, Cumbria LA22 9AY
Tel: 015394 32046
- e-mail: theanchorageguesthouse@hotmail.com
- website: www.theanchorageguesthouse.co.uk

Caravan Park
Greenhowe Caravan Park, Great Langdale,
AMBLESIDE, Cumbria LA22 9JU
Tel: 015394 37231
- e-mail: enquiries@greenhowe.com
- website: www.greenhowe.com

Hotel / Guest House
Mrs Liana Moore, The Old Vicarage, Vicarage
Road, AMBLESIDE, Cumbria LA22 9DH
Tel: 015394 33364
- e-mail: info@oldvicarageambleside.co.uk
- website: www.oldvicarageambleside.co.uk

Self-Catering
43A Quarry Rigg, BOWNESS-ON-
WINDERMERE, Cumbria.
Contact: Mrs E. Jones, 45 West Oakhill Park,
Liverpool L13 4BN. Tel: 0151 228 5799
- e-mail: eejay@btinternet.com

B & B
Amanda Vickers, Mosser Heights, Mosser,
COCKERMOUTH, Cumbria CA13 0SS
Tel: 01900 822644
- e-mail: amandavickers1@aol.com
- website: www.stayonacumbrianfarm.co.uk

Self-Catering
Mrs Almond, Irton House Farm, Isel,
COCKERMOUTH, Cumbria CA13 9ST
Tel: 017683 76380
- website: www.irtonhousefarm.com

Self-Catering
Fisherground Farm Holidays, ESKDALE
Contact: Ian & Jennifer Hall, Orchard House,
Applethwaite, Keswick, Cumbria CA12 4PN
Tel: 017687 73175
- e-mail: holidays@fisherground.co.uk
- website: www.fisherground.co.uk

Farm / Self-Catering
Mr P. Brown, High Dale Park Farm, High Dale
Park, Satterthwaite, Ulverston, GRIZEDALE
FOREST, Cumbria LA12 8LJ
Tel: 01229 860226
- e-mail: peter@lakesweddingmusic.com
- website:
www.lakesweddingmusic.com/accomm

B & B
Paul & Fran Townsend, Pepper House,
Satterthwaite, Near HAWKSHEAD,
Cumbria LA12 8LS. Tel: 01229 860206
- website: www.pepper-house.co.uk

Guest House
Mr Taylorson, Rickerby Grange, Portinscale,
KESWICK, Cumbria CA12 5RH
Tel: 017687 72344
- e-mail: stay@rickerbygrange.co.uk
- website: www.rickerbygrange.co.uk

350 WEBSITE DIRECTORY

Self-Catering
Brook House Cottage Holidays, Bassenthwaite Hall Farm, Bassenthwaite Village, Near KESWICK, Cumbria CA12 4QP
Tel: 017687 76393
- e-mail: stay@amtrafford.co.uk
- website: www.holidaycottageslakedistrict.co.uk

B & B
Greta Naysmith, Cocklake House, Mallerstang, KIRKBY STEPHEN, Cumbria CA17 4JT
Tel: 017683 72080
- e-mail: gretamartensassociates@kencomp.net

Self-Catering
Mrs S.J. Bottom, Crossfield Cottages, KIRKOSWALD, Penrith, Cumbria CA10 1EU
Tel: 01768 898711
- e-mail: info@crossfieldcottages.co.uk
- website: www.crossfieldcottages.co.uk

Inn
The Britannia Inn, Elterwater, LANGDALE, Cumbria LA22 9HP. Tel: 015394 37210
- e-mail: info@britinn.co.uk
- website: www.britinn.co.uk

Self- Catering
Hartsop Hall Cottages, Hartsop, PATTERDALE, Cumbria.
Contact: Mrs F. Townsend, Pepper House, Satterthwaite, Cumbria LA12 8LS
Tel: 01229 860206
- website: www.hartsophallcottages.com

Self-Catering
Mr & Mrs Iredale, Carrock Cottages, Carrock House, Hutton Roof, PENRITH, Cumbria CA11 0XY
Tel: 01768 484111
- e-mail: info@carrockcottages.co.uk
- website: www.carrockcottages.co.uk

Guest House / Inn
The Troutbeck Inn, Troutbeck, PENRITH, Cumbria CA11 0SJ. Tel: 01768 483635
- e-mail: info@thetroutbeckinn.co.uk
- website: www.thetroutbeckinn.co.uk

Golf Club
Seascale Golf Club, The Banks, SEASCALE, Cumbria CA20 1QL
Tel: 01946 728202
- e-mail: seascalegolfclub@googlemail.com
- website: www.seascalegolfclub.co.uk

Caravan & Camping
Cove Caravan & Camping Park, Watermillock, ULLSWATER, Penrith, Cumbria CA11 0LS
Tel: 017684 86549
- e-mail: info@cove-park.co.uk
- website: www.cove-park.co.uk

B & B / Self-Catering
Barbara Murphy, Land Ends Country Lodge, Watermillock, ULLSWATER, Near Penrith, Cumbria CA11 0NB
Tel: 01768 486438
- e-mail: infolandends@btinternet.com
- website: www.landends.co.uk

•DERBYSHIRE

Self-Catering Holiday Cottages
Mark Redfern, Paddock House Farm Holiday Cottages, Alstonefield, ASHBOURNE, Derbyshire DE6 2FT
Tel: 01335 310282
- e-mail: info@paddockhousefarm.co.uk
- website: www.paddockhousefarm.co.uk

Hotel
Biggin Hall, Biggin-by-Hartington, BUXTON, Derbyshire SK17 0DH
Tel: 01298 84451
- e-mail: enquiries@bigginhall.co.uk
- website: www.bigginhall.co.uk

Self-Catering
Mrs Gillian Taylor, Priory Lea Holiday Flats, 50 White Knowle Road, BUXTON, Derbyshire SK17 9NH
Tel: 01298 23737
- e-mail: priorylea@hotmail.co.uk
- website: www.cressbrook.co.uk/buxton/priorylea

Inn
Devonshire Arms, Peak Forest, Near BUXTON, Derbyshire SK17 8EJ
Tel: 01298 23875
- e-mail: enquiries@devarms.com
- website: www.devarms.com

Guest House
Ivy House Farm Guest House, STANTON-BY-BRIDGE, Derby, Derbyshire DE73 7HT
Tel: 01332 863152
- e-mail: mary@guesthouse.fsbusiness.co.uk
- website: www.ivy-house-farm.com

•DEVON

Self-Catering
Helpful Holidays, Mill Street, Chagford, DEVON
Tel: 01647 433593
- e-mail: help@helpfulholidays.com
- website: www.helpfulholidays.com

Self-Catering
Farm & Cottage Holidays, DEVON
Tel: 01237 479698
• website: www.holidaycottages.co.uk

B & B
Lynda Richards, Gages Mill, Buckfastleigh Road, ASHBURTON, Devon TQ13 7JW
Tel: 01364 652391
• e-mail: gagesmill@aol.com
• website: www.gagesmill.co.uk

Self-Catering
Wooder Manor, Widecombe-in-the-Moor, ASHBURTON, Devon TQ13 7TR
Tel: 01364 621391
• e-mail: angela@woodermanor.com
• website: www.woodermanor.com

Hotel
Sandy Cove Hotel, Combe Martin Bay, BERRYNARBOR, Devon EX34 9SR
Tel: 01271 882243/882888
• website: www.sandycove-hotel.co.uk

B & B / Self-Catering
Mr & Mrs Lewin, Lake House Cottages and B&B, Lake Villa, BRADWORTHY, Devon EX22 7SQ
Tel: 01409 241962
• e-mail: info@lakevilla.co.uk
• website: www.lakevilla.co.uk

Self-Catering / Organic Farm
Little Comfort Farm Cottages, Little Comfort Farm, BRAUNTON, North Devon EX33 2NJ
Tel: 01271 812414
• e-mail: info@littlecomfortfarm.co.uk
• website: www.littlecomfortfarm.co.uk

Guest House
Woodlands Guest House, Parkham Road, BRIXHAM, South Devon TQ5 9BU
Tel: 01803 852040
• e-mail: woodlandsbrixham@btinternet.com
• website: www.woodlandsdevon.co.uk

Self-Catering / B & B / Caravans
Mrs Gould, Bonehayne Farm, COLYTON, Devon EX24 6SG
Tel: 01404 871416/871396
• e-mail: gould@bonehayne.co.uk
• website: www.bonehayne.co.uk

Self-Catering / B&B
Mrs Lee, Church Approach Holidays, Farway, COLYTON, Devon EX24 6EQ
Tel: 01404 871383/871202
• e-mail: lizlee@eclipse.co.uk
• website: www.churchapproach.co.uk

Holiday Park
Manleigh Holiday Park, Rectory Road, COMBE MARTIN, North Devon EX34 0NS
Tel: 01271 883353
• e-mail: info@manleighpark.co.uk
• website: www.manleighpark.co.uk

Self-Catering
Mrs S.R. Ridalls, The Old Bakehouse, 7 Broadstone, DARTMOUTH, Devon TQ6 9NR
Tel: 01803 834585
• e-mail: oldbakehousecottages@yahoo.com
• website: www.oldbakehousedartmouth.co.uk

Self-Catering
Mr & Mrs R. Jones, Stowford Lodge, Langtree, GREAT TORRINGTON, Devon EX38 8NU
Tel: 01805 601540
• e-mail: enq@stowfordlodge.co.uk
• website: www.stowfordlodge.co.uk

Hotel
St Brannocks House, St Brannocks Road, ILFRACOMBE, Devon EX34 8EQ
Tel: 01271 863873
• e-mail: barbara@stbrannockshouse.co.uk
• website: www.stbrannockshouse.co.uk

Guest House
Maureen Corke, Varley House, Chambercombe Park, ILFRACOMBE, Devon EX34 9QW. Tel: 01271 863927
• e-mail: info@varleyhouse.co.uk
• website: www.varleyhouse.co.uk

Inn
The Blue Ball Inn, Countisbury, LYNMOUTH, Near Lynton, Devon EX35 6NE
Tel: 01598 741263
• website: www.BlueBallinn.com
         www.exmoorsandpiper.com

Self-Catering
Doone Valley Holidays
Contact: Mr C. Harman, Cloud Farm, Oare, LYNTON, Devon EX35 6NU
Tel: 01598 714234
• e-mail: doonevalleyholidays@hotmail.com
• website: www.doonevalleyholidays.co.uk

Self-Catering
Crab Cottage, NOSS MAYO, South Hams, South of Dartmoor, Devon
Tel: 01425 471 372
• e-mail: 07enquiries@crab-cottage.co.uk
• website: www.crab-cottage.co.uk

Guest House
The Commodore, 14 Esplanade Road, PAIGNTON, Devon TQ4 6EB
Tel: 01803 553107
• e-mail: info@commodorepaignton.com
• website: www.commodorepaignton.com

www.holidayguides.com

WEBSITE DIRECTORY

Guest House
Jane Hill, Beaumont, Castle Hill, SEATON, Devon EX12 2QW
Tel: 01297 20832
- e-mail: jane@lymebay.demon.co.uk
- website: www.smoothhound.co.uk/hotels/beaumon1.html

Hotel
Riviera Lodge Hotel, 26 Croft Road. TORQUAY, Devon TQ2 5UE
Tel: 01803 209309
- e-mail: stay@rivieralodgehotel.co.uk
- website: www.rivieralodgehotel.co.uk

Guest House
Mrs L Read, Silverlands Guest House, 27 Newton Road, TORQUAY, Devon TQ2 5DB
Tel: 01803 292013
- e-mail: enquiries@silverlandsguesthouse.co.uk
- website: www.silverlandsguesthouse.co.uk

Self-Catering
Marsdens Cottage Holidays, 2 The Square, Braunton, WOOLACOMBE, Devon EX33 2JB
Tel: 01271 813777
- e-mail: holidays@marsdens.co.uk
- website: www.marsdens.co.uk

Holiday Park
Woolacombe Bay Holiday Parks, WOOLACOMBE, North Devon EX34 7HW
Tel: 01271 870343
- e-mail: goodtimes@woolacombe.com
- website: www.woolacombe.com/fcw

Caravan & Camping
North Morte Farm Caravan & Camping Park, Mortehoe, WOOLACOMBE, Devon EX34 7EG
Tel: 01271 870381
- e-mail: info@northmortefarm.co.uk
- website: www.northmortefarm.co.uk

Self-catering
Mrs L Hunt, Sunnymeade, Dean Cross, West Down, WOOLACOMBE, North Devon EX34 8NT
Tel: 01271 863668
- e-mail: info@sunnymeade.co.uk
- website: www.sunnymeade.co.uk

•DORSET

Self-Catering
Luccombe Farm Cottages, Luccombe Farm, Milton Abbas, BLANDFORD FORUM, Dorset DT11 0BE
Tel: 01258 880558
- e-mail: mkayll@aol.com
- website: www.luccombeholidays.co.uk

Hotel
Southbourne Grove Hotel, 96 Southbourne Road, BOURNEMOUTH, Dorset BH6 3QQ
Tel: 01202 420503
- e-mail: neil@pack1462.freeserve.co.uk
- website: www.tiscover.co.uk/southbournegrovehotel

Guest House
T. Derby, Southernhay Guest House, 42 Alum Chine Road, BOURNEMOUTH, Dorset BH4 8DX
Tel: 01202 761251
- e-mail: enquiries@southernhayhotel.co.uk
- website: www.thesouthernhayhotel.co.uk

Self-Catering
C. Hammond, Stourcliffe Court, 56 Stourcliffe Avenue, Southbourne, BOURNEMOUTH, Dorset BH6 3PX
Tel: 01202 420698
- website: www.stourcliffecourt.co.uk

Self-Catering Cottage / Farmhouse B & B
Mrs S. E. Norman, Frogmore Farm, Chideock, BRIDPORT, Dorset DT6 6HT
Tel: 01308 456159
- e-mail: bookings@frogmorefarm.com
- website: www.frogmorefarm.com

Chalet Park / Caravans
Owlpen Caravans Ltd, 148 Burley Road, Bransgore, Near CHRISTCHURCH, New Forest, Dorset BH23 8DB
Tel: 01425 672875
- e-mail: owlpen@hotmail.com
- website: www.owlpen-caravans.co.uk

Guest House
Mrs Valerie Bradbeer, Nethercroft, Winterbourne Abbas, DORCHESTER, Dorset DT2 9LU
Tel: 01305 889317
- e-mail: v.bradbeer@ukonline.co.uk
- website: www.nethercroft.com

Hotel
Cromwell House Hotel, LULWORTH COVE, Dorset BH20 5RJ
Tel: 01929 400253
- e-mail: catriona@lulworthcove.co.uk
- website: www.lulworthcove.co.uk

Hotel
Fairwater Head Hotel, Hawkchurch, Near Axminster, LYME REGIS, Dorset EX13 5TX
Tel: 01297 678349
- e-mail: info@fairwaterheadhotel.co.uk
- website: www.fairwaterheadhotel.co.uk

FHG Guides

Self-Catering
Westover Farm Cottages, Wootton Fitzpaine, Near LYME REGIS, Dorset DT6 6NE
Tel: 01297 560451/561395
- e-mail: wfcottages@aol.com
- website: www.westoverfarmcottages.co.uk

Farm / Self-Catering
White Horse Farm, Middlemarsh, SHERBORNE, Dorset DT9 5QN
Tel: 01963 210222
- e-mail: enquiries@whitehorsefarm.co.uk
- website: www.whitehorsefarm.co.uk

Hotel
The Knoll House, STUDLAND BAY, Dorset BH19 3AW
Tel: 01929 450450
- e-mail: info@knollhouse.co.uk
- website: www.knollhouse.co.uk

Hotel
The Lugger Inn, 30 West Street, Chickerell, WEYMOUTH, Dorset DT3 4DY
Tel: 01305 766611
- e-mail: info@theluggerinn.co.uk
- website: www.theluggerinn.co.uk

Guest House / Self-Catering
Olivia Nurrish, Glenthorne, Castle Cove, 15 Old Castle Road, WEYMOUTH, Dorset DT4 8QB
Tel: 01305 777281
- e-mail: info@glenthorne-holidays.co.uk
- website: www.glenthorne-holidays.co.uk

•ESSEX

Farm House B&B / Self-Catering
Mrs Brenda Lord, Pond House, Earls Hall Farm, St Osyth, CLACTON ON SEA, Essex CO16 8BP Tel: 01255 820458
- e-mail: brenda_lord@farming.co.uk
- website: www.earlshallfarm.info

•GLOUCESTERSHIRE

Hotel
The Bowl Inn & Lilies Restaurant, 16 Church Road, Lower Almondsbury, BRISTOL, Gloucs BS32 4DT
Tel: 01454 612757
- e-mail: reception@thebowlinn.co.uk
- website: www.thebowlinn.co.uk

Hotel
Tudor Farmhouse Hotel, CLEARWELL, Forest of Dean, Gloucs GL16 8JS
Tel: 01594 833046
- e-mail: info@tudorfarmhousehotel.co.uk
- website: www.tudorhousehotel.co.uk

Caravan & Camping
Tudor Caravan Park, Shepherds Patch, SLIMBRIDGE, Gloucestershire GL2 7BP
Tel: 01453 890483
- e-mail: info@tudorcaravanpark.co.uk
- website: www.tudorcaravanpark.co.uk

B & B
Anthea & Bill Rhoton, Hyde Crest, Cirencester Road, MINCHINHAMPTON, Gloucs GL6 8PE
Tel: 01453 731631
- e-mail: stay@hydecrest.co.uk
- website: www.hydecrest.co.uk

•HAMPSHIRE

Hotel
Bramble Hill Hotel, Bramshaw, Near LYNDHURST, New Forest, Hants SO43 7JG
Tel: 02380 813165
- website: www.bramblehill.co.uk

•HEREFORDSHIRE

Farmhouse / B & B
Mrs M. E. Drzymalski, Thatch Close, Llangrove, ROSS-ON-WYE, Herefordshire HR9 6EL
Tel: 01989 770300
- e-mail: info@thatchclose.co.uk
- website: www.thatchclose.co.uk

•ISLE OF WIGHT

Guest House / Self-Catering
Frenchman's Cove / Coach House, Alum Bay, Old Road, TOTLAND BAY, Isle of Wight PO39 0HZ
Tel: 01983 752227
- e-mail: boatfield@frenchmanscove.co.uk
- website: www.frenchmanscove.co.uk

Farmhouse B & B / Self-Catering Cottages
Mrs F.J. Corry, Little Span Farm, Rew Lane, Wroxall, VENTNOR, Isle of Wight PO38 3AU
Tel: 01983 852419
- e-mail: info@spanfarm.co.uk
- website: www.spanfarm.co.uk

•KENT

Guest House
S. Twort, Heron Cottage, Biddenden, ASHFORD, Kent TN27 8HH
Tel: 01580 291358
- e-mail: susantwort@hotmail.com
- website: www.heroncottage.info

354 WEBSITE DIRECTORY

Hotel
Collina House Hotel, 5 East Hill, TENTERDEN, Kent TN30 6RL Tel: 01580 764852/764004
- e-mail: enquiries@collinahousehotel.co.uk
- website: www.collinahousehotel.co.uk

•LANCASHIRE

Guest House
Mrs Roslyn Holdsworth, Broadwater House, 356 Marine Road, MORECAMBE, Lancashire LA4 5AQ. Tel: 01524 411333
- e-mail: enquiries@thebroadwaterhotel.co.uk
- website: www.thebroadwaterhotel.co.uk

•LINCOLNSHIRE

Farm B & B / Self-catering cottage
Mrs C.E. Harrison, Baumber Park, Baumber, HORNCASTLE, Lincolnshire LN9 5NE
Tel: 01507 578235/07977 722776
- e-mail: mail@baumberpark.com
  mail@gathmanscottage.co.uk
- website: www.baumberpark.com
  www.gathmanscottage.co.uk

Farmhouse B & B
S Evans, Willow Farm, Thorpe Fendykes, SKEGNESS, Lincolnshire PE24 4QH
Tel: 01754 830316
- e-mail: willowfarmhols@aol.com
- website: www.willowfarmholidays.co.uk

Hotel
Petwood Hotel, Stixwould Road, WOODHALL SPA, Lincolnshire LN10 6QF
Tel: 01526 352411
- e-mail: reception@petwood.co.uk
- website: www.petwood.co.uk

•MERSEYSIDE

Guest House
Holme Leigh Guest House, 93 Woodcroft Road, Wavertree, LIVERPOOL, Merseyside L15 2HG
Tel: 0151 734 2216
- e-mail: info@holmeleigh.com
- website: www.holmeleigh.com

•NORFOLK

Self-Catering
Blue Riband Holidays, HEMSBY, Great Yarmouth, Norfolk NR29 4HA
Tel: 01493 730445
- website: www.BlueRibandHolidays.co.uk

Self-Catering
Sand Dune Cottages, Tan Lane, CAISTER-ON-SEA, Great Yarmouth, Norfolk NR30 5DT
Tel: 01493 720352
- e-mail: sand.dune.cottages@amserve.net
- website: www.eastcoastlive.co.uk/sites/sandddunecottages.php

Self-Catering
Carefree Holidays, Chapel Briars, Yarmouth Road, GREAT YARMOUTH, Norfolk NR29 4NJ
Tel: 01493 732176
- e-mail: tony@carefree-holidays.co.uk
- website: www.carefree-holidays.co.uk

Hotel
The Stuart House Hotel, 35 Goodwins Road, KING'S LYNN, Norfolk PE30 5QX
Tel: 01553 772169
- e-mail: reception@stuarthousehotel.co.uk
- website: www.stuarthousehotel.co.uk

Self-catering
Scarning Dale, Dale Road, SCARNING, Dereham, Norfolk NR1 2QN
Tel: 01362 687269
- e-mail: jean@scarningdale.co.uk
- website: www.scarningdale.co.uk

•NORTHUMBERLAND

Self-Catering
Northumberland Cottages Ltd, The Old Stable Yard, Chathill Farm, CHATHILL
Tel: 01665 589434
- e-mail: enquiries@northumberlandcottages.com
- website: www.northumberlandcottages.com

Self-Catering
Mrs S. M. Saunders, Scotchcoulthard Holiday Cottages, HALTWHISTLE, Northumberland NE49 9NH
Tel: 01434 374470
- e-mail: scotchcoulthard@hotmail.com
- website: www.scotchcoulthard.co.uk

•NOTTINGHAMSHIRE

Caravan & Camping Park
Orchard Park, Marnham Road, Tuxford, NEWARK, Nottinghamshire NG22 0PY
Tel: 01777 870228
- e-mail: info@orchardcaravanpark.co.uk
- website: www.orchardcaravanpark.co.uk

www.holidayguides.com

WEBSITE DIRECTORY 355

• OXFORDSHIRE

Leisure Park
Cotswold Wildlife Park, BURFORD, Oxfordshire OX18 4JN
Tel: 01993 823006
• website: www.cotswoldwildlifepark.co.uk

Guest House
The Bungalow, Cherwell Farm, Mill Lane, Old Marston, OXFORD, Oxfordshire OX3 0QF
Tel: 01865 557171
• e-mail: ros.bungalowbb@btinternet.com
• www.cherwellfarm-oxford-accomm.co.uk

Guest House
Nanford Guest House, 137 Iffley Road, OXFORD, Oxfordshire OX4 1EJ
Tel: 01865 244743
• e-mail: b.cronin@btinternet.com
• website: www.nanfordguesthouse.com

B & B / Self-Catering
Katharine Brown, Hill Grove Farm, Crawley Dry Lane, Minster Lovell, WITNEY, Oxfordshire OX29 0NA
Tel: 01993 703120
• e-mail: katharinemcbrown@btinternet.com
• website: www.countryaccom.co.uk/hill-grove-farm

• SHROPSHIRE

Farm / B & B
Mrs M. Jones, Acton Scott Farm, Acton Scott, CHURCH STRETTON, Shropshire SY6 6QN
Tel: 01694 781260
• e-mail: fhg@actonscottfarm.co.uk
• website: www.actonscottfarm.co.uk

Hotel
Rowena Jones, Longmynd Hotel, Cunnery Rd, CHURCH STRETTON, Shropshire SY6 6AG
Tel: 01694 722244
• e-mail: info@longmynd.co.uk
• website: www.longmynd.co.uk

Self-Catering
Clive & Cynthia Prior, Mocktree Barns Holiday Cottages, Leintwardine, LUDLOW, Shropshire SY7 0LY
Tel: 01547 540441
• e-mail: mocktreebarns@care4free.net
• website: www.mocktreeholidays.co.uk

• SOMERSET

Self-Catering
Westward Rise Holiday Park, South Road, BREAN, Burnham-on-Sea, Somerset TA8 2RD
Tel: 01278 751310
• e-mail: info@westwardrise.com
• website: www.westwardrise.com

Farm / B & B
Mrs M. Hasell, The Model Farm, Norton Hawkfield, Pensford, BRISTOL, Somerset BS39 4HA
Tel: 01275 832144
• e-mail: margarethasell@hotmail.com
• website: www.themodelfarm.co.uk

Farmhouse / Self-Catering
Josephine Smart, Leigh Farm, Old Road, Pensford, Near BRISTOL, Somerset BS39 4BA
Tel: 01761 490281
• website: www.leighfarmholidays.co.uk

Farm Self-Catering
Jane Styles, Wintershead Farm, Simonsbath, EXMOOR, Somerset TA24 7LF
Tel: 01643 831222
• e-mail: info@wintershead.co.uk
• website: www.wintershead.co.uk

B & B
North Down Farm, Pyncombe Lane, Wiveliscombe, TAUNTON, Somerset TA4 2BL
Tel: 01984 623730
• e-mail: jennycope@btinternet.com
• website: www.north-down-farm.co.uk

B & B
The Old Mill, Netherclay, Bishop's Hull, TAUNTON, Somerset TA1 5AB
Tel: 01823 289732
• website: www.theoldmillbandb.co.uk

Farm / Guest House
G. Clark, Yew Tree Farm, THEALE, Near Wedmore, Somerset BS28 4SN
Tel: 01934 712475
• e-mail: enquiries@yewtreefarmbandb.co.uk
• website: www.yewtreefarmbandb.co.uk

Self-Catering
Croft Holiday Cottages, 2 The Croft, Anchor Street, WATCHET, Somerset TA23 0BY
Tel: 01984 631121
• e-mail: croftcottages@talk21.com
• website: www.cottagessomerset.com

Please mention **FHG Guides** when enquiring about accommodation featured in this publication.

• STAFFORDSHIRE

Farm B & B / Self-Catering
Mrs M. Hiscoe-James, Offley Grove Farm, Adbaston, ECCLESHALL, Staffs ST20 0QB
Tel: 01785 280205
- e-mail: enquiries@offleygrovefarm.co.uk
- website: www.offleygrovefarm.co.uk

Self-Catering
Field Head Farmhouse Holidays, Calton, WATERHOUSES, Stoke-on-Trent, Staffordshire ST10 3LB
Tel: 01538 308352
- e-mail: info@field-head.co.uk
- website: www.field-head.co.uk

• SUFFOLK

B & B
Cobbles, Nethergate Street, CLARE, Suffolk CO10 8NP
Tel: 01787 277539
- e-mail: cobbles@cobblesclare.co.uk
- website: www.cobblesclare.co.uk

Guest House
The Grafton Guest House, 13 Sea Road, FELIXSTOWE, Suffolk IP11 2BB
Tel: 01394 284881
- e-mail: info@grafton-house.com
- website: www.grafton-house.com

B & B / Self-Catering
Mrs Sarah Kindred, High House Farm, Cransford, Woodbridge, FRAMLINGHAM, Suffolk IP13 9PD
Tel: 01728 663461
- e-mail: b&b@highhousefarm.co.uk
- website: www.highhousefarm.co.uk

Self-Catering
Windmill Lodges Ltd, Redhouse Farm, Saxtead, Woodbridge, FRAMLINGHAM, Suffolk IP13 9RD
Tel: 01728 685338
- e-mail: holidays@windmilllodges.co.uk
- website: www.windmilllodges.co.uk

Self-Catering
Kessingland Cottages, Rider Haggard Lane, KESSINGLAND, Suffolk.
Contact: S. Mahmood, 156 Bromley Road, Beckenham, Kent BR3 6PG
Tel: 020 8650 0539
- e-mail: jeeptrek@kjti.co.uk
- website: www.k-cottage.co.uk

Self-Catering
Southwold/Walberswick Self-Catering Properties.
Durrants incorporating, H.A. Adnams, 98 High Street, SOUTHWOLD, Suffolk IP18 6DP
Tel: 01502 723292
- website: www.durrants.com

• EAST SUSSEX

Self-Catering
Crowhurst Park, Telham Lane, BATTLE, East Sussex TN33 0SL
Tel: 01424 773344
- e-mail: inquiries@crowhurstpark.co.uk
- website: www.crowhurstpark.co.uk

Self-Catering
"Pekes", CHIDDINGLY, East Sussex
Contact: Eva Morris, 124 Elm Park Mansions, Park Walk, London SW10 0AR
Tel: 020 7352 8088
- e-mail: pekes.afa@virgin.net
- website: www.pekesmanor.com

Guest House / Self-Catering
Longleys Farm Cottage, Harebeating Lane, HAILSHAM, East Sussex BN27 1ER
Tel: 01323 841227
- e-mail: longleysfarmcottagebb@dsl.pipex.com
- website: www.longleysfarmcottage.co.uk

Hotel
Grand Hotel, Grand Parade, St Leonards, HASTINGS, East Sussex TN38 0DD
Tel: 01424 428510
- e-mail: info@grandhotelhastings.co.uk
- website: www.grandhotelhastings.co.uk

Self-Catering Cottage
4 Beach Cottages, Claremont Road, SEAFORD, East Sussex BN25 2QQ
Contact: Julia Lewis, 47 Wandle Bank, London SW19 1DW Tel: 020 8542 5073
- e-mail: cottage@beachcottages.info
- website: www.beachcottages.info

• WEST SUSSEX

Self-Catering
Mrs M. W. Carreck, New Hall Holiday Flat and Cottage, New Hall Lane, Small Dole, HENFIELD, West Sussex BN5 9YJ
Tel: 01273 492546
- website: www.newhallcottage.co.uk

• WARWICKSHIRE

Guest House / B & B
Julia & John Downie, Holly Tree Cottage, Pathlow, STRATFORD-UPON-AVON, Warwickshire CV37 0ES
Tel: 01789 204461
- e-mail: john@hollytree-cottage.co.uk
- website: www.hollytree-cottage.co.uk

• WILTSHIRE

Guest House
Stillmeadow, 18 Bradford Road, Winsley, BRADFORD-ON-AVON, Wiltshire BA15 2HW
Tel:01722 722119
- e-mail: sue.gilby@btinternet.com
- website: www.stillmeadow.co.uk

Guest House
Alan & Dawn Curnow, Hayburn Wyke Guest House, 72 Castle Road, SALISBURY, Wiltshire SP1 3RL
Tel: 01225 412627
- e-mail: hayburn.wyke@tinyonline.co.uk
- website: www.hayburnwykeguesthouse.co.uk

• WORCESTERSHIRE

Guest House
Ann & Brian Porter, Croft Guest House, Bransford, GREAT MALVERN, Worcester, Worcestershire WR6 5JD
Tel: 01886 832227
- e-mail: hols@crofthousewr6.fsnet.co.uk
- website: www.croftguesthouse.com

Self-Catering Cottages
Rochford Park Cottages, Rochford Park, TENBURY WELLS, Worcestershire WR15 8SP
Tel: 01584 781392
- e-mail: cottages@rochfordpark.co.uk
- website: www.rochfordpark.co.uk

Guest House
Moseley Farm B & B, Moseley Road, Hallow, WORCESTER, Worcestershire WR2 6NL
Tel: 01905 641343
- e-mail: moseleyfarmbandb@aol.com
- website: www.moseleyfarmbandb.co.uk

• EAST YORKSHIRE

Guest House / Camping
Mrs Jeanne Wilson, Robeanne House, Driffield Lane, Shiptonthorpe, YORK, East Yorkshire YO43 3PW
Tel: 01430 873312
- e-mail: enquiries@robeannehouse.co.uk
- website: www.robeannehouse.co.uk

• NORTH YORKSHIRE

Farmhouse B & B
Mrs Julie Clarke, Middle Farm, Woodale, COVERDALE, Leyburn,
North Yorkshire DL8 4TY Tel: 01969 640271
- e-mail: j-a-clarke@hotmail.co.uk
- www.yorkshirenet.co.uk/stayat/middlefarm

Farm
Mrs Linda Tindall, Rowantree Farm, Fryup Road, Ainthorpe, DANBY, Whitby, North Yorkshire YO21 2LE
Tel: 01723 515155
- e-mail: krbsatindall@aol.com
- website: www.rowantreefarm.co.uk

Farmhouse B&B
Mr & Mrs Richardson, Egton Banks Farmhouse, GLAISDALE, Whitby, North Yorkshire YO21 2QP
Tel: 01947 897289
e-mail: egtonbanksfarm@agriplus.net
- website: www.egtonbanksfarm.agriplus.net

Self-Catering
Rudding Estate Cottages, Rudding Park Estate Ltd, Haggs Farm, Haggs Road, Follifoot, HARROGATE, North Yorkshire HG3 1EQ
Tel: 01423 844844
- e-mail: info@rudding.com
- website: www.rudding.com/cottages

B & B
Cocklake House, Mallerstang, Near HAWES
Contact: Greta Naysmith, Cocklake House, Mallerstang, Kirkby Stephen,
Cumbria CA17 4JT. Tel: 017683 72080
- e-mail: gretamartensassociates@kencomp.net

Guest House
The New Inn Motel, Main Street, HUBY, York, North Yorkshire YO61 1HQ
Tel: 01347 810219
- enquiries@newinnmotel.freeserve.co.uk
- website: www.newinnmotel.co.uk

Self-Catering
Allaker in Coverdale, West Scrafton, LEYBURN, North Yorkshire DL8 4RM
Contact: Mr Adrian Cave, 21 Kenilworth Road, London W5 5PA Tel: 020 856 74862
- e-mail: ac@adriancave.com
- www.adriancave.com/allaker

Self-Catering
Abbey Holiday Cottages, MIDDLESMOOR. 12 Panorama Close, Pateley Bridge, Harrogate, North Yorkshire HG3 5NY
Tel: 01423 712062
- e-mail: info@abbeyhall.cottages.co.uk
- website: www.abbeyholidaycottages.co.uk

358 WEBSITE DIRECTORY

Farmhouse B&B
Browson Bank Farmhouse, Dalton,
RICHMOND, North Yorkshire DL11 7HE
Tel: 01325 718504
- website: www.browsonbank.co.nr

Self-Catering
Waterfront House, RIPON
Contact: Mrs C. Braddon, Chantry Bells,
Chantry Court, Ripley, Harrogate HG3 3AD
Tel: 01423 770704
- e-mail: chris1.braddon@virgin.net
- website: www.dalesholidayripon.co.uk

Guest House / Self-Catering
Sue & Tony Hewitt, Harmony Country Lodge,
80 Limestone Road, Burniston,
SCARBOROUGH, North Yorkshire YO13 0DG
Tel: 0800 2985840
- e-mail: mail@harmonylodge.net
- website: www.harmonylodge.co.uk

B & B
Beck Hall, Malham, SKIPTON, North
Yorkshire BD23 4DJ. Tel: 01729 830332
- e-mail: simon@beckhallmalham.com
- website: www.beckhallmalham.com

B & B
Gamekeepers Inn, Long Ashes Park,
Threshfield, Near SKIPTON, North Yorkshire
BD23 5PN. Tel: 01756 752334
- e-mail: info@gamekeeperinn.co.uk
- website: www.gamekeeperinn.co.uk

Self-Catering
Mrs Jones, New Close Farm, Kirkby Malham,
SKIPTON, North Yorkshire BD23 4DP
Tel: 01729 830240
- brendajones@newclosefarmyorkshire.co.uk
- website: www.newclosefarmyorkshire.co.uk

Self-Catering
Mrs J. McNeil, Swallow Holiday Cottages,
Long Leas Farm, Hawsker, WHITBY,
North Yorkshire YO22 4LA
Tel: 01947 603790
- website: www.swallowcottages.co.uk

Guest House
Ashford Guest House, 8 Royal Crescent,
WHITBY, North Yorkshire YO21 3EJ
Tel: 01947 602138
- e-mail: info@ashfordguesthouse.co.uk
- website: www.ashfordguesthouse.co.uk

Self-Catering
Greenhouses Farm Cottages, Near WHITBY.
Contact: Mr J.N. Eddleston, Greenhouses
Farm, Lealholm, Near Whitby, North
Yorkshire YO21 2AD. Tel: 01947 897486
- e-mail: n_eddleston@yahoo.com
- www.greenhouses-farm-cottages.co.uk

B & B
Mr & Mrs Leedham, York House, 62 Heworth
Green, YORK, North Yorkshire YO31 7TQ
Tel: 01904 427070
- e-mail: yorkhouse.bandb@tiscali.co.uk
- website: www.yorkhouseyork.co.uk

Self-Catering
York Lakeside Lodges Ltd, Moor Lane,
YORK, North Yorkshire YO24 2QU
Tel: 01904 702346
- e-mail: neil@yorklakesidelodges.co.uk
- website: www.yorklakesidelodges.co.uk

•WEST YORKSHIRE

Farm B & B / Self-Catering Cottages
Currer Laithe Farm, Moss Carr Road, Long
Lee, KEIGHLEY, West Yorkshire BD21 4SL
Tel: 01535 604387
- website: www.currerlaithe.co.uk

•SCOTLAND

•ABERDEEN, BANFF & MORAY

Hotel
P. A. McKechnie, Cambus O' May Hotel,
BALLATER, Aberdeenshire AB35 5SE
Tel: 013397 55428
- e-mail:
mckechnie@cambusomay.freeserve.co.uk
- website: www.cambusomayhotel.co.uk

B & B
Davaar B & B, Church Street, DUFFTOWN,
Moray, AB55 4AR
Tel: 01340 820464
- e-mail: davaar@cluniecameron.co.uk
- website: www.davaardufftown.co.uk

•ANGUS & DUNDEE

Golf Club
Edzell Golf Club, High Street, EDZELL,
Brechin, Angus DD9 7TF
Tel: 01356 648462
- e-mail: secretary@edzellgolfclub.net
- website: www.edzellgolfclub.com

WEBSITE DIRECTORY 359

•ARGYLL & BUTE

Self-Catering
Ardtur Cottages, APPIN, Argyll PA38 4DD
Tel: 01631 730223
- e-mail: pery@btinternet.com
- website: www.selfcatering-appin-scotland.com

Self-Catering
Inchmurrin Island Self-Catering Holidays,
Inchmurrin Island, LOCH LOMOND G63 0JY
Tel: 01389 850245
- e-mail: scotts@inchmurrin-lochlomond.com
- website: www.inchmurrin-lochlomond.com

Self-Catering
Airdeny Chalets, Glen Lonan, Taynuilt,
OBAN, Argyll PA35 1HY Tel: 01866 822648
- e-mail: jenifer@airdenychalets.co.uk
- website: www.airdenychalets.co.uk

Self-Catering
Linda Battison,
Cologin Country Chalets & Lodges,
Lerags Glen, OBAN, Argyll PA34 4SE
Tel: 01631 564501
- e-mail: info@cologin.co.uk
- website: www.cologin.co.uk

Self-Catering
Colin Mossman, Lagnakeil Lodges,
Lerags, OBAN, Argyll PA34 4SE
Tel: 01631 562746
- e-mail: info@lagnakeil.co.uk
- website: www.lagnakeil.co.uk

•AYRSHIRE & ARRAN

B & B
Mrs J Clark, Eglinton Guest House,
23 Eglinton Terrace, AYR, Ayrshire KA7 1JJ
Tel: 01292 264623
- e-mail: eglintonguesthouse@yahoo.co.uk
- website: www.eglinton-guesthouse-ayr.com

Farmhouse / B & B
Mrs Nancy Cuthbertson, West Tannacrieff,
Fenwick, KILMARNOCK, Ayrshire KA3 6AZ
Tel: 01560 600258
- e-mail: westtannacrieff@btopenworld.com
- website: www.smoothhound.co.uk/hotels/westtannacrieff.html

Self-Catering
1 Guildford Street, MILLPORT, Isle of Cumbrae
Contact: Mrs B. McLuckie, Muirhall Farm,
Larbert, Stirlingshire FK5 4EW
Tel: 01324 551570
- e-mail: b@1-guildford-street.co.uk
- website: www.1-guildford-street.co.uk

•BORDERS

Guest House
Hizzy's Guest House, 23B North Bridge St,
HAWICK, Roxburghshire TD9 9BD
Tel: 01450 372101
- e-mail: frankiemcfarlane@btinternet.com
- website: www.hizzys.co.uk

Self-Catering
Glebe House, Hownam, By KELSO,
Borders TD5 8AL
Tel: 07971 522040
- e-mail: enquiries@holidayhomescotland.co.uk
- website: www.holidayhomescotland.com

B & B
The Garden House, Whitmuir, SELKIRK,
Borders TD7 4PZ
Tel: 01750 721728
- e-mail: whitmuir@btconnect.com
- website: www.whitmuirfarm.co.uk

B & B
The Meadows, 4 Robinsland Drive, WEST
LINTON, Nr Edinburgh, Peeblesshire EH46 7JD
Tel: 01968 661798
- e-mail: mwthain@btinternet.com
- website: www.themeadowsbandb.co.uk

Self-Catering
Mrs C. M. Kilpatrick, Slipperfield House,
WEST LINTON, Peeblesshire EH46 7AA
Tel: 01968 660401
- e-mail: cottages@slipperfield.com
- website: www.slipperfield.com

•DUMFRIES & GALLOWAY

Self-Catering
Cloud Cuckoo Lodge, CASTLE DOUGLAS
Contact: Mrs Lesley Wykes, Cuckoostone
Cottage, St John's Town Of Dalry, Castle
Douglas DG7 3UA Tel: 01644 430375
- e-mail: enquiries@cloudcuckoolodge.co.uk
- website: www.cloudcuckoolodge.co.uk

Guest House
Celia Pickup, Craigadam, CASTLE
DOUGLAS, Kirkcudbrightshire DG7 3HU
Tel: 01556 650233
- website: www.craigadam.com

Self-Catering
Barend Holiday Village, Barend Farmhouse,
SANDYHILLS, Dalbeattie, Dumfries & Galloway DG5 4NU
Tel: 01387 780663
- e-mail: info@barendholidayvillage.co.uk
- website: www.barendholidayvillage.co.uk

360 WEBSITE DIRECTORY

Self-Catering
Ae Farm Cottages, Gubhill Farm, Ae, DUMFRIES, Dumfriesshire DG1 1RL
Tel: 01387 860648
• e-mail: gill@gubhill.co.uk
• website: www.aefarmcottages.co.uk

Farm / Camping & Caravans / Self-Catering
Barnsoul Farm Holidays, Barnsoul Farm, Shawhead, DUMFRIES, Dumfriesshire DG2 9SQ. Tel: 01387 730249
• e-mail: barnsouldg@aol.com
• website: www.barnsoulfarm.co.uk

Self-Catering
Hope Cottage, THORNHILL, Dumfries & Galloway DG3 5BJ
Contact: Mrs S. Stannett Tel: 01848 500228
• e-mail: a.stann@btinternet.com
• website: www.hopecottage.co.uk

• EDINBURGH & LOTHIANS

Guest House
Kenvie Guest House, 16 Kilmaurs Road, EDINBURGH EH16 5DA
Tel: 0131 6681964
• e-mail: dorothy@kenvie.co.uk
• website: www.kenvie.co.uk

Guest House
International Guest House, 37 Mayfield Gardens, EDINBURGH EH9 2BX
Tel: 0131 667 2511
• e-mail: intergh1@yahoo.co.uk
• website: www.accommodation-edinburgh.com

• HIGHLANDS

Self-Catering
Cairngorm Highland Bungalows, AVIEMORE.
Contact: Linda Murray, 29 Grampian View, Aviemore, Inverness-shire PH22 1TF
Tel: 01479 810653
• e-mail: linda.murray@virgin.net
• website: www.cairngorm-bungalows.co.uk

Self Catering
Frank & Juliet Spencer-Nairn, Culligran Cottages, Struy, Near BEAULY, Inverness-shire IV4 7JX . Tel: 01463 761285
• e-mail: info@culligrancottages.co.uk
• website: www.culligrancottages.co.uk

Self-Catering
Tyndrum, BOAT OF GARTEN, Inverness-shire
Contact: Mrs Naomi C. Clark, Dochlaggie, Boat of Garten PH24 3BU
Tel: 01479 831242
• e-mail: dochlaggie99@aol.com

Self-Catering
The Treehouse, BOAT OF GARTEN, Inverness-shire
Contact: Anne Mather Tel: 0131 337 7167
• e-mail: fhg@treehouselodge.plus.com
• website: www.treehouselodge.co.uk

Guest House
Mrs Lynn Benge, The Pines Country House, Duthil, CARRBRIDGE, Inverness-shire PH23 3ND
Tel: 01479 841220
• e-mail: lynn@thepines-duthil.co.uk
• website: www.thepines-duthil.co.uk

Self-Catering
Carol Hughes, Glenurquhart Lodges, Balnain, DRUMNADROCHIT, Inverness-shire IV63 6TJ
Tel: 01456 476234
• e-mail: info@glenurquhart-lodges.co.uk
• website: www.glenurquhart-lodges.co.uk

Hotel
The Clan MacDuff Hotel, Achintore Road, FORT WILLIAM, Inverness-shire PH33 6RW
Tel: 01397 702341
• e-mail: reception@clanmacduff.co.uk
• website: www.clanmacduff.co.uk

Golf Club
Golspie Golf Club, Ferry Road, GOLSPIE, Sutherland, Highlands KW10 6SY
Tel: 01408 633 266
• e-mail: info@golspie-golf-club.co.uk
• website: www.golspie-golf-club.co.uk

Caravan & Camping
Auchnahillin Caravan & Camping Park, Daviot East, INVERNESS, Inverness-shire IV2 5XQ. Tel: 01463 772286
• e-mail: info@auchnahillin.co.uk
• website: www.auchnahillin.co.uk

Hotel
Kintail Lodge Hotel, Glenshiel, KYLE OF LOCHALSH, Ross-shire IV40 8HL
Tel: 01599 511275
• e-mail: kintaillodgehotel@btinternet.com
• website: www.kintaillodgehotel.co.uk

Hotel
Whitebridge Hotel, Whitebridge, LOCH NESS, Inverness-shire IV2 6UN
Tel: 01456 486226
• e-mail: info@whitebridgehotel.co.uk
• website: www.whitebridgehotel.co.uk

B & B / Self-Catering Chalets
Mondhuie Chalets and B&B, Mondhuie, NETHY BRIDGE, Inverness-shire PH25 3DF
Tel: 01479 821062
• e-mail: david@mondhuie.com
• website: www.mondhuie.com

WEBSITE DIRECTORY 361

Self-Catering
Innes Maree Bungalows, POOLEWE, Ross-shire IV22 2JU
Tel: 01445 781454
- e-mail: info@poolewebungalows.com
- website: www.poolewebungalows.com

Hotel / Sporting Lodge
Borgie Lodge Hotel, SKERRAY, Sutherland KW14 7TH Tel: 01641 521332
- e-mail: info@borgielodgehotel.co.uk
- website: www.borgielodgehotel.co.uk

• LANARKSHIRE

Caravan & Holiday Home Park
Mount View Caravan Park, Station Road, ABINGTON, South Lanarkshire ML12 6RW
Tel: 01864 502808
- e-mail: info@mountviewcaravanpark.co.uk
- website: www.mountviewcaravanpark.co.uk

Self-Catering
Carmichael Country Cottages, Carmichael Estate Office, Westmains, Carmichael, BIGGAR, Lanarkshire ML12 6PG
Tel: 01899 308336
- e-mail: chiefcarm@aol.com
- website: www.carmichael.co.uk/cottages

Farm B & B
Dykecroft Farm, Kirkmuirhall, LESMAHAGOW, Lanarkshire ML11 0JQ
Tel: 01555 892226
- e-mail: dykecroft.bandb@tiscali.co.uk
- website: www.dykecroftfarm.co.uk

• PERTH & KINROSS

Self-Catering
Loch Tay Lodges, Remony, Acharn, ABERFELDY, Perthshire PH15 2HS
Tel: 01887 830209
- e-mail: remony@btinternet.com
- website: www.lochtaylodges.co.uk

Self-Catering Cottages
Dalmunzie Highland Cottages, SPITTAL OF GLENSHEE, Blairgowrie, Perthshire PH10 7QE Tel: 01250 885226
- e-mail: enquiries@dalmunziecottages.com
- website: www.dalmunziecottages.com

Self-Catering
Ardoch Lodge, STRATHYRE, Near Callander, Perthshire FK18 8NF
Tel: 01877 384666
- e-mail: ardoch@btinternet.com
- website: www.ardochlodge.co.uk

• STIRLING & TROSSACHS

Hotel
Culcreuch Castle Hotel & Estate, Kippen Road, FINTRY, Stirlingshire G63 0LW
Tel: 01360 860555
- e-mail: info@culcreuch.com
- website: www.culcreuch.com

• WALES

Self-Catering
Quality Cottages, Cerbid, Solva, HAVERFORDWEST, Pembrokeshire SA62 6YE
Tel: 01348 837871
- website: www.qualitycottages.co.uk

• ANGLESEY & GWYNEDD

Self-Catering / Caravan Site
Bryn Gloch Caravan and Camping Park, Betws Garmon, CAERNARFON, Gwynedd LL54 7YY Tel: 01286 650216
- e-mail: eurig@bryngloch.co.uk
- website: www.bryngloch.co.uk

Self-Catering
Parc Wernol, Chwilog Fawr, Chwilog, Pwllheli, CRICCIETH, Gwynedd LL53 6SW
Tel: 01766 810506
- e-mail: catherine@wernol.co.uk
- website: www.wernol.co.uk

Caravan & Camping Site
Marian Rees, Dôl Einion, Tal-y-Llyn, TYWYN, Gwynedd LL36 9AJ
Tel: 01654 761312
- e-mail: marianrees@tiscali.co.uk

• CARMARTHENSHIRE

Self-Catering
The Old Stables Cottage, Wren Cottage & The Farmhouse, Sir Johns Hill Farm, Gosport Street, LAUGHARNE, Carmarthenshire SA33 4TD
Tel: 01994 427001
- website: www.sirjohnshillfarm.co.uk

www.holidayguides.com

WEBSITE DIRECTORY

•CEREDIGION

Hotel
Queensbridge Hotel, Victoria Terrace, ABERYSTWYTH, Ceredigion SY23 2DH
Tel: 01970 612343
• e-mail: queensbridgehotel@btinternet.com
• website: www.queensbridgehotel.com
www.queensbridgehotelaberystwyth.co.uk

• PEMBROKESHIRE

Country House
Angelica Rees, Heathfield Mansion, Letterston, Near FISHGUARD, Pembrokeshire SA62 5EG
Tel: 01348 840263
• e-mail: angelica.rees@virgin.net
• website: www.heathfieldaccommodation.co.uk

Hotel
Trewern Arms Hotel, Nevern, NEWPORT, Pembrokeshire SA42 0NB
Tel: 01239 820395
• e-mail: info@trewern-arms-pembrokeshire.co.uk
• www.trewern-arms-pembrokeshire.co.uk

Self-catering
Ffynnon Ddofn, ST DAVIDS, Pembrokeshire. Contact: Mrs B. Rees White, Brick House Farm, Burnham Road, Woodham Mortimer, Maldon, Essex CM9 6SR. Tel: 01245 224611
• e-mail: daisypops@madasafish.com
• website: www.ffynnonddofn.co.uk

Golf Club
Tenby Golf Club, The Burrows, TENBY, Pembrokeshire SA70 7NP
Tel: 01834 842978
• e-mail: tenbygolfclub@uku.co.uk
• website: www.tenbygolf.co.uk

•POWYS

Self-Catering
Mrs Jones, Penllwyn Lodges, GARTHMYL, Powys SY15 6SB
Tel: 01686 640269
• e-mail: daphne.jones@onetel.net
• website: www.penllwynlodges.co.uk

Self-Catering
Old Stables Cottage & Old Dairy, Lane Farm, Paincastle, Builth Wells, HAY-ON-WYE, Powys LD2 3JS
Tel: 01497 851 605
• e-mail: lanefarm@onetel.com
• website: www.lane-farm.co.uk

Caravan Holiday Home
Mr & Mrs P. N. Tolson, The Pines Caravan Park, Doldowlod, LLANDRINDOD WELLS, Powys LD1 6NN
Tel: 01597 810068
• e-mail: info@pinescaravanpark.co.uk
• website: www.pinescaravanpark.co.uk

•SOUTH WALES

B & B / Self-Catering Cottages
Mrs Norma James, Wyrloed Lodge, Manmoel, BLACKWOOD, Caerphilly, South Wales NP12 0RN
Tel: 01495 371198
• e-mail: norma.james@btinternet.com
• website: www.btinternet.com/~norma.james/

Self-Catering
Cwrt-y-Gaer, Wolvesnewton, USK, Monmouthshire, South Wales NP16 6PR
Tel: 01291 650700
• e-mail: info@cwrt-y-gaer.co.uk
• website: www.cwrt-y-gaer.co.uk

•IRELAND

CO. CLARE

Self-Catering
Ballyvaughan Village & Country Holiday Homes, BALLYVAUGHAN.
Contact: George Quinn, Frances Street, Kilrush, Co. Clare Tel: 00 353 65 9051977
• e-mail: vchh@iol.ie
• website: www.ballyvaughan-cottages.com

Looking for holiday accommodation?
for details of hundreds of properties
throughout the UK visit:

www.holidayguides.com

Index of Towns and Counties

Aberystwyth, Ceredigion	WALES
Aldbrough, East Yorkshire	YORKSHIRE
Alnwick, Northumberland	NORTH EAST
Ambleside, Cumbria	NORTH WEST
Appleby, Cumbria	NORTH WEST
Apsley Guise, Bedfordshire	EAST
Ardfern, Argyll & Bute	SCOTLAND
Arundel, West Sussex	LONDON & SOUTH EAST
Ashbourne, Derbyshire	MIDLANDS
Ashford, Kent	LONDON & SOUTH EAST
Ashprington, Devon	SOUTH WEST
Attleborough, Norfolk	EAST
Aviemore, Highlands	SCOTLAND
Axminster, Devon	SOUTH WEST
Aylesbury, Berkshire	LONDON & SOUTH EAST
Aylsham, Norfolk	EAST
Ayr, Ayrshire & Arran	SCOTLAND
Ballachullish, Argyll & Bute	SCOTLAND
Ballater, Aberdeen, Banff & Moray	SCOTLAND
Balterley, Cheshire	NORTH WEST
Banbury, Oxfordshire	LONDON & SOUTH EAST
Banchory, Aberdeen Banff & Moray	SCOTLAND
Barnstaple, Devon	SOUTH WEST
Barton-on-Sea, Berkshire	LONDON & SOUTH EAST
Bath, Somerset	SOUTH WEST
Bathgate, Edinburgh & Lothians	SCOTLAND
Beaminster, Dorset	SOUTH WEST
Bebington, Merseyside	NORTH WEST
Beith, Ayrshire & Arran	SCOTLAND
Belton-in-Rutland, Leicestershire & Rutland	MIDLANDS
Berwick-upon-Tweed, Northumberland	NORTH EAST
Betws-y-Coed, North Wales	WALES
Beverley, East Yorkshire	YORKSHIRE
Bideford, Devon	SOUTH WEST
Biggar, Borders	SCOTLAND
Bishop's Stortford, Hertfordshire	EAST
Blackburn, Edinburgh & Lothians	SCOTLAND
Blackburn, Lancashire	NORTH WEST
Blackpool, Lancashire	NORTH WEST
Blairgowrie, Perth & Kinross	SCOTLAND
Bognor Regis, West Sussex	LONDON & SOUTH EAST
Boscastle, Cornwall	SOUTH WEST
Boston, Lincolnshire	MIDLANDS
Bournemouth, Dorset	SOUTH WEST
Bowburn, Durham	NORTH EAST
Bowness-on-Windermere	NORTH WEST
Bradford-on-Avon, Wiltshire	SOUTH WEST
Brae, Scottish Islands/Shetland	SCOTLAND
Brampton, Cumbria	NORTH WEST
Brayton, Devon	SOUTH WEST
Brechin, Angus & Dundee	SCOTLAND
Brecon, Powys	WALES
Bridlington, East Yorkshire	YORKSHIRE
Bridport, Dorset	SOUTH WEST
Brighton, East Sussex	LONDON & SOUTH EAST
Bristol, Gloucestershire	SOUTH WEST
Bristol, Somerset	SOUTH WEST
Brixham, Devon	SOUTH WEST
Broadford, Scottish Islands/Skye	SCOTLAND
Broadstairs, Kent	LONDON & SOUTH EAST
Brockenhurst, Hampshire	LONDON & SOUTH EAST
Brodick, Ayrshire & Arran	SCOTLAND
Bromsgrove, Worcestershire	MIDLANDS
Broompark, Durham	NORTH EAST
Brough, Cumbria	NORTH WEST
Bude, Cornwall	SOUTH WEST
Bunessan (Argyll), Scottish Islands/Mull	SCOTLAND
Bungay, Suffolk	EAST
Burghill, Herefordshire	MIDLANDS
Burnaston, Derbyshire	MIDLANDS
Burton Joyce, Nottinghamshire	MIDLANDS
Burton-in-Kendal, Cumbria	NORTH WEST
Burwash, East Sussex	LONDON & SOUTH EAST
Burwell, Cambridgeshire	EAST
Bury St Edmunds, Suffolk	EAST
Buxton, Derbyshire	MIDLANDS
Cairndow, Argyll & Bute	SCOTLAND
Caldbeck, Cumbria	NORTH WEST
Callander, Stirling & Trossachs	SCOTLAND
Callington, Cornwall	SOUTH WEST
Cambridge, Cambridgeshire	EAST
Canterbury, Kent	LONDON & SOUTH EAST
Cardiff, South Wales	WALES
Carlisle, Cumbria	NORTH WEST
Carmarthen, Carmarthenshire	WALES
Carrbridge, Highlands	SCOTLAND
Castle Douglas, Dumfries & Galloway	SCOTLAND
Castleside, Durham	NORTH EAST
Charmouth, Dorset	SOUTH WEST
Cheltenham, Gloucestershire	SOUTH WEST
Chester, Cheshire	NORTH WEST
Chesterfield, Derbyshire	MIDLANDS
Chichester, West Sussex	LONDON & SOUTH EAST
Chideock, Dorset	SOUTH WEST
Chinley, Derbyshire	MIDLANDS
Chipping Campden, Gloucestershire	SOUTH WEST
Chorley, Lancashire	NORTH WEST
Chudleigh, Devon	SOUTH WEST
Church Stretton, Shropshire	MIDLANDS
Churchill, Somerset	SOUTH WEST
Clare, Suffolk	EAST
Claverdon, Warwickshire	MIDLANDS
Clitheroe, Lancashire	NORTH WEST
Clun, Shropshire	MIDLANDS
Cockermouth, Cumbria	NORTH WEST
Colchester, Essex	EAST
Colebrook, Devon	SOUTH WEST
Congresbury, Somerset	SOUTH WEST
Coniston, Cumbria	NORTH WEST
Conwy, North Wales	WALES
Corbridge, Northumberland	NORTH EAST

INDEX OF TOWNS AND COUNTIES

Corsham, Wiltshire	SOUTH WEST
Corwen, North Wales	WALES
Coupar Angus, Perth & Kinross	SCOTLAND
Coverdale, North Yorkshire	YORKSHIRE
Cowbridge, South Wales	WALES
Crathie, Aberdeen, Banff & Moray	SCOTLAND
Craven Arms, Shropshire	MIDLANDS
Crediton, Devon	SOUTH WEST
Crewe, Cheshire	NORTH WEST
Crianlarich, Perth & Kinross	SCOTLAND
Crianlarich, Stirling & Trossachs	SCOTLAND
Criccieth, Anglesey & Gwynedd	WALES
Crieff, Perth & Kinross	SCOTLAND
Crosby-on-Eden, Cumbria	NORTH WEST
Croyde, Devon	SOUTH WEST
Cullingworth, West Yorkshire	YORKSHIRE
Culross, Fife	SCOTLAND
Dalry, Ayrshire & Arran	SCOTLAND
Danby, North Yorkshire	YORKSHIRE
Dartmoor, Devon	SOUTH WEST
Dartmouth, Devon	SOUTH WEST
Dawlish, Devon	SOUTH WEST
Derby, Derbyshire	MIDLANDS
Dereham, Norfolk	EAST
Devizes, Wiltshire	SOUTH WEST
Diss, Norfolk	EAST
Dolgellau, Anglesey & Gwynedd	WALES
Doncaster, South Yorkshire	YORKSHIRE
Dorchester, Dorset	SOUTH WEST
Dornoch, Highlands	SCOTLAND
Dover, Kent	LONDON & SOUTH EAST
Driffield, East Yorkshire	YORKSHIRE
Droitwich Spa, Worcestershire	MIDLANDS
Drumnadrochit, Highlands	SCOTLAND
Dufftown, Aberdeen, Banff & Moray	SCOTLAND
Dulverton, Somerset	SOUTH WEST
Dumfries, Dumfries & Galloway	SCOTLAND
Dunlop, Ayrshire & Arran	SCOTLAND
Dunoon, Argyll & Bute	SCOTLAND
Dunsford, Devon	SOUTH WEST
Dunster, Somerset	SOUTH WEST
Durham, Durham	NORTH EAST
Ealing, London	LONDON & SOUTH EAST
Eastbourne, East Sussex	LONDON & SOUTH EAST
Eastleigh, Hampshire	LONDON & SOUTH EAST
Eccleshall, Staffordshire	MIDLANDS
Edinburgh, Edinburgh & Lothians	SCOTLAND
Ellingham, Northumberland	NORTH EAST
Elton, Nottinghamshire	MIDLANDS
Ennerdale Bridge, Cumbria	NORTH WEST
Exeter, Devon	SOUTH WEST
Exmoor, Devon	SOUTH WEST
Exmouth, Devon	SOUTH WEST
Fairford, Gloucestershire	SOUTH WEST
Falmouth, Cornwall	SOUTH WEST
Faversham, Kent	LONDON & SOUTH EAST
Felixstowe, Suffolk	EAST
Fishguard, Pembrokeshire	WALES
Folkestone, Kent	LONDON & SOUTH EAST
Forest of Dean, Gloucestershire	SOUTH WEST
Forres, Aberdeen, Banff & Moray	SCOTLAND
Fort William, Highlands	SCOTLAND
Framlingham, Suffolk	EAST
Frosterley in Weardale, Durham	NORTH EAST
Gainsborough, Lincolnshire	MIDLANDS
Gairloch, Highlands	SCOTLAND
Gatehouse of Fleet, Dumfries & Galloway	SCOTLAND
Gilsland, Cumbria	NORTH WEST
Gilsland, Northumberland	NORTH EAST
Glaisdale, North Yorkshire	YORKSHIRE
Glastonbury, Somerset	SOUTH WEST
Glencoe, Argyll & Bute	SCOTLAND
Glossop, Derbyshire	MIDLANDS
Gloucester, Gloucestershire	SOUTH WEST
Godalming, Surrey	LONDON & SOUTH EAST
Gomshall, Surrey	LONDON & SOUTH EAST
Goodwick, Pembrokeshire	WALES
Grantown-on-Spey, Highlands	SCOTLAND
Grasmere, Cumbria	NORTH WEST
Great Malvern, Worcestershire	MIDLANDS
Hailsham, East Sussex	LONDON & SOUTH EAST
Haltwhistle, Northumberland	NORTH EAST
Happisburgh, Norfolk	EAST
Harrogate, North Yorkshire	YORKSHIRE
Hartfield, East Sussex	LONDON & SOUTH EAST
Hastings, East Sussex	LONDON & SOUTH EAST
Haverfordwest, Pembrokeshire	WALES
Hawick, Borders	SCOTLAND
Hawkshead, Cumbria	NORTH WEST
Haworth, West Yorkshire	YORKSHIRE
Hayling Island, Hampshire	LONDON & SOUTH EAST
Headon, Kent	LONDON & SOUTH EAST
Heddon-on-the-Wall, Tyne & Wear	NORTH EAST
Helmsley, North Yorkshire	YORKSHIRE
Helston, Cornwall	SOUTH WEST
Helton, Cumbria	NORTH WEST
Henfield, West Sussex	LONDON & SOUTH EAST
Henley-on-Thames, Oxfordshire	LONDON & SOUTH EAST
Hereford, Herefordshire	MIDLANDS
Hexham, Northumberland	NORTH EAST
Holmes Chapel, Cheshire	NORTH WEST
Honiton, Devon	SOUTH WEST
Hook, Hampshire	LONDON & SOUTH EAST
Hope Valley, Derbyshire	MIDLANDS
Hopton, Suffolk	EAST
Horley, Surrey	LONDON & SOUTH EAST
Horncastle, Lincolnshire	MIDLANDS
Horseheath, Cambridgeshire	EAST
Howgill, Cumbria	NORTH WEST
Hyde, Cheshire	NORTH WEST
Ilfracombe, Devon	SOUTH WEST
Inveraray, Argyll & Bute	SCOTLAND
Inverness, Highlands	SCOTLAND
Inverurie, Aberdeen, Banff & Moray	SCOTLAND
Ipswich, Suffolk	EAST
Ironbridge, Shropshire	MIDLANDS
Isle of Gigha, Argyll & Bute	SCOTLAND
Jedburgh, Borders	SCOTLAND
Kelso, Borders	SCOTLAND
Kelvedon, Essex	EAST
Kendal, Cumbria	NORTH WEST
Kenilworth, Warwickshire	MIDLANDS
Keswick, Cumbria	NORTH WEST

INDEX OF TOWNS AND COUNTIES 365

Kettering, Northamptonshire	MIDLANDS
Killin, Perth & Kinross	SCOTLAND
Kilsyth, Glasgow & District	SCOTLAND
King's Cross, Ayrshire & Arran	SCOTLAND
King's Lynn, Norfolk	EAST
Kingsbridge, Devon	SOUTH WEST
Kingston-Upon-Thames, Surrey	LONDON & SOUTH EAST
Kingussie, Highlands	SCOTLAND
Kinlochbervie, Highlands	SCOTLAND
Kinlochleven, Highlands	SCOTLAND
Kirkby Lonsdale, Cumbria	NORTH WEST
Kirkby Stephen, Cumbria	NORTH WEST
Kirkby-in-Furness, Cumbria	NORTH WEST
Kirkbymoorside, North Yorkshire	YORKSHIRE
Kirkton, Dumfries & Galloway	SCOTLAND
Kirkwall, Scottish Islands/Orkney	SCOTLAND
Kirriemuir, Angus & Dundee	SCOTLAND
Knaresborough, North Yorkshire	YORKSHIRE
Lairg, Highlands	SCOTLAND
Lake District, Cumbria	NORTH WEST
Lamphey, Pembrokeshire	WALES
Lanark, Lanarkshire	SCOTLAND
Lancaster, Lancashire	NORTH WEST
Langdale, Cumbria	NORTH WEST
Launceston, Cornwall	SOUTH WEST
Leamington Spa, Warwickshire	MIDLANDS
Lechlade on Thames, Gloucestershire	SOUTH WEST
Ledbury, Herefordshire	MIDLANDS
Leicester, Leicestershire & Rutland	MIDLANDS
Leominster, Herefordshire	MIDLANDS
Lesmahagow, Lanarkshire	SCOTLAND
Leven, Fife	SCOTLAND
Lewes, East Sussex	LONDON & SOUTH EAST
Leyburn, North Yorkshire	YORKSHIRE
Lifton, Devon	SOUTH WEST
Lingfield, Surrey	LONDON & SOUTH EAST
Linlithgow, Edinburgh & Lothians	SCOTLAND
Liskeard, Cornwall	SOUTH WEST
Little Watham, Essex	EAST
Liverpool, Merseyside	NORTH WEST
Llanidloes, Powys	WALES
Loch Lomond, Stirling & Trossachs	SCOTLAND
Lochearnhead, Perth & Kinross	SCOTLAND
Lochinver, Highlands	SCOTLAND
London	LONDON & SOUTH EAST
Long Buckby, Northamptonshire	MIDLANDS
Long Hanborough, Oxfordshire	LONDON & SOUTH EAST
Long Stratton, Norfolk	EAST
Longframlington, Northumberland	NORTH EAST
Looe, Cornwall	SOUTH WEST
Loughborough, Leicestershire & Rutland	MIDLANDS
Louth, Lincolnshire	MIDLANDS
Ludlow, Shropshire	MIDLANDS
Lulworth, Dorset	SOUTH WEST
Lulworth Cove, Dorset	SOUTH WEST
Luton, Bedfordshire	EAST
Lyme Regis, Dorset	SOUTH WEST
Lymington, Hampshire	LONDON & SOUTH EAST
Lynmouth, Devon	SOUTH WEST
Lynton, Devon	SOUTH WEST
Maidstone, Kent	LONDON & SOUTH EAST
Malham, North Yorkshire	YORKSHIRE
Malmesbury, Wiltshire	SOUTH WEST
Malvern Wells, Worcestershire	MIDLANDS
Mansfield, Nottinghamshire	MIDLANDS
Market Drayton, Shropshire	MIDLANDS
Market Rasen, Lincolnshire	MIDLANDS
Marlborough, Wiltshire	SOUTH WEST
Maryport, Cumbria	NORTH WEST
Matlock, Derbyshire	MIDLANDS
Mauchline, Ayrshire & Arran	SCOTLAND
Mawgan Porth, Cornwall	SOUTH WEST
Mayfield, Derbyshire	MIDLANDS
Melrose, Borders	SCOTLAND
Melton Mowbray, Leicestershire & Rutland	MIDLANDS
Mere, Wiltshire	SOUTH WEST
Merstham, Surrey	LONDON & SOUTH EAST
Mevagissey, Cornwall	SOUTH WEST
Middlewich, Cheshire	NORTH WEST
Milford-on-Sea, Hampshire	LONDON & SOUTH EAST
Minehead, Somerset	SOUTH WEST
Minster Lovell, Oxfordshire	LONDON & SOUTH EAST
Moffat, Dumfries & Galloway	SCOTLAND
Monmouth, South Wales	WALES
Morecambe, Lancashire	NORTH WEST
Moretonhampstead, Devon	SOUTH WEST
Morpeth, Northumberland	NORTH EAST
Mortehoe, Devon	SOUTH WEST
Much Hadham, Hertfordshire	EAST
Muirkirk, Ayrshire & Arran	SCOTLAND
Mundesley, Norfolk	EAST
Munslow, Shropshire	MIDLANDS
Nairn, Highlands	SCOTLAND
Nantwich, Cheshire	NORTH WEST
Neath, South Wales	WALES
New Forest, Hampshire	LONDON & SOUTH EAST
Newbiggin on Lune, Cumbria	NORTH WEST
Newcastle-upon-Tyne, Tyne & Wear	NORTH EAST
Newport, Pembrokeshire	WALES
Newport, Shropshire	MIDLANDS
Newquay, Cornwall	SOUTH WEST
Newtown, Powys	WALES
North Walsham, Norfolk	EAST
Northallerton, North Yorkshire	YORKSHIRE
Northwich, Cheshire	NORTH WEST
Norwich, Norfolk	EAST
Oban, Argyll & Bute	SCOTLAND
Okehampton, Devon	SOUTH WEST
Oswestry, Shropshire	MIDLANDS
Otterburn, Northumberland	NORTH EAST
Ottery St Mary, Devon	SOUTH WEST
Oxford, Oxfordshire	LONDON & SOUTH EAST
Paignton, Devon	SOUTH WEST
Paisley, Renfrewshire	SCOTLAND
Parkend, Gloucestershire	SOUTH WEST
Pathhead, Edinburgh & Lothians	SCOTLAND
Patna, Ayrshire & Arran	SCOTLAND
Penrith, Cumbria	NORTH WEST
Penzance, Cornwall	SOUTH WEST

INDEX OF TOWNS AND COUNTIES

Perranporth, Cornwall	SOUTH WEST
Perth, Perth & Kinross	SCOTLAND
Peterborough, Lincolnshire	MIDLANDS
Pickering, North Yorkshire	YORKSHIRE
Pitlochry, Perth & Kinross	SCOTLAND
Plockton, Highlands	SCOTLAND
Pluckley, Kent	LONDON & SOUTH EAST
Plymouth, Devon	SOUTH WEST
Polgate, East Sussex	LONDON & SOUTH EAST
Polzeath, Cornwall	SOUTH WEST
Porlock, Somerset	SOUTH WEST
Port Ellen, Scottish Islands/Islay	SCOTLAND
Port Isaac, Cornwall	SOUTH WEST
Portland, Dorset	SOUTH WEST
Portpatrick, Dumfries & Galloway	SCOTLAND
Portsmouth, Hampshire	LONDON & SOUTH EAST
Preston, Lancashire	NORTH WEST
Reading, Berkshire	LONDON & SOUTH EAST
Redruth, Cornwall	SOUTH WEST
Richmond, North Yorkshire	YORKSHIRE
Ringwood, Hampshire	LONDON & SOUTH EAST
Ripon, North Yorkshire	YORKSHIRE
Robin Hood's Bay, North Yorkshire	YORKSHIRE
Romsey, Hampshire	LONDON & SOUTH EAST
Ross-on-Wye, Herefordshire	MIDLANDS
Rothbury, Northumberland	NORTH EAST
Rye, East Sussex	LONDON & SOUTH EAST
Salcombe, Devon	SOUTH WEST
Salisbury, Wiltshire	SOUTH WEST
Saltburn-by-the-Sea, North Yorkshire	YORKSHIRE
Sandown, Isle of Wight	LONDON & SOUTH EAST
Sanquhar, Dumfries & Galloway	SCOTLAND
Saundersfoot, Pembrokeshire	WALES
Saxmundham, Suffolk	EAST
Scarborough, North Yorkshire	YORKSHIRE
Sea Palling, Norfolk	EAST
Seaford, East Sussex	LONDON & SOUTH EAST
Seaton, Devon	SOUTH WEST
Selkirk, Borders	SCOTLAND
Shanklin, Isle of Wight	LONDON & SOUTH EAST
Sherborne, Dorset	SOUTH WEST
Shillingstone, Dorset	SOUTH WEST
Sidmouth, Devon	SOUTH WEST
Skegness, Lincolnshire	MIDLANDS
Skipton, North Yorkshire	YORKSHIRE
Souldern, Oxfordshire	LONDON & SOUTH EAST
South Molton, Devon	SOUTH WEST
Southampton, Hampshire	LONDON & SOUTH EAST
Southport, Merseyside	NORTH WEST
Spennymoor, Durham	NORTH EAST
St Agnes, Cornwall	SOUTH WEST
St Andrews, Fife	SCOTLAND
St Austell, Cornwall	SOUTH WEST
St Boswells, Borders	SCOTLAND
St Ives, Cornwall	SOUTH WEST
Staithes, North Yorkshire	YORKSHIRE
Stamford, Lincolnshire	MIDLANDS
Stanley, Durham	NORTH EAST
Stanley, Perth & Kinross	SCOTLAND
Stanton-by-Bridge, Derbyshire	MIDLANDS
Stepps, Glasgow & District	SCOTLAND
Stoke-on-Trent, Staffordshire	MIDLANDS
Stokesley, North Yorkshire	YORKSHIRE
Stowmarket, Suffolk	EAST
Stow-on-the-Wold, Gloucestershire	SOUTH WEST
Stratford-Upon-Avon, Warwickshire	MIDLANDS
Strathyre, Stirling & Trossachs	SCOTLAND
Stroud, Gloucestershire	SOUTH WEST
Sturminster Newton, Dorset	SOUTH WEST
Surbiton, Surrey	LONDON & SOUTH EAST
Sutton-in-Ashfield, Nottinghamshire	MIDLANDS
Swanage, Dorset	SOUTH WEST
Swansea, South Wales	WALES
Talyllyn, Anglesey & Gwynedd	WALES
Tarbert, Argyll & Bute	SCOTLAND
Taunton, Somerset	SOUTH WEST
Telford, Shropshire	MIDLANDS
Tewkesbury, Gloucestershire	SOUTH WEST
Theale, Somerset	SOUTH WEST
Thurso, Highlands	SCOTLAND
Tiverton, Devon	SOUTH WEST
Tongue, Highlands	SCOTLAND
Torquay, Devon	SOUTH WEST
Totland, Isle of Wight	LONDON & SOUTH EAST
Totnes, Devon	SOUTH WEST
Truro, Cornwall	SOUTH WEST
Tywyn, Anglesey & Gwynedd	WALES
Uist, Scottish Islands/Uist	SCOTLAND
Ullswater, Cumbria	NORTH WEST
Umberleigh, Devon	SOUTH WEST
Ventnor, Isle of Wight	LONDON & SOUTH EAST
Wadebridge, Cornwall	SOUTH WEST
Wakefield, West Yorkshire	YORKSHIRE
Wareham, Dorset	SOUTH WEST
Warkworth, Northumberland	NORTH EAST
Warwick, Warwickshire	MIDLANDS
Wasdale, Cumbria	NORTH WEST
Washford, Somerset	SOUTH WEST
Waterhouses, Durham	NORTH EAST
Wells, Somerset	SOUTH WEST
West Linton, Borders	SCOTLAND
West Lulworth, Dorset	SOUTH WEST
Westbury, Wiltshire	SOUTH WEST
Weston-Super-Mare, Somerset	SOUTH WEST
Weymouth, Dorset	SOUTH WEST
Whitby, North Yorkshire	YORKSHIRE
Whitebridge, Highlands	SCOTLAND
Wigtown, Dumfries & Galloway	SCOTLAND
Winchcombe, Gloucestershire	SOUTH WEST
Winchester, Hampshire	LONDON & SOUTH EAST
Windermere, Cumbria	NORTH WEST
Windsor, Berkshire	LONDON & SOUTH EAST
Winkfield, Berkshire	LONDON & SOUTH EAST
Winster, Derbyshire	MIDLANDS
Wisbech, Cambridgeshire	EAST
Wolverhampton, West Midlands	MIDLANDS
Woodbridge, Framlingham, Suffolk	EAST
Woodhall Spa, Lincolnshire	MIDLANDS
Woodstock, Oxfordshire	LONDON & SOUTH EAST
Wooler, Northumberland	NORTH EAST
Worthing, West Sussex	LONDON & SOUTH EAST
Wroxham, Norfolk	EAST
Wymondham, Norfolk	EAST
Yelverton, Devon	SOUTH WEST
York, North Yorkshire	YORKSHIRE

Other FHG titles for 2009

367

FHG Guides Ltd have a large range of attractive holiday accommodation guides for all kinds of holiday opportunities throughout Britain. They also make useful gifts at any time of year. Our guides are available in most bookshops and larger newsagents but we will be happy to post you a copy direct if you have any difficulty. POST FREE for addresses in the UK. We will also post abroad but have to charge separately for post or freight.

The Original Pets Welcome! — £9.99
- The bestselling guide to holidays for pets and their owners

500 Great Places to Stay in Britain — £7.99
- Coast & Country Holidays
- Full range of family accommodation

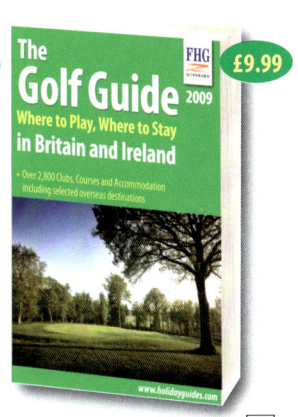

The Golf Guide — £9.99
Where to play, Where to stay.
- Over 2800 golf courses in Britain with convenient accommodation.
- Holiday Golf in France, Portugal, Spain, USA and Thailand.

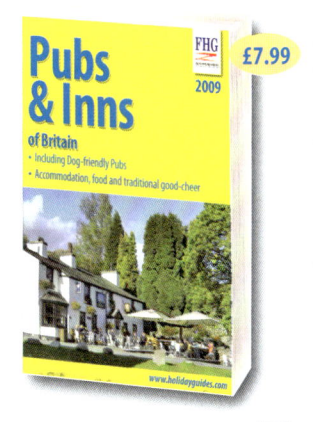

Pubs & Inns of Britain — £7.99
- Including Dog-friendly Pubs
- Accommodation, food and traditional good cheer

Country Hotels of Britain — £6.99
- Hotels with Conference, Leisure and Wedding Facilities

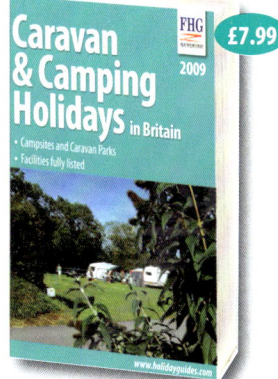

Caravan & Camping Holidays in Britain — £7.99
- Campsites and Caravan parks
- Facilities fully listed

Family Breaks
in Britain
£7.99
• Accommodation, attractions and resorts
• Suitable for those with children and babies

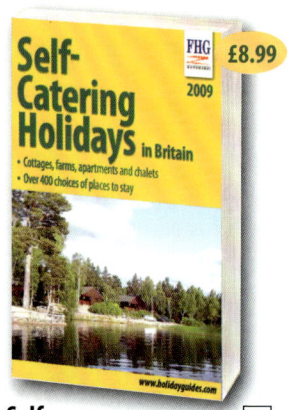

Self-Catering Holidays
in Britain
£8.99
• Cottages, farms, apartments and chalets
• Over 400 places to stay

Weekend & Short Breaks
in Britain
£7.99
• Accommodation for holidays and weekends away

Tick your choice above and send your order and payment to

**FHG Guides Ltd. Abbey Mill Business Centre
Seedhill, Paisley, Scotland PA1 1TJ
TEL: 0141- 887 0428 • FAX: 0141- 889 7204
e-mail: admin@fhguides.co.uk**

Deduct 10% for 2/3 titles or copies; 20% for 4 or more.

Send to: NAME ....

ADDRESS ....

....

....

POST CODE ....

I enclose Cheque/Postal Order for £ ....

SIGNATURE .... DATE ....

Please complete the following to help us improve the service we provide.
How did you find out about our guides?:

☐ Press   ☐ Magazines   ☐ TV/Radio   ☐ Family/Friend   ☐ Other